THE EMPIRE
OF REASON

Henry Steele Commager was born in 1902 in Pittsburgh, Pennsylvania, and did his graduate work in history at the universities of Chicago and Copenhagen. He has taught American history at New York University, Columbia University, and at Amherst College, where he held the position of Simpson Lecturer, teaching until 1992. Mr Commager also held the Pitt Chair of American History at Cambridge University, the Harmsworth Chair at Oxford University, and the Gottesman Chair at Uppsala University. He was an Honorary Fellow of Peterhouse, Cambridge, and held an Honorary Professorship at the University of Santiago de Chile. In 1972 he was awarded the Gold Medal for History by the American Academy of Arts and Letters. Henry Steele Commager died in 1998.

A SELECTION OF WORKS BY HENRY STEELE COMMAGER

America in Perspective (Editor)

The American Mind

America: The Story of a Free People (with J.A. Nevins)

The Blue and the Gray: The Story of the Civil War as
Told by Participants (Editor)

Britain Through American Eyes (Editor)

Commager on Tocqueville

The Commonwealth Learning

The Defeat of America: Presidential Power and the
National Character

Documents of American History (Editor)

The Era of Reform, 1830–1860 (Editor)

Freedom, Loyalty, Dissent

The Growth of the American Republic (with S.E. Morison)

Jefferson, Nationalism and the Enlightenment

Majority Rule and Minority Rights

The Spirit of "Seventy-six: The Story of the American
Revolution as Told by Participants (Editor, with R.B. Morris)

The Struggle for Racial Equality (Editor)

Theodore Parker: A Biography

THE EMPIRE OF REASON

How Europe Imagined and Europe Realised the Enlightenment

Henry Steele Commager

PHOENIX
PRESS

5 UPPER SAINT MARTIN'S LANE
LONDON
WC2H 9EA

For Mary
with Love

A PHOENIX PRESS PAPERBACK

First published in Great Britain
by Weidenfeld & Nicolson in 1978
This paperback edition published in 2000
by Phoenix Press,
a division of The Orion Publishing Group Ltd,
Orion House, 5 Upper St Martin's Lane,
London WC2H 9EA

A CIP catalogue record for this book
is available from the British Library.

Printed and bound in Great Britain by
Clays Ltd, St Ives plc

ISBN 1 84212 076 X

Contents

List of Illustrations

1. Frontispiece for L'Encyclopédie. Designed by Charles Nicolas Cochin III. (*Albertina, Museum.*)
2. Engraving of Buffon by Robert Hart. (*Bettmann Archive.*)
3. Portrait of Carl Von Linne by Alexander Roslin. (*Bettmann Archive.*)
4. Portrait of Sir Joseph Banks by Sir Joshua Reynolds. (*From the Collection at Parkham Park, Sussex [England].*)
5. Portrait of Thomas Paine by Auguste Millière after Romney. (*Bettmann Archive.*)
6. Portrait of Edmund Burke by Sir Joshua Reynolds. (*National Gallery of Scotland.*)
7. Sculpture of Voltaire by Houdon. (*Victoria and Albert Museum.*)
8. Coronation of Gustavus III by Carl Gustav Pilo. (*National-museum.*)
9. Tapestry of *chinoiseries*. (*Kunstgewerbe Museum.*)
10. Miniature portrait of Thomas Jefferson. (*Thomas Jefferson Memorial Foundation.*)
11. Apotheosis of Benjamin Franklin by Fragonard. (*The White House.*)

Preface

The thesis of this book can be stated quite simply: The Old World imagined, invented, and formulated the Enlightenment, the New World—certainly the Anglo-American part of it—realized it and fulfilled it. It was Newton and Locke, and their eighteenth-century successors in Britain and on the Continent—philosophes like Priestley and Bentham, Hume and Monboddo in Britain, Montesquieu, Voltaire, Buffon, and Diderot in France, Christian Wolff and Lessing, von Haller and Goethe in Germany, Genovesi, Filangieri, Beccaria, and Tanucci in the Italian states, and sometimes supporting them, "enlightened" monarchs like Frederick of Prussia, Joseph of Austria, Leopold of Tuscany, and Gustavus of Sweden —who launched the Enlightenment, gave it respectability and, somewhat tentatively, experimented with it. But it was Americans who not only embraced the body of Enlightenment principles, but wrote them into law, crystallized them into institutions, and put them to work. That, as much as the winning of independence and the creation of the nation, *was* the American Revolution.

Although inevitably the Enlightenment took different forms from country to country and from generation to generation, in its dominant and pervasive ideas it transcended national and continental boundaries. Alike in the Old World and the New, it had its roots in the same intellectual soil, and produced a common harvest of ideas, attitudes, and even of programs: recognition of a cosmic system governed by the laws of Nature and Nature's God; faith in Reason as competent to penetrate to the meaning of those laws and to induce conformity to them among societies in many ways irrational; commitment to what Jefferson called "the illimitable freedom of the human mind," to the doctrine of progress, and—with some reservations—to the concept of the perfectibility of Man; an ardent humanitarianism that attacked torture, slavery, war, poverty, and disease; and confidence that Providence and Nature had decreed happiness for mankind.

These were articles of faith among the philosophes on both sides of the Atlantic, but they did not dictate a common program. Almost inevitably the program in the Old World was negative: Its inspiration was Voltaire's *"Écrasez l'infâme"* and its purpose to sweep away tyrannies and iniquities which were deeply entrenched and immensely powerful. Only rarely, and sporadically, could Old World philosophes turn their energies to the tasks of improvement and reform. But in America, where there were no ancient tyrannies to overthrow, no barriers of tradition or poverty or ignorance to surmount, and few iniquities—except the prodigious iniquity of slavery—to banish, the philosophes could devote their energies to realizing the program of the Enlightenment. Because the European philosophes were the intellectual begetters of the new era, we have tended to study the Enlightenment almost wholly in, and on, their terms, and neglected the American Enlightenment, or dismissed it as merely derivative. The philosophical origins were indeed derivative (though the significance of this can easily be exaggerated), but what is important is not so much origins as consequences. For consequences we turn to the Old World almost in vain: There the Enlightenment terminated in the reaction of monarchs like Gustavus, Catherine, and Charles III against the French Revolution, in Burke's flamboyant *Reflections* which quickly took on scriptural authority, in Robespierre's Terror, and in Napoleon's betrayal. But in America, where the Revolution was not followed by a Thermidor, and where the greatest of philosophes was triumphantly elected to the highest office, the Enlightenment not only survived but triumphed.

Contemporaries saw this more clearly than we do now, for time has blurred our perception of that contrast between life in the Old World and in the New which was so sharp in the eyes of the generation that made the American Revolution—a contrast not only in material well-being but in moral. We tend increasingly to interpret the American Revolution and Enlightenment not in eighteenth- but in twentieth-century terms, to see it not against the background of eighteenth-century Europe but against the foreground of our own time, and to be more conscious of its limitations than of its spectacular achievements. We take for granted what neither Americans nor Europeans took for granted in the eighteenth century; not only have we lost that sense of astonishment and exultation that animated Jefferson's generation, we have almost lost our ability to understand it. It is not perhaps surprising that we should be skeptical of a society that preached liberty and practiced slavery, but it is surprising that we should be equally skeptical of a society that achieved a larger degree of political and social democracy, constitutional order, effective limits on the pretensions of government, freedom of religion, freedom of the press, civil liberties, popular education, and material well-being than any other on the globe.

It was not only exiles from the Old World like Crèvecoeur, Paine, Van der Kemp and Dr. Priestley, or cosmopolites like Jefferson and Franklin and Joel Barlow who saw this; even a conservative like John Adams, whose view of human nature was jaundiced, could confess to his beloved Abigail, when he signed the Declaration, that he saw "rays of ravishing light and glory" and, forty years later, after a lifetime of disappointment and disillusionment, could assure his old friend Jefferson that

According to the few lights that remain to us, we may say that the eighteenth century, notwithstanding all its errors and vices, has been, of all that are past, the most honorable to human nature. Knowledge and virtue were increased and diffused; arts, sciences, useful to men, ameliorating their condition, were improved more than in any former equal period.

This volume covers, however inadequately, that body of ideas and institutions which illustrate what we might call The Spirit of the Laws. A second volume, now in progress, will address itself to what might be called the Substance of the Laws: religious freedom, freedom of the press, education, the classless society and the paradox of slavery, the relations of the military to the civilian, and the uses of History.

A book of this kind, in the making for ten years or more, incurs obligations too numerous to detail. My deepest debt is to the librarians of Amherst College and her sister institutions in the Connecticut Valley, of the Massachusetts Historical Society, the American Antiquarian Society, the Boston Athenaem, and Cambridge University, who have for so long borne patiently with my importunate demands. My debt to those affluent scholars who have cultivated the rich soil of Enlightenment history will be apparent on every page: Robert Palmer, Peter Gay, Geoffrey Bruun, Lester Crocker, Caroline Robbins, Frank Manuel, Clarence Glacken, Gordon Wood, Edmund Morgan, Bernard Bailyn, Alfred Cobban, J. R. Pole, Paul Hazard, Daniel Mornet, Franco Venturi among them, and to Julian Boyd, Lyman Butterfield, Leonard Labaree and their associates whose magisterial editions of the papers of the Founding Fathers are one of the glories of modern historiography.

I am indebted, too, to a long procession of students at Amherst College who have, with unfailing kindness, taken on themselves many of the chores connected with historical research: William Weary, John Teague, William Alford, Robert Hawkins, William and Frederick Woolverton, Richard B. Bernstein, and Mark Daniell. To my assistant, Mary E. Powlesland, formerly of the University of California, my debt is incalculable.

HENRY STEELE COMMAGER

Amherst 1976

The
Empire of Reason

CHAPTER ONE

The Enlightenment as an Age of Discovery

It was the age of science, it was the age of philosophy, it was the age of enlightenment. Everywhere the scientists were philosophers, and most of the philosophers were scientists,* while all were enlightened.[1] They had emancipated themselves from all but the classical past (which was not really past at all, but viewed as contemporary)[2]— the past of ignorance, credulity, and superstition—and now with tireless curiosity and feverish impatience they hurled themselves upon a new world and a new universe. They were not interested in the next world; they were interested in the world about them, the world of Nature, society, politics, and law; they were interested in Man, and their most representative literary production was an *Essay on Man*.[3] They sailed the seven seas and others that no one had charted before; they mapped unknown islands and unveiled hidden continents, and they banished some that had been merely imagined like the famous Terra Australis Incognita.[4] They discovered new worlds of flora and fauna, and fitted them all into the great chain of nature and of being.[5] They probed deep into the earth, and the waters, and debated Vulcan versus Neptune[6]; they found new races of men, new marvels and wonders, and what

* The term was not "scientist"—that is a nineteenth-century shift; in the eighteenth century all scientists were "Natural philosophers," and scientific academies were known as Philosophical Societies.

they did not find they imagined, for their imaginations teemed with Utopias. They mapped the heavens, and Herschel alone doubled the expanse of the solar system.[7]

"Order," they knew, "is Nature's first law," and they made it their own, for they were in harmony with Nature. They organized, they systematized, they classified, they codified, and all Nature, the universe itself, fell into order at their bidding. The Encyclopédie, the greatest literary monument of the Enlightenment, was a heroic effort to summarize all scientific and philosophical knowledge, but alas it was disorganized, so Charles Joseph Panckoucke launched an Encyclopédie Méthodique which substituted an analytical for an alphabetical arrangement.[8] Up in Uppsala, Linnaeus classified all the flora of the globe according to a System of Nature, and the Comte de Buffon added the rest of the natural world, man and animals, birds and fishes, and minerals for good measure. The indefatigable Antoine Réamur[9] devoted six volumes to the classification of insects, while in Göttingen, Albrecht von Haller and Johann Blumenbach systematized the study of human anatomy.[10] The whole thing added up, as the Baron d'Holbach made clear, to a vast *Système de la Nature* (1770), and the glib Baron followed this up with a *Système Social*. Who could doubt that there was a social system that corresponded to the natural order? "How exact and regular is everything in the *natural* world," wrote the young Benjamin Franklin:

> How wisely in every part contriv'd . . . All the heavenly Bodies, the Stars and Planets, are regulated with the utmost wisdom! And can we suppose less care to be taken in the order of the Moral than in the Natural System?[11]

Montesquieu imagined an orderly constitution for England and, by sheer eloquence and logic, he almost imposed it upon her; and young Jeremy Bentham tried to codify the chaos of English law and equity into a logical system, as indeed he tried to codify morals, sentiments, and emotions into a logical system.[12] David Hume hoped that politics might be reduced to a science,[13] and Americans demonstrated that it could be by framing constitutions for their states and their nation.

There was order in the architecture of Palladio and of the Earl of Burlington, order in the music of Handel and Mozart, order in the gardens of Capability Brown and of William Chambers, for even when they introduced calculated disorder (as they did in the famous English garden) it was in an orderly fashion.[14] The Duc de Luynes spent a lifetime drawing up an orderly social register for the French aristocracy,[15] and not to be outdone, M. de Chevanne devoted an entire volume to detailing the successive dance steps of the Minuet.[16] There was order even in religion, and Franz Reinhard of Dresden outlined a *System of Christian Morality* in five stout volumes.[17] Indeed, God Himself was admonished to abide by fixed laws, for as Jonathan Mayhew of Boston reminded Him, "the power of this Almighty King is *limited by law* . . . by the eternal *laws* of truth, wisdom, and equity, and the everlasting *tables* of right reason."[18]

What remarkable men they were, these philosophes. Not since the Renaissance had there been such enthusiasm, such curiosity, such courage, such foolhardiness, such versatility. There was a prodigality about them; they recognized no bounds to their curiosity, no barriers to their thought, no limits to their activities or, for that matter, to their authority. They took the whole earth for their domain and some of them the cosmos, for they were not afraid to extend their laws to the universe. Most of them were scientists—they used the word Naturalist—and those who were not, tried to be, for it was science to which they all pledged their allegiance and gave their devotion. "Unless we utilize the compass of mathematics or the torch of experience and physics," wrote Voltaire, "it is certain that we cannot take a single step forward." Voltaire had begun his literary career by introducing Newton to French men and women who knew no science, and he never lost his interest in science.† Rousseau wrote on botany and chemistry; the learned Christian Wolff taught mathematics and phys-

† Unlike his American counterparts, Franklin, Jefferson, and Rumford, he made no contributions to it.

ics at Halle, and wrote on astronomy; Goethe produced books on mineralogy and challenged Newton on optics. Diderot dabbled in physiology and anticipated evolution, and the clergyman Étienne Condillac laid the foundation for the scientific study of psychology, while the Baron d'Holbach wrote on geology and metallurgy. Immanuel Kant lectured on physics and astronomy, Herschel turned from music to astronomy, the Reverend Dr. Priestley wrote a comprehensive *History of Electricity* and discovered a dozen gases, and even Dr. Johnson was addicted most of his life to "chemical experiments." The *Économiste* Quesnay was a doctor, and so also were Louis de Jaucourt, who contributed so much to the Encyclopédie, La Mettrie, Albrecht von Haller of Göttingen, Linnaeus in Uppsala, and Johann Frederich Struensee, the ruler of Denmark. In America such philosophes as Dr. Benjamin Rush, Dr. Manasseh Cutler, Dr. David Ramsay of South Carolina, and Dr. Hugh Williamson of North Carolina were ceaselessly active in public affairs. Dr. Franklin embraced a dozen sciences, and so did Jefferson, and the lexicographer Noah Webster wrote a two-volume work on the history of epidemics. How natural, then, that in the era of the Enlightenment, the scientist should be king.

Although England was a bit outside the Enlightenment, she could be justly charged with responsibility for the whole thing, what with Isaac Newton and John Locke, but by the time of the eighteenth century both were taken for granted and so, too, in a sense, was Enlightenment. In England freedom and toleration flourished—so at least almost everyone on the Continent thought, and philosophes who could agree on little else, agreed in singing England's praises: Voltaire and Montesquieu and Rousseau, Holberg and Haller and, for a time, even Franklin. To be sure, after mid-century all the philosophers seemed to be Scottish—Hume and Ferguson and Hutcheson and Adam Smith and the fantastic Monboddo who was the most original of them all.[19] Perhaps that was because the English had concluded that they had no need of philosophers: after all, they drove Priestley from the country, and

Bentham did not come into his own until the Enlightenment had run its course.

Perhaps the most characteristic figure of the English Enlightenment was neither a philosopher nor a scholar nor even a scientist, but a patron, a spokesman, a representative of them all: Sir Joseph Banks.[20] He wrote no philosophy, he made no original scientific discoveries, he championed no reforms, he led no crusades, he indulged in no eccentricities, or none that were unbecoming, and his philanthropies (one feels) expressed a sense of *noblesse oblige* rather than social convictions. No one was more unlike the ardent Voltaire, the learned Lessing, the vivacious Mazzei, the visionary Condorcet, or the scores of other philosophers who wore at their hearts the fire's center, than this proud aristocrat. Yet Lord Brougham, who knew him well, thought his credentials sound:

> Who better deserved the name of philosopher than he whose life was devoted to the love of wisdom, whose rich reward was the delight of the study, whose more noble ambition left to others the gratification of recording their progress in books?[21]

Born to wealth and position, Banks moved on from Eton to Oxford without any visible intellectual interests. But at Oxford he became fascinated by botany, and when he found that the professor of that subject had no inclination to lecture, he imported—at his own expense—a lecturer from Cambridge.‡ Banks was connected with all the proper families, inherited broad acres in the Midlands, and built himself a splendid mansion in Soho Square which he turned into a combination of club, salon, library, and natural history museum, and where his curator, the famous Dr. Solander, presided over one of the great botanical collections of the realm. A common interest in farming won him the friendship of George III, who made him Keeper of the Royal Gardens; soon they rivaled the Jardin des Plantes, and

‡ The professor "showed his love of science by agreeing to the proposal"—the quote is from Lord Brougham—and the Cambridge don, as a reward for his services, was shipped off on an expedition to the Arctic!

Banks could fancy himself an English Buffon, though he
was not. English to the core—sheriff of Lincolnshire, a
country squire, a mighty fisherman, a great walker—Banks
was at the same time a cosmopolite.
For forty-two years he presided over the Royal Society,
and over the Royal Observatory as well, dispensing hospitality and patronage. He corresponded with Linnaeus,
whose favorite pupil was Dr. Solander, and with the leading
botanists of France, Holland, and America. He accompanied Dr. Franklin to Portsmouth to observe the latter's
experiments with pouring oil on waters—a failure, this, as
the Doctor's parallel attempt in British politics was a failure
—and he later conferred upon Franklin the gold medal of
the Royal Society for his zeal in protecting Captain Cook
during the Revolutionary War. During the long conflict
with France he intervened to save scientists and scientific
collections: the French navigator, La Perouse, the German
Alexander von Humboldt, and many others. He rescued
the geologist Diodet de Dolomieu (who gave his name to
the Dolomites) from a Neapolitan dungeon, for he held
that "the sciences are never at war."[22]
Banks's long career was one of ceaseless activity on behalf of science. As a young man he had explored Newfoundland and Labrador, and had botanized in Iceland, and
years later he was able to save that island from starvation
by persuading William Pitt to lift the blockade he had
imposed on Denmark and her possessions. He visited
M'Fingal's Cave, in the Hebrides, first reciting Ossian's
poems, and then carefully measuring its dimensions. He
had sailed with Captain Cook on that famous voyage of
1769 to the South Seas to observe the transit of Venus—
perhaps the first great international scientific enterprise,[23]
and he brought home with him no less than seventeen thousand new plants to fill the bulging cabinets of his Soho
house. No wonder the great Linnaeus wrote that he was
"the glory of England, and of the whole world."[24] He
made Australia his own, chose Botany Bay—named after
his botanizing*—as ideal for a colony of convicts, and there-

* "The great quantity of New Plants etc. Mr. Banks and Dr. Solander
collected at this place occasioned my giving it the name of *Botany
Bay*."—quotation from Cook's *Journal.*[25]

after was sponsor, spokesman, and benefactor of the colony. He projected other South Seas explorations such as that by Matthew Flinders, who mapped much of the Australian coast, and James Burney compiled his great *History of Voyages in the South Seas* from materials in the Banks library. He sent Captain Bligh to take the breadfruit tree from Tahiti to Jamaica, adding two botanists to the expedition to build up the collections of Kew Gardens, and imported fruit trees from Ceylon and the mango from Bengal, and he experimented with merino sheep to improve the wool of the English breed exported to Australia. He encouraged "Athenian" Stuart to explore the antiquities of Athens and Rome and, as a patron of the African Society, sent the Connecticut-born John Ledyard to search out the headwaters of the Nile and, a little later, financed Mungo Park's exploration of the Niger.[26] Generous, high-minded, adventurous, and imaginative, for half a century Banks devoted his wealth and power to advancing science and the community of learning. If he was not himself a philosophe he deserved the merit of those who were.

On the Continent there was no one whose credentials were more universally acknowledged than the Comte de Buffon, the Newton of the natural world.[27] For fifty years he presided over the Royal Gardens, and as he paced the garden paths he could contemplate his own statue with the unimpeachable inscription, "he embraced the whole of Nature." He not only embraced it, he ruled over it as some enlightened despot. When he wrote, said the Marquis de Chastellux, it was Demosthenes writing down the truths of Aristotle, while Rousseau, not given to praise of others, thought him the finest stylist of the century. He was so great—so thought his contemporaries—that when he and Nature differed, Nature gave way. While others enlarged the world of space, Buffon expanded the world of time; he had extended the age of the earth from six thousand to many millions of years, though publicly he was content to claim only eighty thousand. To be sure, the Church persuaded him to make a retraction of even those modest calculations, but it was a tactical withdrawal, and no one took it seriously, for it was taken for granted that Buffon was right.

Buffon surveyed the whole of Nature and organized it

according to his system; by anticipating evolution he gave
Nature herself a new character and a new shape. He was
perhaps the first—certainly the first whose scientific credentials were unassailable—to challenge the popular theories
of environment and to point out that man could master
environment and, by draining the marshes, building dykes
against the seas, and clearing the forests, "make a new
nature come forth from his hands." He was, at the same
time, the first conservationist who described Man as the
most predatory of animals, and warned that in the not distant future the beaver and the ostrich, the seal and the
walrus would be extinct—an argument which the American
John Lorain was to pick up in his plea for *Nature and
Reason Harmonized in the Practice of Husbandry*.[28]

Sweden boasted Buffon's only rival, Carl Linnaeus, who ruled over the kingdom of plants as Buffon
over the animal and mineral kingdoms.[29] "God," Linnaeus
confessed, "had suffered him to peep into His secret cabinet," and now it was no longer secret. He reorganized Nature, imposed upon her a sexual classification, divided the
whole world of flora and fauna into subdivisions of genera
and species, and gave new names to eight thousand plants.
The inscription under his portrait was more presumptuous
even than that on the Buffon statue: *"Deus creavit, Linnaeus disposuit."* (God imposes, Linnaeus disposes.)
Though Linnaeus accepted without question the Biblical account of creation, his great work, the *System of Nature*,
was banned by Pope Clement XIII because it challenged
the classifications of Moses; fortunately, the new Clement XIV gave way to an authority he could no longer deny,
and removed the ban.

As a young man Linnaeus had given up the luxuries of
Holland for the little town of Uppsala on the turbulent
Fyrisan, and his very presence tripled enrollment at the
ancient University situated there. From America, Siberia,
Africa, students hurried to sit at his feet, and the whole
world poured its botanical riches into his gardens, the
Americans alone sending him over two thousand plants.
The greatest of botanists, he was not merely a botanist,
but a biologist and mineralogist as well, and he taught and
practiced surgery. He was an explorer, too—mostly by

proxy, for though he himself botanized no farther than Lapland, his students sailed with Captain Cook and botanized in America and Japan. Gustavus III visited him at his home in Hammerby, and all Sweden rejoiced in him and honored him, and when he died the Swedes allowed his great collections to be sold to England.

Linnaeus had studied with the incomparable Dr. Boerhaave in Leyden, as had his rival, the great Göttingen savant, the Swiss-born Albrecht von Haller, who had embraced the Baconian admonition to take all knowledge for his province.[30] Haller had been an infant prodigy, and all his life he remained something of a prodigy. He had so many talents that he never quite knew which to cultivate, so he cultivated all of them simultaneously—the literary, the philosophical, the theological, the scientific. He was a poet, perhaps the first romantic poet, for his lyrical description of *The Alps* (1728) had in it much that later romanticism was to embrace, as was also true of his apotheosis of William Tell which nourished Swiss nationalism and deeply influenced Friedrich Schiller.[31] He had read medicine at Tübingen before he went to Leyden, and as his own city of Berne ignored him, he reluctantly accepted an appointment as Professor of Medicine, Anatomy, Surgery, and Botany at the new University of Göttingen. These responsibilities did not exhaust his energies; he created an anatomical theater, set up a lying-in hospital, established a Botanical Garden, edited a learned journal and wrote all of it himself—twelve thousand reviews and articles!

No one more widely honored; the Emperor Francis I ennobled him, and Joseph II made a pilgrimage to his house. But he longed for his native Berne, and returned there to manage the salt works, create another Botanical Garden, found an Economic Society, establish an orphanage, and set up chairs of history and of natural science at the local academy. In between these activities he produced an eight-volume *Elementa Physiologie corporis Humani,* and a multi-volumed *Flora Helvetica,* scores of books on economics, philosophy, and theology, poetry by the ream, and three historical novels that explored the hypotheses of Montesquieu about empires, monarchies, and republics, and made clear that the best government was

very much like that which by good fortune flourished in
Berne.[32] Yet for all this he was not a true philosophe,
but rather a philosophical anti-philosophe. He had no quarrel with the Church or, for that matter, with society or
government; he was orthodox, pious, and respectable, and
he vindicated Special Creation, the Deluge, and the Soul
by science and by logic as he vindicated patrician government by history.

In the breadth and depth of his knowledge, Haller was
perhaps unique, yet he was not untypical of the philosophes
who swarmed over Germany in the eighteenth century.
There were so many States and Courts and Universities,
all the way from Hamburg to Pomerania, from Baden to
Dresden, and, for that matter, in border nations like Austria
and Switzerland and Denmark that were also German, that
the philosophes tripped over one another. Even a tiny state
like Weimar was a veritable Athens.[33] The German philosophers were more scholarly, perhaps, than their French
colleagues, but less given to crusades, and—on the whole—
willing to let the Church alone if it left them alone.[34] Most
of them—as in Scotland and Italy—were connected with the
Universities; that was part of the tradition which the magisterial Christian Wolff had established at Halle, and the Universities were both respectable and powerful. How different
this was from those of England where they were respectable
but not powerful, or those of France where they were
powerful but not respectable. In Germany, too, the Aufklärung (for perhaps we should use the term that Immanuel
Kant picked up from Wolff, rather than Enlightenment)
did not concern itself much with politics; even great men
like Haller and Kant and Lessing were willing to come to
terms with the rulers of their states, who were only spas-
modically enlightened. Goethe at Weimar, Sonnenfels in
Vienna, Rumford in Bavaria, Holberg in Copenhagen, preferred absolutism—even if unenlightened—to popular government. Yet the German philosophers did much to bring
about that thawing of the ice of absolutism and of parochi-
alism, that resurgence of the mind and the spirit which in
Germany merged the Enlightenment with Romanticism
more easily than anywhere else except in America.[35] The
process had been anticipated by Haller, it was encouraged

by Lessing and Herder, by Georg Forster who sailed with Cook, by the historian Augustus von Schlözer, also of Göttingen, and by professor Ebeling of Hamburg.

Christopher Ebeling (1741–1817) came almost too late for the Enlightenment, but then, except for Christian Wolff and Gotthold Lessing and perhaps Johann Basedow—all of whom were sufficiently traditional to write their books in Latin—the Enlightenment itself came late to Germany. Ebeling had all the customary credentials for membership in the academy of the philosophes, and the additional one that his cosmopolitanism was not merely theoretical but practical.[36] Like so many of the German philosophes he was a product of Göttingen, the wonderful new University on the banks of the Leine. It was there that he first conceived that passion for history and geography which was to fill the rest of his life and make him a kind of academic Captain Cook. It was there, too, perhaps, that he developed a devotion to freedom not nearly so common east as west of the Rhine. He was no crusader, to be sure, no reformer; he was content to be a scholar and a discoverer, and to conduct his explorations in the pages of his voluminous books and journals. He was indefatigable. He taught the ancient languages at the Hamburg commercial college; he taught history at the local Gymnasium; he presided over the municipal library of a hundred thousand volumes and advised the universities of Halle and Göttingen on their library collections. He edited geographical and historical journals, and at the age of seventy-five hopefully launched a *Journal for the Knowledge and History of Non-European Lands and Peoples*. He translated books from the Danish and the Portuguese, as well as from French and Italian, and together with his friend Klopstock rendered Handel's "Messiah" into German, for though he was deaf he was a musician as well as a scholar.

These duties and activities did not exhaust his energies. Because he was entranced by the spectacle of freedom and self-government, his course of lectures on the Italian city-states made clear that only those states that respected law, freedom, and peace, could be truly happy. No wonder he thought that "America must give an example to the world,"[37] and set himself the most ambitious of projects:

a history of the new United States which would devote one
volume to each of the thirteen American states. Hamburg
was without the resources to sustain such an enterprise,
but full of confidence in the fellowship of the community
of learning, Ebeling turned to members of the American
Philosophical Society, the American Academy of Arts and
Sciences, and the new Massachusetts Historical Society for
help, and not in vain. All through the tumultuous years
of the Revolutionary and Napoleonic wars packages of
books, newspapers, and maps flowed across the Atlantic
into the library at Hamburg, until in the end Ebeling presided over the greatest library of Americana in the world.
By rising at five in the morning and working until midnight
he managed to produce seven of the projected volumes:
Erdschreibung und Geschichte von Amerika (1793–1816),
the most comprehensive and scholarly history of the American states that had yet appeared.[38] To his friend Joel Barlow he could write truthfully that "I have spent a great
deal of my life and all of my money and even much of
my health" on America.

The *History* was chiefly notable for its wealth of economic and social data—it was, in fact, a kind of statistical
compendium—but it was a document on the literary history
of the Enlightenment, too. It explored the flora and fauna
of the New World, described the culture and habits of the
Indians, explained the political and constitutional institutions of the new nation; it had something of the range of
Raynal's *Philosophical History of the Indies,* and if it
lacked Raynal's liveliness, it had substance where Raynal
had imagination. And at a time when many German intellectuals were deeply suspicious of such notions as republicanism, equality, and democracy, and therefore unfriendly
to the American cause, Ebeling was a staunch partisan of
the young Republic, for he was confident that the United
States was to be "the Mother Country of Liberty." It was
indeed an "arduous task" he had undertaken, but, as he
wrote so touchingly to Ezra Stiles of Yale College, "I was
inclined to persevere by the animating beauty of the object,
the many imperfect and false accounts Europe has of your
country, and the good effect which a faithful picture of
a truly free republic founded upon the most solid founda-

tions, could produce on most parts of Europe so very remote from such happiness as you enjoy."[39]

It was not only books that flowed across the Atlantic—a two-way traffic, this—for Professor Ebeling supplied his American friends with all the latest German publications—seventy-nine volumes of the *Neue Allgemeine Bibliothek* for the polymath Dr. Bentley of Salem, for example, and letters as well. Ebeling's letters to Bentley, to Jeremy Belknap, who had founded the Massachusetts Historical Society and written a *History* of New Hampshire, to Benjamin Smith Barton of Philadelphia, to Crèvecoeur, and scores of others, confessed his own prodigies of research and publication, described the intellectual currents of revolutionary Germany, and raised questions about the new United States that started a score of investigations. At a time when few Americans knew Germany—or Germans, America—Ebeling was the chief interpreter of each to the other.[40] He translated Burnaby's *Travels,* and those of Liancourt; he wrote a biography of the Baron von Steuben, edited two American journals, and welcomed visitors from America to his hospitable library—Aaron Burr, Samuel Williams, the historian of Vermont, and Joel Barlow among them (he even read Barlow's *Columbiad;* what heroism!). How appropriate it was that his great library of over three thousand volumes, thousands of newspapers, and maps, whose creation had truly been a joint enterprise of the philosophes of both continents, should find its final resting place in the library of Harvard College.[41]

Ebeling was merely one of many Old World philosophes who found intellectual excitement and inspiration in the contemplation of the new American Republic. He did not manage to see it for himself, though he probably knew more about it than almost any other European of his time. Many other philosophers, however, did: Crèvecoeur, Barbé-Marbois, Du Pont de Nemours, the Marquis de Chastellux who was an expert on happiness, the botanist André Michaux, and young Albert Gallatin from Geneva. From England came Tom Paine and young Benjamin Vaughan to whom Priestley had dedicated his *Lectures on History,* and eventually Joseph Priestley himself. Edward Fitzgerald from Ireland who died tragically in the uprising

of ninety-eight, and Jefferson's friend Philip Mazzei from
Tuscany, and the intrepid Francis Adrian Van der Kemp
from Holland were also visitors.

Holland did not need an Enlightenment; she was already
enlightened, perhaps the most enlightened country in
Europe, the one whose freedom and religious toleration
flourished most vigorously.[42] Yet Holland had its own
form of intolerance, its own class system, its own political
reaction, and it had, too, its own patriots who looked to
America for guidance. None more eager than young Van
der Kemp, theologian, scholar, soldier, statesman, patriot,
and, in the end, exile.[43] He was a man of the Enlightenment, as truly as Ebeling himself, or Priestley, a clergyman who had no use for the State church; a member of
the aristocracy of Oversyssel, cousin to half the gentry of
Holland, but a champion of the classless society; and a
scholar who compiled studies of military jurisdiction that
changed the law of Holland. Yet he was a soldier, too,
who put himself at the head of the Free Corps, and
fought, in vain, for freedom; an ardent nationalist and a
cosmopolite; familiar with a dozen languages, at home in
many cultures.

Van der Kemp had come out of Leyden, center of
learning and of freedom; he had abandoned the Reformed
Church for Deism, but embraced, in the end, the Mennon-
ite faith. He led the fight on the Corvée and, for composing an *Ode to Freedom*, stood trial before a University Inquisition on ninety-four charges, and emerged triumphant.
"I perceived the forged chains which were to be riveted on
the necks of my countrymen," he wrote, but he did not despair, for he was confident that "the time was fast ap-
proaching when these sacred rights for which the blood of
our ancestors had been shed, might be recovered,"[44] and
he dedicated himself to their recovery. It was the spectacle
of American independence that had most deeply stirred
him, and as he studied the documents that John Adams
made available to him—the Declaration of Independence,
the Articles of Confederation, the Constitution of Massachusetts—his excitement mounted. "In America," he
wrote rapturously, "the sun has risen brightly, a promise to
all of us if we will but see it. . . . America can lift us

up. . . . It is the land of justice, we are a land of sin."
America, he added somewhat wildly, "has been ordained
to heal the wounds of the Netherlands if we but follow her
footsteps, if we but rise up and build anew."[45] He pled the
American cause, and frustrated the plan of the Stadtholder
to use a Dutch regiment in the American war. Soon, with
his cousins, the Van der Capellans, he was leading a campaign to limit the power of the Stadtholder and emancipate
his country from the malign influence of Britain. Shortly
he had put off his clerical gown and donned a military uniform and was deep in revolution. The British rallied to the
cause of the Stadtholder, and the Prussians to the cause of
his wife, the sister of Frederick William of Prussia—how
Burke was to romanticize that[46]—and Van der Kemp was
forced to flee the country.

Where should he go but to America? He bought a farm
in the wilderness of northern New York, built himself a
house and settled down to be an American farmer, like another Crèvecoeur, and to philosophize. Picture him on the
wild shores of Lake Oneida, where his companions were
the painted Iroquois, or, later on, at Oldenbarneveldt
where the Holland Land Company was colonizing Dutch
emigrants, reading his Horace and Seneca, his Grotius and
Rousseau, with new books streaming in not only from Boston and Philadelphia but from Amsterdam and Paris and
Milan. At the same time he was carrying on a busy correspondence with his old friends John Adams and Thomas
Jefferson, and editing the documents of Dutch New Amsterdam—twenty-eight volumes of them. He also found
time to botanize along the banks of the Genesee and the
shores of Lake Ontario, to write essays on the theories of
Buffon, the character of the Achaean Republic, the Mos-
lem invasions of Europe; to study, like Adams, the Canon
Law and the theology of Calvin; and to project, before
anyone else had thought of it, a canal to link up the Hudson and the Great Lakes. No wonder De Witt Clinton
thought him the most learned man in America.[47]

CHAPTER TWO

The Enlightenment Spreads to America

1

America, too, had its philosophes,[1] though for few of them was philosophy, or even science, a full-time activity. For the most part, they were busily engaged in farming or medicine or law or the ministry. More important, they lacked the Courts, the Cathedrals, the Academies, the Universities, and the libraries that provided so large a part of the patronage and nurture of philosophy in the Old World. In their confidence in Reason, their curiosity about the secular world and—with most of them—their indifference to any other, their addiction to Science—if useful—their habit of experimentation, and their confidence in improvement, their humanitarianism, and their versatility, they were much like their European associates. Many of them had studied at Edinburgh or at the Inns of Court in London[2] or even in Leyden; some had found their way to Germany or Italy. They immersed themselves in the history and culture of Europe, and when they returned they brought Europe with them, but in a highly selective fashion, for they saw more to disapprove than to approve. For all their similarities with the philosophes of the Old World, it was the differences that were most striking and, in the end, most consequential.

Much of the American Enlightenment centered on and radiated from Philadelphia and the remarkable American

Philosophical Society over which Benjamin Franklin presided from 1769 until his death in 1790.[3] Philadelphia was not quite London (though it was the second city in the Empire) or Paris; it was rather a kind of American Weimar or, perhaps, in its contributions to science and medicine (though not to theology or philosophy) a second Edinburgh. With its Philosophical Society, its Library Company, its infant college that soon became a University, its hospital, its Botanical Garden, and its museums, it was indubitably the intellectual center (John Adams called it "the pineal gland")[4] of British America. It had never known a religious Establishment, and it had escaped Puritanism; its character was heterogeneous, its temper secular, and its philosophy utilitarian, and it stamped these qualities on the American Enlightenment.

If Philadelphia could not boast such a distinguished literary fellowship as Weimar, with Goethe, Wieland, Schiller, Fichte, and Herder, it had a far greater variety of men of talent and of genius than that famous city-state. It had all started with James Logan,[5] a kind of American precursor to Joseph Banks, who foreshadowed the special character of the American Enlightenment by combining the roles of statesman, administrator, scientist, scholar, businessman, and Maecenas. A trusted adviser to the Penns, he was a member of the ruling Council as well as mayor of Philadelphia; he was, at the same time, the leading botanist in the Colony, a student of Newtonian physics, a distinguished classicist, and a patron of artists and scientists of the next generation. It was in his noble study at Stenton—one of the handsomest houses in the Colonies —that young Thomas Godfrey spelled out Newton's *Principia*—for Logan owned the first American copy of that work—and that John Bartram learned the Linnaean classification of plants.[6]

When Logan died in 1751, Philadelphia boasted a galaxy of talent unmatched elsewhere in America, and unmatched, since then, by any city of its size.[7] There were botanists like John Bartram, who presided over the first Botanical Garden in the American colonies, and the Reverend David Muhlenberg who found almost fourteen hundred species of plants in nearby Lancaster County; it was

to Philadelphia that Peter Kalm first came on his botanical
expedition in the American colonies, and it was from Bartram and his associates that he learned much that he took
back with him to Sweden. There was Thomas Godfrey,
who had "a natural intuitive knowledge of the abstrusest
parts of mathematics and astronomy"[8] and who invented a
new and improved mariner's quadrant, and his son,
Thomas, who produced the first drama written and performed in the American colonies—the *Prince of Parthia*—
and David Rittenhouse who had built the famous orrery
and observed the transit of Venus, and of whom Jefferson
wrote, somewhat wildly, that "the world has but one Ryttenhouse [sic], and never had one before."[9] There was
Charles Thomson, perpetual secretary to the Continental
Congress, an expert in Indian languages, and a classical
and Biblical scholar, too, and provost William Smith, a
product of the University of Aberdeen, who had come to
America in 1751 and whose visionary picture of the *College of Mirania*[10] won him the presidency of the newly established College of Philadelphia, a post that failed to exhaust his cascading energies which found outlets in
politics, science, and controversy.

Philadelphia was the medical center of the English Colonies and—as in so many countries of the Old World—its
doctors were both philosophers and statesmen.[11] Most of
those who dominated the Philadelphia medical scene in the
half century after the founding of the Pennsylvania Hospital (1752) had studied in Europe—in Edinburgh under
Dr. Alexander and Monroe Primus, in London under the
Hunter brothers, and Dr. Fothergill, in Leyden under the
greatest medical teacher of his day, Hermann Boerhaave;
they brought back with them not only medical skills, but
enlightened ideas about medicine and public health that
accounted for the dramatic improvement in the mortality
figures during the second half of the century. The three
men chiefly responsible for the creation of the new College
of Medicine—John Morgan, Edward Shippen, and Benjamin Rush—were all Edinburgh trained; all involved
themselves deeply in public affairs and played an active
role in the struggle for independence and the creation of
the new Republic.

Philadelphia had some claim, too, to be considered the artistic capital of the Colonies and of the new nation.[12] It had discovered talent in young Benjamin West, and sent him on his road to glory which ended with the presidency of the Royal Academy in London and the patronage of the King; it had nourished Matthew Pratt, who painted the Quaker gentry as Copley painted those of Boston, and Henry Bembridge, who studied in Italy where he painted the Corsican chief Pasquale Paoli who gave his name to a town destined for tragedy. It was in Philadelphia that the Swiss-born Pierre du Simitière had set up his primitive American Museum, which displayed not only paintings and statuary but a miscellaneous collection of Indian artifacts, fossils, shells, coins, and medals. There, too, Charles Willson Peale, who—like Stuart—made a career of painting Washington, established his more famous Museum; twenty years later (1805) he succeeded in founding the first permanent Academy of Fine Arts in the new Republic.

Almost from the beginning Philadelphia had been a magnet for the most heterogeneous elements from abroad and from other colonies. Germans, Scots-Irish, Welsh, Huguenots, Swiss streamed into the infant colony, doubling and redoubling its population, and giving Philadelphia the most cosmopolitan character of any American city. At mid-century some five hundred Acadians, expelled from their native Nova Scotia, found refuge there, and half a century later hundreds of refugees from the French Revolution and from the anarchy in Santo Domingo found Philadelphia both hospitable and interesting.[13] The pious Anthony Benezet had come over from Picardy early in the century and devoted himself to good causes—the education of girls, temperance, the welfare of the Indians, peace, and, increasingly, the amelioration of the lot of the blacks, for he was the pioneer American abolitionist. Others from the Old World were to follow his example—Tom Paine and Dr. Joseph Priestley among them. Little wonder that Philadelphia was the most liberal of American cities or that the new Constitution, in which men like Dr. Franklin and Tom Paine had a hand, was the most radical of State constitutions.

Presiding over it all for fifty years was the benign pres-

ence of Dr. Franklin.[14] Franklin was the oldest of the
Founding Fathers—as he is to us the most nearly contemporary. He was a young man setting type in his brother's
printing shop in Boston when Samuel Sewall was keeping
his *Diary* and John Wise penning his *Vindication* and
William Byrd writing his *Dividing Line*.[15] He was the elder
statesman of the Federal Convention when Henry Clay
and John C. Calhoun and Daniel Webster were disporting
themselves innocently in an America still in the making.
He was not only long-lived,[16] he was ubiquitous. Part of
genius (Justice Holmes was to say) "consists in being
there," and Franklin was there. He was there in 1743 to
propose the organization of a society whose purpose was
to embrace in its scope "all philosophical Experiments that
let Light into the Nature of Things, tend to increase the
Power of Man over Matter, and multiply the Conven-
iencies or Pleasures of Life,"[17] and that became, twenty-
some years later, the American Philosophical Society. He
was there at the Albany Congress of 1754 where he
drafted a plan that anticipated the ultimate American confederation; there at the House of Commons to defend the
American distinction between external regulation and internal taxation; there in Carpenter's Hall to help Jefferson
draft a Declaration of Independence; and there, too, on
the committee that drew up Articles of Confederation for
the new nation. He was there at the Court of Louis XVI to
win French support, and there at the peace negotiations
that acknowledged American independence. He was there,
finally, at the Federal Convention that drew up a constitution for the new nation—where he managed to have the
last word, as he had had the first word.[18] As Postmaster
General he had traveled the length and breadth of the
Colonies; he was one of the commissioners assigned the
hopeless task of winning Canada as a fourteenth state; he
was there in England for sixteen years and knew that nation better than any other American; and he was in France
for eight. He was, therefore, part of both the British and
the French Enlightenment. He was the most traveled
American of his day, and the most cosmopolitan.

No one else, except Jefferson, touched American life on
so many sides, or left so lasting an impression on all that

he touched. Printer, journalist, scientist, politician, diplomat, educator, statesman, author of the most popular of aphorisms and the best of autobiographies, he was, or seemed, the complete philosophe, American style, as representative of his nation as Voltaire was of France or Goethe of Germany or Holberg of Denmark or Banks of England. He could contrive, with equal facility, a subscription library or a colonial union; he could fashion a new stove and a new commonwealth; he could draft the constitution of a club, a learned society, or a state; he could organize a fire company, a post office, or a military alliance; he could perfect a new musical instrument, test the winds and the tides, chart the Gulf Stream, and confound mathematicians with magical squares. He could snatch the lightning from the skies and the scepter from the hands of tyrants (*Eripuit coelo fulmen, sceptrique tyrannis,* wrote Turgot, and Houdon chiseled it into immortality). He was a historical Robinson Crusoe, prepared to new-make everything, resourceful, ingenious, inventive, competent, and benevolent, the representative of and the symbol of the Age of Reason. He was reasonable with misguided members of Parliament who were unable to understand American politics—or even their own Constitution—and reasonable with Jefferson about changes in his draft of the Declaration, and with members of the Federal Convention about what they might suppose to be defects in the Constitution. He was reasonable about religious enthusiasm—in others—and he permitted his mythical Polly Baker to triumph over her persecutors by making clear how reasonable it was that she should add each year to the population of Boston. He had a tidy mind and hated to see anything go to waste—time, energy, money, or the opportunity for happiness. He liked to organize everything—even morals. He saw no reason why Philadelphia should not be tidied up and organized, or why the whole of mankind should not be similarly tidied up and organized along sensible lines. He was reasonable enough to conclude that "there never was a good war, or a bad peace," but reasonable enough, too, to fight a war and make a peace. He was the least doctrinaire of men, and his zeal for improvement was a product of common sense, not of fanaticism, and he was assuredly the most amiable of all reformers.[19]

America was to be many things, and Franklin represented most of them. "It seems I am too much of an American," he said to an English friend when he prepared to return to Pennsylvania after many years in Britain, and he reflected, not unhappily, that "old trees cannot be safely transplanted." Certainly Franklin could not be transplanted: He took his America with him—soil, roots, and all—to England and to France.

Almost from boyhood Franklin had espoused one principle central to the Enlightenment: freedom of speech and of the press. Perhaps there was a personal, a professional, ingredient in this conviction. As a lad of sixteen he saw his brother thrown into jail for the crime of criticizing the General Court of Massachusetts; he took over the editorship of the offending paper and promptly inserted from the London *Journal* the defiant argument that "Without freedom of Thought, there can be no such thing as Wisdom; and no such thing as publick Liberty, without freedom of Speech, which is the Right of every Man." And at the close of his long life he could say that

All the heretics I have known have been virtuous men. They have the virtue of Fortitude, or they would not venture to assert their Heresy; and they cannot afford to be deficient in any of the other Virtues, as that would give advantage to their many enemies; and they have not, like orthodox Sinners, such a number of friends to excuse or justify them.

Like Washington—it was one of the amiable foibles of an Enlightenment which was classical-minded—Franklin was apotheosized even before his death. His reputation, wrote John Adams,

was more universal than that of Leibniz or Newton, Frederick or Voltaire, and his character more beloved and esteemed than that of any of them . . . There was scarcely a peasant or a citizen, a valet de chambre, coachman or footman, a lady's chambermaid or a scullion who was not familiar with [his name], and who did not consider him as a friend to human kind. When they spoke of him they seemed to think he was to restore the Golden Age.[20]

The Royal Society had conferred its gold medal on him even during the Revolutionary War—for that was an era when, in the great words of Edward Jenner, "the sciences were never at war." When he and Voltaire embraced on that famous occasion at the Academy of Sciences, all Europe pronounced it the meeting of Solon and Sophocles.[21] Jefferson put it best, Jefferson who felt no envy,

He was our Patriarch, whom Philanthropy pronounced the first of men, and whose name will be like a star of the first magnitude in the firmament of Heaven.

2

Franklin's successor in Philadelphia was Benjamin Rush,[1] as broad in his interests as Franklin, but not in his sympathies. He had studied in Edinburgh and London, but not just medicine, for he found time to hobnob with radicals and reformers in both cities and even visited "that devil Wilkes" in prison. He returned to America in time to become professor of chemistry in the new College of Philadelphia, and a member of the newly organized American Philosophical Society,[2] and plunge into those moral, practical, and political reforms that were to engage him for the rest of his long career. It was characteristic that though he did publish a syllabus of *Lectures on Chemistry* as early as 1770, his other publications, in those early years, were *Sermons* on temperance and exercise, a study of diseases among the Indians, and a polemic against slavery.[3] His years in Britain had served to sharpen his disapproval of the manners and morals—particularly the morals—of the Old World, and to exacerbate his discomfort with the badge of colonialism, and he was early zealous for independence and hot for revolution. He welcomed John

Adams to the First Continental Congress; he inoculated Patrick Henry against the smallpox, he provided Tom Paine with the title *Common Sense* for his pamphlet.[4] He signed the Declaration of Independence and promptly enlisted in the Army, and in the spring of 1777 he was appointed Surgeon General for the Middle Department.

In time the most successful of American physicians,[5] he was never content to be merely a physician; the most popular of teachers, he did not confine himself to teaching only his specialty. "The science of medicine" he wrote, "is related to everything" and he interested himself in everything from psychiatry to cooking, wrote indefatigably on the most miscellaneous subjects—politics, morals, theology, and education[6]—and corresponded with everybody.[7] He was ceaselessly active in politics, state and national; served for forty years as an officer of the American Philosophical Society; helped found a college named after his friend John Dickinson, and then another, chiefly for German youths, named after Franklin. He taught three thousand students, set up the first dispensary, argued for penal reform, and propounded novel ideas about the relation of health to mind. He had novel ideas about so many things, the good Dr. Rush. Thus, he suggested that the black skin of Negroes might be a form of leprosy; cure the leprosy and blackness would disappear![8]

He argued that capital punishment was unbecoming and futile, and so, too, slavery and the slave trade, and he proposed to abolish them all. He thought that in a republic girls and women should be educated as well as boys and men, for they would instruct each new generation in republican virtues, and he wanted American schools to accommodate themselves to this principle.[9] He rejected spirits and tobacco on grounds of health, and the study of Greek and Latin on grounds of practicality, for he preferred that the citizens of a new country should be instructed in such things as agriculture, botany, and geology, and argued that to neglect these for Latin and Greek was "to turn our back upon a gold mine in order to amuse ourselves catching butterflies." His title for Tom Paine's *Common Sense* was, in a way, the title to the American Enlightenment, and in himself he represented what was most uncompromisingly American about that Enlightenment: reasonable revolution, conservative reform, constructive iconoclasm, prudent democracy, secular morality, and practical idealism. Working ceaselessly for the welfare of his beloved city, and for the new nation which he had helped bring to birth, he was always conscious of larger issues. "I was animated constantly," he wrote, "by a belief that I was acting for the benefit of the whole world, and of future ages, by assisting in the formation of new means of political order and general happiness."[10]

Very different was another American philosophe, Joel Barlow, a Connecticut Yankee, graduate of Yale College, and, early in his career, provincial enough to be numbered among the "Connecticut Wits."[11] He was a parson, a soldier, a bookseller, an editor; he was a lawyer who challenged Blackstone with the argument that the laws of Nature were not eternal, but progressive, and a poet who challenged Homer and Virgil with the promise of poetry suffused by a higher morality than they had imagined. He was a land agent, too, a speculator, a gambler in securities and foreign exchange, an agitator, a philanthropist, a diplomat, and a statesman; he was "a volunteer in the cause of humanity."[12] Circumstances—or ambition—had uprooted him from his native Connecticut, and you might meet him in London, Paris, Hamburg, even in Algiers; he was at home everywhere and nowhere, but always eager to remake whatever society he was part of into a replica of that republican society that he remembered from his youth, and wherever he was—in Revolutionary Paris consulting with Tom Paine or Condorcet, in Hamburg talking with Christopher Ebeling, in the Haute Savoie trying (in vain) to get himself elected a member of the French Revolutionary Convention, in the courts of the Barbary pirates, arranging the release of American captives—he yearned for his native Connecticut for he was, so he wrote,

> Doom'd o'er the world thro' devious paths to roam
> Each clime my country, and each house my home.[13]

Very early Barlow had caught a vision of what the New World was destined to be, and he assigned his vision to

Columbus—who else was worthy of it—and for twenty years he belabored the vision with relentless passion, producing in the end a monstrous epic of six thousand lines that surveyed the melancholy history of the Old World and viewed the glorious prospects of the New.[14] For the nobility of his sentiments rather than the beauty of his verse, he was adjudged the first poet of the Republic—there was, after all, little competition—and Byron himself, whether in admiration or derision, called him the American Homer. Yet it was not for the *Vision of Columbus* (later *The Columbiad*) that Barlow was destined to be remembered, but for the simple celebration of *Hasty Pudding*, written, in a moment of nostalgia, in a tavern in the Haute Savoie, where

> tho distant from our native shore,
> With mutual glee we meet and laugh once more,
> The same! I know thee by that yellow face,
> That strong complexion of true Indian race,
> Which time can never change. . . .[15]

Barlow had fought in the American Revolution, and tried to stir up revolution in England, hobnobbing with philosophes like Joseph Priestley, Dr. Price, Horne Tooke, and Tom Paine, who was there at the time, but he found England sunk in inertia, and he crossed the channel to participate in a revolution that promised to be like the American: What a delusion that proved to be, but not a disillusion. A grateful France conferred honorary citizenship upon him, and as the rules of American citizenship were still lax, he saw nothing wrong in standing for office from Savoy. When this failed he settled down to make money in complex and murky speculations, and in that at least he succeeded. A rich man now, his house in Paris was a meeting place for the radicals of three nations: there you could find Tom Paine, Robert Fulton, Count Rumford—who had been driven from Bavaria—and Mary Wollstonecraft and such French philosophes as had survived the Terror. When Tom Paine was thrown into prison, it was Barlow who rescued the manuscript of the *Age of Reason* and saw it through the press—he had drifted far from his Yale piety—and it was Barlow, too, who took up Volney's *Ruins*, partly because it was so much like his own *Vision of Columbus*, and put it into English.[16] He lived on in France through the beginning of the Napoleonic era but was happy to return to his own people who, almost alone in the Western World, had not betrayed their Revolution but instead triumphantly elected their leading philosophe, Thomas Jefferson, to the chief magistracy. Meantime he was busy turning out books and pamphlets: *Advice to the Privileged Orders of the Old World*—telling them to give up their privileges; *Advice to the People of Piedmont*—telling them to join France; and the new version of his epic. He settled outside Washington in a mansion as grand as the White House and with thirty acres of gardens—like Voltaire, he knew how to make and to hoard his money—and he gave his home a Greek name, Kalorama. He drew up elaborate plans for a national University and an Academy, but these came to nothing.[17] When Jefferson and Madison offered to provide him with materials for a history of the American Revolution he failed to embrace the chance to become the American Thucydides. Instead, ever restless, he accepted a mission to Napoleon, followed that monarch to Russia, and met his death in an obscure village in Poland, but not before he had written his best poem *Advice to a Raven in Russia*, calling upon men to

> Hurl from his blood-built throne this king of woes,
> Dash him to dust, and let the world repose.

Like so many of his fellow Americans, Barlow was a transition figure: He belonged to the Age of Reason, he belonged to the era of romance. He composed over three thousand heroic couplets, he early abandoned Calvinism for rationalism and counted himself a philosophe, and it was with the philosophes of two countries that he associated himself. But his life was wildly romantic: the disorderly speculations in western lands from which he somehow escaped unscathed; the improbable speculations in French consols which made him rich; the extravagant forays into the lairs of the Barbary Corsairs, like something out of *The Arabian Nights;* the wild proposal to seize

New Orleans and turn it over to the French—when Aaron
Burr imagined something like that a few years later he was
charged with treason; the building of Kalorama with its
gardens and fountains—as extravagant for America as
William Beckford's Fonthill Abbey—the pursuit of Napoleon through the Russian blizzards and the end as the
ravens circled.

The Reverend Manasseh Cutler was a product of the
same society and the same experiences that had formed
Joel Barlow, and like his friend Barlow, he was indubitably
a member of the American Enlightenment.[18] A Connecticut Yankee and a product of Yale College, he too trained
for the ministry, but unlike Barlow, he was never infected
by the virus of Deism, and it is difficult to imagine him
rescuing the *Age of Reason* from destruction. He was content to be a parish minister in his little town north of Boston, pious and devout, conscious of his Puritan inheritance
and determined to preserve it and to transplant it to new
soil.

The New England of which Cutler was a part was full
of learned clergymen like him, ministers who combined
deep learning and piety with public service and liberal
views. There was the famous Dr. Bentley in nearby Salem,
who knew twenty-one languages and was equally at home
in science and music and kept a famous *Diary;* or there
was the tireless Jeremy Belknap who wrote not only a *History of New Hampshire,* but a novel about it—*The
Foresters*—and founded the Massachusetts Historical Society; there was Dr. Samuel Johnson who fought the Connecticut Establishment, cultivated philosophy—and wrote
it—and was President of King's College in New York, and
the mighty Jonathan Mayhew of Boston who had some
claim to be called the first American Unitarian, and whose
learning was forgotten in his polemics. Or consider President Ezra Stiles of Yale College who was not only a theologian but an orientalist and a scientist and championed
freedom of the press in matters of religion as in politics, or
his successor to that Presidency, the Reverend Timothy
Dwight who was as active in politics as in education and
religion, and wrote better poetry than Joel Barlow, though
not as much, and whose *Travels in New England* were

filled with observations on the Yankee—and the American
—character that were not only shrewd, but original and
profound.[19]

Certainly Manasseh Cutler was far more than a theologian and a shepherd to his little flock in Ipswich. He had
been a soldier, a lawyer, and a doctor, and he was a geographer, a scientist, and something of a diplomat and statesman as well. As a chaplain in the American Army he had
studied medicine and inoculated hundreds of soldiers
against the smallpox; as a lawyer he helped draw up what
he rightly called the greatest contract ever made in America
—a contract on behalf of the Ohio Company for western lands the size of a European duchy; as a statesman he
dedicated the new country to republicanism, and as an educator laid the foundations for a University in the new
Utopia. Like so many of the philosophes on both sides of
the water he cultivated natural philosophy; in America,
more than elsewhere, Nature meant flora and fauna and
Cutler was an indefatigable botanist. He compiled a catalogue of the flora of New England; with Jeremy Belknap
he went botanizing in the White Mountains and on Cape
Cod; he lectured on botany at Yale College and the new
College of Philadelphia and corresponded on botanical
matters with Count Castiglioni of Milan; he visited the famous gardens of William Bartram outside Philadelphia
and those of Gray's Inn, too, with its Chinese bridge,
which he found "very romantic"—surely one of the early
uses of that term in America. Dr. Rush tried to persuade
him to leave Ipswich and become keeper of the Botanical
Gardens of Philadelphia, but in vain, and on his way home
he stopped off to see the gardens of the famous André
Michaux in Newark, now alas overgrown. He was something of an astronomer, too; he described the transit of
Mercury and found—or thought he found—new planets
through his simple telescope, and he borrowed a sextant
from the legal luminary Theophilus Parsons to observe the
conjunction of Jupiter and Saturn. Meantime he was busy
with the private school which he conducted in his parson-
age, teaching boys from the first families of the North
Shore—the Derbys and Silsbees and Cabots and Lowells
among them—not only Greek and Latin but navigation

and lunar observation, for many of them would sail to the Pepper Islands and the Java seas.[20]

Then came the opening up of the Ohio country, and of a new life for Cutler, or perhaps just an enlargement of the old. Like Barlow he was a shrewd businessman, and like Barlow and so many others, he combined private enterprise and public expansion and enlightenment and, for that matter, colonization and botanizing, and one sometimes suspects that the whole Ohio adventure was a kind of by-product of Cutler's passion for botany and for exploring Indian mounds. He lobbied in Congress for the land sale, and it helped that everybody knew him and trusted him; he contributed to the famous Northwest Ordinance[21] with its provision that "religion, morality and knowledge being necessary for good government and the happiness of mankind, schools and the means of education shall be forever encouraged," and what is more, he encouraged them. It was from his parish that the first band of intrepid emigrants set out for the Ohio country with their minister and their Bibles and their muskets, too—new Pilgrims en route to a new world. Soon Cutler joined them, driving all the way in his sulkey, seven hundred and fifty miles over wilderness roads, botanizing on the way and keeping a diary, and once there he helped get a church under way, and schools, and wrote a charter for the new university to be located in a town called Athens, for these Argonauts were confident that

> The *Ohio* soon shall glide by many a town of note,
> Nations shall grow, and states, not less in fame
> Than Greece and Rome of old. . . .

And indeed Cutler himself was rhapsodic when he contemplated the future of his new Eden in the West. "Not far from this spot," he predicted, "will be the seat of Empire for the whole domain," but, better yet, this "errand into the wilderness offered" an advantage which no other part of the earth can boast and which probably will never occur again; that in order to begin *right* there will be no *wrong* habits to combat, and no inveterate systems to overturn."[22] By "inveterate systems" he meant slavery, and with his

friend Nathan Dane of nearby Beverly—the learned lawyer who was to compile the first comprehensive compendium of American law and found a chair of law for
Joseph Story at Harvard College—he helped combat the
worst of all wrong habits, the habit of slavery, for Nathan
Dane wrote into the Ordinance a prohibition of slavery.

Two other philosophes, both scientists and reformers,
reflect the relations between the Old World Enlightenment
and the New: Joseph Priestley, who fled England to
America, and Benjamin Thompson, who fled America for
England—and beyond. Dr. Priestley[23]—for so he was always called—came to America late in life, but in a sense
he had always belonged there, spiritually and intellectually,
and when he finally arrived it was like coming home. He
had met Dr. Franklin at the Royal Society and, often
enough, at dining clubs in London and Birmingham, and
Franklin early formed Priestley's notions of America as in
the end he formed the notions which the whole of Europe
entertained about America. Though a clergyman, Priestley
was himself something of an English Franklin, bustling
about in science, politics, and education, full of benevolence and wisdom, ardent for freedom, confident of progress, the most practical of philosophers. He taught literature and the classics and botany and astronomy and even
anatomy at the famous Dissenting Academy at Warrington
which provided, in its day, quite as good an education as
did Oxford or Cambridge,[24] from whose halls Dissenters
were barred. He gave lectures on modern history—the first
delivered anywhere in England—and dedicated the lectures, when published, to young Benjamin Vaughan who
was later to throw in his lot with the Americans, and then
retire to the wilds of Maine, as Gallatin had retired to the
wilds of Pennsylvania and Van der Kemp to the wilds of
New York. He was a gifted teacher, and formulated a philosophy of education far ahead of his time, for he was
confident that if you provided children with the right environment and the right models, *association* would convert
these into sound habits of thought and morals. It was to
this end that he lectured on history and liberty and ethics,
and to this end, too, that he was the first to conduct laboratory experiments in the schoolroom. He wrote on ora-

tory—like Demosthenes he had overcome a speech impediment—on politics, drawing, and optics, and he compiled a Chart of Biography which won him an honorary degree from the University of Edinburgh. In his laboratory as in his study and his pulpit he was indefatigable. At Franklin's suggestion he wrote a multi-volume *History of Electricity,* and then three volumes on *Air.* These were merely the first installments of an ambitious project, nothing less than a *History of All the Branches of Experimental Philosophy*—pretty good, that, for a country parson with no scientific training! He discovered oxygen, carbon monoxide, hydrochloric acid, and soda water, and he even discovered the usefulness of India rubber for erasing, not that he ever bothered to erase what he had once written—on Phlogiston, for example. No wonder Sir Joseph Banks wanted him as scientific adviser on Cook's second voyage to the South Seas; alas, the clergy vetoed Priestley and the Admiralty vetoed Banks. He was for some years librarian and companion to Lord Shelburne, who was justly suspect by his associates for his intimacy with the radicals and the Dissenters, and he shared the Earl's interest in America and in political reform. When he moved to Birmingham, he was adopted at once into the famous Lunar Society, which included the elder Darwin, Samuel Galton, Josiah Wedgwood, James Watt of steam engine fame, and Dr. Small, who had once taught Thomas Jefferson over in Williamsburgh.[25] Stimulated by this remarkable group Priestley allowed his imagination to range widely over practical problems: He obtained samples of the air breathed by workingmen in factories, sought improvements in fire engines, and experimented with a copying machine. For he was confident that progress was material as well as moral and philosophical, and that Nature would reward her devotees now:

> I view the rapture [he wrote] the glorious face of nature, and I admire its wonderful constitution, the laws of which are daily unfolding themselves to our view. . . . Civil society is but in its infancy, the world itself is but very imperfectly known to the civilized inhabitants of it and we are but little ac-

quainted with the real value of those few of its productions of which we have some knowledge and which we are only beginning to name and to arrange. How must a citizen of the world wish to know the future progress of it?[26]

Yet for all his multifarious interests, Dr. Priestley thought of himself as a theologian; he had all but invented Unitarianism, and he wrote voluminously on religious history and philosophy: three volumes on the *Corruptions of Christianity,* four volumes of *Notes on All the Books of Scriptures,* and a *Disquisition Relating to Matter and Spirit* which proved that God meant men for happiness. He himself found no difficulty in reconciling his enlightened religion with science, and he was taken aback when the philosophes he met on his tour of France and Germany refused to believe that so distinguished a scientist could be a devout Christian. Himself the most benevolent of philosophers, he was militant on behalf of the True and the Just. He attacked David Hume, he attacked William Blackstone, he attacked Edward Gibbon, he championed the American cause, for he held that liberty was not only a natural right but the hallmark of civilization, and he announced—it was almost a commonplace by now, but Jeremy Bentham always gave him credit for the idea[27]—that the happiness of man was the end of government and that the greatest happiness of the greatest number was "the standard by which everything relating to the state must be judged." He defended the French Revolution, and entered the lists against Burke himself, and it was for this final audacity that a Birmingham mob destroyed his house, his library, and his scientific apparatus. So at sixty-one he sailed for America, where he hoped to be free from tyranny and bigotry. Governor Clinton met him in New York harbor; the University of Pennsylvania offered him a chair in chemistry; Jefferson invited him to settle in Virginia where they would discuss religion and education and he could help with the embryo University of Virginia. Priestley chose instead the Pennsylvania frontier, a farm on the banks of the Susquehanna where he hoped that his English friends and disciples might join him in founding a Utopia; just what

Shelley and Southey and Coleridge planned to do.[28] There Priestley built himself a house and lived out the remainder of his days, preaching, writing, and puttering about in his laboratory, working with his son in the fields for he was a kind of philosophical Cincinnatus as Washington was a military and John Adams a political Cincinnatus. There he found time to complete his extensive *General History of the Christian Church,* which he dedicated to Jefferson, and his *Unitarianism Explained and Defended,* and a comparison of the teachings of Jesus and Socrates which induced Jefferson, in turn, to complete his own study of the teachings of Jesus.[29] Whenever he felt the need for intellectual companionship he could visit the Philosophical Society in Philadelphia where he might chance to see Jefferson—for the government was still in Philadelphia—or Dr. Rush, or the incomparable David Rittenhouse, surveyor, astronomer, and public servant, or Dr. Benjamin Smith Barton, who shared his enthusiasm for the study of the climate and soil of the New World.

Dr. Priestley lived to see Jefferson in the Presidency and to console himself that if the revolution had failed in the Old World, it had triumphed in the New. What he had earlier written to the people of Birmingham was a commentary on his own career, and on the career of the philosophes everywhere:

> The present silent propagation of truth may be compared to those causes in Nature which lie dormant for a time, but which in proper circumstances act with the greatest violence. We are, as it were, laying gunpowder, grain by grain, under the old building of error and superstition, which a single spark may hereafter inflame, so as to produce an instantaneous explosion, in consequence of which that edifice . . . may be overturned in a moment, and so effectually that the same foundation can never be built upon again.[30]

Benjamin Thompson of Woburn, Massachusetts,[31] reversed what with Dr. Priestley and Gallatin and scores of others was almost a standard formula, by moving from the

New World to the Old. He was both a cosmopolite and a man without a country, but in this he was typical enough of the European—though not of the American—philosophe. A Loyalist, almost by accident—for at the age of twenty he had caught the eye of Governor Wentworth who dressed him in a scarlet uniform and made him a major—he had been forced to flee his native country for England where, with his genius for making friends, and using them, he was promptly made Under-Secretary of State and appointed to a Colonelcy in the British Army, and he even returned to ravage Virginia and the South. Yet for all his youthful ardor, he had no use for war, or for empire; his passion, as with all the philosophes, was science, his interest to make a more orderly and ship-shape world. Like Dr. Franklin, whatever he saw he had to improve. He improved heating, gunpowder, firearms, and military transport and was elected to the Royal Society at twenty-six and, in time, to all the scientific academies on the Continent. Soon he caught the fancy of the Elector and was off to Bavaria where, an unlikely Minister of War, he reformed the Army, set up industrial schools, abolished beggary, attacked poverty with workshops for the poor, encouraged scientific farming, and introduced the potato;[32] he even concocted a new potato soup which was honored with the name Rumford, for he was now a Count of the Holy Roman Empire and, with curious piety, chose for his title the name of the little New Hampshire town which later called itself Concord. He put idle soldiers to work draining swamps and cultivating gardens—who but an American would have thought of that (unless it was the practical Frederick of Prussia)—and laid out, in Munich, the famous garden called "English" because of its carefully planned disorder; it was equipped with a Chinese pagoda, a Greek temple and ruins, and with nice calculation, a cattle farm which was to pay for the whole enterprise. The new Elector wearied of Rumford's reforms, or of him, and he returned to London where he endowed the Rumford prizes at the Royal Society and graciously accepted the first of them for himself. He founded the Royal Institution, with its emphasis on the useful arts and sciences and on education as a replica of the American Philosophical

Society. He made improvements in heating—for all the world like Dr. Franklin—and installed over one hundred proper fireplaces in the great houses of London, invented a new lamp, experimented with chemical photography and introduced the drip pot for making coffee. He tried to introduce his improvements to Paris, in vain; so he took them to Dublin, instead, where he was received with rapture. He had betrayed America and returned to lay waste her cities. But the Americans bore him no grudges; they invited him to return as superintendent of the new military academy at West Point. Instead he was off to Bavaria where he organized an Academy of Arts and Sciences, and then to Paris where, in time, he married the widow of the great Lavoisier, Priestley's rival as the discoverer of oxygen, who had fallen afoul of Robespierre. Rumford lived on in Paris untroubled by the tyranny of Napoleon as he had been untroubled by the tyranny of the Elector of Bavaria, cultivating his garden and making improvements in carriages and fireplaces. When he died he left part of his fortune as an endowment for a professorship in Harvard College to teach the physical and mathematical sciences and "for the extension of the industry, prosperity, happiness and well-being of Society." In his cosmopolitanism, his delight in titles and in the society of Princes and Lords, his fascination with the military, his lack of local or even national attachments, his indifference to marriage and to conventional morality, Rumford belongs to the Old World Enlightenment. In his single-minded practicality, his zeal for improvement and for reform, his genuine concern for the welfare of the poor, and for his final philanthropic gesture, he is part of America.

Turn, finally, to a philosophe who had no training in philosophy, and no interest in it; a cosmopolite who came out of the most parochial of backgrounds and was never really at home in any culture but his own; and an internationalist who fought in three countries for the Rights of Man but was a zealous champion of isolation for America. In character and in personality Thomas Paine seems an unlikely representative of the Enlightenment—the lack of personal style, the aesthetic insensitivity, the intellectual aridity, the propensity to fanaticism. But in his devotion to principles rather than to men or places, his fascination with Nature and with mechanics, his abiding faith in Reason and in Progress, and his selfless dedication to the public interest—or to the interest of mankind—Tom Paine belongs indubitably in the era of the Enlightenment.[33]

His love of America was deep and abiding. From the beginning he saw America as the hope of the human race, the American a potential Adam, the country itself a potential Paradise. He had a career in America, as penman of the Revolution, no less; another in the England he had abandoned but from which he could never really escape, and a third in the France he never understood, and he had the remarkable fortune of being rejected by all three countries—outlawed in England, imprisoned in France, scorned and rejected in America.

It was in character, perhaps merely in manners, that Paine differed most strikingly from his brother philosophes, for he was wholly lacking in the graces or in grace notes, in that "taste" in which the age put such store. He was at the center of three cultures and associated with some of their most distinguished figures—Franklin in America, for example, Priestley in England, Condorcet in France—but he confessed nothing of that artistic impulse that persuaded Jefferson to gaze all day at the Maison Carrée "like a lover gazing at his mistress," or Diderot to report the salons, or the youthful Rousseau to compose the charming operetta *Le Devin du Village,* or Joseph Banks to create Kew Gardens. The rejection of the arts was deliberate; as a boy Paine recalled, "I had some talent for poetry, but this I rather repressed than encouraged, as leading too much into the field of imagination." There was something of class mentality here, for Paine associated the arts with privilege, and in eighteenth-century England privilege was very much a class affair. Yet it is difficult to avoid the conclusion that if—in one of Paine's more vivid phrases—Burke had "pitied the plumage but forgot the dying bird," he himself resented the plumage and all that it symbolized.

But when it came to those matters that Paine thought really important, there was no one who spoke more authori-

tatively for his Age than this upstart agitator who was almost a professional troublemaker. It is perhaps this very
lack of profundity, of grace notes, and of local attachments that made it possible for Paine to reflect so faithfully the varied intellectual currents of his day, and to re-
state them in a rhetoric and style that everyone could
understand and remember.

For if Paine had genius, it was for popularization without vulgarization. Indeed, of all the philosophes, only Voltaire had a comparable talent for making complex issues
simple and philosophical issues plain in arguments that
were logical, language that was memorable, and passion
that was contagious. He had genius in his eyes, said
Charles Lee, but it was really more in his pen. It was an
age of great literary artists, but for going to the heart of
the matter with aphorisms that everyone could understand,
and no one could forget, Paine had no rival. "These are
the times that try men's souls," and the phrase was designed for immortality as was the reference to "summer
soldiers and sunshine patriots." How much of Paine was,
indeed, destined for the ultimate immortality of being de-
tached from its original association and living a life of its
own!

Society is produced by our wants and government by
our wickedness. . . . Government like dress is the
badge of lost innocence; the palaces of kings are built
on the ruins of the bowers of paradise. . . . There is
something absurd in supposing a continent to be governed by an island. . . . Of more worth is one honest
man to society and in the sight of God than all the
crowned ruffians that ever lived. . . . Through all the
vocabulary of Adam there is not such an animal as a
Duke or a Count. . . . When we are planning for
posterity we ought to remember that virtue is not hereditary. . . . A bad cause will ever be supported by
bad means and bad men. . . . All the great laws of
society are laws of nature. . . . The contrast of
affluence and wretchedness is like dead and living
bodies chained together. . . . Now is the seedtime of
continental union, faith and honor. . . . Tyranny like

hell is not easily conquered, yet we have this consola-
tion with us, that the harder the conflict the more glorious the triumph. . . . There is a morning of reason
rising upon us. . . . What Athens was in miniature,
America will be in magnitude.[34]

You can go on and on, for Paine overflowed with aphorisms as Mozart overflowed with melodies. No wonder Edmund Burke denounced him as an enemy to society, Burke
of whose arguments in *The Reflections* Paine said that he
had been obliged "to tread a pathless wilderness of rhap-
sodies," only to find that, in the end, "they finish with
music in the ear but nothing in the heart."

Almost by instinct—for he was no scholar, or widely
read—Tom Paine embraced and made his own the leading
ideas of the Enlightenment. Thus, he subscribed to the
principle that Laws of Nature presided over and regulated
"the great machine and structure of the universe." He
was confident that Reason could understand and intelligence apply these great natural laws. Did he not, in the
end, give name to that age—*The Age of Reason?* He
popularized, too, a third great concept of the era, natural
rights; surely this principle reached the average Englishman not so much through the writings of John Locke as
through Paine's *Rights of Man,* just as arguments for independence reached the average American not through the
treatises by John Dickinson or John Adams as through
Common Sense. He shared Jefferson's hostility to tyranny
in every form, helped to overthrow the tyranny of George
III in America, and hoped to overthrow it in England—a
very different matter, that, as he speedily discovered; and
he played an active role in the revolt against absolutism
and privilege in France. He shared, too, Voltaire's determination to destroy "the infamy," and if *The Age of Reason*
did not launch a crusade against the Established Church,
that was, perhaps, because by the mid-nineties, the crusade
was no longer relevant, certainly not in America. He professed Franklin's faith in the common sense of the common man, for he was himself very much a common man,
this stay maker and naval rating who had failed at everything he put his mind to in his own country, and if it was

Dr. Rush who provided the title for that great book, it
was, after all, Paine who wrote it. Like so many of the
French and Italian philosophes he was an ardent humani-
tarian, but where so much of the humanitarianism of the
Old World was, of necessity, an attack on ancient wrongs
and sometimes an amelioration of them, with Paine—as
with his fellow-Americans—it could be the achievement of
social justice for white men, anyway, and the improvement
of material well-being. "Establish the rights of man,"
wrote Paine, "enthrone equality; let there be no privileges,
no distinctions of birth; make safe the liberty of industry
and of trade, the equal distribution of family inheritances,
publicity of administration, freedom of press; and, these
things all established, you will be assured of good laws."[35]

Paine shared with most of the philosophes (not all, by
any means) an almost uncritical faith in progress, but
where, in the Old World, progress tended to be an intellectual abstraction or an aesthetic ideal, with him—as with
most Americans—it was practical, material, immediate,
and equalitarian. Part Two of *The Rights of Man* had for
its sub-title "Combining Principle and Practice," and that
is just what Paine did, once he had come over to
America and found that there was no insurmountable barrier between the two. He was among the first to attack
Negro slavery, and had the satisfaction of writing the preamble to the Pennsylvania Act prohibiting slavery in that
commonwealth.[36] He proposed progressive income
taxes, and taxes on inheritances to finance far-reaching
schemes for social welfare: bonuses to the young at marriage to give them a right start in life (what a difference
that might have made to Tom Paine), special grants and
free schooling to the children of the poor, support for
those thrown out of work by the vicissitudes of industrial
change, and freedom of bargaining for working men. And,
what is more, in *The Rights of Man* he worked out practical schemes for financing these proposals, practical certainly for the common men who bore the burden of taxation, though doubtless wildly impractical in the eyes of the
privileged classes who would be required to pay for them
by heavier taxation, or of the King who would be expected

to forego much of his extravagance and live as simply as an American President.[37]

Clearly much of the tyranny of government and the misery of men could be traced to war, for war carried in its womb corruption, extravagance, injustice, ruin, and death. "War," wrote Paine, "is the Pharo-table of governments and nations the dupes of the game." Who knew better than Paine, who at the age of nineteen had served on the warship *King of Prussia,* who had written the *Crisis* papers on a ramhead by the flickering light of camp fires, and who had lived through the wars of the French Revolution and Napoleon, that man would never win his rights as long as nations were at each other's throats. He proposed that nations scrap their navies and form, instead, a federation of nations dedicated to peacekeeping, but meantime he urged that the new United States steer clear of foreign involvements. "Nothing of reform in the political world ought to be held improbable," he wrote, for

it is an age of revolution in which everything may be looked for. The intrigues of courts by which the system of war is sustained, may in time provoke a federation of nations strong enough to abolish it; and a European congress to patronize the progress of free government and promote the civilization of nations, in an event nearer to probability than once were the alliance of France and America, and the French Revolution.[38]

Thomas Paine was a world figure, but it was America that made him. It was in America that he found his mission in life. It was to America he returned, in the end, after both England and France had rejected him. It was on America, too, that his hopes were centered. Everywhere in the Old World "antiquity and bad habits" supported tyranny. Freedom had been hunted round the globe; reason was considered as rebellion. "America was the only spot in the political world where the principles of universal reformation could begin."[39] And Paine was confident that he would live to "enjoy the Happiness of seeing the New World regenerate the Old." Nor did America betray him.

He lived to see the greatest of American philosophes in the White House, the one man who combined in himself all that the Enlightenment thought and all that it felt, and all that it did: what a tribute, that, to the virtue of republicanism! And what a gratification to poor Tom Paine that he had helped bring all this about. Through all the poverty and neglect and contumely of his last years he could reflect that no sooner was Mr. Jefferson in the White House than he brought him back to his adopted country, and in a public ship, too, and with the encomium that "it will be your glory to have steadily labored, and with as much effect as any man living to bring about the greatest of revolutions."[40] Surely that was such triumph as could wear out mere glamor.

CHAPTER THREE

The Enlightenment Unveils a New World of Nature and of Man

1

What had they in common, the philosophes,[1] the encyclo-pédistes, the naturalists, the explorers, the historians, the statesmen? They were a fellowship engaged, so they believed, in a common enterprise and bound together by a common faith.[2] They were launched on a voyage of dis-covery of new worlds, new ideas, new laws, new aspects of nature and of human nature. On these voyages of discov-ery they steered by the compass of Reason, for while they did not disparage the emotions or the passions,[3] they ac-knowledged the sovereignty of Reason, and were confident that with Reason as their guide they could penetrate to the truth about the Universe and about Man, and thus solve all of those problems that pressed upon them so insistently. "Reason is for the philosopher what grace is for the Chris-tian," wrote César Dumarsais; Diderot incorporated the fe-licitous phrase in his essay on *Philosophe* in the Encyl-copédie,[4] and the master plan for that great *Dictionnaire raisonné* allocated to philosophy all that was dependent on reason.[5] Perhaps Voltaire put the matter best, as he put most things best:

God has given us a principle of universal reason, as he has given feathers to birds and furs to bears; and

this principle is so constant, that it subsists despite all
the passions which struggle against it; despite the tyrants who wish to drown it in blood; despite the im-
posters who would employ superstition to bring it to
naught.[6]

It was Reason that guided the legal thinking of Blackstone
and his greatest critic, Jeremy Bentham; Reason that reorganized the national economy in Prussia and Austria and
Denmark; and the great Jacques Louis David asserted that
"the genius of the arts needs no other guide than the torch
of reason."[7] Looking back over half a century of struggle,
the aged Jefferson celebrated the animating principle of his
age. "We believed," he wrote to Justice Johnson, "that
man was a rational animal, endowed by nature with rights
. . . We believed that men, habituated to thinking for
themselves, and to follow their reason as guide, would be
more easily and safely governed than with minds
nourished in error and vitiated and debased . . . by ignorance."[8]
They had confidence, most of them, in progress—
progress, sometimes, in material things like agriculture and
industry, or, more often, in lifting the burdens of life from
the shoulders of men,[9] progress, more commonly, in government, law, and science, even philosophy, the arts, and
morals.[10] They were cosmopolites—citizens of the world, in
Goldsmith's happy phrase—and enlisted in the service of
mankind. "A philosopher," wrote Gibbon, "was to consider Europe as one great republic." Most of the philosophes took in more than just Europe; they could say, with
the great Neapolitan statesman, Filangieri, that "the philosopher is a citizen of the world, not of a single country;
he has the whole world for his country, and earth itself for
his school. Posterity will be his disciples."[11]
Faith in Reason, in Progress, in a common Humanity—
these were the principles that bound together such disparate figures as Voltaire and Diderot, Franklin and Jefferson, Buffon and Raynal, Count Rumford and Josef Sonnenfels, Dr. Price and Jeremy Bentham, Joseph Priestley
and Joseph Banks, Ludwig Holberg and Johann Struensee,
Gotthold Lessing and Adrian Van der Kemp, and scores

like them.[12] These are the men of the Enlightenment, the
men who will chart the new universe that is opening up before their enraptured gaze; they are the first fully to emancipate themselves from religious superstition and to understand the nature of man in the light of science and
reason.[13] Their curiosity is as boundless as their daring. "I
do not know," wrote Charles Duclos, who succeeded Voltaire as royal historiographer, "whether I have too favorable an opinion of my century, but it seems to me there is a
certain fermentation of universal reason which is tending
to develop."[14] So said the youthful Jeremy Bentham, in his
first published work: "The age we live in is a busy age, in
which knowledge is rapidly advancing towards perfection.
On the natural world in particular, everything teems with
discovery and with improvement." And, he added, "Corre-
spondent to discovery and improvement in the natural
world, is reformation in the moral."[15] In his *Essay on the
Elements of Philosophy* d'Alembert asserted that,

> Our century has called itself the philosophic century
> par excellence. . . . from the principles of the pro-
> fane sciences to the foundations of revelation, from
> metaphysics to questions of taste, from music to
> morals, from the scholastic disputes of theologians to
> commercial affairs, from the rights of princes to those
> of people, from the natural law to the arbitrary law of
> nations, in a word from the questions that affect us
> most to those that interest us least, everything has
> been discussed, analyzed and disputed.[16]

Everything discussed and disputed! What a din of controversy and debate, what a clashing of minds, and of tem-
peraments too. What is the nature of the universe and of
the celestial mechanics that God imposed upon it? How
does Man fit into the cosmic system? Is religion necessary,
is Christianity the only true religion? What is the end and
the object of life? Is it happiness, and if so, what is happiness? Is primitive man happier than civilized man? Are the
Chinese the most civilized of men? Is civilization a mistake? What is beauty, what is virtue, what is truth? Are
wars ever justified, are colonies worth their cost? What de-

termines the character of nations? What is the origin of government, what the basis and the limits of government? What are the rights of Man—that cuts close to the bone!

These are the great questions that sent pens scratching across an infinity of pages, that launched a thousand Essays, Discourses, Considerations, Inquiries, and Histories. How they speculated, how they probed, how they wrote! They searched the past, they explored the present, they imagined the future. They contemplated Nature in all her manifestations, but always in relation to Man: they were cosmic philosophers, but they never doubted that Nature was to be judged by her usefulness to Man, and their theologians stood ready to prove that every phenomenon of Nature was designed by Providence for the convenience of Man.[17] They studied history, confident that they could wrest from it great and enduring moral lessons. They analyzed government to ascertain its role in assuring happiness to Man. They charted the economy and their economists were all moral philosophers.[18] With extensive view, they surveyed mankind from China to Peru, and even beyond. They sought the good and the true; they were enraptured with the sublime and the beautiful;[19] they cherished virtue; they pursued happiness. Nothing trivial, nothing parochial; only the greatest questions were worthy of their attention.

Listen to the titles of some of their books, titles that almost take your breath away with their ambition and their presumption. The great Christian Wolff of Halle led the way with *Reasonable Thoughts on God, the World, the Soul of Man, and All Things in General;* perhaps none of his successors staked out broader claims than that, but it was not for want of boldness.[20] Early in the century the Abbé Saint Pierre had produced a *Project for Universal Peace,* and late in life he followed that with a *Project to Perfect the Governments of States.* Montesquieu probed *The Spirit of the Laws,* and Voltaire submitted a long *Essay on the Morals and Character of Nations.* The hapless Morelly who wanders through the century like some frustrated ghost without a Christian name, wrote not only the *Code of Nature,* but an *Essay on the Human Spirit* and an *Essay on the Human Heart.* Up in Scotland Adam

Ferguson undertook a *History of Civil Society*, Francis
Hutcheson proposed a *System of Moral Philosophy*, and
Adam Smith launched his immortal *Inquiry into the
Wealth of Nations*, and the psychologist David Hartley,
admired by Priestley and by Dr. Rush, published *Observations on Man, His Frame, His Duty, His Expectations.*
The Marquis d'Argens produced a *History of the Human
Spirit* and the Marquis de Chastellux concocted two volumes *On Public Happiness.* Gotthold Lessing surveyed
The Education of the Human Race, and Johan G. Herder
put together four volumes of *Ideas on the History of Humanity.* At the age of twenty-three the Marquis Turgot
pronounced a *Discourse on the Successive Advances of the
Human Mind*, and his disciple Condorcet managed, just
before his death, to provide a sketch for an *Historical Picture of the Progress of the Human Mind.* The Baron
d'Holbach outlined, in a few years, a *System of Nature*, a
System of Society, and a *System of Universal Morality*,
and, fittingly enough, at the end of the century Du Pont de
Nemours, who belonged to both Old World and New,
covered the whole ground with *A Philosophy of the Universe.*

Yet even the genius of a Voltaire, a Diderot, a Lessing,
could not really encompass the whole of Nature, or of History. So the philosophes embarked upon great co-operative
enterprises. It was the age of the Encyclopedias, and the
greatest of these, *Encyclopédie, ou Dictionnaire raisonné
des sciences, des arts, et des métiers, par une société des
gens de lettres*, was the representative product of the age.[21]
It had started with Chambers' Encyclopaedia; Diderot and
d'Alembert, who had agreed to revise it for French
readers, wearied of that dull compilation, nor did they
propose to imitate the massive German Encyclopedia with
the characteristic title *Grosses Vollständiges Univer-
sal-Lexikon Aller Wissenschaften und Künste Welche bi-
shero durch senschlichen Verstand und Witz erfunden und
Verbessert worden,** in no less than sixty-four stout
volumes.[22] No, an encyclopedia was not just a device for

* The Great Comprehensive Universal Encyclopedia of Science and
the Arts which have up to the Present been discovered and developed
by the wit and understanding of Man.

putting facts together, though it was that. Nor was it
merely a survey of all the new knowledge that had burst
upon the astonished world in the century since Newton—
though it was that, too. It was a weapon, it was a campaign, it was a crusade;[23] its purpose nothing less than the
regeneration of mankind. The object of the Encyclopédie,
wrote d'Alembert

> is to assemble the knowledge scattered over the sur-
> face of the earth, to explain its general plan to the
> men with whom we live, and to transmit it to the men
> who come after us; in order that the labors of cen-
> turies past may not be in vain during the centuries to
> come; that our descendants, by becoming better in-
> structed, may as a consequence be more virtuous and
> happier, and that we may not die without having de-
> served well of the human race.[24]

Most of the philosophes hurled themselves into the fray—
Diderot, of course, who wrote a good part of it, and
d'Alembert, whose enthusiasm cooled, and Voltaire, Mar-
montel, Rousseau, and the Baron d'Holbach, and the almost forgotten Daubenton, who had worked with Buffon,
and the Chevalier de Jaucourt, who wrote on almost every
subject.[25] Wherever they could manage—they were dis-
creet and even evasive in their articles on religion[26]—the
authors fired off artillery salvos against some ancient injustice, some gross superstition, some palpable absurdity.
Some of these hit home, though many of them were
deflected by that worst of printers, André Francois Le Breton, who, terrified by the threat of censorship, took upon
himself the responsibility for censoring the Encyclopédie,
cutting, hacking, and despoiling the great work just to save
his own skin.[27]

For now, almost everywhere, the philosophers were
straining at the bonds of orthodox Christianity or, what
was worse, undermining it, sometimes in the name of
religion itself. Thus, Matthew Tindal of All Souls, Oxford,
whose justification of Christianity did as much to injure it
as Voltaire's attacks;[28] thus, Soame Jenyns, who proved
the necessity of pain, misery, poverty, and ignorance in the

Divine Order by the argument that "the beauty and happiness of the whole depend altogether on the just inferiority of the parts."[29] Thus, too, Pope, whose *Essay on Man* admonished those who were puzzled by the persistence of evil in the world

> Know thy own point: this kind, this due degree
> Of blindness, weakness, Heaven bestows on thee,
> Submit, in this, or any other sphere
> Secure to be as blest as thou can bear.[30]

Or there was Emmanuel Swedenborg, surely a special kind of philosophe, who conjured up a new Heaven and a new Hell and, for that matter, a new kind of Christianity. In Hamburg there was the inoffensive Professor Hermann Reimarus whose posthumously published *Apology for the Rational Worship of God* undermined much of the Old and some of the New Testament, Original Sin, Miracles, and Revelation, and in making God rational made worship of Him superfluous.[31] Meantime the Deists were launching ceaseless attacks upon the Scriptures and the miracles, from John Toland's *Christianity Not Mysterious* (1696) to Tom Paine's *Age of Reason* a century later.[32] Nor was this the worst that the Church had to endure. As early as 1741 the curious Johan Edelmann of Jena had proclaimed the falseness of God and the Scriptures in his *Divinity of Reason.*[33] Soon David Hume was to dispose not only of miracles but of religion itself, and with admirable impartiality of Reason as well, at least as anything one could rely on.[34] And though Gibbon never counted himself among the philosophes, none of them, not Voltaire, not Lessing, not even Hume, dealt a heavier blow to orthodox Christianity and to the pretensions of the Church than did the author of the *Decline and Fall.* Over in France La Mettrie—Voltaire called him the "King's Atheist in Ordinary"—announced that Man was a Machine, neither more nor less; and indeed if the whole world was a machine, why not man?[35] Soon, too (1770), the Baron d'Holbach, who could be forgiven everything because his hospitality was boundless and his dinners Lucullan,[36] was to explain all

things in simple terms of matter and motion and point out
that

> If we go back to the beginning we shall always find
> that ignorance and fear have created gods; fancy, en-
> thusiasm, or deceit has adorned or disfigured them;
> weakness worships them; credulity preserves them in
> life; custom regards them and tyranny supports them
> in order to make the blindness of men serve its own
> ends.[37]

Two years later d'Holbach rejoiced to publish what was
perhaps the most shocking of all assaults on Christianity,
the *Testament* of the apostate priest, Jean Meslier.[38]

The philosophes were indeed "going back to the beginning" to find the origin of religion, and finding that natural
religion flourished in ancient times and among the most
exotic peoples, in China, Peru, Tahiti, and the forests of
Canada. No wonder they celebrated

> the poor Indian, whose untutored mind
> Sees God in clouds and hears him in the wind.

No wonder they delighted when Diderot reported how the
grave Orou confounded the pious Almoner there under the
bread trees of Tahiti.[39] Skepticism about religion stimulated and gave respectability to the study of primitive man
and exotic societies, and now at last the explorers and navigators had provided abundant material for such study.[40]
How logical of Rousseau to propose that ten-year expedition by scientists and philosophers to study primitive societies; a score of expeditions did just that. And for every
narrative of exploration, there were a dozen fictions and
dramas and imaginary voyages, all designed to bring home
to Europeans that there were many religions besides the
Christian, and many roads to Heaven, too.[41] This conclusion was re-enforced by the writings of the learned Sir
William Jones of Oxford and the Bengal, who laid the
foundations for the study of comparative religion and of
comparative law.[42]

Along with this skepticism about revelation and miracles

—this habit of looking on God as a Master Clockmaker, and of man as a machine—went a new interest in psychology, a study first given vogue by Christian Wolff, and elaborated on by David Hartley with his doctrine of the *Association of Ideas*,[43] and by Étienne Condillac whose *Treatise on Sensations* went well beyond Locke toward materialism.[44] With all this went a more intense study of man, his brain, his nervous system, his instincts and passions and appetites, a study that led such literary interpreters as Restif de la Bretonne and the Marquis de Sade down perverse and labyrinthine ways.[45]

There was a new interest, too, in the mind of primitive man, and a readiness to speculate about intelligence in animals and about possible links between man and the higher animals. The Swiss doctor and psychologist Charles Bonnet surmised that the advance of civilization was a product of successive Deluges or Catastrophes, each one bringing about an improvement in the germs responsible for new life, and predicted that in time "there may be found a Leibniz or a Newton amongst the monkeys or the elephants, a Perrault or Vauban among the beavers."[46] And the fantastic Lord Monboddo in Edinburgh, who wrote six volumes on *The Origin and Progress of Language*, boldly asserted that the orang-outang was part of the human species with not only a mind but even a language, and concluded on a note already becoming widespread, that "there is a progression of our species from a state little better than mere brutality to that most perfect state you describe in ancient Greece, which is really amazing and peculiar to our species."[47] So, just as the scientists turned away from the Biblical account of Creation on 28 August 4004 B.C. to the contemplation of a long progressive evolution, and the historians from their parochial interest in the Mediterranean and European civilizations to the study of the societies and civilizations that flourished on other continents, the philosophers turned from the desperate attempt to rationalize Scriptural miracles to the infinitely more interesting and more rewarding study of man as a product of his material environment.[48]

2

Do not suppose that it was only the philosophes who engaged in this vast inquiry into Nature and Man, government and economy, morals and art, and who launched themselves upon voyages of discovery. It was a universal occupation, it was almost an obsession. Statesmen enlisted eagerly—Turgot, Struensee, Pombal, Sonnenfels, Tanucci in Naples, Campomanes in Spain; and even sovereigns like Frederick of Prussia and Catherine of Russia, both called "the Great," made gestures toward discovering new worlds. In America, needless to say, all the statesmen were philosophers. The historians took part, too: Montesquieu with his study of the *Grandeur and Decadence of Rome;* Voltaire who wrote histories in every form—even his romances and dramas were commentaries on history;[1] the Abbé Raynal whose *Philosophical History of the Indies* was, after Rollin's interminable *Ancient History,* the most popular and possibly the most influential history of the age;[2] David Hume whose *History of England* was as secular as Voltaire's but not as liberal or as entertaining;[3] Ludwig Holberg with his *Histories* of almost everything from *Denmark* to *The World;*[4] Johannes Müller who expressed equal enthusiasm for Frederick the Great and for Liberty, and whose romantic story of the Swiss Confederation helped inspire Schiller's *Wilhelm Tell.*[5] And over in America Jeremy Belknap of New Hampshire and Hugh Williamson of North Carolina wrote local history to illustrate the operation of universal laws of climate and of morals in the New World.[6]

Economists, too, enrolled in the great enterprise, men like Dr. Quesnay who has some claim to be regarded as the father of physiocracy, and his disciple Du Pont de Nemours who ended up in America, and Dr. Richard Price who successfully combined theology with economy and formulated sound principles of insurance, and principles that were optimistic rather than sound for disposing of the national debt. In Glasgow Adam Smith professed Moral Philosophy, and in Italy Antonio Genovesi, de-

barred from a chair of philosophy at the University of
Naples for his heretical notions, held the first chair of economics in all Europe, while his wonderful colleague Gaetano Filangieri covered the whole range of politics, economics, education, and morals in his six-volume *Science of
Legislation*. In Milan the Marquis Cesare Beccaria, whose
Treatise on Crimes and Punishments influenced governments throughout the civilized world, lectured on economics.[7]

Even the artists and art-philosophers joined in the inquiry, seeking general principles and authoritative laws:
Joshua Reynolds and William Hogarth, for example, both
of whom laid down first principles of beauty—how
different their practice!—and Edmund Burke who defined
the Sublime as well as the Beautiful, and William Chambers who thought true beauty was to be found only in
China and tried to transplant some of China to England.
Montesquieu wrote a treatise on "Taste," and Buffon made
"Taste" the subject of his inaugural address as a new
member of the Academy. Diderot launched a "philosophical Inquiry into the Nature of the Beautiful." Johann
Winckelmann's *History of Ancient Art* set standards for a
whole generation, and his fellow-German, the happily
named Raphael Mengs, gave the world *Thoughts on
Beauty and Taste in Painting*.[8]

Meantime, the scientists, navigators, explorers, and adventurers who swarmed over the globe all through the century were giving new dimensions to both Nature and Man.
The astronomers and cartographers had made their contributions earlier—Jean Cassini had solved the mathematical
problem of measuring longitude in the seventeenth century, but it was not until the invention of the mirror-sextant and the chronometer in the eighteenth that the practical problem was solved.[9] In 1772 John Moore issued the
first edition of that *Practical Navigator* which the genius of
young Nathaniel Bowditch over in Salem, Massachusetts,
was to make the *vade mecum* of every sailor on every
sea.[10] And one dread peril of the sea was in process of being
banished: an Austrian doctor and an English surgeon's
mate discovered that lemons could prevent scurvy, and
Captain Cook triumphantly demonstrated it by circum-

navigating the globe without losing a single man to the familiar disease.[11]

Now new worlds sprang up before the enraptured gaze of the philosophers. The fifteenth and sixteenth centuries had been the Age of Reconnaissance and Discovery, yet at the dawn of the eighteenth century most of the globe was still unexplored and much of it even unknown to Europeans.[12] The broad sweep of the Pacific was unmapped, and scores of islands, great and small, that were to be the delight and despair of Europe, were as yet undiscovered, though the vast and mysterious Terra Australis Incognita was located uneasily in the Antarctic. Of the two great American continents only the fringes had been thoroughly exposed; from Hudson's Bay to Tierra del Fuego the shaggy interior was still hidden from the European gaze but did not escape its imagination. Most of Africa, too, was *terra incognita*, for there had been no progress in exploration since the days of Henry the Navigator, and no explorers had yet penetrated to the exotic kingdom of Prester John. China, India, Persia, could not be called unexplored for they boasted ancient civilizations, but only the intrepid Jesuits had penetrated their interior recesses and their secrets; even they had been unable to pry open the kingdom of Japan.

But by the close of the century, what a change! Now explorers, sailing under a dozen different flags, had crisscrossed the Pacific, dotting its map with one island after another, and substituting for the mythical Terra Australis Incognita an Australia that was soon to be an asylum for English felons and failures. The Russians opened up Siberia; the Spaniards launched a succession of expeditions into the American interior, and up the long coast of California where they met the Russians; the French opened up the Great Plains and penetrated into the Rockies, and dauntless Scots conquered the continent west from Michilimackinac and reached the Pacific. Even Labrador was not exempt: Captain Cartwright made six voyages to its barren shores and brought back some Esquimaux who promptly died, and Joseph Banks botanized there, and in Iceland. Africa, too, if not fully explored was becoming known, with the Dutch at the Cape pushing relentlessly into the interior, and greedy slavers plying their nefarious trade along the Gold Coast, and the indefatigable James Bruce exploring to the headwaters of the Nile. India, given over to warring European companies and armies, was remaking the British economy and corrupting British politics, and China, as an idea rather than as a nation, was conquering the European imagination.[13]

Only a tremendous outburst of energy could achieve all this in less than a century. It was inspired chiefly by imperial rivalries, to be sure, and by that search for wealth and markets which was the subject of the Abbé Raynal's eight-volume polemic. But that was not the whole story. It was inspired by scientific curiosity, too. So said President De Brosses of the Parlement of Dijon in his famous *History of Navigations:* "It is not necessary that we concern ourselves overmuch with the advantages we hope to gain from these enterprises. Consider rather the role of scientific curiosity, the contributions to geography, the addition of new lands and new peoples, to the geography of the globe."[14] It was a vast, unplanned and unconscious co-operative enterprise to lay open the whole of the world; to chart the skies, explore the seas, map the land, find new flora and fauna, and new men as well, new civilizations, perhaps, just as Cortes and Pizarro had found new civilizations.

Consider that remarkable international effort to chart the transit of Venus in 1769:[15] Danes, Swedes, French, Spaniards, English, even Americans, who did the best they could—and very good it was, too—all joined in the great adventure. Monarchs were at war and armies clashed, but the explorers and astronomers, zoologists and botanists, united on the common principle that the sciences are never at war, worked together harmoniously to advance knowledge of the universe.[16]

Almost every year some expedition sailed out to circumnavigate the globe, find a new continent or new islands, stake out national claims, open new trade routes, collect botanical specimens or make astronomical observations. As the seventeenth century blended into the eighteenth, William Dampier was adding island after island on the map of the Pacific—Galapagos, New Guinea, New Britain, even Australia. He was a pirate, but he was a Naturalist, too, and a man of letters, and all was forgiven.[17] A few years later Woode Rogers told the story of Alexander Selkirk on his lonely island in the South Pacific, a tale which fired the imagination of Daniel Defoe who became, in time, a kind of fictional Hakluyt.[18] In the seventeen-forties came the exploits of Captain Anson; for four years he sailed the Pacific, from the Ladrones and Formosa to Canton, in between punishing the Spaniards, just on the chance that they were an enemy. Thereafter, one fleet followed another; Captain Byron, grandfather of the poet, who circumnavigated the globe in 1764, and Captain Wallis who discovered Tahiti—what a gift that was to the world of literature—and next the learned Bougainville who described Tahiti as an earthly Paradise and whose description inspired an even more famous description from the pen of Denis Diderot. Bougainville further won immortality by giving his name to one of the most magnificent of flowers.[19] Greatest of them all was Captain Cook who in 1769 sailed to Tahiti to observe the transit of Venus, and in two more voyages, swept the mists from the Pacific all the way from Alaska to Australia, putting an end to the myth of the Antarctic continent and of the Northwest Passage.[20] Now the world imagined by Jonathan Swift was banished: he had located Lilliput between Van Dieman's Land, New Holland, and Brobdignag, the land of giants, east of Japan, and the land of the Houyhyhnms in the Terra Australis Incognita. What emerged from the discoveries of the navigators was scarcely less marvelous than what the misanthropic Dean (Swift) had imagined.

How it all excited the imagination of the men of letters, and how impoverished literature would be without the inspiration of discovery and the response to it! There were a thousand imaginary voyages: to the moon, to Jupiter, to Saturn, to the underworld, to the islands of the Pacific or of the Indian seas, to the mythical kingdoms of Prester John or the real Kingdom of the Incas, or to Arabia Felix. What would the literary scene be without *Robinson Crusoe* or *Captain Singleton, Gulliver's Travels* or *Roderick Random,* Dr. Johnson's *Rasselas* or the wicked Beckford's *Vathek,* Voltaire's *Candide* or Morelly's *Basiliade,* the Abbé Prévost's *Manon Lescaut,* destined for musical immortality, and Saint Pierre's *Paul and Virginia* destined for artistic, Sterne's *Sentimental Journey* and LeSage's *Gil Blas,* the *Marvellous Adventures of the Baron Munchausen,* or Albrecht von Haller's Utopian romances? Many of these imaginary tales were set in the New World, like Mrs. Behn's immensely popular *Oroonoko or the Royal Slave* and, a century later, Chateaubriand's *Atala.* The New World, too, inspired a vast literature of exploration and description, from William Byrd's *History of the Dividing Line* and William Bartram's *Travels in the Carolinas and Florida* to Crèvecoeur's incomparable *Letters from an American Farmer* and the good Dr. Belknap's *The Foresters.*

For from the beginning the literature of America had been in large part a response to the beauties and marvels of Nature and to the dangers and marvels of the Indians: John Smith's immortal story of Pocahontas, and the eloquent journals of William Bradford, Cadwallader Colden's *History of the Five Indian Nations,* and the scores of thrilling narratives of Indian captivity. That obsession with Nature was to dictate the style of much of the literature of the young Republic for years to come, for with independence and the prospect of westward expansion came a flowering of literature celebrating Nature in all of its manifestations.[21] Thus, the poetry of such disparate versifiers as Philip Freneau, whose "Wild Honeysuckle" and "Indian Burying Ground" were destined for a longer life than his political verse, and Alexander Wilson's epic poem, *The Foresters* (did he know of Dr. Belknap's novel?)—just the right poem for the first and in many ways the greatest of ornithologists and a better poem than Barlow's much touted *Columbiad* or Timothy Dwight's relentless *Conquest of Canaan.* Thus, too, the novels of Charles Brockden Brown, who quite deliberately concluded that "the incidents of Indian hostility and the perils of the western wilderness" were the most suitable subjects for the novelist, of Hugh Henry Brackenridge's *Modern Chivalry,* a kind of American *Don Quixote,* and the novels and histories of Washington Irving and Fenimore Cooper.

Now heroic explorers who were both Naturalists and men of letters were adding a special dimension to American literature: Meriwether Lewis and William Clark, whose story of the great expedition to the Pacific Coast took on in time the legendary character of the Odyssey; and John Ledyard, who wrote an account of Captain Cook's last voyage and whose travels took him to every quarter of the globe; and François André Michaux, whose *North American Sylva* was destined to be a classic, and Zebulon Pike, who gave his name to a peak as famous as that on Darien. All of these had been sent out by Jefferson, whose *Notes on Virginia* had some claim to be the best American treatise on "climate," combining as it did geography, botany, ethnology, history, and philosophy, for Jefferson was even a greater patron of exploration than Joseph Banks himself and with sympathies and objectives broader than those entertained by the Maecenas of Soho Square.

In the meantime, two great continents were opened up to science and to settlement. In a burst of energy as spectacular as that which the Spaniards displayed in the sixteenth century, the Russians now thrust one spearhead after another, eastward and northward, into the limitless wastes of Siberia.[22] By the end of the seventeenth century they had reached the Amur and there erected a barrier against the fierce Chinese to the south. During the next century they established themselves on the immense peninsula of Kamchatka which they used as a springboard for the exploration of the north Pacific. In the seventeen-twenties and again in the forties, the Danish navigator Vitus Bering explored these unknown seas east of Siberia, and in 1741 he found the strait which now bears his name and touched on the mainland of America. During the second half of this century the Russians moved along the Aleutians, setting up trading posts on Kodiak and Unalaska islands, and they went onto the mainland where they found seal and otter beyond the dreams of avarice. Swiftly they pushed down the Pacific Coast, setting up permanent posts at Prince William Bay and even at Fort Ross, just north of the Bay of St. Francis. Soon English and French ships were drawn to these shores and harbors, seeking a share in the lucrative trade with China.

At last North America was yielding its secrets. All

through the eighteenth century the Spaniards, French, and English were thrusting into the vast and unknown interior, dispelling the myth of the Northwest Passage, and that other myth of a great river flowing from the headwaters of the Missouri into the Pacific.[23] Animated by missionary zeal, by greed, and by fear of Russia, New Spain sent out expedition after expedition from Mexico, eastward across Texas, northward into Colorado, westward across the most forbidding of deserts into California, and up that long coast until, in 1769, Gaspar de Portola reached the noble bay which he christened San Francisco. Within a few years the coast of California was dotted with missions, from San Diego to San Juan. Still other explorers, by sea and by land, staked out a claim to Nootka Sound and another at Sante Fe.[24] What an Empire it was! Not Alexander's empire, nor the Roman under Diocletian embraced so many races and tribes or so much land, and it seemed to have inexhaustible vigor.

The French, too, were busy unlocking the mysteries of the new continent, and scrambling for its resources.[25] The intrepid La Salle had opened the way; by 1682 he had followed the Mississippi to its mouth and struck off into Texas, where he met his death, but he had planted the standard of Louis XIV that was to wave over New Orleans for a century. Early in the new century Bernard de la Harpe moved out from New Orleans to the plains of Texas, exploring the Red River of the South, which he hoped might link up with some passage to the Pacific, and he fired the French imagination not only with reports of diamond mines, but of unicorns, too. Louis de St. Denis explored westward along the Red River and down to the Rio Grande, and soon the French and Spaniards were competing all along the Louisiana-Texas frontier, with merchandise, or with arms. But though in the seventeen-forties the brothers Mallet fought their way from the Illinois country across prairie and desert and mountain to Santa Fe, the French could not in the long run compete with the Spanish in the southwest, and transferred their attention to the North.

Toward mid-century, the wonderful la Vérendrye family penetrated deep into the West.[26] They crossed the rolling prairies of the Dakota country, where they found the fair-skinned Mandans, indubitably the descendants of Madoc, Prince of Wales! and they caught a glimpse of the Rockies from whose crests they hoped to gaze upon the distant western sea. Meantime, back in France Father Bobé and Guillaume de Lisle, the royal geographer, drew maps showing that there was but a short portage between the headwaters of the Missouri and a series of great rivers flowing into the Pacific. "Nothing easier," wrote Father Bobé, "than to have communication between the two seas by lakes and rivers." Nothing easier, indeed! In a matter of only eighty years or so of incessant exploration and un-paralleled adventure and heroism, the problem was solved, though not at all as Father Bobé and his Parisian map-maker had imagined.

The Scots took up where the French had left off, one dauntless explorer after another: Henry Kelsey who cele-brated his northern explorations in wretched verse, and James Hearne who reached the Arctic at the mouth of the Coppermine River, and Alexander Henry, yet another of Joseph Banks's many protégés, who drafted a plan for "A Proper Route by Land to Cross the Great Contenant [sic] of America," and almost carried it through. The crowning achievement came at the close of the century when the in-trepid Alexander Mackenzie, after giving his name to one of the great rivers of the world, made his way down the misnamed Peace River and then along the Salmon River to the Pacific Coast, and definitely ended the dream of a Northwest Passage already blurred by the findings of Cap-tain Cook. He found the Russians already on the coast; he just missed Captain Vancouver who had planted the Brit-ish flag, and his own name, on the great island opposite the mouth of the Fraser.[27]

The Americans were there too, though theirs was as yet only a kind of token rivalry for empire. Samuel Shaw and "King Derby" of Salem had already opened up that China trade which had for too long been the monopoly of the Russians, and in 1792 Captain Robert Gray entered the mouth of the great river which had been known as the "Oregan," and named it, after his ship, *Columbia*, thus staking out a claim for America to this country which was formally ratified half a century later.[28]

Now at last poor John Ledyard was vindicated.[29] Running away from the infant Dartmouth College, he had shipped as a sailor to the Mediterranean; then in 1776 to London where he talked his way into a berth on Captain Cook's *Discovery*, and he sailed on that famous third voyage to the Pacific. At Unalaska Island he visited with the Russians, and consumed a fearsome meal of bear meat and whale oil; at Nootka Sound he caught a glimpse of the limitless possibilities of a triangular trade in furs from Boston to the Pacific Northwest and on to China. He went back east to plead with ship masters and bankers for support of his vision, but in vain, so he decided to make his way to Nootka Sound and eastward across the continent on foot, just to show that it could be done. Fortune intervened to thwart him, as it was to do again and again, for he seemed marked for failure, this Connecticut Yankee who was something of a mad man and something of a visionary and yet, withall, so sensible and simple. Nothing daunted, he hit on the wild idea of walking across Europe and Siberia to Kamchatka, and thence by boat to Alaska, and down the Northwest coast and across mountains and deserts and plains all the way to Virginia: just the plan to catch the interest of Mr. Jefferson. He almost succeeded in his fantastic scheme, too, reaching Yakutsk in far-eastern Siberia before the Empress Catherine's soldiers caught up with him and hurried him back all the way and decanted him into Poland. In despair he offered his services to Joseph Banks, who persuaded him to try to penetrate the interior of Africa and cross that continent to the mouth of the Niger. He ascended the Nile, succumbed to fever, and was buried there, but Jefferson did not forget him or his plan of crossing the American continent on foot.[30] Who else, even in that age of exploration, and of eccentricity, had seen so much of the globe, or seen it so intimately— America, Europe, Asia, and Africa, and even the islands of the Pacific. Who else had imagined so audaciously and yet so sensibly? How fitting it was, in that age of so many paradoxes, that this great world traveler should come from parochial Connecticut.

Other travelers, scholars, men of letters and of art, rediscovered the Far East—China, India, Burma, and Siam —and wondered if these ancient peoples had not found the secret of happiness. Much of their information came from the *Édifiantes* which the Jesuits had been sending back from these distant lands for over a century. Soon everyone was proclaiming the wisdom of Confucius, or extolling the virtues of Chinese education, or painting in what they took to be the Chinese style, or building Chinese pagodas in gardens landscaped in the Chinese manner, or writing letters from mythical Chinamen which made fun of the absurdities of European society. That was how the dissipated Marquis d'Argens tried to make Paris look foolish and how the upright Oliver Goldsmith advertised the follies of London.[31]

China rapidly captured the imagination of all Europe: Philosophers, men of letters, artists, theologians, even monarchs and their mistresses caught the contagion and rejoiced in this exotic world.[32] As early as 1670 the Jesuit Athanasius Kircher had reported that China "is ruled by Doctors, à la mode of Plato, and according to the desire of divine philosophy; and I hold the ruler to be happy because he is himself a philosopher, or permits a philosopher to govern." Shortly after came another Jesuit, Father Le Comte, who made clear in his *Nouveaux mémoires sur l'état de Chine* that for more than two thousand years the Chinese had in fact practiced all the Christian virtues. The faculty of the University of Paris promptly condemned the book on the logical ground that it made Christianity superfluous.

At the very end of the century the incomparable Leibniz pointed out, in his *Novissima Sinica,* that in all matters of politics and ethics, China was well ahead of Europe, and proposed that the Chinese send missionaries to Europe to teach practical morality. He had even suggested that the Chinese language should be taught as the universal language![33] Another generation passed and the learned Christian Wolff took up the theme and elaborated upon it: The Chinese were really quite as good Christians as the Christians themselves, and were just as highly civilized, too. He was promptly banished from Halle by an outraged

monarch[34] and found refuge in Marburg, but the harm
was already done. Soon the address appeared in England
with the intriguing title, "The Real Happiness of a People
under a Philosophical King Demonstrated; not only from
the Nature of Things, but from the Undoubted Experience
of the Chinese." To dramatize this, as soon as Frederick II
got on the throne, he brought Professor Wolff back to
Halle in triumph! And now Voltaire took up the cause of
the Chinese, as he took up so many causes designed to em-
barrass the Church, and was indefatigable.[35] How better
expose the iniquities and absurdities of Church and King
in France than to show how much better they managed
things in China. "They have perfected moral science," he
asserted, and wrote a drama to prove it, *Orphelia de la
Chine,* and then two famous chapters in his *Essai sur les
Moeurs.* Where Voltaire led, all followed. Helvétius became a Sinophil, so too the Baron d'Holbach, and the Curious Abbé de Pauw who sat up nights discussing China
with Frederick the Great.[36]

China was a new world, but how like Europe, after all;
there was everything to learn from her. There, agriculture
was supreme: The Emperor guided the plow in the spring
with his own hands, and soon Louis XV was to do just that
to prove that he, too, was a wise and virtuous Emperor.
China exalted learning; the state supported the schools,
and all the bright youths were educated by the state, rich
and poor alike, to love wisdom and prize happiness and
serve their fellow men. China achieved beauty without luxury—beauty everywhere, in the houses, temples, furniture,
fabrics, porcelains, above all in gardens. Let us achieve
beauty *à la Chine,* said those who molded the taste of
Europe. Soon all the monarchs and princes were building
palaces or tea-houses in the Chinese style: a Chinese pavil-
ion at Sans Souci, a porcelain palace at Dresden, a Chinese
park in Weimar, and in Drottningholm, outside Stockholm, not only a Chinese palace, elaborately furnished and
decorated, but a whole Chinese village, named Canton.[37]

William Chambers had lived in China and came home
to write a *Dissertation on Oriental Gardening,* and to build
a famous pagoda in Kew Gardens, which he laid out for
the Royal family. There were pagodas, too, in Nymphen-

burg, and outside Cassel there was a Chinese village with
Negro milkmaids because Chinese were not to be found.
The Duke of Cumberland kept a "mandarin" yacht on the
Thames equipped with a Chinese kiosk and even a dragon,
and successive Dukes of Bedford added a Chinese room
and a Chinese Diary to the glories of Woburn Abbey.[38]
The Archbishop of Cologne rode about his diocese in a
Chinese paladin, and Watteau painted the panels of La
Muette in Chinese style. The Pompadour adored goldfish,
which became all the rage, and commissioned Boucher to
do Chinese tapestries, and everyone drank tea from Chinese porcelain cups.

Americans, too, were learning about China, with New
England merchantmen carrying furs from the Northwest
coast to Canton markets and bringing back lacquered furniture and golden wallpaper and porcelain for the new
mansions of the merchant princes of Boston and New
York—just what poor Ledyard had imagined. And soon
the Cherokee rose was spreading acre after impenetrable
acre across the warm soil of the South: Two Scots botanists had brought it home from China in 1794, and within
five years it rooted itself in America, and with an Indian
name, too.[39]

Europe rediscovered the Near East, too, Turkey and
Arabia and Palestine and Persia, what a different East it
was from that of the Scriptures! In a single decade—1720
to 1730—no less than twenty Turkish histories, ten
Turkish romances, and five Turkish dramas clamored for
the attention of the Parisian salons.[40] *The Arabian Nights*
—Antoine Galland had translated them into French early
in the century—had revealed that exotic society to an
enchanted Europe, and now came Laurent d'Arbieux's
Travels in Arabia the Desert—he had lived as a Bedouin—
and Jean la Roque's *Voyage in Arabia Felix,* and William
Beckford located his fantastic *Vathek* in Arabia.[41] The
Danes sent out a scientific expedition to explore Arabia, all
of whose members died except Carstens Niebuhr, who
lived to write about it and to father the historian of
Rome.[42] Even two young Americans, Philip Freneau and
Hugh Brackenridge, who were still in college at the time,

wrote a novel with the unlikely name *Father Bombo's Pilgrimage to Mecca* (1770).[43]

Nor was Africa neglected. Except for the land along the Mediterranean, Africa still lay under the curse of Ham. The Negroes who inhabited this vast continent were somehow excepted from the writ which made other savages Noble; they were, quite clearly, ignoble. As early as the sixteenth century it had been established that among them were tribes of troglodytes, of satyrs, of pygmies, of men with the face of dogs; that they were irremediably primitive; that they were cannibals. By the eighteenth century doubt had crept in, but not enough, as yet, to challenge the assumption of the justice and validity of enslaving them. Defoe's Captain Singleton and his ruffian band crossed Africa on foot, killing the natives who got in their way, picking up gold dust and ivory as they went and loading it onto the blacks they had enslaved for the long trek.[44] In the sixties, just as Captain Cook was heading for the South Pacific, the Scots laird James Bruce penetrated to the headwaters of the Nile and emerged to write five volumes to prove it to a skeptical world; if his Ethiopians were not philosophers like those who inhabited the pages of Dr. Johnson's *Rasselas*, neither were they monsters (except of cruelty) or satyrs or even anthropophagi. In 1788 Joseph Banks founded the African Society, equally interested in science and in trade, and it was Banks who sent poor John Ledyard to Cairo, and death; not long thereafter Mungo Park opened up the interior of the Black Continent.[45]

The exploration was backward in time as well as outward in space. Ancient Greece came into its own, and Republican Rome; there was a renaissance of classical art and literature more widespread than in the fifteenth century, and perhaps more imitative.[46] Now Johann Winckelmann took over, the cobbler's son from Stendal with his unquenchable passion for Hellas who had somehow scrambled his way to Dresden to the Court of that Augustus III who was bankrupting Saxony by buying up art collections from every capital in Europe. By mid-century the ruins of Herculaneum had been uncovered and the temples which the Greeks had built at Paestum. Winckelmann concluded that Pompeii was well worth a mass, so he embraced Ca-

tholicism, and betook himself to Rome where he quickly
won the protection of the blind Cardinal Albani.[47] There
he wrote his masterpiece, *The History of Ancient Art*,
which was to cast a spell over Germany and indeed over
much of Europe for a generation, and reached even America, for Jefferson owned the Italian translation. Now Lessing, whose famous essay on *Laocoön* argued a different philosophy for art and for literature, and Herder, who exulted
that "with Greece the morning breaks," wrote a series of
dramas on Hellenic themes, while Christoph Wieland
wrote novels about the Greeks, which brought down upon
him the wrath of Goethe who fancied himself the first of
German Hellenists.[48]

Scholarship, too, was glorying in the world of Greece
and Rome. Pope translated the *Iliad* and the *Odyssey* into
the language of Pope, and there were new editions of Plutarch, who had captured the imagination of Europe and of
America. The Abbé Jean Jacques Barthélemy wrote an interminable *Imaginary Voyage of Young Anacharsis to
Greece*, which introduced its rapt readers to geography,
politics, war, music, and the arts. The Comte de Caylus
spent a fortune on Greek and Roman archeology and published seven volumes of *Collections of Antiquity*, which
embraced Etruscan and Egyptian as well as Greek and
Roman art. In Göttingen Professor Heyne* lectured on
classical philology and archeology and his pupil, Frederic
Wolf of Halle, whose lectures attracted no other than
Goethe, laid the foundation for all future Homeric scholarship with his *Prolegomena to Homer*.[49] Montesquieu had
speculated on the greatness and decadence of Rome, and
in 1776 Gibbon, the greatest historian of his age, launched
his magisterial history of the *Decline and Fall of the
Roman Empire*.

Musicians, too, turned to classical themes. Handel led
the way with a series of classical operas—*Orestes, Jupiter,
Ariadne, Julius Caesar* and others, and he was followed by
the ever-victorious Gluck: soon *Orpheus and Eurydice*
took Paris by storm.[50] Haydn, too, wrote on the Orpheus

---

* Napoleon spared Göttingen from attack out of respect for the University which boasted Professor Heyne.

theme, which had an irresistible fascination for a generation whose classicism was already blending into romanticism, and so did the Florentine Cherubini, and even the
youthful Mozart.[51] Early in the century Montfaucon's
sumptuous volumes of engravings of Greek and Roman
antiquities had opened up new worlds of ancient art, and a
few years later Caylus was publishing catalogues of Greek
and Roman antiquities—vases, medals, coins, jewels, paintings.[52] Now the Society of the Dilettante in London,
whose President wore a scarlet toga, sent James Stuart and
Nicholas Revett to Greece to study—and reproduce—ancient paintings, and then to Rome to sketch the ruins of
the ancient world. Their *Antiquities of Athens* in five volumes, influenced Robert Adam, who was to create a new
style.[53] By now Greek and Roman ruins were becoming
as popular as Chinese pagodas: Chambers put a ruin in
Kew Gardens along with his famous pagoda, and Wilhel-
mina of Bayreuth traveled through Italy with the scientist
La Condamine and returned to build a Roman ruin in her
garden at the Hermitage.[54] Now the artists turned from
rococo to classicism. From every country of the West
painters and sculptors flocked to Rome, whose glories had
been made known through Stuart and Revett and through
the wonderful engravings of Piranesi—two thousand of
them, no less. Raphael Mengs from Germany and An-
gelica Kauffman from the Grisons made Rome their temporary home. From the wilderness of Pennsylvania came the
young Benjamin West, whom Mengs took in hand, and
whose "Departure of Regulus" caught the fancy of George
III and thus changed the history of English and American
painting for a generation, for half the artists in America
were to study in West's studios and bask in his patronage.[55]

In sculpture it was Antonio Canova who did most to
recreate the classical world and to impose upon it an almost inhuman calmness, purity and tranquility.[56] He immortalized Orpheus and Eurydice, he showed the triumph
of Theseus over the Minotaur, he peopled a hundred gardens with Hebes and Apollos, and when he made a statue
of Washington it was clear that Washington came out of
Plutarch. The Englishman John Flaxman found his way

back to the beauty of ancient Greece through a study of
Greek urns and vases; his contribution was not to sculpture but in the recreation of Greek vases for Josiah Wedgwood and in the delicate engravings with which he revived
the world of Homer.[57] While Flaxman returned from
Rome to London, Bertel Thorwaldsen went down from
Copenhagen and Johan Sergel from Stockholm to join
Canova in imposing the stamp of epicene beauty and
passionless nobility on the ancient world.[58]

Long after Thorwaldsen had gone out of fashion in
Europe, he was being faithfully copied by the Americans
who had studied in his atelier. For it was in the new nation
across the Atlantic that classicism had perhaps its most
striking triumph. Though—thanks to Winckelmann—it was
Greece that dazzled the Germans and Italians, it was
Rome that commanded the admiration of the Americans.[59]
Every schoolboy among them learned Latin, and all the
philosophers read Rollin's *Ancient History* and his *History
of Rome*, and Plutarch, too, for they themselves learned
from Plutarch and practiced all the Roman virtues. The
Maison Carrée that Jefferson loved was Roman not Greek,
and so, too, that Villa Rotunda which served as a model
for Monticello.[60] The very vocabulary of government
was Roman—Constitution, Republic, Federalism, Senate,
Congress, President, Governor, Judiciary; even the mottoes
were Latin—*E Pluribus Unum, Novus Ordo Saeclorum,
Annuit Coeptis*.[61]

3

The ancient world was familiar and reassuring, and that
is perhaps why so many of the philosophes and artists and
scholars turned to it with pleasure. It had those qualities of
symmetry and grace and of order, that the Enlightenment
prized, or those qualities which could, in any event, be im-
puted to it.[1] So, too, with China whose philosophes were
kings and cherished beauty and wisdom above all things.
What is more, China could be transferred to Europe, its
furniture, its porcelain, its gardens, and perhaps even its

philosophy. These forays into distant and exotic lands, these discoveries and recapturings, fitted well into the pattern of the Enlightenment, and required no convulsive effort of accommodation.

But America was another matter altogether.

America was really a new world, and no mere physical conquest, no royal decrees, no literary gestures could assimilate it easily to Europe. That required imagination and time. For America was new in nature, new in people, new in experience, new in history. Nothing had prepared the Old World for what now confronted it, fearfully, alluringly, and implacably.[2]

Wherever the explorers went, from Hudson's Bay to the Straits of Magellan, they encountered marvels. Sailing south from Brazil, Peter Martyr reported giants, one of them so big that "the heads of one of our [sic] men came but to his waste," and "canibales" too.[3] The cannibal theme quickly became familiar, in literature and art. Montaigne seized upon it,[4] and inspired Shakespeare to one of his most memorable creations, and scores of artists titillated the European imagination with drawings of the horrid practices of the anthropophagi.[5] Patagonia—Magellan himself had named the country after its great-footed inhabitants—was a land of giants. Few facts were better authenticated than that, and the only question was whether they were nine feet tall or only eight. Pigafetta, who had sailed with Magellan, started the story and after him there were clouds of witnesses. In 1766 Admiral Byron came back from a trip to the Falkland Islands and the charmingly named Fort *Desire* on the Patagonian coast with evidence of giants so conclusive that there was no longer room for doubt, and Dr. Maty of the Royal Society hastened to write his colleague in Paris, M. de la Lande, that "the existence of the giants is now confirmed. Between four hundred and five hundred Patagonians of at least 8 or 9 feet in height have been seen and examined." A Spanish friar, Joseph Torrubia, wrote a book, *Gigantologia,* proving that giants were in fact to be found in many parts of the New World. The learned President De Brosses of the Academy at Dijon, who had already authenticated Terra

Australis Incognita, found it easy to accept a few giants in that part of the globe, and Maupertius, who had been president of the Royal Academy in Berlin, proposed an international expedition to study the creatures.[6] Best of all, the great Linnaeus made room for them in his analytical table, under *Homo Monstrosus,* along with Hottentots who were "less fertile," and Chinese who had "conic heads," and American Indians who were "beardless."

Far to the north, in the land of the great water, or Michinici, dwelt a nation of pygmies who lived in holes in the ground, descendants, probably, of the Skraelings of Iceland; do not scorn them, for they are rich, and all their tools are made of gold and silver![7] In a place called Estoiland were natives with only one leg; the isthmus of Darien was inhabited by albinos with eyes so weak they could see only at night—so said Buffon, and no one could challenge his authority. Brazil swarmed with single-breasted Amazons, who gave their name to the greatest of rivers; they hated men, but once every year packs of them tracked down helpless males and raped them and thus made sure that the race of Amazons would continue! There were hermaphrodites, too, and cyclopes, and men with heads in their chests, and men with the face of a dog.[8] The natural world was equally marvelous: strange fish, alligators that pursued their prey onto the banks of rivers; sea monsters, equally at home on land and in water; serpents that swung from tree to tree; hippogriffs who descended from the skies to seize their prey; frogs who weighed forty pounds and bellowed like bulls; vast swarms of insects darkening the skies.[9] As late as 1707 the learned Cotton Mather warned against "rabid and Howling wolves"—accurate enough, this—and against "Dragons, Droves of Devils, and Fiery Flying Serpents" in the forests of New England.[10]

Most of this is in America south of the Rio Grande, for it was the vast stretch of Spanish America, with its startling contrasts of the civilized and the primitive, that fascinated the philosophes, the naturalists, and the romancers. For a long time North America lay neglected; it was neglected even by Buffon, and by the editors of the Encyclopédie. Thus, every writer on the New World whom Buffon used was Spanish, or wrote about New Spain and Brazil, and of the six hundred articles in the Encyclopédie touching on the Americas, almost all dealt with the Caribbean and the Southern continent.[11] Perhaps North America was not exotic enough; perhaps it came too late on the historical scene. In any event, it made a very different impression on the Old World imagination than had the fabulous continent to the South that in the end imposed its will on its conquerors.

The wonder of the New World was inexhaustible. Much of it, to be sure, had been anticipated, for in a sense America had been invented before it was discovered:[12] The invention embraced the Blessed Isles, the Fortunate Isles, Avalon, El Dorado and Atlantis;[13] even the sensible Edmund Spenser thought that his countrymen might find Faery Land in the new world.[14]

The wonder of the New World was inexhaustible. When Columbus landed on Hispaniola he found it an earthly paradise,[15] and Ponce de León was sure that the fountain of youth was to be found in one of the islands of the Caribbean, and he searched for it, somewhat wildly, in the happily named Florida. Americans themselves took up the theme, and each generation played new variations on it. Captains Amadas and Barlowe who sailed with Raleigh to Virginia in 1584, were enchanted with Roanoke Island, "where we smelt so sweet and so strong a smel, as if we had bene in the midst of some delicate garden abounding in all kinde of odoriferous flowers," and as for the soil, "it was the most plentiful, sweete, fruitfull and wholsome of all the world," while the natives were "most gentle, loving, and faithfull, voide of all guile and treason, and such as live after the manner of the golden age."[16] So, too, said John Smith, who created Pocahontas, who was, like Smith himself, a blend of fact and fancy;[17] so said John Josselyn and John Pory and William Strachey, and a score of other seventeenth-century explorers,[18] and even William Bradford, who first thought Cape Cod "a hideous and desolate wilderness, full of wild beasts and wild men," in time changed his mind.[19] The English themselves caught the

soft infection. As early as 1610 the anonymous author of
"Newes from Virginia" told of

> Great Store of fowle, of venison,
> Of grapes and Mulberries,
> Of chestnuts, walnuts and such like
> Of fruits and strawberries,
>   There is indeed, no want at all. . . .[20]

And a few years later Michael Drayton hailed Virginia
as

> Earth's only paradise
> Where nature hath in store
> Fowl, venison and fish
>   And the fruitfull'st soil
>   Without your toil
> Three harvests more,
> All greater than your wish.[21]

Even the satirists paid tribute to the beauty and richness of
the New World:

> There twice a year all sorts of Grain
> Doth down from Heaven like hailstones rain;
> You never need to sow nor plough,
> There's plenty of all things enough,
> Wine sweet and wholesome drops from trees
> As clear as crystal, without lees. . . .[22]

"The country is not only plentiful but pleasant and
profitable," wrote John Hammond in *Leah and Rachel,
the Two Fruitful Sisters*. "Pleasant in regard to the
brightnesse of the weather, the many delightful rivers, the
abundance of game, the extraordinary good neighborhood
and loving conversation they have with one another. . . .
Pleasant in observing their stocks and flocks of Cattle,
Hoggs, and Poultry, grazing, whisking and skipping in
their sights."

Maryland moved George Alsop to poetry: "Neither do I
think there is any place under the Heavenly altitude, or

that has footing or room upon the circular Globe of this world, that can parallel this fertile and pleasant piece of ground in its multiplicity, or rather Nature's extravagancy of a super-abounding plenty." William Bartram, who sent seeds to Linnaeus and to Banks, and kept his own botanical garden in Philadelphia, found Georgia prodigal in fertility and beauty. "I ascended this beautiful river [the Altamaha]. . . . My progress was rendered delightful by the sylvan elegance of the groves, cheerful meadows, and high distant forests which in grand order presented themselves to view. The winding banks of the river and the high projecting promontories, unfolded fresh scenes of grandeur and sublimity," and his picture of the Indian was as romantic as anything imagined by John Smith. "What an Elisium it is, where the wandering Seminole . . . roams at large, and after the vigorous chase retires from the heat of the meridian sun. Here he reclines and reposes . . . his verdant couch guarded by the Deity. Liberty, and the Muses, inspiring him with wisdom and valour, whilst the balmy zephyrs fan him to sleep." Traveling along the Shenandoah River, the Reverend Andrew Burnaby rejoiced in the beauty and prosperity enjoyed by those fortunate enough to live in that happy valley—"the most delightful climate, the richest soil imaginable, they are everywhere surrounded with beautiful prospects and sylvan scenes, lofty mountains, transparent streams, falls of water, rich valleys and majestic woods, the whole interspersed with an infinite variety of flowering shrubs; . . . they possess what many princes would give half their dominions for, health, content, and tranquility of mind."[23] And when, a few years later, the pioneers opened the blue grass country of Kentucky, the cycle of paradise began anew. Listen to the enraptured Gilbert Imlay; he was an adventurer, he was even something of a scoundrel, but he knew Kentucky:

Everything here assumes a dignity and a splendour I have never seen in any other part of the world. Here an eternal verdure reigns, and the brilliant sun, piercing through the azure heavens, produces in this prolific soil an early maturity which is truly as-

tonishing. . . . Soft zephyrs softly breathe on sweets,
and the inhaled air gives a voluptuous glow of health
and vigor that seems to ravish the intoxicated senses.
Everything here gives delight.[24]

The French reports on the New World were extensive
but monotonous, for they came chiefly from the indefatigable Jesuits who sent home, over the years, a stream of
Édifiantes[25] recounting their own pious and heroic efforts
to bring salvation to the Indians and compiling, in the
process, the most elaborate and faithful of all accounts of
the savages of the New World. Some of the soldiers and the
fur-traders kept journals, or wrote memoirs that were often
as good as romances. Here is Father Hennepin, no Jesuit
but a Récollect friar, who sailed over to New France with
the Sieur de la Salle and went with him deep into the interior, along waterways swifter than any in the Old World, on
lakes as large as oceans, camping under trees of gigantic
size, living on bear and buffalo and wild turkey, and press-
ing wine from wild grapes and feasting with a dozen tribes
of dusky Indians. La Salle sent him far into the prairies to
seek out the Sioux and they made him a prisoner, but no
matter, it was all stuff for his *New Discovery* (1697)
which told of the "manners, customs and languages of the
several native Indians." He claimed to have discovered the
Mississippi and followed it to its source, and he provided
the world with a description of what the Indians called the
Father of Waters.[26]

How different from the elusive Hennepin was the good
Father Charlevoix, a model scholar, and a model reporter,
too, for his *History of New France*—not really a history
but a record of his own experiences there—was not only
exciting but honest. He had taught Voltaire at the College
of Louis le Grand, and from there the Regent packed him
off to New France to see if he could find a path to the
Pacific. He adapted himself well to the life of the wilderness, and he made his way in a canoe up the St. Lawrence
and along the Great Lakes and down the Mississippi to
New Orleans, where he was wrecked. He managed to survive and returned to France and to his Holy Order, and

wrote histories of Santo Domingo and Paraguay, and, in six volumes, a *History of New France.*[27]

More exciting, certainly, to the mind of the Enlightenment were the *New Voyages to North America* (1703) by the Baron de Lahontan,[28] describing his own wanderings, real and imaginary. There is something of the conquistador about him, but more of the Enlightenment, for he was not only an adventurer but a philosophe. He had fought with Frontenac, he had explored with Tonti and Duluth, he had paddled on the gleaming lakes and along the swift rivers all the way from Quebec to Michilimackinic, and then on to Lake Superior, taking Homer with him, and Lucian, but not Aristotle, who, he wrote, was too heavy for his canoe. He had joined the Chippewa on a war-party against the fierce Iroquois, accompanied by a Huron chief who rejoiced in the name The Rat, and who was soon to be metamorphosed into the lovely Adario of the famous *Curious Dialogues.*[29] Back in France, England, Scotland—for he was always on the run—Lahontan compiled his *New Voyages,* and added to these the *Curious Dialogues;* both presented to the approving eyes of Europe the noble savage who dwelt in happiness and tranquility in his American Eden, a child of Nature, beautiful of form, manly, vigorous, intelligent, and virtuous. How the century delighted in the dialogue between the Baron de Lahontan and Adario, "a noted man among the savages," which showed how truly superior the Indians were to the Europeans in virtue, how much more sensible in their domestic arrangements, how more profound in their philosophy. Just the lesson they needed to learn to prepare them for the *Persian Letters* and the *Chinese Letters,* and the *Supplement to Bougainville* and a hundred similar tracts. To be sure, the reason Adario was so convincing was that he spoke the language of a true philosophe, but perhaps that merely proved that the true philosophe was a child of Nature.

Skeptics might point out that the Baron was something of a scamp, and was not to be trusted. But what was to be said of the revelations of the Abbé Lafitau? His credentials were all in order, he had no grudge against France, his character was exemplary; yet in the end he said much the same thing. His *Customs of the American Savages Compared with those of Earliest Times* (1724)[30] was perhaps the first book of cultural anthropology to be written in and of America. Lafitau, too, took his Homer with him; took with him, indeed, the whole cargo of the classical past. Fifty years before the youthful Benjamin West stared at the Apollo Belvedere and burst out, "My God! how like a Mohawk Indian."[31] Father Lafitau had observed the Mohawks and exclaimed, how like Achilles! Wherever he looked—and where did he not look, this indefatigable observer?—he saw resemblances between the Indians and the Greeks and the Trojans, so strong that they could not be accidental. The forays of the Iroquois into the interior were like those of Herodotus; the voyages of a Huron chief like those of Ulysses; the devotion of two Indian warriors to each other like that of Achilles and Patrocles; the fortitude of the Indian under torture was like that of Scaevola, and his courage in war like that of Hector. The treatment of prisoners was the same, the discipline of children, even the ceremonies attending birth, marriage, and burial. Perhaps, after all, there was something to those theories that the Indians were the descendants of the survivors of Troy who, seeking to escape the wrath of the Greeks, fled the length of the Mediterranean and were blown across the Atlantic to a more hospitable home. Make of all this what you will, but clearly it endowed the Indians with all the virtues, the courage, and the dignity of the heroes of classical antiquity.

CHAPTER FOUR

America Under Attack

1

What were they looking for so tirelessly, the explorers, the naturalists, the historians, the philosophes? Some were looking for God, no doubt, or for salvation, some for gold and empire, some for fame, and almost all for happiness. Whatever their goals, they shared one common quality: intellectual curiosity. They were looking for answers to their importunate questions about Nature and Man. Not about God and Man unless you identify God with Nature, as so many of the Deists did, for most of these thought of God as a kind of cosmic principle or, perhaps—to use the popular metaphor—as a clockmaker. They set afoot a vast inquiry into Nature in all her manifestations; an inquiry into Man —his past, present, and future, his role in history, his potentialities for progress; an inquiry into government, politics, and law, into the economy and the wealth of nations, into the social order and the happiness of mankind. It was an inquiry that placed an enormous responsibility on philosophers and statesmen, for it assumed—for almost the first time in modern history—that men were not the sport of Nature or the victims of society, but that they might understand the one and order the other. This was the starting point of a new philosophy of Progress.[1]

It was an inquiry that, almost everywhere, was marked by two qualities: secularism and rationalism. For now the philosophes could enjoy some measure of freedom from the trammels of religious superstition, and now, too, a vast laboratory lay open to them for observation and experimentation. If the answers were not to be found in Paris or London—as many of them were—perhaps they could be found in China or in Arabia Felix, under the bread-fruit trees of Tahiti, in the lofty mountains of Peru or the trackless forests of Canada, or even on the sylvan farms along the banks of the Connecticut and the Delaware. Now Nature would provide the answers that priests and philosophers had been unable to find in the familiar scriptures; it was on the palimpsest of Nature that you could read the fate of Man.[2]

For if human nature was the same everywhere, and the same yesterday, today, and tomorrow, then the primitive and the pastoral might reveal it in all its nakedness. And who could doubt that human nature was the same—that no matter how various the patterns, the same master hand had designed them all and made them of the same stuff? Churchmen called that master hand God, Naturalists called it Nature; Jefferson combined the two in the felicitous phrase, Nature and Nature's God. It was, in any event, the universal that interested the philosophes, not the particular. It was Nature, Man, Law, Happiness, Beauty, Order. Thus, Alexander Pope proposed to deal with "Man in the abstract" and to draw "a general map of man." Thus, the Baron d'Holbach held forth at the Chateau de Gradval:

> The savage man and the civilized, the white man, the red man, the black man; Indian and European, Chinaman and Frenchman, Negro and Lapp have the same nature. The differences between them are only modifications of their common nature, produced by climate, government, education, opinions and the various causes which operate upon them.[3]

So, too, thought Helvétius, who contended that all infants are equal at birth, that all have equal potentialities, and that all men are animated by the same motives of self-interest, while David Hume observed that "mankind are so much the same in all times and places that history informs us of nothing new or strange."[4] This was the view too that John Adams developed so elaborately in his *Defense of the Constitutions of the United States*—that what had happened in the city-states of Greece, in Rome, Italy, and France was bound to happen in America, if Americans did not heed John Adams. For "all nations, from the beginning, have been agitated by the same passions. . . . Nations move by unalterable rules; and education, discipline, and laws make the greatest difference in their accomplishments, happiness and perfection."[5] Or listen to that expert on happiness, the Marquis de Chastellux. An examination of the laws of nature, he asserted, should be the foundation of all knowledge. "Andeologie, or the knowledge of Man in General" would serve as the basis of medicine, natural history, morality, and conduct, and these would give birth to a scientific politics.[6] The lordly Sir Joshua Reynolds told the Royal Academy, in his Discourse of 1781, that "a history painter paints man in general, a portrait painter a particular man, and consequently a defective model."[7] This was the view of almost all the artists and critics as well. The Danish sculptor Johannes Wiedewelt observed that "the Greek artists purified their pictures of all merely personal idiosyncrasies which might distract our spirit from pure beauty,"[8] and that greater Danish sculptor, Thorwaldsen, carried the process of purification so far as to impose a sexless character on almost all of his mythological figures, and Diderot declared that "beauty is founded on the eternal, original, sovereign, and essential rules of order, proportion, relation and harmony."[9] Dr. Johnson pontificated that literature should avoid the local and the particular. "Poetry," he said, "is to speak a universal language," and Blackstone, though he was commenting on the laws of England, nevertheless addressed himself to "the general spirit of the laws and the principles of universal jurisprudence."[10] Almost all the major political treatises of the age made the same assumptions about the similarity and uniformity of human nature: *The Patriot King, The Spirit of the Laws,* the *Social Compact,* even the Declaration of Independence.[11]

So, said the philosophers, let us study human nature in order to find those ingredients and components that are universal. You will not find these in the sophisticated societies of the Old World: There everything is over-laid by customs and traditions, mannerisms and pretensions, affectations and insincerities; there it is impossible to distinguish between nature and artifice. Turn, rather, to the new-found islands of the Pacific, to the mountains of Corsica, or the glens and cairns of the Scottish highlands, to the misty fjords of Norway, or the forests that crowd the shores of the Great Lakes in new-found America. There, perhaps, we can find man before the Fall, without the taint of artifice, sophistication, and luxury, the social sins and political crimes, that corrupt him in the Western world. By observing primitive man the philosophes might find their way back to that natural man that lay concealed in every human being. Here is how Diderot put it:

> Would you like to know the condensed history of almost all our miseries? Here it is. There existed a natural man; an artificial man was introduced within this man; and within this cavern a civil war breaks out, which lasts for life. Sometimes the natural man is stronger, sometimes he is felled by the artificial, moral man; and in both cases the miserable monster is plagued, tortured, stretched on the rack; ceaselessly lamenting, always wretched whether a false enthusiasm of glory transports him . . . or a false shame bows him down.[12]

Back, then, to original man. Set sail for Tahiti and find some Omai in his island paradise. Penetrate the forests of Canada and find him as God and Nature made him, some noble savage running wild in the woods, just as Dryden had described him in those immortal lines:

> I am free as Nature first made man
> Ere the base laws of servitude began
> When wild in woods the noble savage ran.[13]

Find him among the *banditti* of Corsica: after all the banditry was natural and spontaneous. Recover him in the remnants of the once-proud Incas. Seek him out in the fastnesses of modern Greece, "still flaunting the spirit of ancient Sparta," or resurrect him from the ruins of ancient Greece "so full of beautiful, godlike and youthful forms" —the phrase is from Johan Herder.[14] Or discover him on Nantucket Island or, arrayed in Quaker garb, on the decent streets of Philadelphia. And if he is still not to be found or captured, create him, as Macpherson created Ossian, as Lahontan created Adario, as Diderot created Orou, perhaps, even, as Voltaire created the "good Quaker."

* * *

But come, now, what nonsense is this! How can you assert with a straight face that Man is everywhere the same, when he is palpably everywhere different? How can you exalt the primitive when it is so obvious that the primitive means not innocence and contentment, but brutishness and misery: surely Hobbes made that clear enough! All very well for a Colonel Schuyler to transport three Mohawk Kings, and an Emperor, for the amusement of Queen Anne and the London mobs, or for Henry Timberlake to display his assorted Cherokee chieftains;[15] for the Duke of Grafton to import Paoli from Corsica to London,[16] and for Captain Furneaux to bring the charming Omai all the way from Tahiti to grace the country houses of England.[17] All very well, even, to pretend that Franklin was a kind of homespun philosopher from the backwoods of Pennsylvania. But really, now, what of the wretched Patagonians, who turned out not to be giants at all; what of the flatheaded savages of the Brazilian jungle, the miserable Esquimaux living on blubber all the year round, or the black women of Sennar on the upper Nile, their ears reaching to their shoulders, rings through their noses, and their breasts hanging to their middles.[18] What of the anthropophagi of the Caribbean or the South Seas? How do you fit all these into your moon-struck theories? Surely this is just a game you are playing, and the noble savage is a pawn in that game.

That was a problem, but it was not an insuperable one, not for those philosophes who deigned to notice these ob-

jections. Whatever they might think of the South Seas—
and from Diderot to Herman Melville, Tahiti remained a
special case—or of the Norsemen, who after all became
Norman conquerors, when it came to the New World the
philosophers had their answer ready. All men were originally the same, you can't get away from that, not if you
accept the Biblical story of an original creation[19] (and
even those who were ready enough to throw out the Scriptures somehow took that story for granted); not if you accept the story of the Deluge.[20] Yet though human nature
is, or originally was, everywhere the same, men are no
longer the same, nor are civilizations the same. For men
and societies are subject to forces of nature, and of history, that prosper them or thwart them, and it is these
which account for the immense differences that we observe
between primitive and civilized men—these, and not innate
differences. The learned Jean Bodin had made that clear
back in the sixteenth century,[21] when he pointed out that
men who live in the equatorial regions are quick-witted
and learned, but lacking in courage, while those who live
in temperate regions have "more force than they of the
south and less policie, and more wit than they of the north
and less force." Montesquieu observed, in his *Spirit of the
Laws,* that "mankind are influenced by various causes: by
the climate, by religion, by the laws, by the maxims of
government, by precedents, morals and customs; whence is
formed a general spirit of nations," and he had devoted a
whole book to elaborating on the observations of Bodin.[22] Voltaire simply said that "three things influence
the mind of man incessantly, climate, government and
religion; this is the only way to explain the enigma of the
world."[23] These, then, were the elements that accounted
for the differences in the societies of the Old World and
the New, and as the New World had very little history but
a great deal of Nature, it is "climate" that is decisive there.

Let us start, then, with climate—it was a broad term
which embraced all that was later to be included in the
term environment: heat and cold, rainfall and drought, the
winds and the tides, rivers and lakes, marshes and swamps,
mountains and deserts, volcanoes and earthquakes, the
products of the soil and the animals who lived on those

products, the flora and the fauna, birds, insects and fish—
all the operations and conditions of Nature that affected
the lives of men.[24]* And let us start with the most puzzling
of all problems, and the most challenging. Let us start with
America. For unless America could be explained, it threatened to confound the philosophy of the Enlightenment.

How account for America?

No use saying that America didn't need accounting for;
clearly it did. The contrast between the philosopher of Fer-
ney or the poet at Weimar and the naked savage on the
banks of the Orinoco confounded the Scriptures, and shat-
tered the laws of history.[25]

Why had America come so late on the stage of history?
Why had she played so passive a role? Was America really
a new world, a special creation, centuries after the original
creation which Buffon had now pushed back some eighty
thousand years? Had it emerged late from the Deluge, or
had it perhaps suffered a second deluge from which it was
only now recovering? Why was its climate so different from
that of Europe: the Great Lakes were the same latitude as
Spain but their waters were frozen over for half the year!
Why was so large a part of the New World still immersed
in marshes and fetid swamps, its forests too dense to admit
the sunshine, its soil too moist for husbandry, its very air
filled with noxious vapors? How account for the monsters
who swarmed in its woods, the venomous reptiles, the
clouds of poisonous insects? How account for the savages
of America, primitive, miserable, and impotent? Why was
the population so thin, barely able to reproduce itself?
Why were the natives copper-colored, even in the temperate north, even at the torrid equator, instead of either
white or black? Why were they thousands of years behind
the rest of the world in civilization,[26] all except the Aztecs
and the Incas whose civilizations, for all their splendor,
were so feeble that they were toppled by the first on-
slaught?

There was an even more elementary mystery. Whence
came these savages of America? Were they the descend-

---

* Eventually, as we shall see, the concept of "climate" embraced the
economy, the society, government, laws, customs, and morals.

ants of Ham, working out that primal curse; if so, why were they not black?[27] Were they descended from the lost tribes of Israel? So said the learned Rabbi Manasseh Israel of Amsterdam, who found conclusive evidence in the similarity of Peruvian temples to Jewish synagogues.[28] The widespread practice of circumcision in America re-enforced this explanation, but did not convince Hamon L'Estrange, who wrote a counter book, *Americans no Jewes.* One of his arguments was conclusive: Jews are not permitted to marry whores, all Indian women are whores, thus the Indians could not be Jews! Were they Trojans, then, who had escaped from Troy, as the Abbé Lafitau implied, or Carthaginians, perhaps, who had fled from the wrath of Rome and been blown by favorable winds to the shores of Carolina? So thought the wicked Thomas Morton of the Bay Colony. Were they refugees from the lost continent of Atlantis? It was one of the most popular of all theories, and there was support for it even in Plato's *Timaeus;* in the 1780s, Count Carli, of Milan, refurbished the theory with great learning in two volumes. Were they Chinese who had drifted across the broad Pacific, from island to island, to the shores of Peru, or were they perhaps Polynesians? So said the magisterial Hugo Grotius, who was equally confident that the people of Central America had come from Ethiopia, and those of North America from Norway. Were they the followers of Madoc, Prince of Wales, who had sailed with three thousand men for this western world back in 1170? What other migration was substantiated so circumstantially as this, for now Sieur de la Vérendrye had actually found the descendants there in those Mandan villages on the high plains! Were they Tartars, who had sailed from Kamchatka to Alaska and drifted down the coast of the new continent, spreading out southward and eastward: This was the most generally held theory, and the most common-sensible. Some of the theories were bolder than any of these. There was the notion that the Indians were descended from Noah himself. It was a reasonable enough theory, for Noah was the greatest of all navigators, and sometime during his three hundred years of sailing and colonizing he might well have come to America with some of his many progeny. Or contemplate the even more audacious notion that the American natives were antediluvian or post-Adamite. Surely God had not exhausted his creative capacity with the creation of Adam. A special creation: that is what Bailli d'Engel argued in five stout volumes, and that is what the hapless Isaac de la Peyrere asserted, and that is what even Voltaire surmised.[29]

The dispute persisted all through the eighteenth and into the nineteenth century. President Stiles of Yale was committed to the Lost Tribes theory. Edward Rutledge confessed to Jefferson, in 1787, that he was almost persuaded that the Carthaginian theory was the right one.[30] John Ledyard had satisfied himself by personal reconnaissance that the Indians had crossed the Bering Straits from Siberia, and the learned Dr. Benjamin Smith Barton of Philadelphia accepted this theory, as did Jefferson himself. But the no less learned Samuel Mitchill, who was not only a scientist but a senator,[31] too, was torn between the Tartar, the Norwegian, and the Malaysian origin, while the historian Hugh Williamson somewhat wildly embraced the notion of a Hindoo origin for Americans.[32] Out of all this controversy one thing emerged: The natives of America confounded religion, history, and science. But there they were: How do you explain them?

The explanation was no cool enterprise of science. Not at all. The question of America was part of a galaxy of interlocking questions about which the philosophes were passionate: the quarrel between ancients and moderns, the classic and the romantic, the mercantilist and the physiocratic, the issues of religion, empire, colonialism, and slavery, and a dozen others. America did not fit readily into the patterns imagined by the Enlightenment, but seemed, rather, to confound history, science, and logic. For some of the philosophes it brought out all that was eager, generous, and hopeful; for others all that was impatent, intolerant, and malicious.

For now, after all the bold explorations, all the ingenious theories, all the picturesque fables, from a handful of the philosophes came a harsh verdict. Now the mists of romance rolled away, and America stood revealed in their eyes in all her misery and shame. Blow after blow rained down upon the hapless continents. They were unable to explain themselves; they had failed to fulfill their promises; they had frustrated all hopeful expectations, they were a snare and a mockery; they were a mistake, perhaps the greatest mistake in history. Now, for reasons that were sometimes scientific but more often political or religious or personal, or even for no reasons at all, the lordliest of the French naturalists,[33] the most waspish of the propagandists, the most enthusiastic of the historians, and with them assorted scribblers in neighboring countries, joined in a kind of conspiracy to expose Nature and Man in the New World.

2

How explain America?

Francis Bacon had anticipated both the question and the answer even as his fellow countrymen were busy planting colonies in the New World. "Marvel not," he wrote, "at the thin population of America, nor at the *rudeness* and *ignorance* of the people. For you must accept your inhabitants of America as a *young* people; younger a thousand years, at the least, than the rest of the world."[1]

Here it was, the simplest and perhaps the most logical of all explanations of the backwardness of the American continents, and a secular one, too: that while Heaven had been content to inundate the Old World with one great Deluge, and had permitted Noah and his progeny to start the world anew, it had visited later deluges on the hapless Western World, and the people of America were but the miserable remnants of these successive deluges.[2]

It remained for the mighty Comte de Buffon[3] to provide a scientific basis for this speculation. Buffon had no animosity toward the New World, certainly not toward the French and English portions of it; he was, in any event, far too great for animosities. No, his view of the Americas —their flora, their fauna, their inhabitants—was as objective as was his view of Nature and Man elsewhere on the globe. But somehow the transparent backwardness of the New World had to be accounted for. This is what Buffon proceeded to do. His explanation was both scientific and philosophical. America was, indeed, a New World—just what Francis Bacon had conjectured—for it had emerged from the Deluge later than had the continents of the Old, or it had, perhaps, been visited by repeated deluges. The effects of these were everywhere visible. So swampy was the soil, so rank the vegetation, so thick the forests, so miasmic the air, that the sun could not penetrate to the ground below, and the waters could neither evaporate nor drain away. Inevitably,

> in this state of abandon everything languishes, decays and stifles. The air and the earth, weighed down by the moist and poisonous vapours, cannot purify themselves. . . . The sun vainly pours down its liveliest rays upon this cold mass incapable of responding to its warmth. It will never produce anything but humid creatures, plants, reptiles and insects, and cold men and feeble animals are all that it will ever nurture.

In this "climate" nothing flourishes, nothing but gigantic insects and poisonous snakes. Animals are stunted in growth and so, too, is man—stunted not merely physically but mentally as well—for Nature has treated man in America

> less as a mother than as a step-mother, withholding from him the sentiment of love or the desire to multiply. The savage is feeble and small in his organs of generation; he has neither body hair nor beard, and no ardor for the female of his kind. He is much less strong in body than the European. He is also much less sensitive and yet more fearful and more cowardly; he lacks vivacity and is lifeless in his soul . . .[4]

Here is the real secret of the failure of America: nature that is miserable, animals that are stunted and incapable of growth, man primitive and impotent, scarcely able to reproduce himself and incapable of creating a civilization.

Even as Buffon was bringing out the first of his many volumes of the *Histoire Naturelle,* a young Swedish bota-

nist was confiding to his journal his misgivings about the
fate of Europeans in the New World.[5] Peter Kalm was a
professor at the Swedish University in Abö; he had studied
with Buffon's rival, Carl Linnaeus. And it was Linnaeus
who persuaded the Royal Academy to send him over to
America to find plants that would "improve Swedish husbandry," and embellish his own botanical gardens outside
Uppsala. He traveled widely in the American colonies, met
and consulted with everyone, but particularly with the incomparable John Bartram, whom Linnaeus thought the
greatest "natural botanist" of his age, and who had already
shipped over hundreds of seeds and plants to the gardens
of Europe.[6] What the young Kalm saw tended to confirm
what Buffon had written: that both man and animals were
feebler in the New World than in the Old. The men were
not as large, nor as strong, nor as long-lived; women
ceased bearing children when they were thirty—or forty,
anyway—and while the children were bright enough when
young, they became stupid as they grew older. It was probably the fault of the climate, which was fluctuating and extreme, or perhaps of some lack of nourishment in the
food, or of those fevers and diseases which were so pervasive. The climate diminished animals as well—all but insects and snakes, apparently, for these were both large and
venomous. There were clouds of locusts and beetles and
mosquitoes, swarms of lice and caterpillars, a prodigious
number of rattlesnakes, horned snakes, red-bellied snakes
and green snakes. It was all quite terrifying, and a wonder
that the Swedes along the Delaware didn't want to pack up
and hurry back to Sweden. The soil was rich enough, yet
nothing really grew well:

> Peas cannot be grown on account of the insects which
> consume them. There are worms in the rye seed, and
> myriads of them in the cherry trees. The caterpillars
> often eat all the leaves from the trees . . . and large
> numbers die every year, both of fruit trees and of for-
> est trees. The grass in the meadows is likewise con-
> sumed by a kind of worm; another species causes the
> plums to drop before they are half ripe. The oak here
> affords not nearly so good timber as the European

oak. . . . The houses are of no long duration. The
meadows are poor and what grass they have is bad.
The pasture for cattle in the forests consists of such
plants as they do not like and which they are compelled to eat by necessity . . .[7]

No wonder the Americans were weaker than their Old
World cousins; no wonder they did not live so long. A bit
awkward, to be sure, that when Kalm had time to look
about him—and to talk with Dr. Franklin and Dr. Bartram—he changed his mind, and that soon he was sprin-
kling his pages with examples of longevity in America. But
the damage was done. The *Travels* were translated into
German; they excited interest; they were reviewed by that
indefatigable literary gossip the Baron Grimm, and were
read, doubtless with approval, by seven monarchs![8]
No need to trace this controversy down all its labyrinthine paths—those marked out by the wretched Corneille
de Pauw, whom Franklin characterized as "ill-informed
and malignant," in his three-volume *Philosophical Inquiry
into the Americans;*[9] those pursued, more enthusiastically
but not much more critically, by the famous Abbé Raynal;
those followed by the learned Dr. Robertson of Edinburgh
whose *History of America* was on the whole fair and
learned, but who swallowed the Buffon-De Pauw thesis
pretty uncritically, or by Robertson's colleague at the University of Edinburgh who still thought that "extensive
marshes and decayed forests . . . replenished the air with
noxious vapours" and that the Americans were "sunk in
effeminacy."[10] But how interesting that the greatest philosopher of the age, Immanuel Kant, was prepared to accept
the animadversions of Buffon and to confer on the thesis
of American degeneracy the mark of his approval. The
Americans, he said (and he meant, of course, the natives),

are incapable of civilization. They have no motive
force, for they are without affection and passion.
They are not drawn to one another by love, and are
thus unfruitful. They hardly speak at all, never caress
one another, care about nothing, and are lazy.[11]

Needless to say, all this was not the fault of the native Americans. They were as Nature and Nature's God had made them. No, the fault was with the men, the governments, and the churches of the Old World for violating the purposes of Nature or the will of God by tearing aside the veil which had concealed the New World from the Old. It was not America herself that was a mistake; it was the discovery of America that was a mistake. Nature (and perhaps God as well) had made clear that the New World was not really ready to be brought into the mainstream of history, not ready to be Christianized and civilized. The fault was in the misguided zeal of the Church, the inordinate ambition of monarchs, the cruelty and ruthlessness of conquerors, the venery of soldiers, the greed of merchants and adventurers, who collectively ravaged and destroyed whatever they touched. And at what cost! At the cost of millions of Indians, killed by sword or by disease, whole tribes extinguished and such civilizations as they had managed to create wiped out;[12] of slaves torn from their African homelands to take the place of the Indian victims, and slavery spread over two continents; of incessant wars between great nations—wars for gold and silver, for timber and fur, coffee and tobacco and naval supplies; and, worst of all, of syphilis carried from the New World to the Old and spread throughout Christian society as punishment for its sins! ("A shameful and cruel poison from the New World, which attacks even the sources of reproduction," wrote the Abbé Raynal.)

And what good could ever come out of this enterprise? The conquerors had not Christianized the natives; they had themselves been barbarized by the climate and the temptations of the New World. Europe had not extended its civilization across the oceans and to new lands, for Nature herself had decreed that civilization could not flourish in these lands—for all the forces that had operated to condemn the Natives to barbarism and impotence would operate on the transplanted European. So said the Abbé Corneille de Pauw, and in the Encyclopédie, no less, that the Europeans who had migrated to America had visibly degenerated. "Through the whole extent of America, from Cape Horn to Hudson's Bay there has never appeared a

philosopher, an artist, a man of learning."[13] This sort of
thing invited not so much indignation (though there was
some of that) as satire. Thus, the youthful "Connecticut
wits" responded in *The Anarchiad:*

> . . . Th' inverted optics show
> All nature lessening to the sage De Pau . . .
> His peerless pen shall raise, with magic lore
> The long-lost pigmies on th' Atlantic shore
> Make niggard Nature's noblest gifts decline
> The indical marks of bodies masculine.[14]

There were hints of this disparagement in Raynal,
though he was ready enough to retract once France and
the American states were joined in a common enterprise
against Britain, and in Dr. Robertson, too—after all, with
all those Americans reading medicine at his University, he
should have known better. The attitude persisted even into
the next century, and as late as 1804 the Irish poet
Thomas Moore could write that

> Columbia's days were done!
> Rank without ripeness, quickened without sun,
> Crude at the surface, rotten at the core
> Her fruits would fall before her spring were o'er.[15]

CHAPTER FIVE

The Enlightenment Vindicates America

1

And what of the Americans all this time?

They were not mere auditors, idle spectators, to this drama of conjecture and controversy; it was not like them to be passive. Were the philosophes laying down laws of History and of Nature on the basis of American experience? It was difficult to know whether to be more astonished or disgusted at such a spectacle. How few of them had any American experience, how few of them knew what they were writing about! Peter Kalm did, perhaps, but he can scarcely be included as one of the critics, though he provided ammunition enough for those who were less judicious and less scientific. But after this botanizing Swede with the inquiring mind, who was there? Not Buffon, not De Pauw, not Raynal, who thought of the Americas as a kind of private domain: none had visited America. Not Dr. William Robertson, of Edinburgh, for all his dignity and respectability. His monumental *History of America* had, after all, merely repeated the animadversions of Buffon and Raynal, and besides, he later made amends just as, for that matter, did Buffon and Raynal.[1] Certainly the minor figures who denounced and derided the New World with such miscellaneous and irregular energy, knew little or nothing about it—the hapless Reverend Niels Clausson in Copenhagen, or Simon Linguet in exile in London, or the forgotten Joseph Madrillon—who may have written on both sides of the question just to be sure to be right.[2]

Only the Americans really knew their own world. They saw it, to be sure, through the eyes of affection and of pride, but they saw it through the glasses of science, as well. Almost all the native champions of America were scientists—by vocation or by inclination—and most of them were members of the American Philosophical Society, which came closer to being a national institution than almost anything else, and which was international as well:[3] Benjamin Franklin and Thomas Jefferson, the extraordinary Philadelphia medical trio Dr. Rush, Dr. Barton, and Dr. Currie, Dr. David Ramsay down in Charleston and the Rev. Manasseh Cutler who was a doctor on the side; even the historian Hugh Williamson, who had after all taken a medical degree at Utrecht and was an astronomer to boot.

They had another advantage, too, the Americans. They had a country to defend, a continent, even a hemisphere, but no doctrine, no philosophy, in the formal sense. They did not start with some theory about the New World, but with observation and facts; tables of weights, measurements, records of rainfall, descriptions of flora and fauna, statistics of births and of life expectancy. Occasionally they indulged themselves in theory, or perhaps in moralizing—some of them allowed themselves to make assumptions about human nature or about progress—but their instincts were for the observed reality.[4] Thus, Jefferson, who sometimes did give rein to his fancy, writing to his old friend Charles Thomson about the "antiquities" of the West, expressed a "wish that the persons who go thither would make very exact descriptions of what they see of that kind, without forming any theories. The moment a person forms a theory," he added, "his imagination sees, in every object, only the traits which favor that theory . . . We must wait with patience till more facts are collected."[5]

How fortunate it turned out to be, this felt necessity to vindicate the New World from misunderstanding and calumny. It encouraged Americans, for the first time, to consider their national, and their natural, character. It per-

suaded them to launch their own inquiries into Man and
Nature in the New World. It inaugurated the scientific
study of the Indian: The American Philosophical Society
was the clearinghouse, and Jefferson and his disciple, Gallatin, provided the inspiration and much of the scholarship. It marked the beginning of what we may call American sociology—inquiries into vital statistics, the effects of
social mobility, the impact of countryside and of city on
health and welfare, the social history of diseases and epidemics,[6] the nature of racial differences, and the impact of
social and of moral environment on health and growth. It
inspired that argument which stood De Pauw and Raynal
on their heads, so to speak and that three generations of
poets and novelists were to exploit: the theory of New
World innocence and Old World depravity. It quickened
the American sense of isolation and of special destiny, a
better word, this, than Providence in an age so secular. In
the past Americans had not thought of themselves as a
people apart, but had taken for granted that they were Europeans, but now, what with one thing and another, they
were being persuaded that they were indeed a separate
people.

Now the Americans themselves rallied their resources to
vindicate their environment, their society, their history,
and their civilization. There is no less monotony in the
American defense than in the European attack, for just as
the critics repeated—or plagiarized—each other until their
arguments became shop-worn, so the defenders had recourse to a common arsenal of facts and principles.[7] How
could it be otherwise? It was not new and original ideas
that were needed (though these were not absent) but observation and common sense. And from first to last the
Americans founded their counterattack upon what they
deemed unassailable facts.

Is nature sterile and cruel here in the New World? Contemplate Pennsylvania, a veritable garden of Eden; everyone admitted that, even Raynal.[8] Let us take you to our
streams, swarming with fish; our meadows with their hundreds of song birds—soon Alexander Wilson and Audubon
were to astonish Europe with the pictorial evidence of
their beauty.[9] Contemplate our forests, with the pine trees

piercing the skies—where would the British Navy be without our pine and our oak? Is the soil of the New World
thin and poisonous? Why all Europe comes to us for corn
and tobacco and rice, and every American farmer dines
better than the nobles and princes of the Old World. Is our
climate moist and debilitating? Consider these tables which
demonstrate that there is more rainfall in London and
Paris than in Boston or Philadelphia! Are the vicissitudes
of climate unfriendly to mental or physical welfare? Quite
the contrary—they are stimulating and invigorating—an
even and temperate climate such as you find in the islands
of the Caribbean may be pleasant enough, but it does not
encourage intellectual activity. Is the New World covered
with fetid swamps and miasmal marshes? That has been
vastly exaggerated, but no matter; we can get rid of these
readily enough, and not in "some centuries," as Buffon
predicted, but in a few years.

And look, now, to Man. Are men stunted and feeble in
the New World? Come, stand up and be measured—see
how Franklin and Humphreys and Carmichael tower over
their French hosts.* Is America incapable of producing
men of genius, as both De Pauw and Raynal charged?
Consider Dr. Franklin who wrested the lightning from the
skies and the scepter from tyrants, the Newton and the
Cromwell of his age. Look at David Rittenhouse of Philadelphia, fit to stand with Laplace and Lagrange. "The

---

* There are several versions of the famous dinner in Paris where the
Americans and the French measured up with each other, but that of
Carmichael is the most nearly contemporary. On 15 October 1787, he
wrote to Jefferson: "I do not know whether Dr. Franklin ever men-
tioned to you what passed at a Dinner at Paris in which I was present
. . . I think the Company consisted of 14 or 15 persons. At Table
some one of the Company asked the Doctor what were his sentiments
on the remarks made by the Author of the *Recherches sur L'Amérique*
[by De Pauw]. We were five Americans at Table. The Venerable
Doctor regarded the Company and then desired the Gentleman who
put the question to remark and to judge whether the human race had
degenerated by being transplanted to another section of the Globe.
In fact there was not one American present who could not have tost
out of the Windows one or perhaps two of the rest of the Company,
if this effort depended merely on muscular force. We heard nothing
more of Mr. P's work . . ." Carmichael to Jefferson, 15 October 1787
(XII Boyd's *Jefferson*, 240–41).

world" wrote Jefferson, "has but one Ryttenhouse (*sic*), and never had one before."[10] Or contemplate George Washington, who made every crowned head in Europe look like a valet—it was John Adams who said that, and he knew something about European Kings. "We calculate thus," wrote Jefferson, who was an inveterate calculator, "the United States contains three millions of inhabitants. We produce a Washington, a Franklin, a Rittenhouse. France, then, should have half a dozen in each of these lines, and Great Britain half that number, equally eminent."[11]

From first to last it was Jefferson who directed the counterattack, and who conducted it, too. Better than any other American, except Franklin himself, he combined the sturdy provincialism of the frontiersman with the cosmopolitanism of the philosophe. Had he lived in the Old World he would have been a familiar of Diderot and Voltaire, of Lessing and Goethe, of Filangieri and Beccaria, and—if he could have overcome his inveterate distrust of the English—of Dr. Price and Dr. Priestley, Joseph Banks and David Hume. But imagine any one of these founding a political party or governing an extensive nation! Jefferson knew everything the naturalists and the philosophes knew and responded not only to their ideas and their interests, but to their sentiments as well. He shared Goethe's passion for Italy and, what is more, translated Palladio to Virginia—something Goethe could not do for Weimar.[12] He shared Voltaire's hatred of *l'Infâme* and, what is more, toppled the Established Church in his own Commonwealth.[13] He embraced most of the teachings of the *Économistes*, and helped revolutionize agriculture in America with his plow, his far-reaching experiments with grains and plants and his doubling of the agricultural domain, by the acquisition of Louisiana, and he thought agriculture "a science of the very first order."[14] He matched Beccaria's zeal for penal reform with his own equally humane penal code, and Filangieri's *Science of Legislation* with a comprehensive revision of the laws of Virginia, much of it adopted.[15] His philosophy of education was more sensible than that set forth in Émile and more democratic than that formulated by Diderot or Condorcet, and he managed to

translate it into laws and institutions.[16] In the war between
the ancients and the moderns he preferred the moderns,[17]
but he knew Greek as well as Latin, and that was more
than you could say for most of the philosophes. He did not
need Capability Brown to teach him landscape gardening
or Reynolds to instruct him in the principles of art, or
Rousseau in music, but was familiar with all the Muses
and made some contributions to most of them.[18] In the
realm of natural history he could instruct Buffon, and if he
did not come up to Savigny or Bentham in legal scholarship he had a firmer grasp of legal philosophy than most
of his contemporaries. He was not a systematic political
thinker, but neither were Rousseau nor Voltaire for that
matter; unlike them he proved to be a systematic political
architect. He accepted Turgot's and anticipated Condorcet's philosophy of progress, but with him it was a familiar
reality, not mere rhetoric, nor wistful longing, nor desperate faith.

How natural, then, that it should be Jefferson who formulated the strategy and directed the tactics of the campaign. More, he delivered a first stroke, that proved decisive. Early in 1780 the young French attaché, the Marquis
de Barbé-Marbois, submitted to Jefferson (and to other
governors as well) a series of queries about the character,
history, institutions, and resources of his state. Jefferson's
response was elaborate and historic: *Notes on Virginia*. A
formidable volume this, with notes and appendices it filled
over three hundred printed pages.[19] What a book it was, in
a way not unlike the famous *History of the East and West
Indies*, for it was description, history, politics, philosophy,
and morality all in one. It portrayed the geography of the
state, described its public and private institutions, its customs and manners, its commerce and trade, its wealth and
resources. It argued the importance of education and the
necessity of religious and intellectual freedom. And in the
course of all this it dealt, item by item and charge by
charge, with the animadversions of Buffon, Raynal, and
De Pauw.

Easy enough to dispose of the charge that animals in the
New World did not compare with those of the Old in numbers or in size and strength. Just count, and weigh and

measure and you would confound the most intransigent
Europeans.[20] All very well, but how did Jefferson propose
to meet Buffon's assertion that the New World had nothing
to compare with the lordly elephant or the mighty hippo-
potamus but the ignominious tapir; and nothing to compare with the lion and the tiger. Ah, Jefferson was not to
be caught out that way. We have something just as formidable: the Great Claw or Megalonyx. "What are we to
think of a creature whose claws were eight inches long,
when those of the lion are not 1½ inches; whose thigh-
bone was 6½ in diameter, when that of the lion is not 1½
inches?" Jefferson asked Dr. Rush, who quite agreed with
him that there was nothing to say as the facts spoke for
themselves.[21]

More important, indeed quite conclusive, was the discovery of the mammoth, an animal clearly (notwithstanding Buffon) indigenous to the New World.[22] Jefferson
had come across the giant fossil bones of this creature as
early as 1780, and thereafter he was fascinated by the implications of his find. It was a creature "of unparalleled
magnitude," five or six times the size of an elephant—
imagine that! And its existence "should have sufficed to
have rescued the earth it inhabited and the atmosphere it
breathed from the imputation of impotence in the conception and nourishment of animal life on a large scale; to
have stifled, in its birth, the opinion of a writer [Buffon]
the most learned, too, of all others in the science of animal
history, that in the New World *La nature vivante est
beaucoup moins agissante, beaucoup moins forte,*' that nature is less active, less energetic, on the one side of the
globe than on the other."[23]

This was but the beginning. Soon Jefferson was in Paris
where he could personally supervise the conversion of the
Comte de Buffon. He inundated the hapless Comte with
evidence that he could not ignore: the skin of a panther;
the horns of an elk, and for good measure, of a roebuck, a
caribou, and the spiked horn buck as well; a beaver; a
brace of pheasant and of grouse. The search for a moose
with which to confound Buffon took on epic proportions.
Jefferson entrusted the task to his old friend General Sullivan of Maine, who embarked upon a regular campaign to

track down some lordly bull moose that would forever silence the skeptical Buffon. "The troops he employed sallied forth," wrote Jefferson, "in the month of March—much snow—a herd attacked—one killed—in the wilderness—a road to cut twenty miles—to be drawn by hand from the frontiers to his house—bones to be cleaned, etc., etc." That etc., etc. covered a lot of ground, but in the end the much-traveled moose arrived, a bit the worse for wear, but no less conclusive for that, and Jefferson thought the sixty-five guineas it had cost him well spent.[24]

Thus, Jefferson vindicated the flora and fauna of the New World. He vindicated the native races, too. . . . All this time we have neglected the Indians who had, in a sense, ignited the whole dispute. No fear that the Americans would neglect the Indians. They were fascinated by them.[25] Cadwallader Colden, who has some claim to be considered one of the first American philosophers, had written a *History of the Five Indian Nations* early in the century,[26] and the naturalist John Bartram—it was to him Peter Kalm had come for knowledge of the New World—made a series of "Observations" about the Indians, more intimate, if less historical. Half a century later his son William wrote a famous report on his travels through the south that was to stir the imagination of a whole generation of poets.[27] Doctors Rush and Barton both studied the health and habits of the redmen, and so, too, the versatile Reverend Ezra Stiles up in Newport.[28] No one was more fascinated by the Indian than Jefferson, and no one contributed more to Indian studies, directly through the *Notes on Virginia*, indirectly through such explorers as John Ledyard, André Michaux, and Zebulon Pike, and finally, the indomitable Lewis and Clark.

What, then, of the Indian? Is he degenerate, as Buffon and De Pauw had asserted? Is he feeble, beardless, impotent? What nonsense. Come and fight him, that will teach you to sing a different tune. Or let us read you the speech of Logan, chief of the Mingoes: since Demosthenes where can you match that for eloquence?[29] And as for ardor and virility, the Indians have the passions and the powers that their circumstances dictate, neither more nor less, and their bodies and their minds are as well adapted to their environment as are the bodies and minds of Europeans to the environment of civilization. "It is true" wrote Jefferson's friend Charles Thomson in an Appendix to the *Notes*, "they do not indulge those excesses nor discover that fondness which is customary in Europe, but this is not owing to a defect in nature but in manners. Their soul is wholly bent on war."[30] That charge of impotence was on a par with the charge that they were beardless. "Had Mr. Buffon known the pains and trouble it costs the men to pluck out by the roots the hair that grows on their faces he would have seen that Nature had not been deficient in that respect."[31]

This is all very well, but when you look closely at the American defense of the Indian is it not clear that the Americans are hoist on their own petard? Like Buffon, they were environmentalists, and they made clear that the Indian was a natural and logical product of the American environment. If the New World environment was as propitious as they asserted—and proved—then why was it that, after thousands of years, it had produced only the American Indian, and not many of him, even in the wonderfully rich environment of the Northern continent, whereas the less beneficent environment of the Old World had produced, after all, a great galaxy of geniuses and of civilizations? And if after thousands of years, the American environment had produced only the American Indian, what reason was there to suppose that in the long run it augured well for Europeans in the New World? Would not the same climate, the same soil, the same products of Nature that had formed the Indian out of the miscellaneous stocks which had peopled America work slowly but irresistibly to form something very like the Indian out of the miscellaneous European stocks—European and African—who had now supplanted the original natives?

Nor was this the whole of the difficulty: There was a moral problem as well. If the red men had all the virtues that Jefferson and Charles Thomson and other Americans ascribed to them, what right had Americans to seize their lands, destroy their villages, kill their warriors, yes, and their women and children, too?[32] Even as Jefferson was extolling the courage and wisdom of the Indians, American frontiersmen were waging relentless war upon them, driving them out of their ancestral lands, debauching them with fire-water, and infecting them with smallpox.[33] In the beginning the American justification had had much in common with that which many Spaniards had invoked: the Indian was not quite a human being; he was a heathen, and one who proved stubbornly unwilling to embrace the true faith.[34] Thus John Winthrop of the Bay Colony could write exultantly that "the natives are all neare dead of the smallpox . . . the Lord hath cleared our title to what we possess."[35] Some Puritans and most Quakers tried to deal justly with the Indians, tried to convert them, to educate them, to give them the protection of English laws and justice. The failure was not so much of law as of imagination, and it was a failure not of Church or State, but of frontiersmen greedy for land, impatient of restraint or resistance, and convinced that they were soldiers of the Lord and advance agents of civilization.[36] Thus, a century and a half after Winthrop, James Sullivan of Maine—he who had procured the mighty moose—brushed aside sympathy with the Indian as sentimental:

> His agonies, at first, seem to demand a tear from the eye of humanity; but when we reflect that the extinction of his race, and the progress of the arts which give rise to his distressing apprehensions, are for the increase of mankind, and for the promotion of the world's glory and happiness; that five hundred rational animals may enjoy life in plenty and comfort, where only one savage drags out a hungry existence, we shall be pleased with the perspective into futurity.[37]

And down in Charleston the enlightened Dr. David Ramsay said much the same thing:

> The earth was made for man, and was intended by the creator of all things to be improved for the benefit of mankind. The land which could support one savage in his mode of living, is capable of supporting five hundred under proper cultivation. These wild lands

therefore were not the separate property of the few
savages who hunted over them, but belonged to the
common stock of mankind. The first who possessed a
vacant spot, and actually cultivated it for some time,
ought to be considered as the proprietor of that spot,
and they who derive their titles from him have a valid
right to the same.[38]

This was not, to be sure, the vocabulary of Raynal or
De Pauw, but did it not confess much the same animus,
was it not much the same argument? The Indian is inferior; it is right and just that he should give way to those
who are superior, and whose claims are more righteous in
the sight of God and of history?[39]

There was really no easy way out of this dilemma. If the
Indians were as splendidly adapted to their environment as
Bartram and Jefferson and Dr. Rush and others asserted,
then the Europeans had no right to take their lands away
from them and kill them off. If the Europeans did have
this right, was it not on the assumption that Buffon and De
Pauw and Raynal were sound critics and true prophets?

Out of all this came an uneasy compromise which
satisfied neither Jefferson's generation nor its successors.
Clearly, the Indian was not degenerate and Nature had not
condemned him to impotence. Just as clearly he was not
Noble—not John Smith's Pocahontas, nor Lahontan's
Adario, nor even Mr. Jefferson's Chief Logan. Just because the Americans rejected the untamed primitivism of
the Rationalists did not mean that they were required to
embrace the idyllic primitivism of the Romantics. The
choice was not really between De Pauw and, let us say,
Chateaubriand; there was a third choice, that made by
Jefferson and Gallatin, that celebrated a generation later in
the realistic pages of Fenimore Cooper.

Thus, Crèvecoeur, who called himself *"un cultivateur"*
—the term is really better than "farmer"—had little use
for the frontier; what he really admired was Nantucket Island, so neat and tamed and respectable, an island "which
seems to have been inhabited merely to prove what mankind can do when happily governed," and the significant
word is "governed."[40] Nor was he truly romantic about

the Indians; he knew them too well for that. They were, in their own way, happy—he admitted that readily enough. They were even, in their way, superior. Thus:

> Without temples, without priests, without kings, and without laws, they are in many instances superior to us; and the proofs of what I advance are that they live without care, sleep without inquietude, take life as it comes, bearing all its asperities with unparalleled patience; and die without any kind of apprehension for what they have done, or for what they expect to meet with hereafter.[41]

But that did not make them noble, not even generous or wise or humane; it did not temper their ferocity or abate their cruelty, and Crèvecoeur's chapter on the Wyoming Massacre throws a lurid light on the character of the red men, in some respects so admirable.[42]

So, too, Philip Freneau, though long inclined to sentimentalize the Indian, concluded, in the end, that he did not yield himself either to romanticizing or to civilizing; he was what he was, and could not be fitted into European categories.

> Of different mind, he sees not with your sight.
> Perfect, perhaps, as viewed by Nature's light;
> By Nature's dictates, all his views are bent,
> No more imperfect than his Author meant.[43]

Or—to adopt some other test than the Indian—Jefferson was enchanted with his views westward over a sea of virgin forests, but Monticello was no log cabin, but a monument to Palladio, and its gardens were not "English," pretending to be wild, but orderly and trim.[44] Fresh from the courts of Europe John Adams might yearn for a bit of pomp and circumstance in the Vice-Presidency, but he had really been revolted by the immoralities of Paris and London, and what he treasured most deeply was the farmhouse in Braintree.[45] Joel Barlow might conjure up the wildest visions of Columbus, but when he found himself

under the smoky rafter of a Savoyard inn, what he longed
for was a dish of Hasty Pudding.[46] When he translated
Volney's romantic *Ruins* he dedicated it to the Father of
the Steamboat, and when he returned from his long exile
in France it was not to plunge into the western wilderness
but to build his palatial Kalorama on the outskirts of the
capital city.[47] And though Gallatin did betake himself to
the banks of the turbulent Monongahela, it was he who
sponsored the first great program of internal improvements
designed to enable civilization to triumph over Nature.[48]

2

Turn now to the second American argument, one which
most eighteenth-century economists and philosophers regarded as conclusive: population.[1] "I am constantly astonished," wrote Rousseau, "that people could fail to recognize or that they should have the bad faith not to agree
upon, a sign that is so simple. What is the purpose of political association? It is the preservation and prosperity of its
members. And what is the most certain sign that they are
living and prospering? It is the number and increase of
population . . . Other things being equal, that government
under which the citizens live and multiply most is infallibly
the best."[2] The Abbé Raynal put it even more simply:

> But it will be asked whether a great degree of popula-
> tion is of use to promote the happiness of mankind.
> This is an idle question. In fact the point is not to
> multiply men in order to make them happy; but it is
> sufficient to make them happy, that they should mul-
> tiply.[3]

No wonder that the elder Mirabeau's book, *L'Ami des
Hommes,* should display a sub-title, "A Treatise on Population."

It was a well-nigh universal preoccupation,[4] this matter
of population. Goldsmith had made clear—it was in
1769—that

Ill fares the land, to hast'ning ills a prey
Where wealth accumulates, and men decay . . .
Princes and lords may flourish, or may fade,
A breath can make them, as a breath has made.
But a bold peasantry, their country's pride,
When once destroyed can never be supplied.[5]

Most European states seemed bent on proving how right
he was. In the countryside and the villages population held
its own, and a bit more, but everywhere towns and cities
were draining away the peasantry, and that was fatal, for
if births outnumbered deaths in the country, it was the
other way around in the cities. London, Paris, Amsterdam,
Vienna, Breslau, wherever you went in the great cities,
death triumphed over life. The philosophes were quite
clear about this. It was Buffon who demonstrated that the
population of Paris had barely maintained itself over the
past half century, and this notwithstanding the thousands
who flocked in from the provinces.[6] It was Dr. James Anderson who found that in London deaths exceeded births
by five to four, year after year; even with all the influx
from the countryside, London had added only two thousand to her population in the first half of the century.[7] The
Reverend Dr. Price presented figures which proved that
the situation was even worse in Berlin and Amsterdam:
one hundred and thirty-five deaths for every hundred
births in Berlin and no less than one hundred sixty-nine in
prosperous Amsterdam—that was hard to believe! Everywhere the toll on infants was cruelly high.[8] Even in England and France one sixth of the babies did not survive
their first year, and in some communities, Flanders for example, or Vienna, the mortality was even higher. Thus, in
Breslau five out of twelve children died before they
reached the age of five.[9] And when it came to foundlings,
the chances of survival were indeed thin: only one out of
four babies committed to the new London Foundling Hospital survived its fifth year.[10]

From time to time—when the harvests were good, when
there was a long era of peace, or even of freedom from the
ravages of invasion, when smallpox and typhus and ma-
laria withheld their toll, countries could show a modest in-

crease in population: Ireland, for example, and Prussia,
after the Seven Years' War, and Finland through most of
the century. Notwithstanding dire oppression and frequent
economic crises and substantial emigration to the New
World, Ireland managed to increase her population by
three-quarters of a million in the first seventy years of the
century. In the same period Finland almost doubled her
population—a record, that, for Europe, though maybe it
had something to do with the way the statistics were kept.[11]
Mostly, however, the nations of Europe barely held their
own. Thus, for all their prosperity and good fortune, England and Wales added only a little over a million to their
population in the first two generations of the century.[12]
Between 1750 and 1800 Denmark increased from eight
hundred thousand to less than one million, and in the same
half-century Norway added barely one hundred thousand
to her population. For long stretches of the seventeenth
and eighteenth centuries, Spain, Portugal, and some of the
German states and Italian provinces actually lost population. France, the most powerful and the richest country on
the continent, made a poor showing indeed, and it was one
that American visitors observed with interest. She had
counted some twenty-two millions at the beginning of the
century, but only twenty-seven millions ninety years later,
on the eve of the Revolution. Or there is Lombardy, as fertile as any region in Europe, with a population of one million at the beginning of the century and one hundred thousand more after seventy years. Tuscany, too, added one
hundred thousand in seventy years. Portugal did a little
better, notwithstanding the Lisbon earthquake, increasing
her population by one-third in seventy years.[13] No wonder
the Marechal de Saxe, who was something of a philosophe
and who was sure that the happiness as well as the strength
and prosperity of the state required large families, proposed
that women should be permitted to mate with whoever
could beget children; in less than two hundred years, he
concluded, one million women would produce a population of nine hundred and seventy-eight millions![14]

Now look across the Atlantic, and what a spectacle
greets the enraptured eye of the economist and of the philosophe. Everywhere, from Massachusetts to Georgia, in

town and in countryside, among the Negroes as among the whites, the story is the same: the Americans are obeying the Biblical injunction to multiply and replenish the earth. Look at it any way you will and it points to the same inescapable conclusion.[15] At the beginning of the century the English colonies counted some 250,000 white inhabitants, no more. Sixty years later and their number had mounted to one million six hundred thousand, a five-fold increase. And when Americans took their first census in 1790 they counted almost four million inhabitants.[16] Never before in history had there been anything like this. Consider the birth rate. Franklin had estimated, back in the fifties, that the population of Pennsylvania was doubling every twenty years, and as it turned out, that was about right. And it was not a matter of immigration, either, though that told its own story—after all how few migrated eastward across the Atlantic! No, the reasons were clear: "the salubrity of the Air, the healthiness of the Climate, the Plenty of good Provisions, and the Encouragement to early Marriages by the certainty of Subsistence in cultivating the Earth"— there was your explanation.[17] Even marriage was not always necessary, and Franklin concocted the famous legend of Polly Baker to make clear that a sensible society (like the American) should prefer fecundity to morality, a story which all Europe greeted with credulity and rapture![18] Jefferson's statistics for Virginia pointed to the same conclusion: he estimated the population doubled there every twenty-seven years; and what was surprising was that the slaves increased even more rapidly than their masters, a testimony to the beneficence of Nature rather than to the benevolence of the institutions.[19]

Yet all this was mostly conjecture, though well-reasoned conjecture.[20] But here is Dr. Benjamin Smith Barton with the facts. "Observations on the Probabilities of Human Life, and the Progress of Population in the New World," he called it, and it was to his uncle, David Rittenhouse of the Philosophical Society that he addressed his Observations.[21]

A remarkable man this Dr. Barton, another of those cosmopolites who seem to swarm across the stage of eighteenth-century America, another of those Philadelphia scientists who like Dr. Franklin, James Logan, Rittenhouse, Benjamin Rush, and Samuel Currie somehow found time for politics and scholarship and philosophy along with science.[22] As a lad he had accompanied his uncle on one of his many surveying expeditions, and "in this wilderness" he recalled, "he first fostered my love and zeal for natural history." Young Barton had gone off to Edinburgh to study medicine, and then to London where he formed a friendship with the famous Joseph Banks, whose house in Soho Square was a Mecca for all scientists; then on to Göttingen—at least so it was said—the first American to receive a medical degree from that illustrious University.[23] Back, then, to Philadelphia, where he taught botany and medicine at the University, wrote a *Materia Medica*, edited a medical journal, compiled the first textbook on botany, set forth "New Views" on the origin of the American Indian and—for us—most important of all, observed "The Progress of Population in the United States of America."

"Numbers of people," he began oracularly, "constitute the strength and riches of a state; that country whose population is rapidly advancing may fairly be said to be increasing in both concomitants of national prosperity." Apply this test to the United States and it is evident that "this country possesses, in a superior degree, an inherent, radical, and lasting source of national vigor and greatness . . . in no other part of the world is the progress of population so rapid as in these states." And the reasons were not only the familiar ones of climate and soil, but—a new note here—virtuous morals, and the benign influence of government.

And here is the evidence to prove it all, miscellaneous, to be sure, but no less conclusive. In London, Paris, Berlin, Amsterdam, Copenhagen—everywhere in the Old World —each marriage produces, on the average, four children; in Massachusetts the average is more than six. In the healthiest parts of Europe there are four and a half persons to a house, but in America the number is closer to six and one-half. Or consider the birth rate: in England one birth to every twenty-six inhabitants, but one death for every thirty or so—the precise number is in dispute. But in America there is one birth for every twenty inhabitants and one death for every forty; what a difference! In all the great cities of Europe deaths exceed births, but in American towns there are twice as many births as deaths.

More children survive, that much is clear, and those who survive live longer than their European cousins. The average length of life in Europe is a mere thirty-two years, but in America it is no less than forty-five years. This is, of course, merely an average; actually a good many Americans can confidently expect to survive long past the Biblical three score and ten. Look at the trim little state of Connecticut, and you will discover that one out of thirteen of its fortunate inhabitants can expect to live to eighty, and one out of thirty lives to be ninety; match that in the Old World if you can. Clearly Franklin and Jefferson were right all along.

What does all this mean? Does it not prove conclusively that the American environment is the most salubrious of all, the vicissitudes of temperature stimulating "to the generative principle of animal nature;" the earth, the waters, the skies, bountiful? And Dr. Barton concluded on a note of exultation:

> Must not the mind of every American citizen be impressed with gratitude, and glow with emotions of a virtuous pride, when he reflects on the blessings his country enjoys?[24]

Meantime Dr. Barton's colleague, Dr. Samuel Currie, had reënforced this argument on fecundity and longevity with a study of the relation of climate to disease.[25] The American climate, Dr. Currie readily admitted, was not in itself superior to that of other countries, but the Americans enjoy other advantages that guarantee them superiority and progress: immunity from volcanoes, hurricanes, earthquakes, from deluges and from droughts; a fertile soil; an enlightened society and a beneficent government.

For government is part of the environment. Dr. Currie put it perspicaciously:

> North America is the only portion of this spacious globe where man can live securely, and enjoy all the

privileges to which he has a native right. In this envia-
ble and favoured region there is no proud usurping
aristocracy, no ecclesiastical orders with exclusive
privileges, no kings with arbitrary power or corrupting influence, no venal parliaments composed of
different ranks and opposing interests . . . None of
the enervating refinements of luxury or dissipation are
to be found here; but here all the necessaries and con-
veniences of life abound, and a pleasing equality and
decent competence are everywhere displayed. Here
the dignity of the human species is restored, and man
enjoys all the freedom to which he is entitled; for
here he is a member of the government he obeys, and
a framer of the laws by which he is governed.[26]

Here was a new note—there had been anticipations, to
be sure, in Franklin and Jefferson, Crèvecoeur, and Tom
Paine—and it was one that would resound with increasing
frequency and resonance in the coming years. Do not
think of environment purely in terms of climate, soil, flora,
fauna; society and government, too, are essential parts of
environment. The New World possessed not only the most
favored of natural environments; it had constituted for itself the most favored of social environments—one of freedom, toleration, and equality. That is, of course, what
Jefferson had in mind when he wrote to the delicious
Maria Cosway: "They tell me *que vous allez faire un en-
fant* . . . You may make children there, but this is the
country to transplant them to. There is no comparison between the sum of happiness enjoyed here and there."[27] It
is what Brissot de Warville wrote when he visited America
just the year the new government got under way—that "if
you apply moral and political considerations to the United
States you must conclude that there cannot be any country
in which life expectancy is longer for, in addition to all
their natural advantages, the people enjoy the benefits of a
liberty unequaled anywhere in the Old World, and it is
Liberty which is the source of health."[28] And it was in that
same year that Dr. Rush, conducting his far-ranging Medical Inquiries, confirmed this connection:

There is an indissoluble union between social, political, and physical happiness [he wrote], and if it be true that elective and representative governments are most favourable to the individual as well as national prosperity, it follows of course that they are most favourable to animal life. But this opinion does not rest upon an induction derived from the relation which truths upon all subjects bear to each other. Many facts prove animal life to exist in a larger quantity and for a longer time, in the enlightened and happy state of Connecticut, than any other country upon the surface of the globe.[29]

Hugh Williamson the historian of North Carolina, endorsed this interpretation when, in his old age, he came to consider the effect of climate on the New World. An extraordinary figure, Williamson, and no wonder: His mother had been kidnapped by no other than the pirate Blackbeard! He had studied in Philadelphia and in Utrecht, and then involved himself in the Hutchinson-letters imbroglio in London. He was a veritable philosophe: a professor of mathematics, an astronomer who observed the transit of Venus, and a theologian who observed the Heavens; a surgeon general of North Carolina troops during the Revolution; a statesman who represented his state in the Federal Convention; an economist and a historian. When he retired from Congress, in 1793, he stayed on in New York where he composed his *History of North Carolina*. It was not soil and climate alone that determined the character of people, he wrote, in a preliminary essay, but

The habits and manners of every nation take their form and impression from the spirit of the government under which they live, or from the administration of that government. They are diligent or indolent, ignorant or well-informed, according to the privileges they enjoy. The very consciousness of being free excites a spirit of enterprise and gives a spring to the intellectual faculties . . . If I could speak of our liberties as we speak of the climate and face of the country; if I could speak of their duration as we speak of things that are permanent in nature; I should venture with confidence to predict that in the scale of science the American states, in a few ages, would not shrink from a comparison with the Grecian republics, or any other people recorded in history.[30]

3

All this was sufficiently conclusive, but the Americans had still another weapon with which to thwart their assailants. They had not forged it, to be sure, but it was they who first used it, and revealed its potentialities. This was the argument that "climate" was not something forever fixed, but something that man himself could make and remake. Man was not passive in the face of nature;† he commanded Nature and could control her.[1] Montesquieu, who saw so much, had seen this, too. "Men by their care, and by the influence of good laws, have rendered the earth more proper for their abode. We see rivers where there have been lakes and marshes . . . Thus as destructive nations produce evils more durable than themselves, the actions of industrious nations are the source of blessings which last when they are no more."[2] And Buffon was confident, too, that

Some centuries hence, when the lands are cultivated, the forests cut down, the course of the rivers properly directed, and the marshes drained . . . this country will become the most fertile, the most wholesome and the richest in the whole world.[3]

All well enough, but would it really take centuries? Americans knew better. Indeed, the process of transformation was already under way, after only a few score years. As the remarkable Reverend Jared Eliot of Connec-

† Thus anticipating by a century the thesis that the father of American Sociology, Lester Ward, developed in a series of magisterial volumes designed to liberate Americans from the prison of Spencerian Social Statics. See Commager, ed. *Lester Ward and the Welfare State* (Indianapolis, 1967).

ticut—he was theologian, doctor, and scientist all in one—
wrote, at mid-century:

> Take a View of a Swamp in its original Estate, full of
> Bogs, overgrown with Flags, Brakes, poisonous Weeds
> and Vines . . . Behold it now cloathed with sweet
> Grass, adorned with the lofty wide-spreading well-set
> Indian-Corn; the yellow Barley; the Silver-coloured
> Flax; the ramping Hemp, beautified with fine Ranges
> of Cabbage; the delicious Melon, and the best of Tur-
> nips, all pleasing to the Eye and, many, agreeable to
> the Taste; a wonderful Change, this, and all brought
> about in a short Time; a Resemblance of Creation, as
> much as we, impotent Beings, can attain to, the happy
> Product of Skill and Industry.[4]

All brought about in a short time, and all by "Skill and Industry!" That was the point, that was what so many of the
Old World critics had overlooked. Yet even Raynal had
seen this when he wrote, in the revised edition of his *History of the Indies,* that in the British settlements in
America:

> Man appeared, and immediately changed the face of
> North America. He introduced symmetry by the as-
> sistance of all the instruments of art. The impene-
> trable woods were instantly cleared . . . the wild
> beasts were driven away . . . while thorns and briars
> made way for rich harvests . . . Thus the New
> World, like the Old, became subject to Man.[5]

Brissot noted an improvement even in Pennsylvania—that
was almost like improving upon Eden! The marshes had
been drained, floods had subsided, forests had been re-
placed by cultivated fields, and the health of the settlers
had visibly improved. "Pennsylvanians are growing healthier," he wrote, with a bow toward Peter Kalm, "as more
lands are being cleared; in the last thirty to forty years
people's faces have become less pale; for some time the
number of centenarians has been increasing, and sep-
tuagenarians are very common."[6] Even harsh and inhospi-

table Vermont yielded to the benign operations of man, and Ira Allen—brother to the blasphemous Ethan—rejoiced that "Man sees the effect of his own powers . . . the stagnant air vanishes with the woods, the rank vegetation feels the purifying influence of the sun . . . putrid exhalations flit off on lazy wing, and fevers and agues accompany them."[7]

Of all the American philosophes, it was Jefferson who was most indefatigable in bringing about the transformation from wilderness to cultivation, and who contributed most to the process, Jefferson with his inexhaustible ingenuity, his sleepless curiosity, his countless experiments, his boldness and vision, his instinct for the practical and the useful, and for the beautiful, too. He experimented with kale and cabbages and Jerusalem artichokes, with walnuts and pecans and almonds and pistachios, with figs from France and rice from Africa and Italy—the last he smuggled out himself[8]—and mulberry trees and cork trees, and even the India-rubber tree. He tried to introduce the olive tree to Virginia, for he thought the olive the most beneficent of fruit, and he sat up all night watching Lombardy peasants make cheese so that he could introduce the process into America.[9] He brought in merino sheep and Algerian bantams and tried, in vain, to domesticate the nightingale. Discussing the possibility of introducing the breadfruit tree, which Captain Bligh had already transplanted to the West Indies, he wrote that "one service of this kind rendered to a nation is worth more than all the victories of the most splendid pages of their history."[10]

Men could remake their environment, and that is just what the Americans set out to do. Few, to be sure, planned as audaciously as Jefferson, who as early as 1786 was speculating about the advantages which might follow the opening of a canal through Panama—among them: "The gulph stream on the coast of the United States would cease, and with that those derangements of course and reckoning which now impede and endanger the intercourse with those states; the fogs on the banks of Newfoundland would disappear . . ."[11] Meantime, Jefferson's fellow citizens addressed themselves to the immediate and the practical. They drained the swamps and cleared the forests, built

roads and canals, imported new plants and new breeds of
cattle and sheep, and experimented with new techniques of
farming. All this required an enlightened citizenry, and
that is just what the American states possessed: the enraptured author[12] of *American Husbandry* returned again and
again to this circumstance as he demonstrated the superiority of American to English husbandry. It required science, and where do you find more ingenious and adept scientists than in America, above all in Philadelphia, with
Franklin and Bartram, Godfrey and Rittenhouse, Doctors
Rush, Currie, and Barton, and all the others who helped
make the American Philosophical Society one of the
glories of the New World?[13] It required habits of co-operation, and this was a specialty of the Americans: That had
been the price of survival in a world that was new and
strange. It required self-government, and here again, did
not the Americans have longer and richer experience in
self-government than any other people?[14]

To transform Nature required space, too; space for experiments, space for expansion, space for growth. That
was something the new United States had in ample measure. Montesquieu had asserted that great territory was a
handicap, nay a danger, to a republic, and his generalization had become almost hackneyed by repetition.[15] But
not so: America was to disprove all that. "We can no
longer say there is nothing new under the sun," wrote
Jefferson to Dr. Priestley. "For this whole chapter in the
history of man is new. The extent of our republic is new.
Its sparse habitation is new."[16] Great size offered the possibility of an almost limitless choice of environments. Alas,
for the French, the Germans, the Spaniards, they have but
one climate, and that was the end of the matter—unless, of
course, they decided to emigrate to America. That is just
what many of them did. The surprising thing, said Dr.
John Mitchell, was that anyone would remain in the Old
World when the New offered so many advantages:

It is astonishing any men of small fortunes . . .
should remain in such countries that deny them most
of the comforts, enjoyments and security of life. On
the contrary these southern colonies . . . hold forth

the very contrast to the unhappiness they experience
in Europe. They may have whatever land they please
at a price next to nothing; that land is as rich . . . as
in any country in the world; in a climate that produces . . . a plenty not to be equaled throughout any
other countries on the globe, and at the same time
that both soil and climate, and plenty of land join to
yield such advantageous offers; the government is the
most mild in being; liberty reigns in perfection . . .
no oppression to enslave the planter and rob him of
the fruits of his industry. When all these great and
manifest advantages are considered, I think it must
appear surprising that more emigrants from different
parts of Europe are not constantly moving from
thence to America.[17]

Americans had their choice of climates,[18] for the United
States was born the largest nation west of Russia, and in
no time at all—thanks again to Jefferson, who had no misgivings about size—it had doubled its territory. Thus, the
new United States boasted, eventually, as many climates as
the whole of Europe. Is the soil thin and sterile in Vermont? You can migrate to the Mohawk Valley of New
York, a veritable farmer's paradise. Is all the good land
taken up in Pennsylvania?—here is Ohio waiting to welcome all comers. Do marshes and mountains usurp the soil
of North Carolina? Move on then to the bluegrass of Kentucky, the richest land that man had ever known. And if
this new West, across the Appalachians, filled up too
quickly, what with the doubling of population every generation, look across the broad Mississippi, west, and ever
west, across prairie and plain and mountain all the way to
that famous river which Captain Gray had discovered and
named Columbia.

So, in the end, it was not logic that settled the great controversy over the value of America, it was history. And it
was history as future, not history as past. Perhaps history
did not so much settle the controversy, as make it obso-
lete.‡ For now the whole issue took on a new character.

‡ Thus anticipating by a century George Santayana's perspicacious
observation that we Americans "do not nowadays refute our predeces-
sors, we pleasantly bid them good-bye."

America, as it were, turned the tables on Europe. She got the upper hand, and kept it. Was America a mistake? How can you ask, when this new nation is overthrowing the greatest of world powers and setting up on her own, arrayed in the garments of honor and of wisdom? Did the New World drain away the strength of the Old? Say rather it has regenerated the Old, infusing it with new vigor, inspiring it with new ideas, firing it with new expectations. See how quickly the lines reform. Raynal could write in one breath that no man could conceivably desire the discovery of America and—in almost the next—he could predict that

> a new Olympus, a new Arcady, a new Athens, a new Greece will perhaps give birth on the continent, or on the neighboring islands, to new Homers, new Theocrites, and new Anacreons. Perhaps there will arise another Newton in New England. It is in British America—let there be no doubt about that—that the first rays of knowledge are to shine if they are at last to dawn under this long-obscured sky.[19]

Turgot could say, more simply, that "this people is the hope of the human race. It may become the model,"[20] and Condorcet could submit the example of America as evidence of the reality of the idea of Progress, the highest stage that civilization had yet attained.[21] Now the critics broke ranks, threw away their weapons, and abandoned the contest, all but a few of the most perverse. And when a new phalanx of philosophes came in battle array to vindicate the New World, they found that the enemy had disappeared, and that no one now could quite remember what the conflict had been about.[22]

But that was not to be the end of the matter. There are always fresh issues to be disputed, and now there was a new problem, less profound than the old, and certainly less fundamental, but more meaningful and more urgent. Here was an independent United States—the first colony to set up on its own, the first self-made nation; what did it portend? What would be the consequences of the American Revolution, what would be the consequences of an independent United States, panoplied with constitutions and bills of rights? What would happen to the Old World when every breeze that blew from the west carried with it not only the hope of freedom, self-government, and equality, but the reality as well?

That is another story.

CHAPTER SIX

The Enlightenment Celebrates the Spirit of the Laws

1

All the philosophes were statesmen, or thought they were, ready to draw up a new constitution, draft a new code of laws, or design a new commonwealth on demand. Climate, religion, history, customs (the untranslatable *moeurs*)— all of these were important, but their importance was to be read in terms of law. It was in politics and government that you could trace the course of history and read the destinies of nations. "Politics are the divine science, after all," wrote John Adams, and a few years later he complained that "the world has been too long abused with notions that climate and soil decide the characters and political institutions of nations," and it was to make clear the primary role of government in advancing the happiness and security of men that he wrote those encyclopedic volumes which he called a *Defense of the Constitutions of the United States.* Voltaire, too, rejected climate as the key to history, as, indeed, he rejected most of Montesquieu:[1] It was government, religion, and education that were responsible for the happiness or unhappiness of society. So, too, said David Hume, who pointed out that over the centuries climate remained the same, but people did not and that, for that matter, "no one attributes the difference of manners in Wapping and St. James's to a difference of air or climate."[2] "Climate sets the stage," wrote Hume's fellow-philosopher in Glasgow, Adam Ferguson, "and men are what government makes them."[3] So, too, said Joseph Priestley in his *Lectures on History:* "Of all things which contribute to the happiness of states, GOVERNMENT is the first that offers itself to our notice."[4] The Abbé Raynal wrote eight volumes on the influence of climate and environment, but confessed, nevertheless, that "men are what government makes them."[5] Late in life Rousseau confessed that he had been unable to complete what he had hoped to be his masterpiece: ". . . the one at which I worked with greatest inclination, to which I wished to devote myself all my life and which, in my own opinion, was to set the seal upon my reputation . . . my *Institutions Politiques*." For, he added, "I had come to see that everything was radically connected with politics, and that however one proceeded, no people would be other than the nature of its government made it."[6] What would we not give for a continuation of the Social Contract!

Government, constitutions, codes, how the age delighted in them. It was the Age of Buffon, to be sure; it was the Age of Voltaire; it was the Age of Pope; but it was the Age of Montesquieu as well.[7] "Mankind had lost its rights; Montesquieu found and restored them," wrote Voltaire, and it was true that *The Spirit of the Laws* had almost the authority of the *Principia*. Everywhere the philosophes asked the most searching questions about politics and government and law. What was the origin of government? Did it really originate in a state of Nature, and by Compact or was it perhaps a Divine creation? What was the nature of Law? Did civil law differ from Natural Law, and if it did which was superior? Were the laws that governed society like gravity or the flowing of the tides, or were they made by man and to be unmade by man at his pleasure? What was the best form of government: a monarchy, an empire, a despotism, perhaps a republic, or were there different forms suited to different peoples, at different times in history? Is it true that empires require despotic rule, and that republican governments flourish only in small states? Is it true that honor is the distinguishing prin-

ciple of monarchical government and virtue of republican?
Is government designed to represent the will of the people,
and who are the people? What are the rights of man, if indeed he has any rights, that rulers are bound to respect,
that Nature and Heaven are bound to respect? Where do
we find answers to these questions? Let us study primitive
societies. Let us contemplate China. Let us look to the
Greeks, who invented politics, let us look to the Romans
who invented effective government. Let us study the Italian
city-states, let us comment on *Davila,* let us reinterpret *The
Spirit of the Laws.* Let us consider the promise and failure
of all confederations; let us contemplate the rise and decline of empires!

How they studied, how they reviewed, how they observed, how they new-fashioned the laws. Every people
had something to contribute, even the Germans who could
not solve their own problems, even the Italians whose philosophies so out-ran their performances, but particularly
the Scots, the English and the French. In the years between Leibniz and Goethe, Christian Wolff dominated the
mind of Germany with his *Sagacious Thoughts* on the
greatest variety of subjects: *On God, On the World and
the Souls of Men, On the Operations of Nature, On the
Conduct and Indulgence of Men Designed to Prosper their
Happiness.* The Scots, who had never really been able to
manage their own politics, were nevertheless the most profound of political philosophers. For dignity, judiciousness,
and intellectual vigor, what other country could match
Francis Hutcheson's *System of Moral Philosophy,* or
Adam Ferguson's *Principles of Moral and Political Science,* or Adam Smith's *The Wealth of Nations*—as much a
political as an economic treatise—or David Hume's magisterial Treatises and Enquiries *Concerning Human Understanding of Human Nature.* The extraordinary Lord Monboddo, he who dressed in white velvet and dined Roman
style on a floor strewn with roses, was perhaps neither
dignified nor judicious, but his six-volume study *Of the Origin and Progress of Language* which linked the ourang-
outang with the human species was perhaps the most original work to come out of Scotland.

The Swiss were experts on liberty, and on federalism—

or so they thought. Jean Jacques Burlamaqui laid down the
Principles of Natural Law, and Emmerich de Vattel formulated the *Law of Nations* while Johann Zimmermann
laid bare the true nature of *National Pride*—doubtless his
intimacy with Frederick the Great was helpful here, for he
was Frederick's physician. In the realm of speculation, it
was France that was the most prolific. Montesquieu wrote
little, but what he wrote was classic. The Baron d'Holbach
who wrote on almost everything, wrote an *Essay on Natural Law*, and in 1776—what a year that was for treatises
on politics!—the indefatigable Abbé Mably drew up a
Treatise on Legislation. Or contemplate Real de Curban's
eight-folio volumes on *The Science of Government* which
made clear that it was better to stay on familiar paths than
to venture into even the most alluring wilderness, and he
anticipated by more than half a century Lord Melbourne's
preference for the Order of the Garter because "there's no
damned merit in it." Down in Italy—how easy it is to
overlook Italy—where they were busy setting up the first
university chairs of politics and economics, Giovanni Vico
was writing his profound essays on history and jurisprudence, and Beccaria that seminal study of *Crimes and
Punishments* that was to change penal codes everywhere in
the Western World, and Gaetano Filangieri, whom Goethe
called "worthy of all esteem," a five-volume study of *The
Science of Legislation*—poor Filangieri, dead at thirty-six
with only half his many enterprises completed.[8] The English had had their revolution and were confident that they
already possessed the most perfect of constitutions and
that further political thought was largely irrelevant; their
political literature, after Locke, was romantic, as with Bolingbroke's *Patriot King*, or complacent as with Blackstone's *Commentaries on the Laws of England*. Yet there
were undercurrents of dissent—currents on which Gordon
and Trenchard launched *Cato's Letters* and James Burgh
his famous *Political Disquisitions* and Thomas Pownall his
Administration and Mrs. Macaulay her Whig histories and
Dr. Price and Dr. Priestley their voluminous writings;
these currents flowed across the Atlantic.

The Americans were more political-minded than any
other people. The whole of their philosophy—now that

Jonathan Edwards was out of the way—was really political philosophy, and the whole of their literature, too, or all of it that counted, in the long run. Even their imaginative literature had political implications, John Trumbull's *M'Fingal,* or Crèvecoeur's *Letters,* or Barlow's *Vision of Columbus.* How impressive the three volumes of John Adams's *Defense of the Constitutions of the United States,* even though they were not original;[9] or Tom Paine's vindication of the *Rights of Man,* which was; or the *Federalist Papers,* all in all the most significant political treatise of the century and the one with the longest influence. The issues raised by John Locke, by Rousseau, by Tom Paine, were given a dusty answer, though not a final one, in Mr. Burke's *Reflections on the Revolution in France.*[10] That signalized the end of the Enlightenment in the Old World, for a long time, but not in the New, which stubbornly preferred Tom Paine in adversity to Edmund Burke in triumph.

Almost everyone, it seemed, tried his hand at writing a new constitution or drawing up a new code of laws. Rousseau prepared a constitution for Corsica, and drew up one for Poland, too.[11] So did the "celebrated" Mrs. Macaulay, the historian and friend to America—alas no one thought to ask her to draw up a constitution for America, or even for Massachusetts! Turgot prepared a model constitution for France, but did not dare present it to his King.[12] Frederick the Great promulgated his Code Frederic in 1751, Sonnenfels drew up a code for Austria, and Morelly —the poor man has no other name—formulated an elaborate *Code of Nature* which contained a model constitution suitable for all commonwealths and "conformable to the intentions of Nature."[13] And that Abbé who wanted to get rid of all the institutions of property, the Abbé Mably, drafted a constitution for Poland and another for the various American states; he persuaded himself that John Adams had asked him for it, but Adams thought him officious.[14] What fun to draw up constitutions! You could give your imagination free rein, you could construct utopias, you could be as bold as you wished and no danger that you would ever be found out—not in Europe, anyway. In the New World things were a bit different. There, when

you drew up a constitution, it was likely to be adopted, so
you had to know what you were about.

Even in the Old World it was not all just a matter of
speculation, for politics was becoming a serious matter,
and half the philosophes were political. Plato had looked
to the time when philosophers would be kings. Now, if the
philosophers were not kings, surely the Kings were all philosophers, or if they were not, they hastened to attach philosophers to their courts so they could be respectable.
Look at Frederick of Prussia, the model and the envy of
all the enlightened despots; did not Voltaire and Diderot
and Lagrange and Maupertius—the President of Frederick's
Academy—all testify that he was a philosophe as well as a
King. What is more, he wrote philosophy—the *Anti-
Machiavel*, edited by no other than Voltaire—and the famous *Political Testament* which set forth the duties and responsibilities of a King.[15] Or consider Catherine of Russia;
she combined the wisdom of Solon with the justice of
Lycurgus—so said Diderot who ought to know; so said the
Baron Grimm who gave her all the literary gossip for
twenty years; how happy for her to have corresponded
with Diderot and the Baron Grimm! She invited Voltaire
to come to her court, in vain; she invited d'Alembert to
tutor her grandson, and when he refused she imported the
brilliant Frederic La Harpe from the Vaud, the young man
who had just won a prize for the best address on the subject of peace: just the thing that most interested Catherine!
She invited Beccaria from Milan to reform her penal code,
and he had the good sense to refuse. She even had Diderot
draw up a model educational scheme, which she promptly
forgot.[16] And up in Stockholm was Gustavus III, the Sun
King of the North. He had seized the reins of power; he
had knocked Hats and Caps off hard Swedish heads; he
had established freedom of the press, and ended torture,
just like his uncle Frederick down in Sans Souci. He
founded the Swedish Academy; he patronized poets, especially the gifted Karl Bellman who was a kind of Swedish
Ossian; he encouraged music and adored the theater and
the opera, and the Muses rewarded him with immortality
by turning his murder at a masked ball into just such an
opera as would have delighted him.[17]

What a wonderful age when despots were everywhere enlightened. There was Joseph II in Austria, determined to sweep aside the ruins of the old fabric, and build a new one, but who—as it was said—built the roof before he built the foundations. There was his brother Leopold in Tuscany who abolished torture, held the Church in check, and issued edicts against luxury—imagine that in Florence! —and who has some claims to be the most consistent of all enlightened monarchs.[18] There was Charles Frederick of Baden who wrote a book on physiocracy and who was so enlightened that he determined to make his subjects into "free, opulent, and law-abiding citizens, whether they liked it or not." There was Charles William Ferdinand of Brunswick, equally talented in the arts of war and of peace; he played chess for relaxation, called Lessing to preside over his library at Wolfenbüttle, and for a quarter of a century he made his little principality an oasis of freedom and enlightenment. Carl August ruled in tiny Weimar, and made that town the showcase of all Europe, what with Goethe and Schiller and Wieland and the philosophers Herder and Fichte: "Now he would be in the conservatories, where he knew every plant and moss and flower [it is his mistress who is describing him] now in the gardens and the park, now with the professors of Jena, now at one of his farms, now parleying with the artists, now exchanging views with poets, now viewing pictures, now buying antiques."[19]

And where the Kings weren't sufficiently enlightened (some of them had the habit of going mad*) their ministers were—the mighty Pombal in Portugal,[20] the shrewd Floridablanca[21] in Spain, and the incomparable Josef von Sonnenfels in Vienna,[22] the most successful of them all. In Denmark Johann Friedrich Struensee turned everything upside down in two years,[23] and in Bavaria the New Hampshire youth who became so improbably the Count Rumford of the Holy Roman Empire brought Yankee practicality to the solution of the problems of Munich.[24] And it was all mutual admiration society. The Kings indulged the philosophes, the philosophes extolled the wisdom and vir-

* George III of England, Christian VII of Denmark, Karl Eugen of Württemberg, the Duke of Merseberg, John V of Portugal among them.

tue of their sovereigns; all worked together for the happiness of their subjects—and of Man.

2

It is all too good to be real. Alas, it is not real. The play is so brilliant, the lines are so witty, the plots so intricate, the acting so polished, the costumes so splendid, the music so enchanting, that we sit enthralled through it all. Then the last lines are spoken and the actors depart and the lovely tunes are only an echo lingering in our minds, and the whole thing is a dream. We look at the stage and it is no longer a stage. It is no longer the Seville of the Barber; it is the Seville of the Inquisition, once again in power and using its power; no longer the London of the *Beggar's Opera*, but of Gin Alley; no longer the Naples of *Cosi fan Tutti*, but of Ferdinand IV crushing the revolution, Filangieri's books publicly burned, and the romantic Prince Caracciolo hanging from the yardarm of Lord Nelson's *Minerva*,[1] victim not of judicial murder but of naval murder. It is no longer the Venice of Goldoni, but of Giorgino Pisani, who had appealed to the populace against the fearsome Inquisitors, and was hustled off to jail for his temerity, and allowed to rot.[2] Catherine the Great no longer plays the role of the Semiramis of the North to the plaudits of Diderot and Voltaire: when the ardent young Novikov who had founded an orphan school and dabbled in freemasonry and single-handed doubled the number of books published in Russia, espoused too many liberal reforms, she banished him to Siberia for fifteen years, and when the philosophe—one of the very few—Alexander Radischev wrote a book depicting the wretchedness of the serfs and the tyranny of petty officials, Catherine objected that he was obviously "tainted with the French madness," and he too was bundled off to Siberia for a long exile. Worse yet, she banished all her busts of Voltaire to the cellars of her palaces.[3] Charles III had brought the Enlightenment with him from Naples, with its famous Illuministi, to Spain; he expelled the Jesuits and dabbled in physiocracy and allowed Aranda and Floridablanca to push through astonishing reforms, but with the American Revolution he became alarmed, and when the enlightened Pablo Olavide, who had reformed the ancient University of Seville, became too ostentatious in his familiarity with French philosophy, he was handed over to the Inquisition which beggared him and banished him to a monastery.

Gustavus III played at Enlightenment, but it was mostly play. He had decreed freedom of the press, but speedily regretted that indiscretion, and Raynal's *History of the Two Indies* was one of the first of enlightened books to fall under his ban. He lost enthusiasm, too, for the Americans, if indeed he had ever really had any, and in 1778 he informed Louis XV that his American policy "deviated from the principles of justice. I cannot admit" he asserted somewhat gratuitously, "that it is right to support rebels against their king."[4] Over in Norway there was a stout leader of the peasants, Christian Lofthuus, who deluded himself that he had a mandate from the King in Copenhagen to speak for his countrymen. Doubtless that was a misunderstanding, but such misunderstandings were not to be tolerated, and he was tried and found guilty of sedition and for ten years he was chained to a block of stone in the frowning fortress of Akerhus in Christiana: that was the way Denmark put down discontent after Struensee.[5]

What everybody does—*cosi fan tutti*—is no longer to play at love and war. The bugles that sound are real bugles, and the drum beats will soon roll across the whole of Europe. The armies march, and Poland is dismembered. Now Goldoni is dead, and the Venetian Republic is no more, and Wordsworth can write those elegiac lines. In far-away Quito the patriot Dr. Espejo is tortured to death for reprinting the Declaration of the Rights of Man, and in Portuguese Bahia four radicals who called for "the imaginary pleasures of a Democratic Republic in which all should be equal" were hanged and quartered.[6] England had "the best and the most noble constitution in the world," but Tom Paine was outlawed for advocating the rights of man, and up in Scotland poor Thomas Muir sentenced to fourteen years in the penal colony of Australia for urging parliamentary reform.

Now reality takes over. The armies that march are real

armies; cities are put to the torch; nobles ride heedless
over the fields of the peasants; the Irish cotters starve to
death by the thousand, and in Russia Empress Catherine
and Emperor Paul add millions to the number of serfs and
state peasants. Negroes are kidnapped on the coasts of
Africa and transported to the New World, rotting in the
noisome holds of slave ships; the Church hunts down heretics and destroys them, and heretics and prisoners alike are
broken on the wheel. That is the real world, long after
Frederick and Catherine and Joseph and Gustavus have
had their day.[7]

The comedy is over, and reality takes charge. That is
why, in the end, it is not the wicked Giovanni descending
into Hell while all the happy maids and swains stand singing in the courtyard, or Floristan rescued from his dungeon, or Casanova with still another conquest and still another fortune. In the end it is "infuriated man seeking
through blood and slaughter his long-lost liberty,"[8] seeking
and not finding. For in the end the philosophers were not
kings at all: Turgot dismissed, Necker dismissed, Tanucci
dismissed, Count Rumford expelled by the dissolute Karl
Theodore, the mighty Pombal disgraced, Struensee be-
headed, Gustavus himself murdered, Lord Edward Fitzgerald betrayed and killed, Priestley mobbed and driven
into exile, Brissot guillotined, Condorcet dead in that jail
in Bourge l'Égalité, a copy of Horace in his pocket. The
few who survived in power—Sonnenfels in Vienna, Pitt in
London, for example, conveniently forgot most of their
liberal opinions for, like their masters, they were frightened out of their wits by the spectacle of reforms translated from philosophy to politics.[9]

Was Gibbon right, then, that history was but the record
of the follies and vices of man? Did the future belong to
Edmund Burke, to Friedrich von Gentz, to Napoleon?

So it seemed, in the Old World. But to look across the
Atlantic was to find a different answer. For if the waves of
reaction lapped even the distant American shores, they did
not inundate them. It was Thomas Jefferson who was
elected to the Presidency in 1801, not Aaron Burr, not
Fisher Ames.

CHAPTER SEVEN

"The Uncorrupted New States and the Corrupted Old"

1

The philosophes thought the world a machine, and Man too: that was the title of Julien de la Mettrie's scandalous book, *L'homme machine.* They mixed up Man and Nature, Nature and Law, Man and Law, and why not? All were parts of the cosmic mechanism. Government, too, was a machine. Here was Morelly with his *Code de la Nature,* a code of laws which conformed to the dictates of Nature and was equally valid for all civilized societies; here was Holbach with his *Système Sociale,* which set forth the natural principles of politics; here was Filangieri with his *Science of Legislation,* and Real de Curban with his *Science of Government,* and David Hume with his most unscientific argument "that Politics may be reduced to a Science," and scores of other pamphlets and books with the same theme.

Clearly laws, constitutions, and forms of government were important. But it was easy to exaggerate their importance, to read into them a vitality that was not there. How wrong Montesquieu was about England, for example. "It does not belong to me to examine whether the English actually enjoy liberty or not," he wrote magisterially. "It is sufficient to say it is established by their laws."[1] But surely just the opposite was true. The English did enjoy liberty, a greater measure of it than the French, the Germans, the Spaniards, and others. That was no credit to their laws; rather to their customs, their habits, their common sense. Tom Paine, who knew England rather better than did Montesquieu, saw this clearly enough. "The plain truth is," he said, "that it is wholly to the constitution of the people, and not to the constitution of the government that the crown is not as oppressive in England as in Turkey."[2] Indeed, one might say that in England there were no fundamental laws in the sense in which Americans used the term, for Parliament was supreme, and Parliament could make and unmake the laws: No constitutional barriers there! Nor did the laws effectively curb the monarchy; limited monarchy was a product of history rather than of law, and even the limitations were not firm.[3] As for the courts, even Montesquieu did not pretend that they were truly independent, nor could he imagine anything remotely like judicial review of the acts of the other branches of the government. As Destutt de Tracy wrote in his *Commentaries* on Montesquieu's *Spirit of Laws*—Jefferson thought him "the greatest writer living on intellectual subjects:"[4]

> If Montesquieu had bestowed more attention on their laws, he would have discovered that among the English there exists really no more than *two* powers, instead of three: that these two powers exist only when both are present, because one has all the real force and no public attachment, while the other possesses no force, but enjoys all the public confidence; that these two powers, by uniting, are legally competent to change the public established laws, and even those which determine their relations and their existence, for no law obstructs them, and they have exercised this power on various occasions, so that in fact liberty is not truly established by their political laws; and if the English really enjoy liberty . . . it has reference to certain, received usages of their civil and criminal proceedings, rather than to positive laws; as in fact it is altogether without law established.[5]

"Received usages"—that was what was decisive, though even these could be overruled and violated by a willful King. Was not Pope right, after all, in that most familiar of epigrams,

> For forms of government let fools contest,
> Whate'er is best administered is best.

That, in any event, represented a pervasive sentiment, if not a principle, of the Enlightenment in the Old World; more, it represented reality. What difference, after all, did the forms really make in the states of Europe? The forms had already crystallized and, short of revolution, there was little you could do to change them. The Monarch was there, King or Emperor, Prince or Duke, it made little difference; quarrel with that reality and you might end up on the gallows. The Estates and the Parliaments and the Diets were there, on paper anyway; all there was to debate was whether they should be summoned or not; mostly they were not.[6] The hierarchy of government and society was fixed: the great nobles and the lesser nobles, the Magnates here and the Regents there, and elsewhere the *noblesse de la robe*.[7] What chance was there for a change, what room, even, for discussion? No wonder so many of the philosophes took refuge in ideal commonwealths, concocted imaginary constitutions, played happily with Codes and Laws. But the more practical reformers—Turgot and Necker, Pombal and Floridablanca, Struensee and Coccoji, Sonnenfels and Rumford, devoted their talents to administration. Increasingly the Enlightenment encouraged, developed, and relied on bureaucracy, which increasingly frustrated it. Special faculties of the University of Vienna and Halle trained civil servants for the Empire and for Prussia.[8]

But in America the pattern was still to be traced, the die was still to be cut. The Americans struck to the very heart of the matter. They discovered, or rediscovered, fundamental law; they drew up constitutions; they forced administration (such as it was) to fit itself to the law, and not administration alone but even Governors and Presidents, as Jefferson himself could testify.

Of what use to fix the forms of law? Why of every use. It was raising a standard to which the good and the wise could repair, it was setting a pattern to which future generations must conform, it was making a religion of the law, and every man an acolyte. So they wrote constitutions which were "the supreme law of the land," and were "framed for ages to come" and "designed to approach immortality."[9] They decreed that constitutions were *law*, and to assure the supremacy of constitutions over ordinary politics and administration, they invented judicial review—and thus a veto—of acts of legislatures and of the executive whenever these transgress fundamental law.[10] The Swiss publicist, Jean de Lolme, so infatuated with the English constitution that he thought all popular governments predestined ruin, pointed out that "the judicial power, that sure criterion of the goodness of government," was always, *in a popular government*, the instrument of tyranny:[11] He had forgotten Lord Bacon and Judge Jeffreys and the Star Chamber in the non-popular government of his adopted country. It was the Americans who made the judicial power an effective curb on tyranny, and even on such mild transgressions of the law as would not, in the Old World, have worn the guise of tyranny.

"Whate'er is best administered is best" might do for the despots of the Old World, for that axiom freed them from the limitations of the law and enabled them to justify almost anything on the plea of efficiency. It freed them, too, from the obligation to consult the people themselves, for the King, with or without assembly, parliament, or council, made the law, and bureaucrats administered it. "Everything for the people, nothing by the people," might have been the motto of the Enlightened Despots. Frederick made that clear in his *Political Testament*, and so did Catherine in her *Instructions for Composing a New Code of Laws*. "A society of citizens," she wrote, "requires a certain fixed Order. There ought to be some to govern, and others to obey."[12] No doubt, in Russia, which was which. No doubt in Prussia, either. "The prince is to the society which he governs what the head is to the body," wrote Frederick the Great.[13] Or remember Charles Frederick of Baden determined "to teach his subjects, even against their will, how to order their domestic affairs."[14] Here is the philosopher, G. G. Lamprecht of Halle, outlining a program of enlightened government for Prussia, which set the state "the task of making the citizens in every regard more well-behaved, healthier, wiser, richer, and more secure." All towns were to be of precisely the same size; all streets and roads were to meet at right angles; mothers were to nurse their babies, and the coloring of Easter eggs was forbidden![15] Struensee was determined that the Danish people should be free and happy, and he all but drowned them in a torrent of Cabinet Orders—1,800 of them—imposing freedom and happiness upon them.[16] Even in England the people as a whole were supposed to be passive; as Bishop Horsley said in the debate on the Treasonable Practices Act of 1795, "he did not know what the mass of the people in any country had to do with the laws, but to obey them."[17] What it all added up to was clear: the great principles of law were no doubt universal and eternal, but the enlightened application of these principles was something that must, of necessity, be left to the judgment of Kings and their Ministers.[18]

Even the recalcitrant Abbé Raynal accepted this principle as a matter of course. "The happiest of all governments," he wrote in the first edition of his *History of the East and West Indies,* "is that of a just and enlightened despot." This represented, fairly enough, the views of many of the philosophes, witness Voltaire's admiration for Frederick, Diderot's adulation of Catherine, Möser's devotion to Sonnenfels. But it would be difficult to find a phrase, or a principle, that illustrates more luminously than Raynal's the gap between the Old World concept of the Enlightenment, and the American.

2

Americans took seriously the principle of government by laws and not by men, and what is more they institutionalized that principle in their constitutions. Easy enough, thought some of the Old World philosophes who were, themselves, quite as ready to dash off a Constitution for Massachusetts or Pennsylvania as for Poland or Corsica or for some Utopian community of their own invention. Some of the French philosophes were impressed, and hurried to translate the State constitutions for the edification of their countrymen—Franklin had a hand in that; but on the whole European statesmen were not impressed: after all, they had managed well enough without constitutions for some centuries. When Edmund Burke came to reflect on the French Revolution, he disdained to mention any of the American experiments, but asserted quite simply that men could not make government, that men could not write constitutions, that revolutions could not succeed. No doubt the Americans were politically experienced, but their experience was limited to the simple problems of a frontier society. They lacked a historical past which could provide them with guidelines, lacked a ruling class which could provide them with leadership, lacked a trained bureaucracy, lacked those resources of statesmanship which sustained the more affluent and sophisticated countries of the Old World.

No one could deny that the Old World misgivings were reasonable. Americans did display a certain innocence and virtue, a naïve faith in the authority of laws and constitutions and a tradition of managing their simple local affairs, but they were lacking in true sophistication and in national leadership.

But that is not the way it turned out. Americans had their innocence and their sophistication, too, while the Old World, for all its centuries of experience, for all its great cities, universities, academies and ruling classes proved politically bankrupt.

To the astonishment of contemporaries—and of history —it was precisely in statesmanship that the new nation was richest. How paradoxical that the nation most deeply committed to the supremacy of Law over government, should be perhaps the only one where the principle was not really needed. How paradoxical, too, that the nation whose people were most deeply suspicious of power in government was the only one whose leaders seemed immune to the temptations of power.

How paradoxical, too, that from this almost primitive

society of one half to three quarters of a million adult white men[1] spread thin over an immense territory, and lacking most of the appurtenances and institutions of a high civilization which Europe had so long enjoyed, came the most distinguished galaxy of statesmen produced by any nation in any one generation of modern history. What a calendar an American Plutarch might have compiled: Franklin, Washington, Jefferson, Hamilton, John and Samuel Adams, John Dickinson, Tom Paine, James Wilson, George Wythe, James Madison, George Mason, John Jay, John Marshall—this does not by any means exhaust the list. When was a nation ever so fortunate in its political talent? And, no less astonishing and even more clearly a manifestation of that Providential favor which so gratified the Founding Fathers, the generation that presided over the birth of the infant republic lived on to direct its destinies for half a century![2]

How explain this efflorescence of political talent without precedent, without parallel, and without recurrence? The incidence and explanation of genius is a difficult question whether for fifth-century Athens, Renaissance Florence, Elizabethan England, the Low Countries in the seventeenth century, Denmark in the early nineteenth; it is no less difficult for the American colonies and states in the last quarter of the eighteenth.[3]

Consider first this matter of size: three million Americans, ten million Britons, twenty million Frenchmen. Clearly, as Jefferson pointed out,[4] that meant logically that Britain should produce three Washingtons and Franklins, and France six, and all other European nations in the same proportion. That was perhaps a *jeu d'esprit*—though it was advanced soberly enough. America, in any event, overcame the handicap of size by the simplest of all methods: She used the whole of her resources. Europe wasted its resources: Britain, France, Spain, all the nations of the Old World, chose their statesmen, bishops, judges, generals and admirals, from the upper tenth of their population, disqualifying the other nine tenths on grounds of class or birth or wealth or religion.[5] But in America the only effective disqualification was color. As Jefferson pointed out, in his argument for universal public education, "By that part

of our plan which prescribes the selection of youths of
genius from among the classes of the poor, we hope to
avail the State of those talents which Nature has sown as
liberally among the poor as among the rich, but which per-
ish without use."6 The Americans chose their statesmen,
judges, and generals from among the whole of their white
male population. Thus, in effect, they had a larger pool of
talent on which to draw than Britain, France, or Spain. It
was as if the new United States enjoyed a population not
of three or four but of twenty or thirty millions.

America overcame the handicap of a small population,
and very soon it was no longer a handicap, for it was no
longer small. Just so, she overcame another and more serious handicap, turning it—how familiar this—into a positive advantage. In the Old World a young man, if he had
the proper credentials, could pretty much take his choice
of careers: the Court, the Church, the Army, Society, and
even some of the respectable professions such as the law or
medicine. Even if he had the bad luck to be born into the
lower orders he might still find an outlet for his talents in
art, or literature, or learning: thus a Mozart or a Beetho-
ven in music, a Thorwaldsen or a Sergel in sculpture, a
Boucher or a Hogarth in painting, a Smollett, a Diderot, or
a Winckelmann in literature. But the New World offered
few opportunities for a career or for fame, except in politics. American society was simple and undifferentiated,
American economy pastoral and modest, the American
mind provincial and unsophisticated. There was no glittering Monarchy to serve, no fashionable Society in which an
adventurer might disport himself, no Church with its imposing hierarchy of Bishops and Deans, and its monas-
teries and nunneries to draw off the unwary; no Military to
absorb the talents of younger sons; no great merchant
Companies to send young men to India or the Levant to
carve out fortune or empire; no august Law Courts7 in
which to win reputation and office. There were not even
affluent patrons for architects, artists, or musicians; for
that, talented young men like Benjamin West and John
Copley and John Middleton8 had to go abroad. Nor was it
practicable, except perhap in Maryland, Virginia, and
South Carolina, for a gentleman to live a life of leisure,

spending his inheritance on lavish entertainments, palaces, the arts, or mistresses.

America offered few opportunities for the display of talent, except in the public arena, and presented few temptations to distract talent from that arena. Except in land speculation—a chancy business as Robert Morris and James Wilson learned—it offered but meager rewards and no easy way to wealth. By European standards there were no men of wealth in America. There were modest fortunes to be made in trade, to be sure: the slave trade, until the laws put a stop to it, the Mediterranean and Baltic and, later on, China trade. But many of those who carried the American flag into the Baltic or the China seas thought themselves engaged in a kind of national service, just as did some of the servants of the East India or the Hudson's Bay Company. There were few fields for military glory or adventure; the challenge of adventure was there, but with no promise of reward—witness the fate of John Ledyard, Meriwether Lewis, or William Clark, and, later on, of Aaron Burr and his imperial designs. Soldiers who had served their country faithfully ended their days in penury, while officers who had thought to enjoy the modest riband of the Order of the Cincinnati found themselves regarded as monsters of depravity. Society offered no distractions, for that was a function of Courts, palaces, great cities, country houses, and a class system, and America had none of these. How amusing the failure of John Adams to obtain any title for the President except that of Mr. President;[9] how illuminating Jefferson's rejection of the rule of precedence for the "rule of *pêle-mêle*."[10] In the Old World young men of talent and address, even without family, might become courtiers or adventurers, but it is as difficult to imagine a Chesterfield, a Struensee, or a Casanova in America as to imagine a Madame de Barry, a Lady Hamilton, or a Franciska von Hohenheim. Men who yearned for adventure, like the second William Byrd or Benjamin Thompson or Aaron Burr or Lewis Littlepage, headed for Europe, and often stayed there.

Not only were Americans unsophisticated by European standards; they were undifferentiated as well. What variety in Europe! How different London from Paris, Berlin from Naples; how different, too, the monarchs and statesmen, the bishops, the artists, the men of letters. By comparison, the American scene seemed uniform and almost monotonous:* all the citizens belonging, in effect, to the same class, no dramatic contrasts between Magnate and peasant, a merchant prince and a limey, an officer glittering in his uniform and a common soldier. Even the churches were the same; you could not tell one denomination from another, and there was not a cathedral in the whole of English America.

This outward uniformity reflected a general uniformity of character and philosophy, and this, too, helps explain the high standard of public service. The Americans themselves, to be sure, conjured up deep differences between their chosen leaders—a Jefferson and a John Adams, for example—as they conjured up differences between parties and even between classes, and with immense ingenuity, they contrived differences between religious faiths. But after all Jefferson and Adams subscribed to a common philosophy, worked together harmoniously for independence and the establishment of the nation, and served together under Washington, and their long friendship contributed a felicitous chapter to American literature. The Founding Fathers did not need to exhaust their energies finding some common ground; they already stood on common ground.[11] They did not need to bridge social differences or heal religious animosities; such differences as there were made no difference.

How alike, too, were the constitutions of the States; how similar the Bills of Rights—state and federal—but very different from the English.[12] How monotonously familiar, from Massachusetts to North Carolina the arguments for and against ratification of the Federal Constitution, how superficial the criticisms, how insignificant the proposed amendments, how interchangeable the two factions—Federalist and anti-Federalist—when they became parties![18] Of this whole generation we can confidently say that the

* Just what Tocqueville said fifty years later: "the sight of such universal uniformity saddens and chills me."

things that divided them were negligible and the things that united them were fundamental.

One of the things that united them was a common political tradition and political education. The tradition began, in a sense, at Jamestown and in the hold of the *Mayflower*, the tradition of association for salvation, self-government, defense, for creating a church or building a school or founding a college. The American took naturally to politics in part because he had no alternative course of action —Franklin's familiar observation that if the Americans didn't hang together they would hang separately contained a larger and prophetic truth. The habits of leadership, so astonishing in the eyes of the Old World, were formed in the town meetings and the county courts, in service with the militia, or on committees of correspondence. The rough and tumble of local politics, too, nourished special talents for management. So said John Adams, at the beginning of the Revolution:

> the division of our territory, that is our counties, its townships, empowering towns to assemble, choose officers, make laws, mend roads and twenty other things, gives every man an opportunity . . . and makes knowledge and dexterity at public business common.[14]

And so said Jefferson, forty years later, in a remarkable letter to Joseph Cabell:

> Where every man is a sharer in the direction of the ward-republic, or of some of the higher ones, and feels that he is a participator in the government of affairs, not merely at an election one day in the year, but every day; when there shall be not a man in the State who will not be a member of some one of its councils, great or small, he will let the heart be torn out of his body sooner than his power be wrested from him by some Caesar or Bonaparte.[15]

This was the situation that made possible the careers of Benjamin Franklin and Charles Thomson in Pennsylvania,

Samuel Adams and Joseph Hawley in Massachusetts, Alexander McDougall and Aaron Burr in New York, Patrick Henry and Edmund Pendleton in Virginia, Willie Jones in North Carolina, and Aedanus Burke in South Carolina. In the Old World, these, and others like them, would have been excluded from politics,[16] or if they had somehow forced their way in, they would have been regarded as were Wilkes, Horne Tooke, and Cartwright in England, Brissot in France, Struensee in Denmark—as interlopers and demagogues. Just what John Adams warned against, in his *Thoughts on Government* and, more elaborately, his *Defense of the Constitutions*—that agitators and demagogues would destroy the nice balances of the Constitution. His fears were groundless, though he did not for that reason abandon them; of all the spokesmen for the people (and surely he himself was one), only Aaron Burr, who had some claims to being a member of the privileged orders, was seduced into demagoguery, and he ended his life in futility and disrepute.

Education, too, formal and informal, taught disinterested service to the commonwealth. "From infancy," wrote the Pennsylvania Farmer, John Dickinson, "I was taught to love humanity and liberty." In the Academies and Colleges (and those who had attended neither, like Benjamin Franklin or Edmund Pendleton, more than made up for the deprivation) they studied the history and literature of the ancient world, and the political philosophy of seventeenth-century England. All of them had read Plutarch and Thucydides, Tacitus and Polybius; all knew at first hand, or merely as the common sense of the matter, John Locke and Algernon Sidney, Montesquieu and Hume, and Cato's letters.[17] Almost every one of them might have said with the Reverend Jonathan Mayhew of Boston that "having been initiated in youth in the doctrines of civil liberty, as they are taught in such men as Plato, Demosthenes, Cicero, and other persons among the ancients, and such as Sidney and Milton, Locke and Hoadley among the moderns, I liked them; they seemed rational."[18] Almost every one might have provided in his will, as did young Josiah Quincy, "I leave to my son, when he shall have reached the age of fifteen, the Works of Alger-

non Sidney, John Locke, Bacon, Gordon's *Tacitus* and
Cato's *Letters*. May the spirit of Liberty rest upon him."[19]
Samuel Adams was devoted to Plutarch, and the *Quaestio*
he submitted for his Master's degree at Harvard College
was drawn straight from that historian and moralist. John
Adams had concluded his youthful *Dissertation on the
Canon and Feudal Law* with the appeal that "the colleges
join their harmony in the same delightful concert [for
liberty]. Let every declamation turn upon the beauty of
liberty and virtue and the deformity of turpitude and
malignity of slavery and vice."[20] Twenty years later he
wrote in his *Defense* that "the history of Greece should be
to our countrymen what is called . . . the boudoir, an oc-
tagonal apartment in a house with a full length mirror on
every side and another in the ceiling, so everywhere we
look we can see ourselves reflected in the history of
Greece."[21] Richard Bland of Virginia cast his *Inquiry into
the Rights of the British Colonies* in classical form, and
weighted it down with allusions to Tacitus, which is just
what John Dickinson did in his *Farmer's Letters*. Years
later Jefferson could write to his old friend John Adams—
their correspondence was practically a running commentary on the classics—that "I have given up newspapers in
exchange for Tacitus and Thucydides . . . and find myself
much happier."[22]

The ancient world, to be sure, had not practiced democracy as the Americans knew it and practiced it, but the
Greeks, the Romans in the era of the Republic, and the
English Commonwealthmen, had carried the practice of
democracy beyond anything that contemporary Europe
was prepared to try, outside Holland, perhaps, and some
of the Swiss cantons.

It was the practice of democracy that was important,
and it was in the heat of the conduct of practical affairs
that American leadership was forged. The American
spokesmen did not regard themselves as philosophes but as
public servants. Where do you find a more commonsen-
sical fellowship of politicians, empirical in philosophy, ingenious and hard-headed in practice? All of them were students, but none except perhaps the young Madison smelled
of the lamp, and for all their learning, not one of them

wrote in a language or a style that his countrymen could
not understand. They were, almost all of them, men of
affairs. They were farmers, not in absentia like the great
landlords of France and Italy, but in the fields, some of
them, like John Adams, happy to pitch hay with his help.
They were businessmen like Hancock in Boston, Stephen
Hopkins in Providence, or Franklin, and even Rittenhouse,
in Philadelphia, busy with their ships, their counters, their
shops, and their ledgers. They were lawyers like John
Adams, who was the most successful young attorney in
Massachusetts and who was appointed Chief Justice of the
state, or like Mr. Jefferson who gave up a brilliant career
at the bar for public service, or Hamilton who would have
made a great chief justice had he not preferred to be a
great financier. They did not live apart from the people at
some luxurious Court, or some bustling capital, but lived
where they worked and worked where they lived.[23] Their
politics were practical; they wanted results, and got them.
Where a Montesquieu, a Bolingbroke, a Hume, a Rousseau, a Filangieri, a Kant formulated political philosophies
for some ideal society or some remote contingency, the
Americans dashed off their state papers to meet an urgent
crisis or solve a clamorous problem: Dickinson's *Letters
from a Farmer in Pennsylvania*, John Adams's *Thoughts
on Government*, Jefferson's *Summary View*, Paine's *Common Sense*, the *Federalist Papers*. How realistic, too, those
debates in the Federal Convention where the accepted
principle was: "reason may mislead us, experience must
be our guide!" And there was always one consideration
that restrained the American spokesmen from taking refuge in the abstract or the doctrinaire, and required them to
be tough-minded and realistic. In Europe the philosophes
took their case to a small segment of the body politic, in itself a small segment of the whole people—the intellectuals,
the professional classes, the dissenters, perhaps the merchant class. As for the Monarchs and their ministers, they
did not need to take their case to anyone, except perhaps
in Britain and the Low Countries. But in America nothing
went by default, nothing was conceded to rank or to dignity; there you had to submit your case to the people, and

win on merit: no better school than this for making leaders.

For the leaders of the new nation did not hold office by divine right, or by favor of some prince or cardinal, or perhaps some prince's mistress. They did not inherit office or buy it or usurp it. They were chosen by their fellow citizens, some by direct election, some by indirect, but no matter, all derived their titles and their authority from the people themselves. Leadership in America was a product of popular suffrage and, for better or for worse, a monument to it.

3

In the eyes of the Old World most of this was absurd. The business of government was so arduous that you could not trust the common people to do it; the demands were so insistent that you could not expect the common people to meet them; the responsibilities were so heavy that you could not require the common people to fulfill them. Nothing about America excited more surprise, or scorn, than the spectacle of farmers and cobblers, merchants and inn-keepers, setting themselves up as statesmen. Put an end to New England town meetings, cried Lord George Germain; "I would not have men of a mercantile cast every day collecting themselves together and debating about political matters; I would have them follow their occupations . . . and not consider themselves as ministers."[1] The Tory Thomas Chandler was "ravished and transported" at the spectacle of an American aristocracy. "The Committees of Correspondence will furnish us with marquises, and the Committees of Observation with earls. The viscounts may consist of heroes that are famed for their exploits in tarring and feathering," he wrote with exquisite satire,[2] while a French officer reported with incredulity that "our inn-keeper was a captain, . . . there are shoemakers who are Colonels, and it often happens that the Americans ask the French officers what their trade is in France."[3] No one caught more unerringly the scorn of the gentry for the po-

litical pretensions of plebeians than Jonathan Trumbull's
M'Fingal:

> Each leather-apron'd dunce, grown wise,
> Presents his forward face t'advise;
> And tatter'd legislators meet
> From every workshop through the street;
> His goose the tailor finds new use in,
> To patch and turn the Constitution;
> The blacksmith comes with sledge and grate,
> To iron-bind the wheels of state . . .
> The tinker quits his moulds and doxies,
> To cast assembly-men and proxies.[4]

The solution was obvious: limit government to the rich
and the wellborn; limit it to an aristocracy—a nobility with
at least sixteen quarterings; that would give you security!
Limit it to those who lorded over great estates, and who
understood the connection of property with morality and
order. That was the way God had arranged the affairs of
men, said the monarchs and their ministers; that was the
only possible way, said the patricians, the regents, the magnates, the magistrates, the men of substance. That was certainly the best way said even the philosophes, who accepted,
unquestioning, Montesquieu's principle that "honor" was
the animating principle of a monarchy. After all what
did a commoner know about honor; you could not meet
a commoner on the field of honor; you sent your lackeys
to whip him.[5] Frederick the Great put the matter succinctly: "I always chose my officers from the nobility,"
he said, "for nobility nearly always has a sense of
honor. . . . If a noble loses his honor he is ostracized by
his family; whereas a commoner who has committed some
fraud can continue to run his father's business."[6]
    Here is the forgotten Real de Curban, who produced a
monument to *The Science of Government.* "In making
politics depend on birth," he wrote, "we soothe the pride
of the inferiors, and make high positions much less
difficult to accept. There is no shame in yielding when I
may say 'this I owe to my birth.' This argument convinces
the mind without injuring it by jealousies."[7] Besides, if

1. Frontispiece designed by Charles Nicolas Cochin III for Diderot's monumental work L'Encyclopédie. *(Courtesy of the Albertina Museum, Vienna.)*

2. Engraving of Buffon, French naturalist and philosophe, by Robert Hart. *(Courtesy of the Bettmann Archive.)*

3. Portrait of Carl Von Linne, botanist and founder of the binomial nomenclature method of classification, by Alexander Roslin. *(Courtesy of the Bettmann Archive.)*

4. Portrait of Sir Joseph Banks, patron and spokesman for the
English Enlightenment, by Sir Joshua Reynolds. *(From the
Collection at Parham Park, Sussex [England].)*

5. Portrait of Thomas Paine, champion of reason, progress, and revolution, by Auguste Millière after Romney. *(Courtesy of the Bettmann Archive.)*

6. Portrait of Edmund Burke, friend to America but opponent to all revolutionary change, by Sir Joshua Reynolds. *(Courtesy of the National Gallery of Scotland.)*

7. Marble sculpture of philosopher and savant François Marie
Arouet de Voltaire by Houdon. *(Courtesy of the Victoria and
Albert Museum. Crown copyright.)*

8. Painting of the coronation of Gustavus III, Swedish enlightened despot, by Carl Gustav Pilo. (*Courtesy of the Nationalmuseum, Stockholm.*)

9. Tapestry of *chinoiseries* reflecting oriental influences in the West during the eighteenth century. Believed to be the work of a Soho factory. *(Courtesy of the Kunstgewerbe Museum.)*

10. Miniature portrait of Thomas Jefferson, model and spirit of the American Enlightenment. *(Courtesy of the Thomas Jefferson Memorial Foundation.)*

offices were to be thrown open indiscriminately, even
scholars and intellectuals might obtain them, "men with
more Latin than Property!" Blackstone thought Oxford the
best place for the study of law because there the gentlemen
who were destined to govern Britain would associate only
with gentlemen of their own rank.[8] Edward Gibbon made
clear that one of the causes for the decline of the greatest
of empires was the equality of all Roman citizens, and he
rejoiced that "two hundred families . . . supply the second
branch of the English legislature which maintains, between
the King and the Commons, the balance of the Constitution." How right he was to refuse to listen to Franklin
when that equalitarian offered to provide him with material for a history of the decline and fall of the British Empire! Here and there, in Vienna under Sonnenfels, in Prussia under Frederick the Great, or in Holland, office might
go by merit rather than by rank, and in England men of
the middle class could go far if they made a fortune in
India or won the patronage of some great Lord. But generally "there was no damned nonsense about merit."[9] Even
commoners, when they came to power—a Struensee in
Denmark, a Rumford in Bavaria, a Sonnenfels in Austria
(his father had been ennobled, but he had been a Jewish
rabbi), a Süss Oppenheimer in Württemberg—did not propose to extend the suffrage to the body of the people, or
open offices indiscriminately to men of all classes. Nor, for
that matter, did the British radicals: Thomas Hollis, who
spent his energies and his fortune supplying libraries everywhere with the writings of libertarians, thought that the
masses should be kept illiterate.[10]

Nowhere, in fact, did Enlightened Monarchs of the
eighteenth century actually enlarge the existing political
community by extending suffrage to the common people
or, in other ways enlisting them in the affairs of government. Indeed, except in England, the Low Countries, and
some of the Swiss cantons, the very notion of suffrage was
without meaning, and even in these countries the suffrage
was narrow and ineffective. England was the model and
the envy of all the philosophes, from Montesquieu to De
Lolme: what freedom, what tolerance, what enlightenment, what a perfect balance of executive and legisla-

ture, Lords and Commons; how admirable the rule of law, how honorable the principles of justice. Even some Americans joined in the paeans of praise: Hamilton, Gouverneur Morris, Langdon Braxton, Charles Pinckney among them.

But, in fact, the British system was in many ways closer to that of France or Sweden than it was to that to which the people of Connecticut or Pennsylvania had become accustomed. Certainly George III was closer, psychologically, to Louis XVI or Gustavus III than he was to, let us say, George Washington and John Adams. Thus, when, in 1793, Charles James Fox proposed a toast at the Whig Club, "the sovereignty of the people of Great Britain," the King struck his name off the list of privy councilors, and he punished the powerful Duke of Norfolk the same way for a similar toast: "Our sovereign's health: the majesty of the people."[11] And even a literary attack upon the King was still treasonable, as Tom Paine learned when he was outlawed for *The Rights of Man*.[12] Less than one twentieth of the people of England ruled the other nineteen twentieths. Out of a total population of perhaps nine million, in Britain—without Ireland—perhaps two hundred thousand were entitled to vote, but even these voters were heavily concentrated in a few counties and were shockingly underrepresented in the Commons, and as no new towns had been admitted to representation since 1678, most of the townspeople outside London were wholly without political representation. Even those who voted were not free agents. As Lewis Namier delicately says, "people in dependent positions could seldom exercise a free choice."[13]

Thus, an exiguous minority cast all the votes, filled all the offices of government, staffed the Army, Navy, Church, law courts, and the colonial administration, and except in Scotland, they alone had access to the Universities.[14] When agitators like Thomas Muir and the Reverend Fyshe Palmer proposed universal suffrage, they were clapped in jail, and Lord Abercromby charged the jury "to consider whether telling the people that they have a just right to what would unquestionably be tantamount to a total subversion of this constitution" was not treasonable.

He was right; they were found guilty of seditious libel and sentenced to transportation. It is not recorded that the Duke of Richmond experienced any unpleasantness when he made a similar proposal in 1780![15]

The Commons was the glory of the British political system, but the Commons did not represent even the voters, much less the whole people. Out of 558 English members of the Commons, 442 sat for boroughs, most of them with less than one thousand population, and some, like the notorious Old Sarum, with none. Nor was Old Sarum alone in its distinction. As late as 1793 no less than seventy members were returned by thirty-five places with no electors at all, and ninety by forty-six places with less than fifty electors; Manchester, Birmingham, Sheffield, and Leeds had no representation. Scotland returned forty-five members, but in all Scotland there were less than three thousand voters, and of these only half were genuinely qualified—the others had their qualifications provided for them by patrons, as was the amiable custom in eighteenth-century Britain. In 1780 the Duke of Richmond charged that six thousand men returned a majority of all members of the Commons, but even this may have put too favorable a construction on the situation. In 1793 the Friends of the People concluded that 154 patrons returned 307 members of the House, and a few years later the learned Dr. Oldfield presented evidence that 218 members were returned by eighty-seven peers and 137 by ninety commoners, and an additional sixteen by the Crown, a total of 371—a sizable inequity.[16]

It was the boast of the Commons that whatever their election base, they represented—virtually was the key word—all the people of Britain, and not of Britain alone, but of the far-flung Empire, for the colonies, too, were *virtually* represented. The Americans, at least, were too hard-headed to be taken in by that specious argument. Whom did the Commons represent? In the first Parliament of George I, 237 members were alleged to have held their places through the influence of the Crown; as late as 1770 almost two hundred officeholders sat in the Commons.[17] That did not mean that the King automatically controlled the House, far from it. Sometimes he had to go out and

fight for seats, and sometimes he lost them. A member of
the House was required to have a six-hundred-pound freehold. At mid-century only 2,800 men in all England, so it
was estimated, could fulfill this requirement. But no matter; the King could supply the freehold, if necessary, or
some of the great patrons. In 1780 George III spent
£8,000 on the election in Westminster, £4,000 on the
election in the City, and another £4,000 on an election in
Surrey; all in vain.[18] Some of the patrons were even more
extravagant in contesting elections: in 1768 the Duke of
Portland spent £40,000 on Westmoreland and Cumberland; in 1779 a Mr. Chester all but bankrupted himself
by spending £30,000 in a contest for Gloucestershire; a
decade later Lord Penrhyn threw away a comparable sum
contesting the seat for Liverpool.[19] Few others had, or
were prepared to spend, such sums, nor did they need to.
The Duke of Norfolk could control eleven seats, Lord
Lonsdale nine, Sir James Lowther nine—they were popu-
larly known as his "ninepins"—Lord Darlington seven, the
Marquis of Buckingham six, and others down the scale.[20]
Sometimes, to be sure, the choice of a member was more
widely distributed: twenty-five men in Edinburgh controlled the choice of a member of the House; at Bath it
was the mayor and thirty-four other city fathers; and at
Salisbury no less than fifty-six voters were involved in the
election! In some districts all freeholders could vote, thus
in Tavistock, but there were only ten; thus in St. Michael,
but there were only seven![21]

Meantime, fifty or sixty great patrons monopolized
the control of Irish members. This control over the Irish
delegation at Westminster merely mirrored an even more
effective control over the Irish Parliament in Dublin.
"Everything," said Edmund Burke, "was sweetly and
harmoniously disposed through both islands for the . . .
communication of English liberties."[22] The Irish themselves did not think "liberties" the *mot juste*. Ireland was
Catholic, but no Catholic could vote or hold office. A hundred great patrons, headed by John Ponsonby with twenty-
two and the Duke of Leinster with eleven seats, controlled
two thirds of the members of the Irish House, while the
Lords was made up of Irish peers and Anglican Bishops.[23]

It was a model of colonial administration not lost upon American observers.

The Crown, the nobility, the patriciate, the gentry, were even more firmly in the saddle in the other countries of the Old World than in Britain. In some—Russia for example, or Prussia or Denmark—the monarchy ruled without any need to consult Diets or Estates.[24] France was ruled by the King, in alliance with a large and miscellaneous nobility— the hereditary nobility, the military nobility, the nobility of the robe who monopolized membership in the provincial parlements, and many others. Membership in the *noblesse de race* was limited to those who could trace their lineage back to 1400, and beyond—perhaps one thousand families in all. For membership in the *noblesse de robe,* or office in the Army, you had to show no less than sixteen quarterings—four generations of noble forebears. Offices were hereditary and, as elsewhere, a species of property. That was true even in England: Pitt's Parliamentary reform bill of 1785, which proposed to abolish thirty-six rotten boroughs, provided compensation of one million pounds to the bereft owners of the borough nominations.[25] Hungary boasted perhaps the largest nobility in Europe. There 75,000 Magnates, and lesser gentry, had things their own way. They owned all the land, had exclusive right to office, filled all the places in the Church, the Army and the Universities; like nobles elsewhere they were exempt from all regular and most special taxes.[26] Germany presented a kaleidoscope of states and principalities, large and small, and of governments, too, but for all their bewildering differences of character, they had one common denominator: Nowhere was there any hint of popular rule or, except in the Hansa towns and Frankfurt, of rule by the burghers. Here and there—in Württemberg for example, or in some of the states of Prussia—provincial Diets dragged out a dubious existence, but mostly the petty sovereigns dispensed with these and ruled arbitrarily: the journalist, A. G. F. Rebmann, described the Diet of Saxony as "a farce performed every six years in which all the actors have to say is Yes."[27] The Margrave of Ansbach shot one of his huntsmen who contradicted him; the Count of Nassau-Diegen executed a peasant just to prove that he could do what he

pleased;[28] and Frederick's famous observation, "my people
and I have come to an amiable understanding; they say
what they please and I do what I please," was more than
an amusing *bon mot*. Twenty patrician families ruled
Nuremberg; their sons studied at public expense and their
daughters drew dowries from the public treasury. The
thirty-five thousand inhabitants of the Free City of Frankfurt were divided into five classes: all offices were monopolized by members of the first, made up of the patriciate
with patents of hereditary nobility, and burghers whose
families had sat on the town *Rat* for a century; each class
wore a distinctive dress, and the numerous colony of
Jews was consigned to a ghetto and denied citizenship.[29]
Yet in Frankfurt, as in Amsterdam, Genoa, Copenhagen,
Bristol, and other trading cities an outsider could achieve
position and his grandchildren could become insiders: witness the experience of the innkeeper, Friedrich Goethe,
whose grandson became a Minister to the Duke of Saxe-
Weimar and was permitted—when duly ennobled—to play
cards with the ducal family![30] The Landstag of Württemberg, which was chosen by the burghers (for the patricians had their own Senate, which did not function),
was one of the most powerful on the Continent, yet it
could not prevent the deprivations of Süss Oppenheimer,
nor curb the excesses and tyrannies of Karl Eugen. When
the famous Johann Jacob Moser protested against these, he
was condemned to solitary confinement for five years for
his audacity.[31] No one was admitted to the masked balls of
Mainz unless he could prove sixteen quarterings of nobility; at the princely Karlsschule in Württemberg noble students not only wore different dress and wigs from commoners, but bathed in a different part of the river.[32]

The pattern of Italy was as diverse as that of Germany,
but, as with the German, there was a common denominator of privilege and of arbitrary rule. Venice was a
Republic, but scarcely "the eldest child of liberty," and so
were Genoa and Lucca; all three were governed by tight
little oligarchies. The Venetian nobility—it was too proud
to bear titles—numbered scarcely more than one hundred
in 1796, but twelve patrician families really controlled the
state, and all offices were the prerogative of the patriciate.

Of a population of perhaps one hundred and thirty thousand, only 1,218 were entitled to attend the meeting of the Great Council, which presumably included all citizens.[33] Luxury and immorality sapped the energies of the patricians, while poverty and oppression were the lot of the great mass of the population; in the twenty years after 1741 seventy-three thousand people were executed or condemned to the galleys for life.[34] In republican Genoa, too, all power was in the hands of an hereditary aristocracy; they made up the membership in the Senate and in the two great Councils that managed all the affairs of the city and the state, monopolized all the offices, and all the wealth. When Corsica got troublesome, Genoa simply sold it to France. There were perhaps a thousand noble families in Milan and Lombardy; three hundred of the most ancient administered the government, filled the Senate, sat on the judicial benches, owned most of the surrounding lands, and dominated the cultural life of the State. In their temporal capacity the Popes wielded absolute power over the extensive but impoverished Papal States.[35]

Since 1665 Denmark had been ruled by a King more absolute than Louis XIV; Christian succeeded Frederick and Frederick Christian with monotonous regularity while the business of government was carried on by an aristocracy imported from Germany: Moltkes and Rantzaus, Schimmelmanns, and Bernstorffs. The peasants were bound to the soil, while the merchants of Copenhagen, many of them great landlords as well, had influence rather than power. When, in 1770, Struensee sought to modernize Denmark in a whirlwind of reform, he, too, used the machinery of absolutism. Struensee was overthrown but not absolutism; though Denmark achieved some freedom and considerable enlightenment in the following decades, absolutism was not ended until 1834.[36]

Both Sweden and Poland rejoiced in legislative bodies powerful enough to curb royal pretensions, but the result was very far from the English or American notion of representative government. The Swedish Riksdag, alone of those in Europe, actually permitted representation of peasants, but the effective conduct of all political affairs was allotted to the nobility and the Church, and nobles alone could sit on the Royal Council.[37] Legally the Diet was all-powerful in Poland. Chosen by a numerous aristocracy, petty and high, it in turn elected a King, who was usually a foreigner and who thereafter depended on some foreign power—Saxony, France, or Russia—for support. Meantime, notwithstanding the efforts of a few enlightened families like the Czartoryskis, the Diet clung stubbornly to the principle of unanimity, the famous *liberum veto*, thus condemning itself to futility and Poland to anarchy.[38]

Everyone sang the praises of Switzerland, and with some justification, for most of the people of the Swiss cantons enjoyed freedom and tolerance, after a fashion, and the contrast between the luxury of the rich and the poverty of the peasant or the artisan was not as glaring as elsewhere on the Continent. The Swiss towns indulged in self-government, to be sure, but it was a very restricted form of self-government and a far cry from democracy, just as the Swiss *Eidgenossenschaft* was a far cry from true federalism. For two centuries the larger towns had been absorbing the cantons and dependent territory, and for almost that long the city patricians had been aggrandizing power within the towns, excluding not only non-citizens (and citizenship was guarded so jealously that in some towns no new citizen had been admitted for a century) but the lower classes of their own citizens as well. Two hundred patrician families of Bern filled all the posts in the Council; monopolized all the valuable offices, and lorded it over the non-citizens and the rural areas dependent on the city. When, in 1723, the people of Vaud, discontented with the autocratic rule of Bern, turned to Lausanne, their leader, the devout Abraham Davel, was seized and executed. A quarter century later the city fathers expelled Samuel Henzi, a Bernese from the lower middle classes, who proclaimed the doctrines of the philosophes. Returning to agitate for a broader franchise, he was apprehended and executed, and the Bern patriciate hardened its heart and closed its mind against reform.[39]

There was a bit more elbow room in Basle, but there, too, the hereditary patricians, in alliance with the Bishop, kept a close hold on government, economy, and society, putting down upstarts from the trading classes. Rousseau

thought Geneva an ideal commonwealth and did not for-
give Voltaire his attack upon it, but it was Voltaire who, as
usual, saw through the patriotic haze to the reality.[40] The
inhabitants of Geneva and its canton were divided into five
orders; only the first, and smallest, had the right to hold
office, and only the first and second—a total of some
fifteen hundred—enjoyed the suffrage. The patriciate governed well, but there were some drawbacks for those who
were excluded from that order as mere "natives." One native languished six months in prison for singing a satirical
song in a cafe, and another was banished for his failure to
add the word "native" to his name, while a native who
dared fish in Lake Leman—a private preserve for the patricians—was packed off to jail.[41] No wonder Voltaire supported the uprising of the lower orders in 1770, and young
Albert Gallatin preferred the more democratic air of Pennsylvania. As for Spain and Portugal, Russia, the Two
Sicilies, and the Papal States, there was, in effect, no political life at all.

Perhaps in the seven provinces of the Netherlands you
could find an approach to democracy, those provinces famous for religious toleration and political freedom. They
had overcome the tyranny of Spain; they had provided an
asylum for Huguenots and Pilgrims, and for the perse-
cuted of many nations; their press was free, and their
Universities, and they boasted perhaps the highest standard
of living and—with Sweden—of literacy in Europe. The
provinces were governed by Estates, and the Third Estate
represented the Burghers. They were, to be sure, only one
fourth of the population, but where else, in the Old Regime, would you find so large a segment of the people
participating in the business of government? Look more
closely, however, and it is clear that the Prince dominates
the Third Estate, and the *Stadtholder* and the Regents have
things pretty much their own way. Amsterdam, for example, was ruled by thirty-six men who inherited their office,
and held it for life: they picked the burgomaster, and
elected the deputies to the Estates and controlled the whole
civil administration of the province with perhaps thirty-five
hundred offices at their disposal. And so it was in most of
the great trading towns. In the eighties a group of burghers

and patricians who called themselves Patriots—men like
Van der Kemp and Van der Capellan and Peter Ondaatje
—tried to assert the authority of the middle class over the
Third Estate, but in the face of the dire threat to order and
stability the *Stadtholder* and the Regents made up their
differences and closed ranks against the democrats.[42] What
is more, they brought in British money and Prussian
might. The Patriots had actually stopped the carriage of
the Princess of Orange and forced her to return to Nimw-
jegen where they could keep an eye on her; ample cause,
that, for war, especially as the Princess was sister to the
King of Prussia! Twenty thousand Prussian troops
promptly put an end to the democratic threat in the Netherlands. Edmund Burke described it all with an elegance
and an accuracy that excited universal admiration: "A
chivalrous king, hearing that a princess had been affronted,
takes his lance, assembles his knights, and determines to do
her justice."[43]

4

A kaleidoscopic pattern, this, with innumerable and
shifting local variations. Yet for all the differences that distinguished Holland from Poland, Venice from Sicily, Sweden from Portugal, there was a larger harmony that
stamped a common character upon them all. Everywhere
Europe was ruled by the well-born, the rich, the privileged,
by those who held their places by divine favor, inheritance,
prescription, or purchase. They had no misgivings about
their good fortune, their position, or their power, for their
Pope had duly admonished them that the privileges they
enjoyed and the power they exercised were all part of Nature's plan:

> Order is Heav'ns first law; and this confest,
> Some are, and must be, greater than the rest,
> More rich, more wise. . . .

And elsewhere he pointed the great moral lesson that

> Extremes in Nature equal good produce,
> Extremes in Man concur in general use.[1]

Might it not, then, be assumed that these darlings of fortune—or of Heaven—so secure in their positions, were
above all vulgar ambition, immune alike from corruption
and from the temptation to pander to the popular will?
How ingeniously Nature and History had contrived that
government should be in the hands of those best fitted to
administer it, and that whatever they did for their own advantage made ineluctably for the happiness and well-being
of society and, what is more, was in harmony with great
universal laws! How sensible, too, that the common people
should not be permitted to meddle in matters that they
could not understand, or be exposed to temptations that
they could not resist. For, as the infatuated Soame Jenyns
pointed out:

> The universe resembles a large and well-regulated
> family, in which all the officers and servants . . . are
> subservient to each other in a proper subordination;
> each enjoys the privileges and perquisites peculiar to
> his place, and at the same time contributes, by that
> just subordination, to the magnificence and happiness
> of the whole.[2]

The argument is familiar and the logic persuasive, but,
alas, wholly divorced from reality. Privilege and power did
not make for good government. It was rather the other
way around: the greater the privilege, the more absolute
the power, the worse the government. The best governments—best by standards of honesty, peace, prosperity,
and the well-being of the people—were not France, Spain,
Russia, Denmark, but rather those little islands of republicanism and freedom like the Swiss cantons, the Low Countries, and the American States. Not only were these the
best; they were—as history proved—the strongest and the
most durable. Cato had made this clear in one of the most
memorable of his essays, pointing out how "free States
have conquered the greatest Princes, but the greatest
Princes have never been able to conquer Free States," and

now the Americans added another to his long list of examples.[3]

Instead of being a barrier against corruption, privilege was rather a gateway to corruption. Montesquieu who saw so much, saw this, too, and explained it. Honor, he said, is the principle of a monarchy and of aristocracy, and there is room for virtue, too, but not in excess. "As virtue is necessary in a popular government," he observed, "it is requisite also in a monarchy," but "in the latter it is not so absolutely requisite," and the sagacious Baron, himself a member of the privileged orders, elaborated upon this principle in a chapter entitled, "That Virtue is not the Principle of a Monarchical Government." The reason is plain: "honor—that is the prejudice of every person and rank—supplies the place of the political virtue. . . . Hence they are almost all good subjects, but very few are good men." Aristocrats are indeed, almost by definition, courtiers, and in the courtier—Montesquieu assures us that he is not writing satire—

> ambition is idleness; meanness mixed with pride; a desire for riches without industry; aversion to truth; flattery, perfidy, violation of engagements, contempt for civil duties; fear of the prince's virtue, hope from his weakness . . . above all a perpetual ridicule cast upon virtue.

No wonder that "when virtue is banished"—and pretty clearly it is—"ambition invades the minds of those who are disposed to receive it, and avarice possesses the whole community."[4]

Ambition and avarice, were those not the dominant and pervasive attributes of the aristocracy of the ancient regime? Everywhere, except in Frederick's Prussia, office was regarded not as an opportunity for service but as a species of property, even military office. In France, Spain, Sicily, even in England, the tradition that every noble owed military service to his prince had gone by the board, and it was rather the State that owed military commissions to the nobles; for an army of 170,000, Choiseul provided no less than sixty thousand officers whose pay and mainte-

nance absorbed half the entire military budget.[5] Bribery
and corruption were so pervasive, from monarchs down to
servants and hangers-on, like Figaro, that they achieved a
kind of official sanction. Almost everything was for sale.
Louis XV bought the support of Saxony, Württemberg,
and Bavaria during the Seven Years' War for something
like a hundred million livres—a bad bargain, this;[6] in the
Palatinate you could become a Count of the Holy Roman
Empire for a thousand florins; seats in the House of Commons went for two or three thousand pounds, and were
worth more.[7] The rich Count von Walsegg even tried to
buy the *Requiem* from Mozart, and palm it off as his
own.[8]

Compared with French or Italian government and society, British was honest. The long rule of Robert Walpole
had transformed corruption from an indulgence to a system, and even given it a curious kind of legitimacy, but if
Cato's warnings and Bolingbroke's animadversions (he
himself had purchased his return from exile by a bribe of
ten thousand pounds to one of George I's mistresses[9])
were ineffectual at home, they made a lasting impression
on Americans, confirming them in their conviction that
British politics were hopelessly corrupt.[10] Thus, the Virginia aristocrat, Landon Carter, who had lived sixteen
years in England, wrote that George III was "one grand
corrupter of mankind," and that "pensions and places in
government are like Opiates and other various forms, not
administered to remove but to stupify some painful sensation of a disorder."[11] Just what Lord Shelburne charged,
in his scathing attack on the Civil List in 1777:

> The whole mass of the people were corrupted or cor-
> ruptible. No man scarcely possessed a political right
> . . . who did not wish to part with it, or sell it, for as
> much money as it would bring at market. The nation
> was composed of buyers and sellers. . . . What can-
> not be effected by fraud, corruption or force, is
> brought about by various other methods. Contracts
> and contractors, and the inexhaustible source of
> influence derived through these fruitful channels have
> done wonders, and have succeeded in places where

bribes, places and pensions must have forever failed.[12]

No one could challenge the accuracy of this, yet when, a few years later, Lord Mahon brought in a bill to prevent bribery at elections, he ran into a stone wall of opposition and was forced to withdraw it.[13]

Meantime many lesser offices, especially those involving service overseas—and thus away from both the glitter and the opportunities of the Court—were regarded as sinecures, and those who held them hired deputies to perform the duties or simply farmed out the office. Many Colonial governors stayed on in England, drawing their salaries while lieutenant-governors struggled with recalcitrant assemblies;[14] thus George Germain, Junior, was appointed Receiver to one of the West Indian islands at the age of six but farmed the office out to some place hunter and pocketed the difference, which came to £2,000 annually! Ireland was forced to pay for an army of officeholders, most of whom resided in England and returned no services for their lavish salaries; an example not lost on Americans. Admirals and generals, if successful, could expect not only promotion and peerages, but glittering financial rewards as well: General Albemarle and Admiral Sir George Pocock who commanded the successful assault on Havana in 1762 each received £122,000 in prize money; the naval ratings who did the fighting were not forgotten; they received four pounds each.[15] Broken down peers, discarded officeholders, friends, and companions, had to be taken care of —as they were indeed taken care of in all governments: an obscure office like that of Auditor of Receipts in the Treasury was worth twenty thousand pounds a year; the keeper of Hyde Park drew a salary of £2,200 for duties that were purely honorary, and the Secretary to the abortive Congress of Augsburg of 1762 drew a salary of £2,800, which he lost when he had the temerity to vote against the Government.[16]

Meantime the pension list to favorites and mistresses and the grants to cover the gambling debts of the Prince of Wales took more than the government could hope to earn from Stamp taxes or Townshend duties in America.[17] The

Duchess of Kendall, mistress of George I, enjoyed a pension of five thousand pounds; Lady Yarmouth, one of the mistresses of George II, received four thousand, while Madame de Waldmoden had to be content with three thousand. As for the incorrigible Prince of Wales, he had to jog along on an annuity of sixty thousand a year, which was more than doubled after his marriage, while a grateful Parliament paid off gambling debts of over eight hundred thousand pounds.[18] It was this spectacle which moved Franklin to write, in 1774, that

> when I consider the extream Corruption prevalent among all Orders of Men in this old rotten State, and the glorious publick Virtue so predominant in our rising Country, I cannot but apprehend more Mischief than Benefit from a closer Union. I fear they will drag us after them in all their plundering Wars, which their desperate Circumstances, Injustice and Rapacity may prompt them to undertake, and their wide-wasting Prodigality and Profusion is a Gulph that will swallow up every Aid we may distress ourselves to afford them. Here Numberless and needless Places, enormous Salaries, Pensions, Perquisites, Bribes, groundless Quarrels, foolish Expeditions, false Accounts or no Accounts, Contracts and Jobbs, devour all Revenue, and produce continual Necessity in the Midst of natural Plenty.[19]

It was France that Montesquieu knew best and that most fully vindicated his analysis. Nowhere was honor more highly esteemed than in France, but it was a private, not a public, virtue, and one that seemed to find more ostentatious expression in manners than in morals. Successive Kings set an example of self-indulgence and extravagance; the nobility ignored its obligations but was tenacious of its privileges; the Church—or at least churchmen—competed with the nobility in extravagance and self-indulgence. Thus, early in the era of the Regency it had cost the French people over three hundred thousand pounds to obtain a cardinal's hat for the Abbé Dubois,[20] and at the end of the *ancien régime* the Cardinal de

Rohan, who enjoyed a revenue of two and one half million livres from his estates and kept an army of six hundred peasants as beaters for his game, was involved in the unsavory affair of the Diamond Necklace.

Two great Ministers, Turgot and Necker, tried to save Louis XVI from the consequences of folly, extravagance, and corruption, but in vain; the evils that afflicted the *ancien régime* were ineradicable. Thus Royal pensions alone amounted to 28 million livres annually; "I doubt if all the sovereigns of Europe combined pay more than half this in pensions," wrote Necker wistfully, but the King would not, or could not, economize at the expense of his dependents. As the national debt soared toward five billion livres and carrying charges reached the fantastic sum of 320 million livres, the nation faced bankruptcy. Over the years tax collectors had systematically mulcted the government, as they had fleeced the people; some were venal, others incompetent; still others victims of official chicanery, and the majority were seriously in arrears on payments to the exchequer, but again nothing could be done because reform would impair privilege.[21] Indeed, when it was clear that the proposed reforms of Turgot and Necker threatened the interests of the nobility and the Church, these rallied to preserve their privileges; the King sided with them and dismissed his Ministers. In a desperate effort to stave off catastrophe, Necker's successor, Calonne, negotiated a series of loans; in this hour of peril two brothers of the King, Monsieur and the Comte d'Artois insisted on a rake-off of twenty-five and fifty-six millions for themselves. When, faced with Revolution, Calonne persuaded the King to convene the Assembly of Notables, they too chose to defend their own privileges rather than the commonwealth, and forced his dismissal. It was all part of the *ancien régime's* interpretation of honor.[22]

No need to trace this pattern elsewhere in Europe; the differences were of degree rather than of kind. Every Court aped Versailles; few could match it in extravagance, but some did in corruption and immorality. Indeed, if you wanted power unrestrained, privilege unalloyed, immorality uninhibited, you would turn to the Courts of St. Petersburg or Stuttgart, Warsaw or Naples, rather than to Versailles. Of the major states only Prussia under Frederick II celebrated those virtues associated with austerity. Almost everywhere—even in Prussia—monarchs plunged their countries into wars and the peoples into ruin for territorial or dynastic ends, and where, as in Poland, monarchs did not have power, the great princely families played the same game. Almost everywhere nobles, dedicated to honor, betrayed King and country, and church, unhesitatingly putting personal interest above loyalty to nation. Confronted by the prospect of ruin, the great magnates of Poland refused to give up the *liberum veto,* and for that matter, the amiable King Poniatowski, who had been spoiled by Catherine, refused to give up his own revenues which amounted to one third of all the revenues of the state but were still insufficient to pay his enormous debts.[23] In Russia the nobility collected the taxes, but only one third of what they collected found its way to Moscow. Struensee was one of the most dedicated of the enlightened reformers, but he persuaded an imbecile King to give him a present of sixty thousand dollars, and an equal sum to his favorite, Enevold Brand.[24] Süss Oppenheimer provided an efficient administration for Württemberg but could not refrain from collecting a fortune for himself in the process.[25] The nobility of Sweden regarded themselves as the guardians of the liberties of their nation, but they sold their votes to Britain, France, and Russia—modestly enough, to be sure, the British Minister wrote that he was subsidizing two hundred of them for three pounds ten shillings a month each.[26] The Sicilian nobility, who neither performed military duty nor paid taxes, fought Caracciolo's reforms and in the end defeated them and kept Sicily in its medieval backwardness.[27]

Monarchical honor, wrote Montesquieu, "allows of gallantry when united with the idea of conquest: this is the reason why we never meet with so strict a purity in morals in monarchs as in republican governments."[28] From Augustus the Strong of Saxony, with his two or three hundred bastards, to Louis XV with his Deer Park, monarchs and nobles allied gallantry with conquest. The youthful Christian VII of Denmark early dedicated himself to a career of debauchery, while his favorite, Johann Struensee,

set an example to the public by seducing his Queen. The
gallantries, and conquests, of Catherine the Great matched
those of any other monarch in Europe, and were as expensive: five successive Orlovs were enriched by a total of seventeen million rubles while the pampered Potemkin made
a fortune of fifty million rubles out of his attachment.[29]
Princes in Naples kept harems of Ganymedes as well as of
Hebes, and J. F. Dupaty wrote of Genoa that "there was
so much libertinage that there are no prostitutes, and so
many priests that there is no religion."[30] Karl Eugen of
Württemberg "shared his heart between one hundred
mistresses," mostly recruited from the theater, which all
but bankrupted his Duchy, while the enlightened Margrave
Charles III of Baden counted no less than one hundred
and sixty girls in his private ballet.[31] Even in classical
Weimar, Goethe's friend, Jacob Lenz, proposed that the
Grand Duke protect the honor of girls of good family by
attaching a regiment of strumpets to his little Army.[32] It is
all familiar enough in the novels of Fielding and Smollett,
Restif de Bretonne and Alessandro Manzoni, the memoirs
of a Casanova or a Baron von Pöllnitz, the *Journals* of
Boswell and the *Letters* of Horace Walpole, the dramas of
Gay and of Goldoni, the drawings of Hogarth and Gilroy,
the paintings of Pietro Longhi and Francisco de Goya—
good historians, all of them.

How austere, by contrast, the social life of Geneva and
Berne, Amsterdam and Leyden, Boston and Philadelphia:
Perhaps there was some truth in Montesquieu's argument
that virtue was the animating principle of republics.

5

Everywhere, in politics, as in morals, the contrast between the Old World and the New was dramatic. The
same people (for all white Americans were relative newcomers from Britain and the Continent), the same history,
the same religion, and, until they moved to America, the
same institutions! But how differently it all worked out on
the two shores of the Atlantic!

Take this matter of government. There was democracy

in the New World from the very beginning, at Plymouth, in the Bay Colony, in the River towns of Connecticut, and —if that term means not only making government but the practice of self-government—even in the Royal colonies.[1] By the time of independence New England had developed something close to manhood suffrage, and so, too, Pennsylvania, Virginia, North Carolina, Vermont, and Georgia, while everywhere, except in New York, Maryland, and South Carolina, power was actually in the hands of the majority of the white adult males, or of such as chose to vote. Except for Iceland and a few of the smaller Swiss cantons, America was the only country on the globe of which this could be said.[2]

Consider Massachusetts, which had contributed so much to the philosophy of self-government. Well might Governor Hutchinson complain that every Tom, Dick, and Harry attended town meetings, and swamped the sober voice of authority. Every town, he said, was "an absolute democracy" where "anything with the appearance of a man" was allowed to vote, for it was "rare that any scrutiny is made into the qualifications of voters."[3] John Adams, who thought poorly of the principle of universal suffrage, said much the same thing: "Our people have never been very rigid in scrutinizing into the qualifications of voters and I presume"—this was in 1776—"will not now begin to be so."[4] Two years later Adams broadened this generalization to embrace the whole of the country. "The truth is," he wrote, "that the people have ever governed in America; all the force of royal governors and councils has never been able to get the advantage of them."[5]

There were, to be sure, property qualifications for voting in Massachusetts—a forty pound freehold or forty shillings rent—and these were, in effect, re-enacted by the Constitution of 1780.* But what is most interesting is that the requirements were waived for voting on the Constitution itself, and after that, under the new constitution,

---

* The Constitution of 1780 required a sixty pound freehold rather than the earlier forty; this was not a reactionary gesture but a realistic recognition that owing to inflation sixty pounds was roughly equivalent to the earlier forty.

they remained largely ineffective. Town elections were open to all who had paid a poll tax, and in many towns almost every adult male actually voted.[6] Suffrage qualifications were enforced by town officials who were mostly neighbors or friends. Thus, the requirement of a freehold of the value of three pounds annually was interpreted to mean the ability to earn three pounds a year, a requirement which all but vagabonds could meet. All this did not mean that the majority of men actually voted; either out of indifference or of satisfaction with existing conditions or because of the sheer difficulties of getting to the voting place, few of those entitled to vote bothered to do so. Not until 1787 did more than 25 per cent of the voters of Massachusetts go to the polls, while in Connecticut the proportion voting was substantially lower—2 per cent of those qualified voted in the Congressional election of 1790 and 14 per cent in the hotly contested election of 1800.[7] Yet Oliver Wolcott later recalled that property qualifications for voting in Connecticut had been "essentially nugatory," and that "few men of decent character have failed at some time to acquire the qualifications."

Elsewhere, too, voting—or the right to vote—was widespread. New Hampshire abandoned its freehold qualification for suffrage in 1775 and permitted all taxpayers to vote, while the new state of Vermont did away with suffrage qualifications altogether, as did that other new state, Kentucky, and neither appeared to suffer for its boldness. We think of Virginia as an aristocratic state dominated by a low-country planter class, but the situation there differed little from that in New England. By 1785 the requirements for voting in the Old Dominion were easy enough to meet: twenty-five acres of improved or fifty of unimproved land, or a house twelve feet by twelve, or a fifty pound estate or, if none of these were available to town dwellers, a five-year apprenticeship which would normally have been served before the age of twenty-one. Actually, a substantial majority of all white men could vote in Virginia, and what is more, a substantial number of them actually did—rather more than in the democratic states of New England.[8] Georgia and North Carolina extended the franchise to all taxpayers and, in Georgia, to mechanics as well; no wonder Governor Wright had complained that "by far the great number of voters are of the inferior sort of People." Such fragmentary statistics as we possess suggest that a larger number of people voted in North Carolina than elsewhere in America, which means than elsewhere in the world.[9] Aristocratic South Carolina required a hundred acre freehold, or payment of a tax of ten shillings, but whatever the formal requirements, voting was said to be "open to anyone who approached the polls."[10] Pennsylvania was, in many ways, the most radical of the American states—as it was, after Connecticut, the most nearly idyllic. Its constitution announced that "all men having a sufficient evident common interest with and attachment to the community have a right to elect officers and to be elected to office." That was, to be sure, in the Declaration of Rights. The provision on voting was not quite so liberal; it called for the payment of taxes as a prerequisite, though "sons of freeholders of the age of twenty-one years shall be entitled to vote although they have not paid taxes."[11] Paupers and vagabonds, Negroes, and indentured servants were still excluded from the suffrage, but the total number who voted was larger than in Massachusetts or Connecticut—from one third of the adult men in 1790 to over two thirds in the hotly contested gubernatorial election of 1808.[12]

When it came to office holding, Americans were a bit more circumspect than in the matter of voting: the stake-in-society principle, which dictated the exclusion of vagabonds, paupers, and indentured servants, operated here to exclude those without visible property.[13] Nowhere, to be sure, was office holding limited to a legal aristocracy for the elementary reason that there was no such thing in America. Both religious and property qualifications, however, lingered on from the colonial era, though the first, at least, seems to have insinuated itself into the state constitutions more out of respect for tradition than out of conviction.[14] Almost all state constitutions contained some sort of religious qualification: belief in the "being of a God and a future state of rewards and punishments," as in South Carolina, or belief in the Trinity and the inspiration of the Scriptures, as in Delaware. Even liberal Pennsyl-

vania required that all officeholders accept the truth of the
Protestant religion and affirm their belief in the divine inspiration of both Old and New Testaments. It is probable
that such requirements were a gesture toward convention
and not meant to be taken either literally or seriously for
there is no instance, during these years, of any important
elected official being denied the right to hold office on
religious grounds, and even the skeptical Franklin who
certainly did not believe in the divine inspiration of the
Old Testament, managed to qualify as President of Pennsylvania! Property qualifications were, for a time, a more
serious matter, and they lingered on in some states for another generation. The Governor of Massachusetts was expected to own a thousand pound freehold, and aristocratic
South Carolina required that its governor be ten times that
rich, though equally aristocratic Virginia did not require
that her governors have any property at all. There were
substantial property qualifications for members of some
state legislatures. A member of the lower house in Massachusetts was expected to have a hundred pound freehold,
while those who aspired to the Senate were required to
own a freehold of three hundred pounds or an estate of six
hundred. Southern constitution framers were even more
property-conscious. A member of the upper house of
South Carolina was required to have a five-hundred-acre
freehold or property to the value of two thousand pounds,
and members of the Maryland Senate were not only required to possess property to the value of one thousand
pounds but to be "men of the most wisdom, experience
and virtue." Even equalitarian North Carolina expected
members of its lower house to own one hundred acres of
land and members of its senate three hundred acres. Some
of these requirements, to be sure, were drastically reduced
within a few years; thus, by 1790 South Carolina had
deflated her requirement for governor to a modest fifteen
hundred pounds, and for Senators to three hundred.[15] And
it is relevant to observe, too, that in most states land was
both abundant and cheap, and that few of those who
would in any ordinary circumstances be chosen to represent a town or parish or county failed to qualify. Perhaps a
more serious discrimination against the poor was the high

cost of travel and of residence in the State capital, and the meager per diem allowance, for the British theory of unpaid public service was long accepted uncritically in the United States. It was this rather than inability to meet property qualifications that chiefly accounts for the failure of so many New England towns to send representatives to the state assemblies.[16]

Offices ran in families, particularly in Connecticut, New York, and the South, but only where the families commended themselves to the voters, and nowhere outside Connecticut—regarded by foreigners as the very model of a democratic community—could it be said that offices were in any sense hereditary.[17] John Adams was very conscious of the role of family in Massachusetts, but not very perceptive about it. "You and I," he wrote his cousin Samuel, "have seen four noble families rise up in Boston—the Crafts, Gores, Dawes and Austins. These are as really a nobility in our town as the Howards, Somersets, Berties, etc. in England."[18] Alas for the Adams argument, none of these families was able to sustain "nobility" or even any great eminence; it was the upstart Adams who founded something like an hereditary nobility. Jefferson saw more deeply. "A Randolph, a Carter, or a Burwell," he wrote to Adams, "must have great personal superiority over a common competitor to be elected by the people, even at this day."[19]

More instructive and more characteristic because free from the influences of habit and tradition that operated so powerfully in the States, were the arrangements worked out by members of the Convention that drafted the Federal Constitution. Here were the best minds in the country, here judgment matured by thirteen years of discussion, experimentation, and independence; here standards to which the "good and the wise" might repair. That "assembly of demigods"—the phrase is Jefferson's—was chosen by the people, not directly, but by their representatives, and the finished product went back to the people for approval or disapproval. What did these representatives of the people†

† From every State except Rhode Island, which would scarcely have introduced an aristocratic note had it been represented!

—most of them, inevitably, men of substance and position
—do about suffrage and office holding? They provided, for
the first time in history, that all offices, from the highest to
the lowest, would be open to all men. Madison put it,
somewhat rhetorically, in *Federalist Paper* No. 57. Who,
he asked, are the electors? "Not the rich more than the
poor; not the learned more than the ignorant; not the
haughty heirs of distinguished names more than the hum-
ble sons of obscure . . . fortune." The new Constitution
contained no restrictions on voting or on office holding.
Here is the President—the equivalent of a monarch in the
Old World; he must be native-born and thirty-five years
old. That is the beginning and the end of the matter. Here
are the judges of the highest court, who were expected to
be independent enough to resist pressures from President
and Congress and from the States, too: They can be paupers, native or foreign-born, Protestant or Catholic, or
atheist. Indeed, it was the *absence* of religious qualifications that gave pause to many of the members of ratifying
conventions, who conjured up the horrid consequences of
infidelity. As one delegate from North Carolina asserted—
he must have been persuasive for that state voted against
the Constitution as it stood—"the exclusion of religious
tests meant that pagans, deists, and Mahometans might obtain offices among us, and that the senators and representatives might all be pagans."[20] So indeed they might,
for their office, too, was innocent of qualifications. What
the States did about selecting their Senators was, of course,
their own affair, but nothing in the Constitution of the
United States excluded the poor, the foreign-born, or the
irreligious. Needless to say, there were no federal restrictions on voting; that, too, was left to the States. It is sometimes asserted that the Founding Fathers left these matters
to the States because they trusted the States to be properly
conservative and see to it that voting and office holding
were limited to the men of substance and of property. But
by 1787 most of the restrictions on voting, except those of
sex and color, had gone—or were going—by the board,
and the evidence from the embryonic new states, as from
the old, that all would disappear in the foreseeable future,
was irresistible. A convention that distrusted democracy

would have written safeguards against such a contingency into the constitutional document, but that was never seriously considered.[21]

6

How audacious to entrust the whole of government to the mercies of the common man; how reckless to permit him not only to select his magistrates, but to be the magistrate! That was unprecedented in modern history. How was this to be reconciled with the maxim that man was everywhere the creature of interests and passions, ambitions and greed? How was it to be squared with the irrefutable lesson of history that power always corrupts? That was the argument John Adams tried to bring home to his countrymen, his pen driving over those hundreds of pages, night after night, to produce the *Defense of the Constitutions* in time for the Philadelphia Convention—that men could never be trusted with power, not even the best of them; only a government intricately checked and balanced could save society from itself.[1] That was what Hamilton said, in the Convention and again in the *Federalist Papers:* "an hereditary monarch," he wrote, blandly ignoring some famous chapters of English history, "has too much at stake . . . to be corrupted by foreign powers," but for a man chosen from the people and possessed of but a moderate or slender fortune, the situation is very different. "An avaricious man might be tempted to betray the interests of the state to the acquisition of wealth; an ambitious man might make his own aggrandisement . . . the price of his treachery. . . . The history of human conduct," he concluded, "does not warrant that exalted opinion of human virtue which could make it wise" to put too great faith in any executive. Just so, with shrill reiteration, said a veritable phalanx of "men of little faith"‡ in the state ratifying conventions, men who were sure that all but they were corrupt. The upright George Mason of Virginia, who was never tempted by power, nevertheless gravely

‡ The phrase is Cecelia Kenyon's.

warned of that "natural lust of power inherent in man," and Luther Martin of Maryland harped on "the ambition of man and his lust for power." James Winthrop argued that "the experience of mankind has proved the prevalence of a disposition to use power wantonly," and in New York, Melancton Smith confessed that "fickleness and inconstancy were characteristic of a free people."[2] Even Jefferson, when he consulted his fears instead of his hopes, endorsed these misgivings. In one of the greatest of his state papers he wrote that "it would be a dangerous delusion were a confidence in the men of our choice, to silence our fears for the safety of our rights. . . . Confidence is everywhere the parent of despotism; free government is founded in jealousy, not in confidence; it is jealousy which prescribes limited constitutions to bind down those whom we are obliged to trust with power."[3]

Were these fears and misgivings justified? Did those in power seek to enlarge their power? Did the American Governors turn into tyrants, or judges abuse their authority; did the military try to seize the reins of power and subvert the civil authorities? The record, in the United States, told a very different story and long continued to do so. So reluctant was the Congress to exercise even those powers clearly assigned to it—to regulate commerce, control immigration, enlarge the role of the courts—that those essential functions were allowed almost to go by default.[4] And so powerfully was the fear of the abuse of authority stamped upon the American imagination that when, in the eighteen-fifties, the Union was threatened, the executive stood aside, bewildered and impotent; when at last the nation was forced to fight for its life, another and stronger President conducted four years of war with a respect for law and constitution almost unprecedented in history. Though the Supreme Court early asserted its authority to nullify acts of Congress, it exercised this authority only twice in seventy years and, on the first of these occasions only to reject a power which the Congress had sought to confer upon it.[5]

So, too, with those who in other countries were called "rulers," and who, if no longer hedged about with Divinity, were hedged about with every appurtenance of dignity

and luxury and every instrument of power. In the United
States the term "public servant" was a literal description.
The demands of public service were arduous and urgent;
the rewards were meager, even the rewards of public ap-
probation, for each of the first three Presidents left office
under a cloud of public disapproval. No wonder Washington was reluctant to resume the burdens of office in 1789,
and happy to surrender them eight years later. No wonder
John Adams persuaded himself, if not others, that he was
happier on his farm in Braintree than in the Courts of
Europe or the Presidential mansion in Philadelphia,* and
Jefferson longed for the peace and beauty of Monticello.
None in that age (the qualification is important) grew
rich in the service of the United States, either in politics or
in war; indeed an oath of service to the United States was
almost equivalent to a vow of poverty in one of the Catholic orders. This was an experience which Jefferson and
Hamilton shared and a principle on which they agreed.
"Our public economy," wrote Jefferson, "is such as to
offer drudgery and subsistence only to those entrusted with
its administration,"[6] and after he had worn himself out
serving as Secretary of the Treasury, Hamilton confided to
a relative in Scotland that "public office in this country has
few attractions. The pecuniary emolument is so incon-
siderable as to amount to a sacrifice to any man who can
employ his time with advantage in any liberal profession."[7]
Washington served without pay in the Army and in the
Presidency, while his plantations fell into ruin, and when
he set out for New York to be inaugurated President he
had to borrow five hundred dollars to pay his expenses;
that had not been the fate of the victorious Marlborough!
When Jefferson sold his magnificent library to the new Library of Congress, for half its value, he was reviled like a

---

* "He has finally returned to his home, amidst the acclaim of his
fellow citizens. I have seen him by his rustic penates at Braintree,
where he is busy tending his farm, oblivious of the time when he struck
down the pride of his king, who had put a price upon his head and
who later was forced to receive him as the ambassador of a free
country. He is like one of the generals or ambassadors of the golden
ages of Rome and of Greece, an Epaminondas, a Cincinnatus, or a
Fabius." So wrote Brissot de Warville about John Adams. *New Travels
in the United States of America,* 1788, 102, ed. Echeverria.

common thief;[8] after more than half a century of public
service, he had to petition the legislature of Virginia to
permit a lottery on his plantations to rescue him from
bankruptcy. Hamilton, too, died a near-bankrupt, and
friends had to come to the aid of his family; how unlike
the careers of a Henry Fox in England, a Necker in
France, a Sonnenfels in Austria, a Pombal in Portugal.
Robert Morris, "the financier of the Revolution," spent
some years in debtors' prison, and James Wilson of the
Supreme Court, one of the authors of the Constitution,
was in flight from importunate creditors; partly their own
fault, no doubt, but that is not what grateful monarchs
said to their Ministers in Europe or Parliament to the Regent. George Rogers Clark, who had "won" the Northwest
—if it did not stay won, that was not *his* fault—spent his
old age in penury; how unlike the lot of a Clive or a Has-
tings. The upright Edmund Burke enjoyed a modest sine-
cure of four thousand pounds a year and was able to buy
himself a handsome country estate, but Tom Paine, who
did as well by his country, and better by mankind, eked
out a miserable old age in a shack outside New York. The
Lord Chancellor of England enjoyed an income of twenty
thousand pounds, while the Chief Justice of the United
States had to be content with four thousand dollars, and
some of the chief justices of state supreme courts were
paid less than half that sum.[9]† The Governor of the
Northwest Territory, a territory more extensive than most
Old World nations, was paid two thousand dollars a year,
which might be compared with the salary of some forty
thousand pesos—plus provision for a staff of one hundred
or so—for the Viceroy at Peru.

"The only use which the people ever make of their
power," wrote the greatly admired Jean De Lolme, "is either to give it away, or allow it to be taken from them."
And as for the tribunes of the people, he added, they were
invariably corrupt. "We do not find that they ever employed the power of the people in things really beneficial
to the people."[10] Franklin was, as usual, more perspicacious. "It will scarcely be credited," he wrote to his

† The Justices of the Supreme Court of Kentucky received $999.63.

friend Joseph Priestley, "that men can be as diligent with us from zeal for the public good, as with you for thousands per annum. Such is the difference between the uncorrupted new states, and corrupted old ones."[11]

* * *

What an education was all this immense political activity—the winning of independence, the creation of new states and a new nation, the writing of constitutions and Bills of Rights, the administration of government at every level, and the organization of parties, the day-by-day participation in voting and town meeting and county court and caucus, and the training in office holding! In the Old World the philosophes discussed politics in a vacuum—Rousseau with his constitution for Corsica and his solemn advice to the Poles, Mably with his ideal constitution for Massachusetts, Morelly with his fantastic Code. Happily no one invited them to put these plans into effect. In the rare cases when the philosophes did have a chance to play a political role, they almost invariably chose, or were forced, to recite familiar lines and make familiar gestures. (Struensee in Denmark, Count Rumford in Bavaria, and Caraccioli in Sicily are perhaps the only exceptions.) But in the American states the situation was entirely different. The constitutions, which American philosophers wrote, were adopted, the laws they formulated were enacted, and they themselves were drafted to run the governments and administer the laws: John Adams in Massachusetts, Nathaniel Chipman in Vermont, William Livingston in New Jersey, Franklin in Pennsylvania, Jefferson in Virginia, Willie Jones in North Carolina, Charles Pinckney in South Carolina, and many others, down into the new century. Plato was vindicated; for the first time in history philosophers were kings.

Of an absolute monarchy or an aristocracy it cannot be said that the people get the government they deserve, but of a representative government that can be said. Was it not a tribute then to the political maturity of the Americans of this generation that they deserved the government they made for themselves—the constitutions, the Bills of Rights,

the federal system, the dual judiciary crowned by a supreme court, the simplicity and honesty that pervaded
every branch of administration! Was it not a tribute that
they deserved Washington and John Adams and Jefferson
and their colleagues, in state and national governments!

This is doubtless what Samuel Williams—himself a
minor philosophe—had in mind in one of the more eloquent passages of his *Natural and Civil History of Vermont;* he was writing of his own homespun state, but what
he said applied to most of the newly united States:

> The system of government . . . in America is not
> derived from superstition, conquest, military power,
> or a pretended compact between the rulers and the
> people; but it was derived from nature and reason;
> and is founded in the nature, capacities, and powers
> which God hath assigned to the race of men. . . .
> Made equal in their rights by nature, the body of the
> people were in a situation nearly similar with regard
> to their employments, pursuits, and views. Without
> the distinctions of titles, families, or nobility, they ac-
> knowledged and reverenced only these distinctions
> which nature had made, in a diversity of talents, abili-
> ties and virtues. There were no family interests, con-
> nections, or estates large enough to oppress them.
> There was no excessive wealth in the hands of a few,
> sufficient to corrupt them. . . . Nothing remained for
> such a people but to follow what nature taught.[12]

CHAPTER EIGHT

Americans Bring Forth a New Nation

1

It took centuries for the peoples of Britain, France, Spain, and Denmark to establish national monarchies and governments, develop a sense of community, and acquire an awareness of common nationalism. It took even longer for those of Italy, Germany, Austria, and Russia. But Americans brought forth a new nation in a single generation. How did it happen that as early as 1775 the ardent Patrick Henry could declaim, however rhetorically, that "the distinctions between Virginians, Pennsylvanians, New Yorkers and New Englanders are no more," and that the newcomer Thomas Paine could write, more accurately, that "our citizenship in the United States is our national character. . . . Our great title is Americans."?[1] How did it happen that the miscellaneous British and European peoples who had transplanted themselves to the New World and spread out over an area larger than that of any two Western nations, acquired a sense of nationalism, vindicated that nationalism on the battlefield and in diplomacy, organized it into political and administrative institutions, and provided it with so many of the essential cultural ingredients—myths and legends, heroes and villains, symbols and mottoes, the consciousness of a meaningful past, and the assurance of a glorious future—all in two or three decades?[2]

Not only was American nationalism achieved with a swiftness unprecedented in history, but what was achieved was a new kind of nationalism. It was not imposed by a conqueror or by a monarch. It was not dependent on an Established Church at whose altars all worshipped alike, or upon the power of a ruling class. It did not draw its inspiration from a national past or its strength from a traditional enemy. It came from the people; it was an act of will.

There were, needless to say, antecedents and anticipations. The most important of these were rooted not in history but in circumstances: the separation from Europe, and the "climate" of the new land. The settlement of America was indeed the unsettlement of Europe;[3] for perhaps the majority of newcomers it was a repudiation, conscious or unconscious, of the Old World. It was not just a migration; it was, more often than not, a flight. No one saw this more clearly than the "American Farmer," Hector St. John de Crèvecoeur, whose *Letters* are the first perceptive study of the American character:

> In this great American asylum, the poor of Europe have by some means met together; . . . to what purpose should they ask each other what countrymen they are? Alas, two-thirds of them had no country. . . . Urged by a variety of motives, here they came. Everything has tended to regenerate them: new laws, a new mode of living, a new social system; here they are become men . . . by the power of transplantation, like all other plants, they have taken root and flourished.
>
> What attachment can a poor European have for a country where he had nothing? The knowledge of the language, the love of a few kindred as poor as himself, were the only cords that tied him; his country is now that which gives him land, bread, protection, and consequence. *Ubi panis, ibi patria*, is the motto of all emigrants.[4]

That among the more sophisticated and literate Americans there was pride in the British connection and loyalty to the British Crown cannot be gainsaid;[5] that this pride inspired farmers and fishermen and indentured servants, the Germans who had been driven out of the Palatinate and the Scots who had fled after the Forty-five, seems improbable. Such loyalties as these had were to their adopted country: *Ubi panis, ibi patria.*

If there was one common denominator more powerful than any other that united farmers and workingmen, merchants, lawyers and clergy, the English, the Germans, the Scots-Irish, and the Huguenots, it was quite simply the recognition that America was not Europe, but something new in history. The sense of uniqueness came before the reality.[6] America was not Europe! Here men and women, if white, were free to live where they would and as they would and to marry whom they would; free to worship in their own churches—or not to worship; to work at their own trades, to go to their own schools and colleges; free to have souls and minds of their own and, what is more, to bare their souls and speak their minds. Even the most cosmopolitan among them could rejoice that here they could escape the luxury which enervated society in the Old World and the corruption that debased it. For the repudiation of the Old World was not just political, or religious, economic or social; it was—or sought to be—moral. Thus, on the eve of the war Franklin could deplore "the extream Corruption prevalent among all Orders of Men in this old rotten State" with its "desperate Circumstances, Injustice, and Rapacity."[7] Thus, Jefferson blessed "the Almighty Being who in gathering together the waters under the heavens in one place, divided the land of your [Old World] hemisphere from the dry land of ours."[8] The poet-editor, Philip Freneau, had recourse to almost the same metaphor:

> Blest in their distance from that bloody scene,
> Why spread the sail to pass the Guelphs between?

And the puritanical Dr. Rush advised that Americans cultivate an indifference to Europe; what concern, he asked, do we have with "the quarrels or the vices of the old world, with duels, elopements, the kept mistresses, the murders, the suicides, the thefts, the forgeries, the boxing matches, the wagers for eating, drinking . . ."?[9]

The America into which men and women of the Old World escaped was new in a more positive sense than in being merely not-Europe. It was new in its spaciousness— land enough, Jefferson was to say, for our descendants to "the thousandth and thousandth generation." By comparison with Europe, that spaciousness was so astonishing that it took on not just a quantitative but a qualitative character. Together with freedom from the limitations of class and from the demands of the military, it accounted for that mobility which was social as well as geographical: It provided not only an economic safety valve but a psychological one. This, too, Crèvecoeur perceived that "There is room for everybody in America," and added that

> An European, when he first arrives, seems limited in his intentions as well as in his views; two hundred miles formerly appeared a very great distance, it is now but a trifle. He no sooner breathes our air than he forms schemes, and embarks in designs he never would have thought of in his own country. There the plenitude of society confines many useful ideas, and often extinguishes the most laudable schemes which here ripen into maturity. Thus Europeans become Americans.[10]

Like the land, the Indians belonged to what the philosophes called the "Climate" of the New World, and it is difficult to exaggerate their contribution in war and in peace to the growth of the sense of American community.[11] There they were, from the first landfall of the English, all the way from Massachusetts Bay to Georgia, and in the new territory that was added from the Appalachians to the Mississippi and beyond. They were there to give us the Pocahontas story and the story of the wonderful Squanto of the Pawtuxet tribe who taught the Pilgrims "how to set their corne and where to take fishe";[12] they were there as guides into the wilderness and as instructors in the trapping of beaver and the fashioning of canoes. They were there to be converted to Christianity and to "civilization"

—an enterprise that enlisted the talents of John Eliot with his Indian Bible in the 1660s and of the most enlightened of amateur ethnologists, Thomas Jefferson, through much of his life.[13] They provided the colonials with what they otherwise lacked for effective unity—a national enemy, and one who, after the mid-seventeenth century, carried with him a providential guarantee of victory for the white invaders. They presented the paradox, dear to the Enlightenment, of a savage Satanic in his cruelty but at the same time Noble; the savage who inflicted fiendish tortures on his victims, and who—through the high-minded Chief Logan—pronounced one of the most eloquent declamations in the history of oratory; we have Jefferson's word for that![14] Everywhere they taught the lesson of co-operation, whether by the model of the Iroquois Confederacy and the formidable alliance that Chief Pontiac welded together, or by the inescapable logic of necessity: The Confederacy of New England in the mid-seventeenth and the Albany Plan of Union in the mid-eighteenth centuries were called into being by threats of Indian warfare. More than anything except Nature herself they fired the imagination of poets and storytellers, historians and ethnologists, and provided the stuff for myth and legend. From John Smith's *General Historie of Virginia* and Thomas Morton's *New English Canaan* to the *Travels* of John Bartram and Jefferson's *Notes on Virginia;* from Robert Rogers's *Ponteach—* which has some claim to be the first drama written in America—and the innumerable captivity narratives, to the Indian poems of the gifted Philip Freneau; from John Lawson's *New Voyage to Carolina* to the *Journals* of the Lewis and Clark expedition, they provided a voluminous and a romantic library of American literature. They wrote their names indelibly on the land: half the states east of the Mississippi bear Indian names, and rivers and lakes from the Kennebec to the Suwannee, the Susquehanna to the Ohio, and so too most of those we call the "Finger" and "Great" Lakes.[15] More than any other element except Nature herself, they furnished the materials for romanticism in literature, history, and mythology. From Powhatan to Geronimo they were part of the American experience, and after they ceased to be a danger they became part of the American imagination; generations of children built tents in their back yards and played at being Indians, and their parents satisfied their yearning for excitement by reading narratives of Indian captivity or of frontier wars. When that, too, passed, the Indian lingered on as a problem both of politics and of conscience.

All of these pressures for unity were circumstantial; something inherent in the flight from Europe, the settlement of America, the immensity of the continent, and the westward sweep of population with its inevitable conflict with the Indians over the control of their hunting grounds. They set the stage for nationalism; they did not call it into being.

It was institutional pressures that nourished and eventually created an American nationalism. Of these perhaps the most important at the outset was religion.[16] We are in the presence here of a paradox: Where in the Old World religious differences divided society and were thought pernicious, in the New they made for unity. By mid-eighteenth century not only did a score of religions flourish in the American colonies, but a substantial majority even of those who attended any church,* worshipped outside the Congregational and Anglican Establishments. Presbyterians, Baptists, Dutch Reformed, Quakers, Catholics, Lutherans, and other German sectaries outnumbered those who enjoyed official support—a situation inconceivable in the Old World.† Imagine Huguenots outnumbering Catholics in France, or Lutherans outnumbering Catholics in Bavaria!

Even the regional pattern was a variegated one. The Congregational Church was established in most of New England, but the Baptists dominated Rhode Island, and there were large numbers of Presbyterians, Baptists, and Anglicans in the other New England colonies. The Quakers had founded Pennsylvania, but they were by now greatly outnumbered by Presbyterians and by German sectaries. Even in South Carolina, where the Anglican Church

* Even in devout New England there was apparently only one church member to every eight persons.
† Except, of course, in Ireland where the religion of the majority was ruthlessly suppressed.

had power, wealth, and distinction, it could not hold its own numerically with Piedmont and up-country "dissenters"; though the Constitution of 1778 reaffirmed the Anglican Establishment, that of 1790 swept it away—and it went without a struggle.[17] Increasingly throughout the eighteenth century churches ignored colonial and state boundary lines and built up loose intercolonial networks; as religion was the chief preoccupation of Americans in these years,[18] the religious connections often proved stronger than the political divisions.

In this development the Great Awakening, which swept the colonies in the second and third quarters of the century, played an explosive role.[19] It was not only a vehicle for the expression of new religious enthusiasm, but for social and political as well. It was—to invoke Edmund Burke's phrase—a kind of dissent from dissent; it arose spontaneously as a reaction to the formalism even in dissenting churches (the New England revival led by Jonathan Edwards in Northampton is an exception here); it was led by newcomers—self-appointed revivalists, most of them drawn from miscellaneous backgrounds, and often without ardent denominational loyalties, like Gilbert Tennent, Devereux Jarrett, and George Whitefield himself. It swept the colonies like a prairie fire, overleaping both political and denominational barriers; it turned away from the religion of the pulpit and the Seminary to the religion of inspiration and the open fields. It rallied dissenters of all denominations against all Establishments, and inevitably attacked political establishments as well as religious; it was democratic in its origins, its inspiration, and its appeal. It made Philadelphia a religious before it became a political capital and created new colleges that drew students from all of the Colonies and sent them out to carry the Gospel to distant frontiers—the College of New Jersey, which became Princeton, the College of Rhode Island, which became Brown, the Hampden-Sydney College in Virginia, which opened the year of the Declaration—and it reinvigorated older colleges like Yale. In George Whitefield, who was surely its most eloquent spokesman, and whom many thought the greatest orator of his age, it gave colonial America the only "national" figure to rank with Benjamin Franklin.[20]

Meantime, Americans were learning to work together in other areas than religion. Of these the military and the political were the most enduring and the most importunate. It was the New England Colonies which had banded together to capture the frowning fortress of Louisbourg in 1745—only to see it handed back to the French. All the colonies were involved (though in varying degrees) in the French and Indian War, the first major enterprise that can be called truly "continental," and it was that war which transformed George Washington from a Virginia surveyor and planter into a continental figure, thus giving Americans not only their first native military hero but also their most durable.[21]

The Revolution itself was perhaps the most powerful instrument in creating a sense of common destiny and of nationalism—the Revolution with its fears and hopes, its defeats and victories, its anguish and glory; with heroes and villains, symbols and legends. Americans from every state fought side by side all through the years that tried men's souls. Old World wars did not customarily inspire or strengthen a national spirit; they were fought, for the most part, by professional soldiers or by mercenaries—over one-half the Danish Army, for example, were mercenaries, and the language of the Army was German; they were fought at the will of the King, not by decision of the people; and they were fought in distant lands for purposes exotic and obscure. But the Revolutionary War was not something imposed upon the American people; it was, if not quite spontaneous, largely voluntary, and the American imagination is not wholly misguided in dwelling with affection on the Minute Men who gathered at Concord Bridge, the Green Mountain Boys who fought at Bennington, the Mountain Men who repulsed Major Ferguson at King's Mountain, or the Swamp Foxes who followed General Marion. The War, too, affected every part of the country (though unevenly) and every segment of a literate and knowledgeable society. It was an experience that might have fragmented the nation, but that provided, rather, the

sinews for unity; the flight or expulsion of some eighty
thousand loyalists contributed here. It was almost inevitable that after Yorktown, the most passionate spokesmen
for a stronger union were those who had served "their
country" during the war, in the Army or the council:
Washington himself, Hamilton, Pickering, Knox, McHenry,
Franklin, Jefferson, Madison, Tom Paine, and Robert
Morris among them.[22]

The War gave Americans a common cause, one that
could be both rationalized and sentimentalized. The ration-
alization could be read in those state papers that were to
constitute an American Testament; the sentiment in the
legends that clustered about Washington and Valley Forge,
Marion and Mad Anthony Wayne, Nathan Hale who had
but one life to give for his country, and John Paul Jones
who had just begun to fight; in the symbols of the flag and
the bald eagle and in the seals and the mottoes—three of
them, no less—and in patriotic poems, jocular like *Yankee
Doodle* or elevated like Timothy Dwight's

> Columbia, Columbia, to glory arise,
> The Queen of the world, and the child of the skies

or, at the end of the era, Joseph Hopkinson's exultant national anthem

> Hail, Columbia, happy land!
> Hail, ye heroes! heaven-born band!

What country before 1776 had equipped itself with all this
patriotic paraphernalia in one generation?[23]

The war provided an enemy, too, one more formidable
than the Indian, and more worthy, for the distinction of
defeating Britain on the battlefield, and in the pages of history, was more exalted by far than that of overcoming
even the fiercest of Indian tribes. Surprisingly, it vindicated
American nationalism abroad even before it had been vindicated at home. Franklin and Adams, Jefferson and Jay,
spoke for the United States as a nation, and it was as representatives of a nation that they were accepted and won

allies.[24] Tom Paine put this well, as he put everything else
well:

> That which includes and renders easy all interior con-
> cerns is the UNION OF THE STATES. On this our
> great national character depends. It is this which must
> give us importance abroad and security at home. It is
> through this only that we are, or can be, nationally
> known in the world; it is the flag of the United States
> which renders our ships and commerce safe on the
> seas. . . . All our treaties . . . are formed under the
> sovereignty of the United States, and Europe knows
> us by no other name or title.[25]

Political experience was intertwined with military. That
had been true for the making of Dutch nationalism in the
seventeenth century; it might have been true of the Irish
and the Scottish revolts, had they been successful. Elsewhere, in eighteenth-century wars, political like military di-
rection came from the Crown, not the people. Franklin
and his associates had projected something very like a colonial government as early as 1754 with the remarkable
Albany Plan of Union. A decade later came the Stamp Act
Congress which brought together delegates from nine
colonies; among the delegates were many who were to play
stellar parts in the Revolution, even some who were to be
Founding Fathers:[26] James Otis of Massachusetts, Robert
Livingston and Philip Livingston from New York, John
Dickinson from Pennsylvania, Caesar Rodney—whose all-
night ride was to swing the vote for Independence—from
Delaware, and Christopher Gadsden and John Rutledge
from South Carolina. A few more years and Committees
of Correspondence[27] wove their network from colony to
colony. By the time of the First Continental Congress most
of the colonial leaders knew one another, and something
like an American party had come into existence. Formal
union did not come until the ratification of the Articles of
Confederation in 1781, just six months before Yorktown;
had there not been an effective union before this, there
might never have been a Yorktown.[28]

As an organized Church attracts inchoate religious sentiments and institutionalizes them into good works, and as a political party absorbs miscellaneous political sentiments and directs them to governmental purposes, so the first formal union, for all its inadequacies and infirmities, provided a focal point for latent and overt Continental sentiments. As the residuary legatee of the British Government on a continental scale, the Association and the Confederation almost inevitably concentrated and institutionalized all the potential forces of nationalism.[29] Somewhat surprisingly, Americans found themselves with a government that had, or assumed, authority to conduct a war and to make peace, own and dispose of a national domain as large as the original thirteen states, exercise jurisdiction in a score of interstate disputes, and attract to its services some of the ablest minds in the nation. They found themselves thinking "continentally"—there was a Continental Congress and a Continental Army whose soldiers were called quite simply Continentals; currency was called Continental, and there was even a Continental Fast and a Continental Thanksgiving. There was a national capital more like those of the Old World than Washington was to be for half a century, for Philadelphia was not only the political but the religious and cultural center of the nation and, for a time, its financial center as well as its most populous city.[30] And, what with the war and the Congress and the Convention, Americans found themselves with leaders who were indubitably national, and with a ready-made set of Founding Fathers, headed up by the God-like Washington.[31]

* * *

It was a revolutionary and a spectacular achievement, this creation of a nation overnight. Many of the ingredients of nationalism long thought to be essential were lacking from the beginning: no King, no Court, no aristocracy, no Capitol, no body of laws, no professional Army, no Established Church, no history, no tradition, no usable past, and as for that most essential element—territory—here was so much of it that it constituted a danger rather than an immediate asset. But if these ingredients were lacking, so thought many of the shrewdest Old World observers,

the essentials were lacking, and hopes for creating a durable union were illusory. "As to the future grandeur of
America, and its being a rising empire under one head,"
wrote Dean Josiah Tucker of Gloucester—he had opposed
the war all along and thought it as absurd as the Crusades—"it is one of the idlest and most visionary notions
that was ever conceived."[32] So, too, said the great financier
Turgot, an ardent friend of America: "in the general
union of the States I do not see a coalition, a melting of all
the parts together, making but one body, one and homo-
geneous; it is only an aggregate of parts, always too separate and preserving always a tendency to division. . . . It
is only a copy of the Dutch republic."[33] And even that ardent patriot Patrick Henry lamented that a republican government on a continental scale was "a work too great for
human wisdom."[34]‡

But it turned out that Americans could manage very
well with such ingredients as they had, and could create
the others on order. From the most heterogeneous elements, they welded together a people. Crèvecoeur himself
was able to conjure up the image of a "melting pot." They
set up independent state and national governments. Thanks
to the far-sighted provisions of the Northwest Ordinance,
extensive road building, a river system which made it easy
to link up the seaboard and the interior, and, within a few
years, steamboats and canals, they made their extensive
territory an asset rather than a debit. They got along without an Established Church, and their morals did not suffer.
They got along without a military too, and thanks to geographical isolation and to the preoccupation of Old World
powers with the French Revolution and Napoleon, they
were secure until the crisis of 1812, and thereafter for a
generation. Jefferson could say in his First Inaugural Ad-

‡ Note Alexis de Tocqueville's prediction half a century later:
  "Whatever faith I may have in the perfectibility of man, until human
nature is altered, and man wholly transformed, I shall refuse to
believe in the duration of a government which is called upon to hold
together forty different peoples, disseminated over a territory equal
to one-half of Europe in extent, to avoid all rivalry, ambition and
struggles between them, and to direct their independent activity to
the accomplishment of the same designs." (*Democracy in America*,
Vol. I.)

dress that "this is the strongest government on earth . . .
the only one where every man, at the call of the law,
would fly to the standard of the law and would meet invasions of the public order as his own personal concern."
The War of 1812 was to prove that rhetoric romantic
folly, but it proved, too, that distance and size were indeed
a protection. Needless to say, they got along without a
monarchy: as Tom Paine put it, in America the Law is
King.[35] They even got along for some time without a
real capital, and if the peevish Tom Moore could write of
the residents of Washington that

> . . . nought but woods and Jefferson they see,
> Where streets should run, and sages ought to be[36]

Americans themselves were quite content with the woods,
and with Mr. Jefferson, too. They needed History and Traditions, and manufactured these more expeditiously than
any people had ever done before, so that past and present
telescoped, and yesterday became antiquity; thus Jefferson's reference in 1787 to the Articles of Confederation of
1781 as, "the good, old and venerable fabric."[37]

To an extent unimaginable in the Old World, American
nationalism was a creation of the people themselves: it was
self-conscious and self-generating. Elsewhere nationalism
was cultivated and sustained by Kings and Barons, Mar-
shals and Admirals, Prelates and clergy, Judges and Magistrates, Landlords, Proprietors, Magnates, Junkers and Sei-
gneurs, all of whom looked to the Crown and the Church
for their support. They professed loyalty to the nation as
embodied in monarch and Church, and in symbols and
traditions. They served its government, its church, and its
armed forces. Increasingly, in the eighteenth and nineteenth centuries, they were joined by the merchants,
traders, and bankers who helped formulate a special economic philosophy designed to prosper nationalism and
their own interests.

What the new United States lacked in such contributions, it made up in a popular participation, which involved most of its free population. Here it was the farmers
and frontiersmen, the fishermen and woodsmen, the shop

keepers and apprentices, the small-town lawyers (there were no barristers), the village clergy (there were no bishops), the country schoolteachers (there were no dons) who provided the warp and the woof for the fabric of nationalism. Only the large slaveholders represented the kind of widespread and continuous special interest that sustained the State or the Monarch in Europe, and these, as it turned out, contributed as much to the disintegration of the nation as to its nourishment. It was women as well as men who made the nation, for from the beginning they played a more active role in society and the economy, and even in the Church, than had been their lot in the Old World. And children, who were not only more numerous than elsewhere—for most of them survived infancy—but enjoyed greater freedom and more expansive education than did their European cousins, were prepared from childhood to take their place as citizens in a republic. It was indentured servants who, after they earned independence, blended imperceptibly into society and were accepted as equals; it was newcomers from abroad who found room (though not always welcome) in all the colonies, and who—as with the Germans and the Scots-Irish—all but created their own commonwealths within existing commonwealths. All worked the land together; they intermingled in churches and town meetings and militia training; they fought side by side against Indians and British; they moved down the valleys and across the mountains, setting up new communities and States. They erected churches and imported preachers who did not suffer for their nonconformity; they built schoolhouses where their children learned a common language and a common history out of Mr. Noah Webster's Blue-Backed Spellers and Readers. They conducted their public and private affairs under a common law and an equity which they could, themselves, change by statute, and they were guided by the same Bible where they read—in different tongues—the same moral precepts. All of this, as it turned out, provided a foundation for national unity quite as firm as that provided by Monarchy, History, and the Church in the Old World.

Nation making in the United States was not only new

and democratic, it was enlightened. If Americans did not write upon paper that was blank, neither were they condemned to be content with marginal annotations to the black-letter books of the past. Antiquity was picturesque and edifying, but originality and invention had more substantial advantages. In the Old World nations were encrusted with centuries of tradition, bound by a thousand commitments, imprisoned by a thousand precedents, hobbled by a thousand compromises, bemused by a thousand memories. The new-made nation was as yet innocent of traditions, commitments, or memories, although these were speedily provided. It was rooted not in the exhausted soil of some remote past, but in the virgin land of a new continent; it found inspiration not in dubious mythology masquerading as history (that, too, was to come) but in the public will openly proclaimed. Its institutions were fashioned not by the vicissitudes of history, but by the laws of Reason and the dictates of Common Sense. Because the United States was really new, it was free from most of those inherited ambitions and animosities which had for so long made a shambles of many of the nations of Europe. How striking that with the exception of Aaron Burr the new nation did not produce a single adventurer* of the type so familiar in the Old World—an upstart Struensee, an incendiary Wilkes, an imperious Napoleon, a quixotic Miranda.[38] Where it was unable, or unwilling, to free itself from the past—as with the iniquity of slavery—it paid a high price for its failure, a failure all the more tragic in that Jefferson and his co-workers had opened the path to emancipation and freedom. And because the nation was deliberately new-made, in the full light of day, it escaped most of the mysticism and romanticism that suffused those new nations which were quickened into life by the revolutionary spirit blowing out of France. There was romanticism, to be sure, especially in the South, which in its class structure and its yearning for the past, gravitated more and more toward the Old World; the romanticism of New England tended to be transcendental rather than traditional. It

---

* John Paul Jones, perhaps, but it can scarcely be said that the new nation produced him. He arrived in America in 1773 and left it, pretty much for good, in 1783.

required centuries of history to confer sanctity on the State, and America had no such history, so the American State escaped anything remotely resembling sanctity. Centuries of history hedged monarchy about with divinity, but there was nothing divine about the office of the President, and although Washington was doubtless immortal—Parson Weems made that clear—he was wholly unable to transmit any of his majesty or his immortality to his successors, as Bourbon did to Bourbon, Hapsburg to Hapsburg, and even, by some strange alchemy, Tudor to Stuart and Stuart to Hanoverian.

CHAPTER NINE

Americans Realize the Theories of the Wisest Writers

1

It is only against the background of the Old World Enlightenment that we can appreciate the political achievements of the men who were to be immortalized as Founding Fathers of the new Republic, their resourcefulness, their ingenuity, their wisdom, their sagacity, their virtue. Where most of the philosophes of the Old World were recruited from Naturalists and doctors and ecclesiastics—how the Abbés disported themselves in the pages of the Encyclopédie!—in America most of them were students of the law. Law was the common denominator of Jefferson and Madison, of George Mason who wrote Virginia's famous Bill of Rights and George Wythe who presided over her highest court, of Alexander Hamilton and of John Jay, of John Adams who was the chief justice of his state (he never took office, to be sure) and Roger Sherman and Oliver Ellsworth of Connecticut, and the American Blackstone, James Wilson, and his fellow commentator on the Constitution, Nathaniel Chipman of Vermont, and the two brilliant Pinckneys of South Carolina, and even of the educator and lexicographer Noah Webster. And even those who were not trained to the law, like Franklin, Dr. Rush, and Tom Paine, were more than lawyers, they were political philosophers. It was the lawyers who had written the Declaration of Independence and the Northwest Ordinance —and it was mostly lawyers who drafted the Constitutions of the States and of the new United States. For forty years every President of the new nation, with the exception of Washington himself, and every Vice-President and Secretary of State, without exception, was a lawyer. In America politics was the universal preoccupation, legislation the universal resource, and Constitutions the universal panacea.[1]

Almost everywhere in the Old World politics was the business of those who sat in the seats of power and proposed to remain there; it was the instrument of those who were entrenched in authority. How did it happen that where in Britain, Germany, France, Spain, the Law—like the Church—was an arm of the ruling classes, in America law could be independent and even radical? Perhaps it was because in colonial America the ruling class was so often associated with external authority, and once Americans had achieved their independence, politics, laws, and constitutions were cleansed of their association with King and Bishop and Class and taken over by the people. Perhaps it was because lawyers had commonly sided with the people in revolt against authority. Constitutions were not inherited, they were new-made; politics was not the private preserve of a tiny ruling class, but of a ruling class that embraced most of the population. No wonder the whole people was an interested party; no wonder politics and law were a universal preoccupation; no wonder all the philosophy was political, and all the literature, too. The imaginative writings of the English, the French, the Italians, the Germans, compare favorably with their political writings, but Revolutionary America had no imaginative writings to compare to the political writings of a Jefferson, a John Adams, a James Madison, a Tom Paine, or a James Wilson.

What a political-minded people Americans were, and legal-minded, too. They consolidated and concentrated the law, doing away with so much of the *disjecta membra* of Old World law—ecclesiastical law, administrative law, even chancery law—and they limited the reach of the common law. They invented the principle of judicial supremacy, and its instrument, judicial review; they invented an unsuspected merging and blending of the separation of powers and the balance of powers. For that matter, they invented the law school and consolidated the offices of barrister and solicitor into that of lawyer. They invented office without pageantry, administration without bureaucracy, and even—for a time—government without taxation.* They invented the modern political party.

Politically it was, quite simply, the most creative generation in modern history, and its accomplishments the most lasting. There were antecedents, to be sure: there was the deep indebtedness to the Puritan Revolution and to the "great Mr. Locke," and there was some, perhaps, to Montesquieu and to the philosophes. There was a literary and a moral debt to the ancient world, and especially to Republican Rome.[2] But what impresses us most as we reflect on Old World gestures and New World achievements is the validity of Tom Paine's observation that

> the case and circumstances of America present themselves as in the beginning of a world. . . . We have no occasion to roam for information into the obscure field of antiquity, nor hazard ourselves upon conjecture. We are brought at once to the point of seeing government begin, as if we had lived in the beginning of time.[3]

Let us, then, turn to some of the great questions that the philosophes were asking, and see how Americans answered them.

Take, for a starter, this matter that Tom Paine is speaking of, the origin of government. How the philosophers had speculated about that, Locke and Rousseau, of course, and the learned Blackstone, and the later Burke, but how blind they were, or how parochial, never looking at what was going on across the ocean. All agreed to start with Nature, and go on from there. The theme is familiar enough: how man in a state of Nature was subject to anarchy, and how men came together and drew up compacts to establish

* Needless to say, the patents on these inventions ran out long ago!

governments able to protect them. The philosophers may
not have believed it literally, but it was one of those
agreed-on fictions that enabled them to get on with the job,
and it had, besides, a romantic simplicity about it.

But in America, perhaps only in America, that was just
the way government had originated, and the way it continued to originate all through the eighteenth century and
well down into the nineteenth as well. Surely the first authenticated instance of government by compact was that
formed by the Pilgrims in the hold of the *Mayflower,* off
what William Bradford called "a hideous and desolate wilderness, full of wild beasts and wild men."[4] There men
joined together voluntarily to set up a government, writing
down the terms of the agreement and, what is more, abiding by them. Again there were antecedents: in church
compacts, in the "sea laws" of earlier centuries, in the
charters of joint-stock companies, but none of these were
directly political, and none had brought lasting governments into being. All through the colonial era Americans
went from compact to compact—the Fundamental Laws
of Connecticut of 1639, the "Solemn Compact" at Portsmouth of 1638, and its successor the Charter of the Providence Plantations of 1647, the Pennsylvania Charter of
Privileges of 1701[5] (not quite so clear a case, to be sure),
and thereafter a score of compacts and agreements on one
frontier after another. How familiar it all is, this spectacle
of simple farmers gathering together, even under the oak
trees that a Locke and a Rousseau imagined,[6] and resort-
ing to first principles to draw up solemn compacts of
government.[7] Here are the people of the three Connecticut
River towns providing themselves with Fundamental Orders:

> Well knowing that where a people are gathered to-
> gether the word of God requires that to mayntayne
> the peace and union of such people there should be
> an orderly and decent Government established ac-
> cording to God, to order and dispose of the affayres
> of the people at all seasons as occation shall require;
> doe therefore assotiate and conjoyne our selves to be
> one Publick State or Commonwealth. . . .[8]

And how simply John Clarke and his Narragansett associates put it in their Plantation Agreement:

> It is agreed by this Present Assembly thus Incorporate, and by this present Act declared, that the Forme of Government Established in Providence Plantations is Democraticall; that is to say, a Government held by ye Free and Voluntarie Consent of all, or the greater Parte of the Free Inhabitants.[9]

Or listen to the citizens of the little town of Petersham, resolving on the new Constitution of Massachusetts of 1778, which had been submitted to them for approval or rejection:

> The Inhabitants humbly show, that it is their opinion that it will be of little avail for this people to shed their blood and spend their treasure in opposing foreign tyranny, if after all, we should fix a basis of government partial, unsafe, and not fit for the enjoyment of free and virtuous men. We think that God, in his providence has now opened a door, possibly the only one that this state will ever have, for the laying of a foundation for its prosperity, peace and glory.[10]

More familiar is the formal, almost sedate language of George Mason in the Virginia Bill of Rights, familiar, but still able to stir us:

> That Government is . . . instituted for the common benefit, protection, and security of the people, nation, or community; of all the various modes and forms of government, that is best which is capable of producing the greatest degree of happiness and safety, and is most effectually secured against the danger of maladministration; and that when any government shall be found inadequate or contrary to these purposes, a majority of the community hath an indubitable, unalienable, and indefeasible right to reform, alter or abolish it. . . .[11]

So said the Founding Fathers of Maryland: "All government of right originates from the people, is founded in compact only"; so said the Constitution makers of Massachusetts: "the body politic is formed by a voluntary association of individuals; it is a social compact by which the whole people covenants with each citizen, and each citizen with the whole people. . . ." It was, in short, the common sense of the matter.[12]

How moving, too, is the spectacle of state making on the Kentucky frontier of 1775. Richard Henderson had called a meeting of delegates from the four tiny settlements—Boonesboro, Harrodsburg, Boiling Springs, and St. Asaph's Station—and thus addressed them:

> You are called and assembled at this time for a noble and honorable purpose. . . . You perhaps are fixing the palladium of the future. . . . If any doubt remain amongst you with respect to the force of efficacy of whatever laws you now or hereafter make, be pleased to consider that all power is originally in the people . . . and that it is not to be supposed that a people anxious and desirous of having laws made who approve of the method of choosing delegates or representatives to meet in general convention for that purpose, can want the necessary and concomitant virtue to carry them into execution.[13]

Down in frontier Georgia a group of patriots called upon all the men of the Province to foregather at the Liberty pole in front of Tondee's Tavern, in Savannah; those who met found in the laws of Nature authority to call another meeting which, in defiance of the royal governor's fulminations, set up a provisional government.[14] The process continued all across the continent as a spontaneous, almost an instinctive, gesture. The pioneers of Texas, when threatened by the armies of Santa Anna, gathered at the happily named village of Washington and found authority in public support to declare independence and draw up a constitution.[15] Out in California a small group of "peaceable and good citizens" took it upon themselves to establish a "Republican government which shall secure to us Civil & Religious liberty, which shall encourage virtue and literature, which shall leave unshackled by fetters Agriculture, Commerce and Mechanism."[16] Less concerned for "literature and virtue," but clearly more for unfettered Agriculture, Iowa squatters set up their own governments to protect them against the pretensions of existing law.[17] And in distant Oregon settlers along the banks of the Willamette organized "Wolf meetings" which were somehow transformed into constitutional conventions and anticipated the actions of the United States Congress.[18] Along the road to Oregon, pioneers contrived both law and courts to deal with the special problems of the Trail,[19] and in rowdy mining camps of the Far West argonauts imagined a mandate to write their own laws. For, as Senator William Morris Stewart, himself a miner, recalled, they

> found no laws governing the possession and occupation of mines but the common laws of right. . . . They were forced to make laws for themselves. The reason and justice of the laws they formed challenge the admiration of all who investigate them. Each mining district . . . formed its own rules and adopted its own customs. . . . These regulations were thoroughly democratic in character.[20]

What John Jay had said to the people of New York was both history and prophecy:

> The Americans are the first people whom Heaven has favored with an opportunity of deliberating upon, and choosing, the forms of government under which they shall live. All other constitutions have derived their existence from violence or accidental circumstances, and are therefore probably more distant from their perfection, which, though beyond our reach, may nevertheless be approached under the guidance of reason and experience.[21]

And Dr. Ramsay congratulated the people of South Carolina in almost the same words:

> We are the first people in the world who have had it in their power to choose their own form of govern-

ment. Constitutions were forced on all other nations
by the will of their conquerors, or they were formed
by accident, caprice, or the influence of prevailing
parties or particular persons. Our deliberations . . .
were directed . . . by the polestar of the public
good.[22]

True enough, for from the very beginning all of this
state making had been institutionalized. That was, everywhere, the most remarkable achievement of the Americans
—they took old familiar ideas that no other people had
ever put into effect, and institutionalized them.[23] The institution here was, of course, the constitutional convention. It
was John Adams who, more than any other individual, put
it all together and gave it that form which it was to retain
for generations—Adams who had little faith in democracy,
but none in any other principle of government.[24] The constitutional convention, which has some claim to be the
most original political institution of modern times, legalized revolution. It enabled men to do what they had not
before been able to do peacefully and legally—alter or
abolish government, and institute new governments "deriv-
ing their just powers from the consent of the governed." It
was Massachusetts that provided the model, under the
prodding and guidance of Adams. "We had a People of
more Intelligence, Curiosity, and Enterprise," said he,
"who must all be consulted, and We must realize the
Theories of the Wisest Writers, and invite the People to
erect the whole Building with their own hands, upon the
broadest foundation."[25] And that is just what they proceeded to do. Freemen over twenty-one came together in
their town meetings and voted whether to call a convention to write a Constitution. The vote of the towns was
affirmative, and delegates chosen for the task of constitution making, and for no other, met in convention and
drew up a Constitution. That Constitution was then sent
back to the people, assembled once again in their town
meetings, to be debated and voted upon, clause by clause.
What eloquence and what wisdom in the resolutions from
these towns, framed, many of them by men who were simple and almost unlettered, but who had, nevertheless, a

firm grasp of the fundamental principles of politics. Hear the yeomen of Berkshire county:

> In free States the people are to be considered as the fountain of power. And the social Tie as founded in Compact. The people at large are endowed with alienable and unalienable Rights. Those which are unalienable are those which belong to Conscience respecting the worship of God and the practice of Christian Religion, and that of being determined or governed by the Majority in the Institution or formation of Government. The alienable are those which may be delegated for the Common good, or those which are for the common good to be parted with.

Or listen to the farmers of Pittsfield instructing their delegates:

> You will endeavor that all those unalienable and important rights which are essential to true liberty and form the basis of government in a free States, shall be inserted: particularly that this people have a right to adopt that form of government which appears to us most eligible, and best calculated to promote the happiness of our selves and posterity; that as all men by nature are free, and have no dominion one over another, and all power originates in the people, so, in a state of civil society, all power is founded in compact; that every man has an unalienable right to enjoy his own opinion in matters of religion and to worship God in that manner that is agreeable to his own sentiments without any control whatsoever. . . .[26]

The first Constitution was turned down, but after another try a Constitution was duly adopted.[27] "The people of Massachusetts,"† wrote Thomas Dawes, Jr., "have reduced to practice the wonderful theory. A numerous peo-

---

† We should not be too romantic about this. "The people of Massachusetts," indeed, but probably only one out of every four adult males entitled to vote in Massachusetts proper bothered to do so, while in Maine the vote was not more than one out of twenty.

ple have convened in a state of nature and, like our idea of
the patriarchs, have deputed a few fathers of the land to
draw up for them a glorious covenant. It has been drawn.
The people have signed it with rapture."[28]

Over in Manchester the firebrand Thomas Cooper—he
was already planning to migrate to America—wrote if not
with rapture, then with some enthusiasm:

> While the fermentations of a civil and reactionary
> contest were yet operating upon their minds, amidst
> the warmth of feeling incidental to that state of
> things, they have examined with sober attention the
> imperfections of their national and subordinate civil
> establishments; they reflected with due seriousness on
> the numerous inconveniences which those imper-
> fections had produced, and upon the awful scenes in
> which they would probably be called upon to suffer
> or to act if their civil constitutions should continue
> unamended; and they have since exhibited to the
> world the new and interesting spectacle of a whole
> people meeting, as it were, in their political plain, and
> voluntarily imposing upon themselves the wholesome
> and necessary restraints of just governments.[29]

"Exhibited to the world." But not all the world paid attention or understood the moral. "The very idea of the fabrication of a new government is enough to fill us with dis-
gust or horror" wrote Edmund Burke in 1790.[30] For him
the constitutional conventions had labored in vain.

2

Suppose you fabricate a fundamental law, is it binding
forever? Do the dead govern the living?[1] So said Edmund
Burke: Mankind is bound by its original compact "to the
end of time," and an agreement, once made is sacred and
perpetual, its validity warranted not by popular approval
or ratification but by the most sacred of all principles, that
of prescription. Prescription justified, nay exalted, ancient
wrongs as ancient rights. It threw an aura of rationality

over the irrational, transformed prejudice into respect for tradition, outlawed innovation and excommunicated the innovators. To Burke, prescription was the most valid of all titles, "not only to property but to government." Away, then, with the notion that men could contumaciously break with the past, that they could new-make constitutions and laws, for "to discredit the only form of government which we either possess or can project, what is this but to destroy all government? And this is anarchy."[2]

But to most Americans the idea of revision and amendment seemed the common sense of the matter. They were not assigned by Nature, nor committed by principle, nor conditioned by experience to an inherited order of things, or to a constitution that was fixed and unalterable. They lived in a world that was open and malleable, a world of their own making if they but set themselves to the task. Their own lives, and the lives of their forebears, in the New World had been a continuous break with the past, a continuous revision of inherited institutions and constitutions, a continuous exercise of resourcefulness, and they took for granted that those swift currents of change which had brought them to the New World and had transformed their way of life, would flow as swiftly in the future as in the past. Their whole experience was new, their coming to America and their enjoyment of inexhaustible bounty; religious liberty was new, as was self-government and a classless society. Prescription—it was a term they never used—did not justify the continuation of old methods and practices in a new world; after all, why come to America if you assumed that everything was to go on as it always had in the past? Was Crèvecoeur's Farmer supposed to accept that notion when he carved out a farm for himself from the wilderness—a farm happily free of quit rents and allodial dues? Was the printer's apprentice Benjamin Franklin supposed to accept that, when he "stood before five kings, and sat down with one," or when he signed— one might almost say dictated—a treaty of peace with a government resting on Prescription? Was Colonel Washington supposed to acquiesce in that when he found himself outranked by the veriest lieutenant in an Army gov-

erned wholly by tradition? Was Jefferson to believe that
when he looked westward from Monticello and dreamed
of the day—a day he himself ushered in—when there
would be land enough for his descendants "to the thousandth and thousandth generation?"[3] Was the dismissed
exciseman, Thomas Paine, to endorse that principle when
he became the penman of the American Revolution and
the prophet of an English revolution *manqué?* In 1795
he told the Dutch that

> Every age and generation is, and must be, as a matter
> of right, as free to act for itself in all cases, as the age
> and generation that preceded it. The vanity and pre-
> sumption of governing beyond the grave is the most
> ridiculous and insolent of all tyrannies. Man has no
> property in man, neither has one generation a prop-
> erty in the generations that are to follow.[4]

Clearly the New World was the worst possible market to
which you could carry this shop-worn bric-a-brac of Prescription and Tradition. Americans could build on precedent when they wanted to, and they did, in their Constitutions;‡ but they took care to provide a method for
rejecting precedent and altering constitutions. After all,
while law was doubtless made by God or Nature, constitutions were made by men, and could be unmade by them
—that is what Jefferson meant when he spoke of "altering
or abolishing government and instituting new government." As early as 1785 he had elaborated on this idea,
and thereafter it became with him something of *idée fixe.*
It was Dr. Richard Gem[5] who first raised the problem with
him in a practical fashion—the eccentric English physician
who preferred the company of the French philosophes and
who, like Tom Paine and Barlow and Jefferson himself,
meddled in French politics. "Sir," he was accustomed to
say, "I am of a very serious turn," and one of the things
he was very serious about was this question whether one

‡ Indeed, in time precedents came to loom larger in American law
than in English, and certainly than in continental: to this day American judges cite precedent more frequently than do English.

generation had a right to bequeath its debts to succeeding generations—debts contracted, more often than not, for useless wars, immoral extravagances, or corruptions. The more Mr. Jefferson thought over this problem, the larger the dimensions it took on, for clearly any principle that controlled the right of the dead to assign debts to the living must control other and more fundamental relations between the dead and the living. He was thinking of France rather than of the United States, but it was to his friend Madison that he communicated his conclusions. "The earth belongs always to the living generation," he wrote from Paris in 1789.

> They manage it, then, and what proceeds from it, as they please, during their usufruct. They are masters, too, of their own persons, and consequently may govern them as they please. But persons and property make the sum of the objects of government. The constitution, and the laws of their predecessors are extinguished, then, in their natural course with those whose will gave them being.[6]

What this meant was that "every generation and every law naturally expires" after thirty-four years. A new and better calculation quickly reduced this to nineteen years!

Madison protested that the application of such a principle would be both unjust and impracticable, but he did not challenge the validity of the abstract principle. "On the contrary," he wrote,

> it would give me singular pleasure to see it first announced to the world in a law of the U. States and always kept in view as a salutary restraint on living generations from unjust and unnecessary burdens on their successor.[7]

But, he added with characteristic realism, that "this is a pleasure however which I have no hope of enjoying." On the matter of debts, Jefferson was persuaded and perhaps too on the matter of practicality. But on the larger issue he did not give way; if anything, his convictions hardened over the years:

> Some men look at constitutions with sanctimonious reverence [he wrote to Samuel Kercheval in 1816] and see them, like the Ark of the Covenant, too sacred to be touched. They ascribe to the men of the preceding age a wisdom more than human, and suppose what they did to be beyond amendment. . . . But I know that laws and institutions must go hand in hand with the progress of the human mind. As that becomes more developed, more enlightened, as new discoveries are made, new truths disclosed, and manners and opinions change with the change of circumstances, institutions must advance.

And from this it follows that

> Each generation is as independent of the one preceding as that was of all that had gone before. It has then, like them, a right to choose for itself the form of government it believes most promotive of its own happiness . . . and a solemn opportunity of doing this every nineteen or twenty years should be provided by the constitution so that it may be handed on, with periodic repairs, from generation to generation.[8]

And shortly before his death, Jefferson asked his old friend Major Cartwright, over in London—there is something very touching about this exchange between two friends who had fought for freedom, each in his own way, for sixty years—

> Can one generation bind another, and all others in succession forever? I think not. The Creator has made the earth for the living, not the dead. . . . Nothing is unchangeable, but the inherent and unalienable rights of man.[9]

Although to most Europeans the difficulties of new-making government seemed insuperable as well as intolerable, they did not, in fact, prove in the least serious. In the Old World—certainly on the Continent—there was no way to change fundamental law except by violence: that was the method the French used, and others, too, in the Age of Revolution. But Americans made clear that you could legitimize revolution. "Show another government," said Dr. Charles Jarvis in the Massachusetts ratifying convention,

> in which such wise precautions have been taken to secure to the people the right of making such alterations and amendments, in a peaceable way, as experience shall have proved to be necessary. In other countries . . . the history of their respective revolutions had been written in blood; it is only in this that any great or important change in our political situation has been affected without political commotions.[10]

The learned James Wilson—James the Caledonian he was called—was even more lyrical as he contemplated the deliberate creation of a national constitution:

> The science, even of government itself, seems yet to be almost in its state of infancy. Governments, in general, have been the result of force, of fraude, and accident. After a period of six thousand years has elapsed since the creation the United States exhibit to the world the first instance . . . of a nation, unattacked by external force, unconvulsed by domestic insurrections, assembling voluntarily, deliberating fully, and deciding calmly concerning the system of government under which they would wish that they and their posterity should live.[11]

In fact, both the constitution-making process and the amending process proved simple, and even, in time, rather dull: who now notices state conventions looking to revising fundamental law or thinks them revolutionary? South Carolina, the most conservative of American States, managed to get herself no less than three constitutions (that is, to abolish governments and set up new governments) during the Revolutionary years; Georgia required two conventions to get herself one new Constitution, just as Massachusetts had required three conventions to get her Constitution. Pennsylvania got rid of the Constitution that had caused both John Adams and the Abbé Mably such anguish, and got herself a respectable one.[12] As for Amendments, eight of the original States made Constitutional provision for amendments or for general Constitution revision: two of these—Pennsylvania and Vermont—created Boards of Censors which were to report on the health of the Constitution and make recommendations for amendment or revision. It is a commentary on the self-constraint of American democracy that all of these called for more than a simple majority to change the constitution and that some required action by successive legislative bodies.[13] Mr. Burke should have noticed that when legalized, and institutionalized, revolution could be conservative.

That is one reason a true conservative like General Washington could rejoice in the American technique of revolution. "Whether the constitutional door that is opened for amendment," he wrote, in that portion of his Inaugural Address which he failed to use, "be not the wisest and apparently the happiest expedient that has ever been suggested by human prudence, I leave to every unprejudiced mind to determine."[14] And, as if to vindicate him, the very first Congress, certainly a body of prudent men, added no less than twelve amendments to the Constitution, ten of which were eventually ratified by the States. These amendments were designed not to enlarge the scope of government, but to restrict its powers: so much for John Adams's argument that government is always eager to aggrandize power.

3

Clearly, Tom Paine was right when he asserted that it was the UNION OF THE STATES that was essential for the creation of an American nation and an American character. But how create a union out of thirteen States, each with its own history and its own character, and each proclaiming its own independence and sovereignty and writing that principle into the Articles of Confederation? Yet the Articles were themselves ambiguous. The same article that asserted that "each State retains its sovereignty, freedom and independence," also hedged by adding that each State retained only those powers and rights "not by this Confederation expressly delegated to the United States," and what is more, another provision of the Articles required that "every state shall abide by the determination of the United States in Congress assembled on all questions which by this confederation are submitted to them," and, added that "the Articles of this confederation shall be inviolably observed by every State, and the Union shall be perpetual." (Art. 13.)

All very confusing, this. Was the new United States a confederation or was it a nation? That was a fascinating question, and as it turned out, later generations were to return to it in crisis after crisis, most fatefully in 1860. Was there, perhaps, something between a confederation and a nation, something that could preserve at once State sovereignty and national sovereignty?

It was clear enough by the time of the Treaty of Paris that the loose confederation of States was not working very well; it was equally clear that Americans were not yet prepared to embrace, as an alternative, the Old World model of centralized nation-states. Was there perhaps something in between—something that could satisfy the interests and quiet the fear of particularism and fulfill the demands of nationalism without sacrificing those liberties for whose vindication the Americans had fought a war of independence? Could they solve that problem which had for centuries baffled and confounded statesmen of the Old World: the problem of imperial organization or—to put it in American terms—of federalism?[1]

They could and they did.

If Americans did not actually invent federalism, they were able to take out an historical patent on it. Nothing more familiar than the history of federalism in ancient Greece, and the Fathers never tired of ringing the changes on the Amphictyonic, the Lycian, the Achaean, and the Aetolian Leagues.[2] Madison prepared himself to be Father to the Constitution by an intensive study of all confed-

erations, ancient and modern: you can read the results in
three learned papers of the *Federalist*.³ The Fathers knew,
too, the sorry story of the Italian, the Hanseatic, the Hel-
vetic Leagues, the Confederation of the United Netherlands, and the history of the Holy Roman Empire, even
then in such disarray. All of these had suffered from the
same defect. They were too weak to protect themselves
against foreign aggression or domestic dissension. That was
not surprising—not to John Adams and James Wilson, or
James Madison, for they saw what European students had
failed to see, that none of these unions were true federalisms but mere associations or confederacies, and that the
difference between confederation and federalism was not
one of degree but of kind. It remained for Americans to
create a federal government strong enough to maintain itself against both foreign and domestic foes, but not too
strong for the liberty of its citizens or the prosperity of
local self-government.

It all seems easy enough, now that it has been done and
has spread around the globe. But it was not easy at the
time, and it is relevant that for all their experience in politics, for all the wisdom of their statesmen and philosophes,
and for all the clamorous importunity of the problems that
challenged them, neither the Germans nor the Italians nor
the British had been able to imagine or to fabricate a federal system.

Two problems confronted those delegates to the Federal
Convention in Philadelphia who were to be rewarded for
their labors by becoming Founding Fathers. First, a good
federal system required a careful and judicious distinction
between general and local powers and the proper alloca-
tion of each to the appropriate government. By 1787 the
Fathers had enough experience with this problem—after
all it was the central issue of the debate with the Mother
Country—to work out a sensible solution which held up
very well until the Civil War. Even then the failure was
not in the division of authority between central and state
governments, but in the inability of the central government
to persuade or coerce recalcitrant States to abide by the
terms of the division. That was the second and, as it turned
out, by far the most difficult problem: sanctions. For sup-

posing an ideal division of authority between local and national governments, what guarantee was there that each government (or complex of governments) would confine itself to its proper sphere and fulfill its obligations in that sphere? And was it not inevitable that spokesmen for state and nation would differ on what were the proper spheres of action and the proper limits on action, as they would differ on both the scope and the thrust of those powers which, of necessity, they shared? Was it not instinct in all governments to aggrandize power at the expense of both people and governments; was it not inevitable that the national government and the States would all seek to enlarge their powers at the expense of the others, and that the liberties of the people would be the victims of these rivalries, confusions, and lust for power?

If you accepted the Old World as your model and your guide, all this was indeed inevitable. But suppose, instead, you repudiated the experience of the Old World, ancient and modern alike, and struck out on your own. What the Fathers did when confronted by this ancient problem of confederations, alliances, leagues, was to work out a new principle and translate it into a new institution. The new principle was simple enough, but it was one of the supreme strokes of genius in the history of politics. It was to substitute for the rival authorities and claims of state and nation a single authority—the people of the United States, from whom came all power, and who, in their sovereign capacity, delegated appropriate powers to state and nation. What emerged was not conflicting sovereignties, but a single sovereign capable of solving conflicts within its jurisdiction. Those conflicts were to be solved not by the use of force, but by law: as Alexander Hamilton put it, "the mild influence of the magistracy for the violent and sanguinary agency of the sword."[4] Force was not to be used against state or nation, but against individuals who violated the law of the land. Hamilton put that well, too: "The great and radical vice . . . in the existing confederation," he wrote, "is in the principle of legislation for States or Governments, in their corporate or collective capacities, and as contradistinguished from the individuals of which they consist."[5] The new institution was American federalism, and what distinguished it from all previous federalisms, was precisely this recognition that, as Madison pointed out, "the federal and state governments are in fact but different agents and trustees of the people, constituted with different powers, and designed for different purposes."[6] Or, as he explained more simply to Mr. Jefferson over in Paris:

> It was generally agreed that the objects of union could not be secured by any system founded on the principle of a confederation of Sovereign States. A voluntary observation of the federal law by all the members could never be hoped for. A compulsive one could evidently never be reduced to practice, and if it could, involved equal calamities to the innocent and the guilty, the necessity of a military force . . . and, in general, a scene resembling much more a civil war than the administration of a regular Government. Hence was embraced the alternative of a Government which, instead of operating on the States, should operate without their intervention, on the individuals composing them.[7]

Congeries of states, like the Italian or the German, had never heretofore been able to contrive anything like a real federal union, nor had confederations like those of the Low Countries or Switzerland solved the problem. Philosophically, the basic reason for their failure was not so much in the strength of particularism, as in the elementary fact that their collective imaginations could not conceive of a political system in which a sovereign people delegated powers to governments. The Americans were able to solve the problem with greater ease in part because local attachments were not so deep-rooted, in part because their long experience in the Empire had familiarized them with the distribution of powers along central and local lines, but primarily because the notion that sovereignty—or power—is inherent in the people was easy for them to understand and to apply.

Federalism contributed greatly, if inadvertently, to the solution of that problem to which Montesquieu had devoted some of his most luminous pages, and which had so troubled John Adams that he had dedicated to it over a thousand pages, vastly informative but not luminous—the problem of balance in government. It was not the purpose of the authors of the new United States Constitution to vindicate Montesquieu, nor to assuage and support Mr. Adams, and, notwithstanding his obsessive preoccupation with balance, Adams himself had, rather oddly, not thought of federalism as a method for achieving that balance which would secure a sound foundation for government. If he had, perhaps he would not have laid waste his powers quite so extravagantly on the issue of a unicameral versus a bicameral legislature, as if that made any real difference.[8] As it turned out, the rise of the political party —another thing which Adams had not foreseen—played hob with those balances implicit in the separation of powers.[9] But federalism provided a new and more powerful balance than had as yet been contrived or even imagined, a balance between states, between sections, and between state and nation.

Madison who, in his quiet way, saw so much farther than Adams, saw something of this. "In a single republic," he wrote,

all the power surrendered by the people is submitted to the administration of a single government; and the usurpations are guarded against by a division of the government into distinct and separate departments. In the compound republic of America, the power surrendered by the people is first divided between two distinct governments, and then the portion allotted to each subdivided among distinct and separate departments. Hence a double security arises to the rights of the people. The different governments will control each other at the same time that each will be controlled by itself.[10]

Montesquieu had taught that large territories must inevitably be ruled by despotic governments. By fragmenting the American empire into manageable units, each in charge of its own internal affairs, American federalism made that principle an anachronism. Federalism contrib-

uted no less dramatically to the development of democracy
in the New World. By fragmenting territory and diffusing
political and constitutional authority into scores of centers,
it enlarged and energized the effective scope of self-government. Just as Americans had compensated politically for
their meager population, by involving in their governmental enterprises almost the whole of the white adult
population, so they compensated for their lack of great
sophisticated centers of power like London and Paris, and
for a ruling class of Magnates or Lords or bureaucrats, by
creating first fourteen and then—within the lifetime of
Jefferson and Adams—another twelve centers of political
authority, each with its own problems, its own interests, its
own parties, and its own leadership, and each capable of
developing independent political enterprises and experiments. Thus, by a single stroke, as it were, the Americans
provided a new foundation for self-government.[11]

Closely related to the problem of imperial organization
was the problem of colonialism—a problem so immense
and so disorderly that not a single European power had
come up with anything remotely like a solution to it. Britain had done a bit better than most, but as the American
Revolution testified, she had not done well enough. How
troublesome colonialism had been, ever since the beginning of European expansion into the New World—how
troublesome it was to be for centuries to come, with European expansion into the continents of Africa and Asia;
how it had confounded not only statesmen, administrators,
and economists, but theologians and philosophers as
well.[12] Each of the great powers had its own string of
colonies scattered about the globe, and some of the smaller
nations, too, Portugal and Denmark among them and Holland whose empire was so prosperous. Every government
expected colonies to fit into a system profitable for the
Mother Country, and every European people took for
granted that Providence had somehow given them the right
to rule over distant peoples and to exploit them at will.[13]
What Franklin said of the English was even more true of
the French, the Spanish, the Dutch, that "Every Man in
England seems to consider himself as a piece of a Sovereign over America; seems to jostle himself into the Throne

with the King, and talks of OUR Subjects in the Colonies."[14]

You might think British rule in America benevolent enough, and so it was most of the time, but it was not mere rhetoric to say that the Americans "snuffed the approach of tyranny in every tainted breeze," for they knew that the breeze that blew across Ireland was heavy with the taint of tyranny and corruption,[15] and if Ireland, why not Massachusetts! And what was one to say of the practices and malpractices of colonialism elsewhere—the Spanish and Portuguese in America and Africa, and the Dutch in the East Indies; what of the rule of the Russians and the Turks over their conquered and subject peoples—not colonies, these, but part of the Empire and deserving of something better than tyranny.[16] Or what of the slave trade—a trade foisted on colonies by parent countries? The Abbé Raynal wrote his *History of the Indies* in large part as an attack on the wickedness of imperialism and colonialism and slavery, but all in vain.[17] Everyone applauded Raynal, but what power gave up its colonies, or its slave trade? Denmark alone, and that because they were too costly.[18]

Were colonial possessions, then, an insoluble problem, either because of inherent difficulties of dealing with distant and subject peoples, or because of human nature?

Not at all. For American colonialism proved the easiest of all major problems to solve, and they solved it so simply that to this day not one American in a hundred knows that his country ever had colonies, much less a colonial problem.[19] They solved it by eliminating it—much the best way to solve problems—all in one decade, with a few simple resolutions and laws: the Congressional resolution of 1780, the Land Ordinances of 1784 and 1785, the Northwest Ordinance,[20] and the provisions of the Constitution for the admission of new States. And once you rid yourself of the notion that colonies were there for your benefit, and that colonials were, somehow, inferiors, how simple it all was. Then what a metamorphosis: Western territories were no longer colonies, but "distinct Republican States," with "the same rights of sovereignty, freedom and independence, as the other States," and their inhabitants were not "colonials" but free and equal citizens.

What a difference when you repudiate all the false notions of Empire, the pernicious shibboleths of Authority, the pomp and circumstance of Power, and embrace the simple principle of equality! A Viceroy of New Spain like Antonio Bucareli,[21] and the first Governor of the Northwest Territory, Arthur St. Clair,[22] ruled over domains equally extensive, and on paper they had much the same authority, but contrast their state, their repute, their dignity—and their rewards! The Viceroy had, as of right, a sumptuous palace; the Governor had to content himself with a log cabin. The Viceroy was surrounded by a swarm of servants, who ministered to his every whim, but Governor St. Clair had neither servants nor staff, though he was vouchsafed, by a niggardly government, a few deputies and interpreters to deal with a score of far-flung Indian tribes. The Viceroy ended his life loaded with honors, and with wealth, but St. Clair ended his career in bankruptcy, and his life in abject poverty, but remembering, perhaps, those words with which the inhabitants of the Ohio country had greeted him when he first took office:

> The task is truly arduous and the undertaking great, to come to so remote a country as this, to reduce forests to proper cultivation and to rear towns and cities in places explored only by natives and wild beasts; but if we persevere as we have begun, we have but little to fear.[23]

They did persevere, pioneers and politicians alike, and they had little to fear, for the United States had less trouble with successive colonies, all the way from the Ohio to the Pacific, than England had with Ireland in any decade of the century.

CHAPTER TEN

The Blessings of Liberty

1

Granted you can bring forth a nation and make a government and provide it with all the institutions essential to effective administration. But what is government without liberty, and does not history teach that whatever its form or its inspiration, government is the enemy of liberty? That is what Tom Paine pointed out in the opening lines of *Common Sense,* that "society is in every state a blessing, but government, even in its best state, is but a necessary evil; in its worst state, an intolerable one. . . . Government, like dress, is the badge of lost innocence."[1] It was not an original observation, but, alas, familiarity did not stale it.

Americans could make governments and provide them with constitutions, administration, and even political parties. But could they limit the power of the governments they made? That was, after all, the most fundamental problem: how to preserve liberty from the ravages of government. It was a problem that had engaged the anxious concern of philosophers for more than two thousand years, but it had never yet been solved to the satisfaction of those most deeply concerned: the people themselves. Everyone acknowledged that government was limited—that principle had long been a commonplace in American thought and

rhetoric, and in English, too, for that matter. As early as
1654 Roger Williams could boast that "we have long
drunk of the sup of as great liberties, as any people we can
hear of under the whole heaven."[2] A century later James
Otis defied Parliamentary authority in that speech on the
Writs of Assistance which, John Adams later recalled,
opened the Revolutionary struggle.[3] At the close of that
struggle an American, resident in London—his identity is
still uncertain—summed up America's exemption from the
burdens of the British system:

> When she was settled, . . . she was invested with the
> democratic parts of the English constitution. . . . Lit-
> tle of the personal idea of a King ever obtained in the
> western world. The Aristocratic branch of the English
> constitution . . . was there unknown. . . . She
> reaped in her humble career . . . every solid advan-
> tage which flowed from her political inheritance,
> without suffering those evils which that part of the
> parental constitution which she did not possess was
> designed to prevent. She tasted largely of political
> freedom. What never can be enjoy'd in England, she
> possessed: the freedom of Democracy without its An-
> archy.[4]

Power was limited—that was the principle that the Americans grappled to their souls: the power of Kings, of legislators, of Bishops; even God himself "is limited by law, by
the eternal laws of truth, wisdom and equity, and the everlasting tables of Right Reason."[5]

However it might be with the power of God, no secular
government in the Old World was thus limited. Imagine restraining Frederick the Great; why even Voltaire was unable to do that! Imagine trying to impose limits on the will
of Catherine the Great; not even Stanislas Poniatowski,
not even Gregory Orlov, two lovers she loaded with
honors and gifts, could do that. Imagine defying Duke
Karl Eugen of Württemberg; when the great Johannes
Moser tried that, he ended up in solitary confinement in
the fortress of Hohenweil.[6] Challenge these rulers if you
wish, but you might pay for your temerity with your head!

But the English, who had solved so many problems, had solved this one as well: how the Enlightenment adored the English! In law, no doubt, Parliament was supreme, but the power of government was in fact limited by the simple device of balancing all the interests of the realm—those of the one, the few, and the many—and of separating the executive, the legislative, and the judicial authorities. All of this was, after all, in accordance with an ancient and universally accepted principle, one that came, as Joseph Addison aptly said, "with the authority of the greatest philosopher, the most impartial historian, and the most consummate statesman of all antiquity," and everyone knew that these phrases embraced Aristotle, Polybius, and Cicero. James Harrington had celebrated the principle of the separation of powers in his *Oceana*—an idealized and not wholly fictionalized England, so widely read in America that one infatuated member of the Massachusetts Constitutional Convention had proposed that the name of the Commonwealth be changed to *Oceana*. "Government," wrote Harrington,

> is of three kinds, the government of one man, or of the better sort, or of the whole people; which, by their more learned names, are called monarchy, aristocracy and democracy. These (so the ancients) hold, through their proneness to degenerate, to be all evil. . . . The corruption of monarchy is called tyranny; that of aristocracy, oligarchy; that of democracy, anarchy. But legislators, having found these three governments at the best to be naught, have invented another, consisting of a mixture of them all, which only is good.

And more recently that Lord Bolingbroke, whom John Adams knew by heart, had pointed out that "in a constitution like ours, the safety of the whole depends on the balance of the parts, and the balance of the parts on their mutual independency of each other."[7]

But it was Montesquieu, above all, who made clear that this principle of the separation of powers was indeed the distinguishing feature of the British Constitution, Lords,

Commons, and Crown, each restraining the other, the judiciary independent, all the interests of the Kingdom beautifully balanced in the process, and liberty rising triumphant from it all. How discerning of Montesquieu to see this, and how wise of the British thus to fragment political power in order to frustrate tyranny. And what an incalculable debt Americans owed to Montesquieu, and to the Mother Country, for setting so improving an example to them, and to the rest of the world.[8] How odd, too, that with all these limitations on the abuse of power, it should have been necessary for the Americans to revolt!

When we look more closely into the British situation, we discover that there was no such separation of powers as Montesquieu imagined, and for that matter, no such balance of interests as a hundred complacent Englishmen boasted. For Britain had, after all, no fixed constitution—that was one thing the Americans were constantly complaining about—and the Declaration of Rights did not in fact go very far, nor, for all its moral authority, did it command legal sanctions. Parliament was, after all, supreme. "True it is," wrote Professor Blackstone, "that what the Parliament doth, no authority upon earth can undo."[9] Certainly that was true for the colonies; just read the Declaratory Act of 1776, with its resounding assertion that "Parliament . . . had, hath, and of right out to have, full power and authority . . . to bind the colonies and people of America . . . in all cases whatsoever."[10] To which branch of the government were the Americans to appeal against that sweeping legislative fiat? And as for a balance of interests, even as the British were congratulating each other on the perfect balance of interests that reflected, in government, the mechanisms of Nature herself, George III was mixing freely in legislative business, spending lavishly from his civil list to buy seats in the House, and using his vast patronage to corrupt members. Not to be outdone, Lords and Nabobs vied with each other to make sure that the constitutional independence of members of the Commons would give way, when desirable, to the wishes of patrons.[11] Edmund Burke fulminated against this perversion of principle in his "Letter to Gentlemen in Brisol," but he lost his seat for his folly.[12] And as for the vaunted independence of the judiciary, could that be seriously maintained when for over a century no Court dared challenge an Act of Parliament, and when the great Mansfield thought it quite proper to retain his chief-justiceship even after he entered the Ministry as a member of the Cabinet? Even Montesquieu admitted that the judiciary of Britain was, "in some measure, next to nothing."[13]

At the very beginning of the century one Humphrey Mackworth observed that the separate powers of Kings, Lords and Commons, "are like the three perfect conchords in musick, which being exactly tuned to one another upon proper instruments make admirable harmony."[14] That was all very well for those who accepted the "principles of harmony" that had been formulated by the three players. But what if you did not? What if you challenged both the principles and the "conchords" that were based upon them? That is what happened, not in America alone, but in Ireland where the word harmony was rather a bad joke, in Scotland which was increasingly neglected, even in England itself where large segments of the people were excluded from the performance altogether.[15]

It was natural, almost inevitable, that Americans should be persuaded by the wisdom of Harrington, the authority of Locke, the eloquence of Bolingbroke, the insight of Montesquieu, to accept the twin doctrines of separation and of balance. But was it not all an illusion, this vast intellectual fabric, an illusion designed to lull its victims into a state of euphoria? For when you looked at the workings of the British political system quite simply, and through your own eyes, what was it that you saw? Not a separation of powers, and not a balance of interests, but powers constantly invaded by their rivals, and interests that, far from being balanced, were not even represented at all.

The classical principle of balance of interests[16] was based on a series of assumptions that were questionable and, in all likelihood, mistaken, and was supported by results that did not actually prosper the commonwealth but only a handful of self-selected beneficiaries. There was first the assumption of the innate and ineradicable depravity of man. It was a familiar Christian doctrine, reinvigorated now by Puritan theology. Listen to "the judicious Hooker" on *Ecclesiastical Polity:*

> Laws politic, ordained for external order, are never framed as they should be, unless presuming the will of man to be inwardly obstinate, rebellious and averse from all obedience unto the sacred laws of his nature [and] man to be in regard to his depraved mind little better than a wild beast, they do accordingly provide . . . so to frame his outward actions that they be no hindrance unto the common good for which societies are instituted.[17]

How could this gloomy doctrine survive in the sunlight of the Enlightenment? Yet it did. It cast off its religious cowl and took on secular garb, and with this challenge it suffered a certain loss of dignity and of intellectual toughness and took on a narrow and even a vindictive character. More, it laid itself open to the suspicion of insincerity. For did Bolingbroke, did Pope, did Alexander Hamilton and John Adams really believe that they themselves were depraved? Probably not, but they believed that the rest of mankind was depraved and formulated their political philosophies on the basis of that assumption.

Or there was the assumption that power inevitably and invariably corrupts, and that all men in high office would abuse their power. History provided some support for this hypothesis, to be sure, but even Plutarch had not fallen into the error of supposing that all of his Noble Greeks and Romans were monsters of depravity, and English and American readers alike rejoiced in Lycurgus and Themistocles and Aristides the Just, in Cato and Cincinnatus and Marcus Aurelius; when they appeared as writers, they liked to assume these Greek and Roman names. And if the English stage was not quite so crowded with such paragons of virtue, the American was: How could Adams or Hamilton and the other "men of little faith" believe that Washington was depraved or Jefferson corrupt?

Equally popular, but equally fallacious, was the assumption that the body politic is irretrievably divided into warring interests—the interests of the one, the few, and the many; of the rich, the middling, and the poor; of land, trade and finance; of the orthodox and the dissenters—and that each of these could be controlled only by being counterpoised to the others.[18] Where, then, was the commonwealth? For this assumption conceded that each major interest in society was, in a sense, sovereign, and that each must be represented as a quasi-sovereign body dealing with the others, as sovereign nations dealt with each other, and that out of this intricate balance would emerge if not a peace then at least a *modus vivendi*.

Perhaps most illogical of all was the assumption that you could frustrate the ambitions, tame the passions, circumvent the selfishness, greed, and vanity of corrupt men by resort to mechanical contrivances, as if the contrivances themselves would not be controlled precisely by the men who were selfish and greedy and corrupt!

Whatever might be said for "balance" in England, it was clearly inapplicable to the realities of American life and alien to the emerging American character. The idea of a division of society into the one, the few, and the many simply had no meaning in America. The American theory recognized but one society (among whites), one body politic, and one sovereignty—the people. It was, according to the theories that Americans were busy translating into constitutional reality, the whole people that delegated the exercise of sovereignty to various functionaries, executive, legislative, and judicial. These functionaries had no inherent power, only delegated power. They were not expected to represent independent interests, but were presumed to represent the common interest. James Madison put it with characteristic directness: "In Europe charters of liberty have always been granted by power. America has set the example of charters of power granted by liberty."[19]

The difference, too, was one of principle. The purpose of balance was to protect traditional interests; the purpose of separation was to protect the liberties of the people against the usurpations of government. Because balance represented existing interests and institutions, it inevitably favored and sustained whatever was prescriptive and vested: separation of powers left it up to the people to nourish or advance such general interests as they cherished, while preserving the liberties of the individual against those who championed special interests. The British system was based on a recognition of exterior divisions which might just as easily set interest against interest as reconcile them; the American, on interior or structural divisions designed to control the mechanisms of government, not to be the government. On the surface, the system of balance seemed dynamic and organic and that of the separation of powers static and mechanical. But as it turned out it was the American that was organic and the British that—during the Revolutionary era—was static. It was the American that accommodated itself most readily to the will of the people, the British that limited the expression of that will.

Nor had the American experience with balancing interests between Mother Country and colonies been such as to encourage imitation. Were the interests of Virginia planters, New England merchants, pioneer farmers, wilderness fur traders, really balanced against those of British factors, merchants, shipbuilders, and land speculators, by the magic of "virtual representation"? Were the interests of the colonials in freeing themselves from the curse of slavery fairly balanced against the importunate claims of the Royal African Company which found expression in the repeated exercise of the Royal Disallowance?[20] Or were the interests of Presbyterians in Pennsylvania and Baptists in North Carolina nicely balanced against the claims and prerogatives of the Church of England in these Colonies? Not at all. "They have been deaf to the voice of justice and consanguinity"—that was the verdict of Jefferson's Declaration on Parliament and the interests it represented, and it was a verdict endorsed by representatives of every one of the colonies and—where the slave trade and religious establishments were concerned—by History, too.

It would of course be absurd to suppose that America was free of conflicting interests; what other country had so many sections, so many regions, so many political divisions, so many religions, so many languages and races, so many local concerns? But Americans saw, as by a kind of instinct, that the price of nationhood was not to distinguish and divide but to reconcile and unite, and that statesmanship did not single out each interest as a kind of sovereign power, infuse it with a life of its own, and endow it with institutional form and authority, but strove rather to weaken, to blur, and to mediate. It strove to cancel out the myriad interests of a rapidly growing people who were swarming over a vast continent with an energy unprecedented in history, and to provide in their place common denominators.[21] And, as Madison saw, the very multiplicity of interests, the chameleonlike changes that freedom of economic, social, and religious choices permitted, and the mobility that geography encouraged, helped create a situation fundamentally different from that in the Old World.

The Fathers did in fact try their hands at some balances, but their experiments were not successful. Several of the states followed the Adams philosophy by trying to balance an upper House which should represent the rich and the well-born against a lower House which was to represent the people. But as it turned out, the constituents were not really different, nor were the legislative bodies: certainly no American state developed a House of Lords and a Commons. The struggle between Large States and Small in the Federal Convention led to the famous Connecticut Compromise—a balance that assured the small states equal representation in one house and the large states proportionate representation in the other. Yet once again, the wrong things were in balance. There were no real differences of interest between Rhode Island and Massachusetts, Delaware and Pennsylvania, New Jersey and New York, Virginia and Georgia, and this particular balance was quickly drained of meaning though, to be sure, it took on other and perhaps more dangerous meanings. Nor did the third gesture toward balance work out any better: the balance of popular vote and Electoral College vote in Presidential elections. As early as 1800 that balance pretty much lost its significance: The Electoral College lingered on as an anachronism—and an expensive one. As the balances did not represent genuine interests, they did not perform genuine functions.

The astute and learned James Wilson—like Hamilton a Scotsman who had been born a British subject, but wholly without Hamilton's infatuation with the British Constitution—had already swept aside the analogy of Britain. "The British Government," he said, early in the debates in the Convention, "cannot be our model. We have no materials for a similar one. Our manners, our laws . . . the whole genius of our people, are opposed to it."[22] But this was so casual, so much of an aside, that it made little impression. It remained for the precocious Charles Pinckney of Charleston to establish, beyond argument, the irrelevancy of the British model.

A remarkable young man, Pinckney, an aristocrat, like Charles James Fox, but one who knew that an American aristocracy was indeed but the shadow of a dream, and who eventually abandoned his high-toned Federalism and threw in his lot with the rising Jeffersonians. Pinckney was the spokesman for the South Carolina delegation in the Convention, and an ardent nationalist, but he was not prepared to accept either John Adams's theories of checks and balances, or Hamilton's notions of nationalism. When, on 25 June, he addressed himself to the various plans that had been submitted to the Convention—he had submitted one himself—he was replying, in a sense, to Adams's *Defense of the Constitutions*, which had just that spring reached Philadelphia[23] and which, with its animadversions on democracy, created quite a stir. For Adams, who had long been convinced that all men were naturally "beasts of prey," had recommended a constitution that would accept the fact of the depravity of men and incorporate whatever checks and balances were necessary to circumvent it. Without "three orders, and an effectual balance between them," Adams warned, "America was destined to undergo incessant disorder, turmoil and revolution!" More specifically, however, Pinckney was replying to Alexander Hamilton's powerful speech of the week before (18 June), that speech in which the brilliant young delegate from New York had paid tribute to the beauty and symmetry of the British Constitution, to the House of Lords as "a most noble institution," and to the Monarchy as "the best of all models" for the executive authority of a government, and had adjured his fellow delegates to devise a Constitution which would incorporate the features that had made the British Government "the best in the world."[24]

11. Benjamin Franklin exalted in an allegorical painting by Fragonard. *(Courtesy of The White House, Washington, D.C.)*

12. Portrait of Captain James Cook, explorer and circum-navigator, by Nathaniel Dance. *(Courtesy of the National Maritime Museum, Greenwich Hospital Collection.)*

13. Portrait of Benjamin Thompson, who became Count Rumford of the Holy Roman Empire, by Thomas Gains-borough. *(Courtesy of the Fogg Art Museum, Harvard University, Cambridge.)*

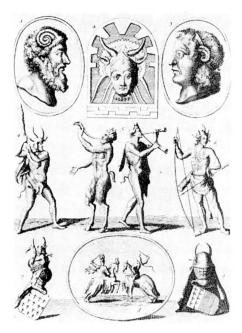

14. Engraved illustration of cultural similarities between America's "savages" and the "heroes" of antiquity noted by Lafitau in his book *Moeurs des sauvages amériquains comparées aux moeurs des premiers temps. (From* THE NEW GOLDEN LAND: *European Images of America from the Discoveries to the Present Time by Hugh Honour, copyright © 1975 by Fleming Honour Ltd. Reproduced by permission of Pantheon Books, Inc.)*

15. Tapestry of America done by Beauvais in the late eighteenth century, after Jean-Jacques François le Barbier. *(Courtesy of Artemis, S.A.)*

16. Portrait of Joel Barlow, author of the *Columbiad,* by Fulton. Taken from title page of the *Columbiad* by S. L. M. Barlow.

17. Portrait of Francis Hopkinson, composer, by Robert Edge Pine. *(Courtesy of The Historical Society of Pennsylvania.)*

18. Portrait of William Bartram, botanist, by Charles Willson Peale. *(Courtesy of Independence National Historical Park Collection.)*

19. Portrait of Joseph Priestley, during an early visit to America, by Sharples. *(Courtesy of the Bettmann Archive.)*

20. University of Virginia. Nineteenth-century print. *(Courtesy of the Thomas Jefferson Memorial Foundation.)*

21. Engraving by Paul Revere of the colleges in Cambridge, New England. *(Courtesy of the American Antiquarian Society.)*

22. Portrait of David Rittenhouse, American astronomer and inventor of the orrery, by Charles Willson Peale. *(Courtesy of the Independence National Historical Park.)*

23. David Rittenhouse's first orrery photographed after its reconstruction in 1953. *(Courtesy of the Princeton University Library.)*

24. Three American philosophes (John Adams, John Jay, and Benjamin Franklin) meet in Paris for preliminary peace treaty negotiations. Painting by Benjamin West unfinished due to British negotiator's resistance. *(Courtesy of The Henry Francis du Pont Winterthur Museum.)*

25. Painting of the drafting committee presenting the Declaration of Independence to Congress, by John Trumbull. *(Courtesy of the Yale University Art Gallery.)*

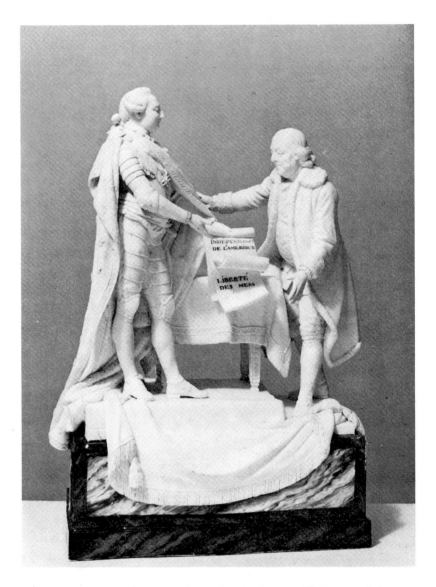

26. Statuette of Louis XVI and Benjamin Franklin in porcelain.
(Courtesy of The Henry Francis du Pont Winterthur Museum.)

Pinckney's speech of 25 June was one of the most re-markable delivered in the Convention in the whole of that long, hot, summer. Let us listen to him: "The people of the United States," he began loftily,

> are perhaps the most singular of any we are ac-quainted with. Among them are fewer distinctions of fortune and less of rank, than among the inhabitants of any other nation. Every freeman has a right to the same protection and security; and a very moderate share of property entitles them to the possession of all the honors and privileges the public can bestow; hence arises a greater equality than is to be found among the people of any other country, and an equal-ity which is more likely to continue. I say this equal-ity is likely to continue because in a new country, possessing immense tracts of uncultivated lands where every temptation is offered to emigration and where industry must be rewarded with competency, there will be few poor and few dependent. Every member of the society, almost, will enjoy an equal power of arriving at the supreme offices and consequently of directing the strength and sentiments of the whole community. None will be excluded by birth, and few by fortune. . . .

How clear, then, that

> the "distinguishing feature" of the British Consti-tution cannot possibly be introduced into the Ameri-can system, that its balance between the Crown and the People cannot be made a part of our Constitution—that we neither have nor can have the members to compose it, nor the rights, privileges and properties of so distinct a class of Citizens to guard—that the mate-rials for forming this balance or check do not exist, nor is there a necessity for having so permanent a part of our Legislative, until the Executive is so con-stituted as to have something fixed and dangerous in its principle. By this I mean a sole hereditary, though limited, executive.

And why is it that the much vaunted English system of balance is so irrelevant to America? It is, quite simply, because the people of the United States are more nearly equal than are the people of any other country.

> They have very few rich among them . . . perhaps there are not one hundred . . . on the continent. . . . The genius of the people, their mediocrity of situation and the prospects which are afforded their industry in a country which must be a new one for centuries are unfavorable to the rapid distinction of ranks. The destruction of the right of primogeniture, and the equal division of the property of intestates, will also have an effect to preserve this mediocrity. . . . The vast extent of unpeopled territory which opens to the frugal and industrious a sure road to competency and independence, will effectually prevent for a considerable time the increase of the poor or discontented, and be the means of preserving that equality of condition which so eminently distinguishes us.

But if equality is the leading feature of American society, where then, Pinckney asked, are the interests that the Senate is supposed to represent?

> They are in the great body of the people, among whom there are no men of wealth, and very few of real poverty. If under the British government for a century . . . no change was probable, I think it may be fairly concluded that it will not take place while even the semblance of Republicanism remains.

On this point, Pinckney continued,

> the policy of the United States has been much mistaken. We have . . . considered ourselves as inhabitants of an old instead of a new country. We have adopted the maxims of a state full of people and manufactures, and established in credit. We have deserted our true interest, and instead of applying closely to those improvements in domestic policy

which would have insured the future importance of our commerce, we have rashly and prematurely engaged in schemes as extensive as they are imprudent.

We are not Athens or Sparta, we are not Rome, we are not Britain. We must be true to our own genius. Our true situation is this,

a new, extensive country, containing within itself the materials for forming a government capable of extending to its citizens all the blessings of civil and religious liberty, capable of making them happy at home. This is the great end of Republican Establishments. . . . We must [Pinckney concluded] suit our government to the people it is to direct. These are as active, intelligent, and susceptible of good government as any people in the world.[25]

2

None saw more clearly than Pinckney, but James Madison saw farther. It was Madison who translated the English concept of balance of interests into the American political vernacular, who understood the true character of American federalism, and who persuaded the first Congress to impose formal limits on the federal government by drafting a Bill of Rights and adding it to the Constitution.

Of course there were diverse interests in every community, Madison conceded—the rich and the poor, creditors and debtors, farmers and merchants, slave owners and those who abjured slavery, Protestants and Catholics, the orthodox and the dissenters; how could it be otherwise in a free society, how could it be otherwise in a nation as large and as heterogeneous as the American? But union and security were not to be achieved either by trying to wipe out these differences, or by arming each interest with its own political and constitutional weaponry and transforming the political arena into a kind of *Champ de Mars*. Statesmanship does not destroy these disparate interests, for that

would be to destroy the very liberty which government ex-
ists to protect; it seeks to reconcile them.

Happily, this is not difficult in America, for thanks to its
immense size the whole of the United States is, in a sense,
a safety-valve for divergencies and antipathies. How mistaken Montesquieu was with his theory that an extensive
territory required a military despotism, and that a republic
must, of necessity, be small as the Greek city-states were
small, or the republics of eighteenth-century Italy. "The
smaller the society," wrote Madison in the tenth Federalist
paper,

> the fewer probably will be the distinct parties and in-
> terests composing it; the fewer the distinct parties and
> interests, the more frequently will a majority be found
> of the same party; and the smaller the number of in-
> dividuals composing a majority and the smaller the
> compass within which they are placed, the more eas-
> ily will they concert and execute their plans of op-
> pression. Extend the sphere, and you take in a greater
> variety of practice and interests; you make it less
> probable that a majority of the whole will have a
> common motive to invade the rights of other citizens;
> or, if such a common motive exists, it will be more
> difficult for all who feel it to discover their own
> strength and to act in unison with each other.

In the equally perspicacious fifty-first Federalist paper
Madison returned to a consideration of how you made
differing interests and factions a source of strength rather
than of weakness: These, he wrote,

> necessarily exist in different classes of citizens. If a
> majority be united by a common interest, the rights of
> the minority will be insecure. There are but two
> methods of providing against this evil; the one by cre-
> ating a will in the community independent of the
> majority—that is, of the society itself; the other by
> comprehending in the society so many separate de-
> scriptions of citizens as will render an unjust combina-
> tion of the majority of the whole very improbable, if

not impracticable. . . . [This] method will be ex-
emplified in the republic of the United States. Whilst
all authority in it will be derived from and dependent
on the society, the society itself will be broken into so
many parts, interests, and classes of citizens, that the
rights of individuals, or of the minority, will be in little danger. . . .
    In a free government the security for civil rights
must be the same as that for religious rights. It consists in the one place in the multiplicity of interests,
and in the other in the multiplicity of sects.

There spoke the man who had pushed the Statute of
Religious Liberty through the General Assembly of Virginia just two years earlier. For assuredly it was the long
experience with sectarianism and denominationalism that
taught Americans that investing a privileged church with
power—as in Britain and her colonies—produced nothing
but resentment and acrimony, but permitting competing
denominations to balance themselves under a broad tent of
toleration and equality prospered both them and society.
Doubtless toleration of religious factionalism was easy
enough for a Franklin or a Jefferson, who did not confess
very ardent religious beliefs; what is illuminating is how
early a New England Puritan like Ezra Stiles—he was
later to serve as President of Yale College—arrived at a
realization that competing sects could flourish side by side
with no harm either to religion or to morals. As early as
1760, while the winds of the Great Awakening were still
ruffling the surface of New England Congregationalism,
Stiles delivered a *Discourse on the Christian Union* which
asserted that "Providence has planted the British America
with a variety of sects, which will unavoidably become a
mutual balance upon one another. Their temporary colli-
sions . . . after a short ebullition, will subside in harmony
and union, not by the destruction of either but in the
friendly cohabitation of all . . . Resplendent and all-per-
vading TRUTH will terminate the whole in universal
harmony."[1] And to a fellow Congregational minister, Stiles
confided that "our great security is in the multitude of
sects and the public Liberty necessary for them to cohabit

together. In consequence of which the aggrieved of any communion will either pass over to another, or rise into new sects and spontaneous societies."[2] When he was invited to draw up the charter for the new College of Rhode Island, Stiles provided for representation on the Board of Trustees of Baptists, Congregationalists, Friends, and Episcopalians:[3] imagine anything like that at an Oxford College!

Separation of church and state, Americans perceived, did not weaken religion or impair morals; it did not even weaken those churches that had heretofore enjoyed special privileges. Though the Anglican Church suffered temporary setbacks in the South, where it had enjoyed the advantages of Establishment, and the Congregational in New England, both emerged stronger under a system of voluntarism and independence than they would have been under exposure to the ceaseless turmoil and assault that must have been their fate had they been permanently "established." The analogy of separation of Church and State and separation of powers was not lost on Americans of that generation. So, notwithstanding the despairing expostulations and solemn warnings of John Adams, they rejected formal balance of interests for formal separation of powers. The balance, as practiced in the Mother Country, which guaranteed power to privileged interests, and the system of Estates, as in France, which recognized the Church as the very first order, were not only devices for perpetuating religious Establishments but for perpetuating social orders. Would they not have operated the same way in the New World, as in the Old?

The American rejection of fixed Orders, formal Interests or legal Establishments reflected not only geographical and natural realities, but deep-seated social habits and instincts, and pervasive economic options. How do you maintain standing Orders when anyone could pull up stakes and move off to another community or even another State? How do you maintain formal interests or traditional Establishments when these could be controlled, and even overthrown, by a suffrage that was well-nigh universal among white men? How few families, after all, retained their eminence for more than two generations; how few business or commercial interests could count on avoiding ruinous competition from more favored regions of the rapidly growing union and of patterns of population that were constantly shifting. How few churches could be exempt from the implications of the separation of Church and State or of the vagaries of denominational competition not only unregulated but encouraged by government. Nor can we overlook the iconoclastic impact of a freedom of thought and of expression, unknown elsewhere, on traditional ideas and institutions.

It was all part of a fundamental revolution. For now it was not government seeking, usually in vain, to limit and control the conflicting ingredients of the social order, but society limiting government through "charters of power granted by liberty." John Adams and Alexander Hamilton and Gouverneur Morris might conjure up dangers from the people, but what the vast majority of Americans feared was danger from government. The balance of interest doctrine, certainly in its American formulation, was not really a device for checking here the merchants and there the planters, here the land speculators and there the financiers, here the military and there the Church. No, it was a device for checking the will of the majority or, as it was long popular to say the tyranny of the majority.* Even Jefferson—mostly when his opponents were in power—frightened himself with what he otherwise dismissed as the "raw head and bloody bones" of majority tyranny. He had objected to the first Constitution of Virginia because it appeared to concentrate all powers in the legislative branch. "One hundred and seventy-three despots," he wrote,

> would surely be as oppressive as one. Let those who doubt it turn their eyes on the republic of Venice. As little will it avail us that they are chosen by ourselves. An *elective* despotism was not what we fought for, but one which should not only be so divided and balanced among several bodies of magistracy as that no

---

* The idea of tyranny of the majority was elaborately developed by John Adams in his *Defense of the Constitutions,* but the phrase itself was popularized by Tocqueville who devoted two chapters of his *Democracy in America* to this bogey.

one could transcend their legal limits without being
effectually checked and restrained by the others.[4]

But Jefferson came in time to believe that there was no
effective alternative to majority rule, and that the dangers
of minority rule were infinitely greater than those of rule
by majorities. It was, he said in his Inaugural Address, a
"sacred principle." "Where the law of the majority ceases
to be acknowledged," he wrote, a few years later, "there
government ends." And at the close of his life he assured
his friend Alexander von Humboldt that "the best principle of republicanism is that the *lex majoris partis* is the
fundamental law of every society. . . . To consider the will
of the society announced by the majority of a single vote
as sacred as if unanimous, is the first of all lessons in
importance."[5] But there was always the assumption, sometimes articulate, usually inarticulate, "that the will of the
majority to be rightful must be reasonable." It was an in-
dication of a certain shallowness in Jefferson's political
philosophy—or perhaps merely an impatience with theory
—that he never inquired too closely into this paradox.

It was the State constitutions that first institutionalized
the principle that government can be limited by the separation and independence of departments, leaving to the play
of the federal system, of political parties, of competing
economic interests, and of education, the task of limiting,
as best they could, local and popular tyrannies. This was a
policy that worked well until slavery became a class rather
than a popular interest (which is not to say that it did not
achieve popular support), and regional rather than merely
local. Thus, the Virginia Constitution pioneered with the
principle that "the legislative, executive and judicial departments shall be separate and distinct, so that neither exercise the powers that properly belong to the others; nor
shall any person exercise the powers of more than one of
them at the same time." Thus, the Maryland Constitution
repeated that "the legislative, executive and judicial powers
of government *ought to be* forever separate and distinct
from one another" and that "the independence of the judiciary was essential to the impartial administration of justice." Thus, the Massachusetts Constitution provided that

"in the government of this commonwealth the legislative department shall never exercise the executive or judicial powers, or either of them; the executive shall never exercise the legislative and judicial powers, or either of them; the judicial shall never exercise the legislative and executive powers, or either of them; to the end that it may be a government of laws and not of men."[6]

To be sure, these ringing declarations of equality and independence were widely dishonored in other provisions of the constitutions themselves and, even more, in the practices of powerful state legislatures. Hostility to executive power—so easily associated with royal power—was deep and pervasive, and to most Americans self-government meant government by elected representatives. The story of legislature usurpation and aggression is too familiar to rehearse. Legislatures kept a tight rein on governors, most of whom were limited to two years service; they kept a tight rein, too, on courts. They played fast and loose with the very structure of the judiciary; meddled constantly in judicial affairs, nullified court verdicts, vacated judgments, remitted fines, dissolved marriages, and relieved debtors of their obligations almost with impunity. For a brief period it looked as if the new commonwealths were moving toward a parliamentary system of government notwithstanding all the firm constitutional declarations to the contrary.[7] Why did this not happen?

Four considerations are relevant here. First, it is by no means clear that the aggrandizement of legislative power at the expense of the other branches was the product of a conscious repudiation of the principle of equality among departments rather than a kind of vestigial remnant of the long controversy with royal governors. Second, within two or three decades greater political maturity (and perhaps even greater constitutional conservatism) dictated changes in many of the early constitutions which looked to a restoration of genuine equality among departments and which went far to restore independence to the Courts. Look at the Constitutions of the new States and you see popular election of governors, longer terms of office, eligibility for re-election, and, increasingly, the veto power. And though most of the new states provided for election of Judges by

the legislature, once elected they enjoyed long terms of
office—usually during "good behavior." Third, the Federal
Convention made clear its commitment to the principle of
equality and independence of the departments. It gave
broad if vague powers to the President—how could you do
otherwise with Mr. Washington in the chair!—and placed
no limit on his terms of service. It made clear, both in Article III and in Article VI, that the judiciary would be
truly independent and that it would exercise judicial review, and two years later Congress, in the Judiciary Act of
1789, spelled out these powers in great detail. And fourth,
it is relevant to recall that notwithstanding fear of strong
executives and suspicion of strong Courts, the people
chose Presidents, Governors and—where that was called
for—judges who were able, powerful, and distinguished.
Indeed, in historical perspective the rapidity and vigor with
which the Revolutionary generation accommodated its
practices to the principle of the independence of the three
branches of government is far more impressive than the
departures from that principle during the early years of experimentation in the states.[8]

* * *

In the light of their experience with the Mother Country, and of history, it is easy to see why the Revolutionary
generation displayed such zeal in placing limits on governments. Was that zeal misdirected? was it excessive? The
first question is philosophically the most interesting. In
their distrust of popular majorities did not the Constitution
makers acknowledge themselves disciples of John Adams,
who saw corruption in every heart and ambition in every
spirit, and who made distrust of human nature the foundation of his political philosophy, rather than of Franklin,
who was prepared to take mankind as he found them, or
of Jefferson, who was confident of progress in the moral
and in the material sphere?[9] So it would seem, but we
must remember John Jay's sage observation that it took
time to make subjects into citizens. More serious, as it
turned out, was the confusion—almost inevitable—between what we may call philosophical and mechanical limi-

tations. Constitution makers confused limitations on the sphere or the scope of government with limitations on the energy of government, and this confusion was to haunt constitutional history for another century. To deny government any authority whatever over religion was both logical and sound, but to restrain or hobble the operations of government where it did rightly have power—as in the realm of taxation, or the conduct of foreign affairs—was neither. Philosophy dictated the exemption of speech or the press from governmental control, but it did not dictate annual elections, or a bicameral legislature, or substantive limits on legislative authority in the realm of social welfare.

Logically a separation of powers as absolute as that required by the Constitutions of Virginia and Massachusetts would have led to governmental paralysis. Happily, the constitution makers did not permit their more extreme theories—the kind of theory we associate with Tom Paine's "government like dress is the badge of lost innocence"—to get in the way of that common sense which Paine also extolled. "The true meaning of [separation of powers]" wrote Madison, "is entirely compatible with a partial intermixture of those departments for special purposes. . . . This partial intermixture is, in some cases, not only proper but necessary."[10] What impresses us most now is not so much the independence as the successful intermixture: the executive, with a veto which assured him legislative power; the legislature, with power to appropriate money, to confirm appointments, and—on the federal level —to participate in the making of war and of peace; the judiciary, with legislative powers implicit in judicial review; and everywhere, throughout the national political system the intermixture of federal, state, and local political activities, and of these with the activities of private associations in the public arena. "Experience must be our guide," had said John Dickinson in the Federal Convention. "Reason may mislead us." Americans had the best of the worlds of Reason and of Experience. Reason dictated the logic of their institutions; Experience made them work.

3

Nothing dramatized the principle of limitations on government more strikingly than Bills of Rights attached to or incorporated into most of the new State Constitutions. It was the spectacle of the American people acting, almost spontaneously, to fix limits on government—that is, on themselves—that impressed Old World observers of the American scene even more than did the fabrication of State Constitutions. After all, no people had ever done this before, and the notion that any people would in fact impose restrictions on themselves, and honor those restrictions, flew in the face of all political theory and experience. There were, to be sure, persuasive arguments against the new American experiment: If the people were sovereign, how could they place limits on the sovereign will? If the earth belonged to the living not the dead, what right had one generation to impose its will on future generations? But these arguments were not vigorously agitated—even Jefferson abandoned his proposal for a new constitution every twenty years. All went smoothly because ever since, in 1634, the freemen of Watertown had demanded "to see the charter" of the Massachusetts Bay Company, most Americans—certainly most New Englanders—had taken for granted that government was bound by the terms of compact to which all, presumably, had consented.†

Then, and since, Americans traced their Bills of Rights to English antecedents: Magna Carta, the Petition of Rights of 1628, the immortal Bill of Rights of 1689. These did indeed provide rhetorical precedents, but they did not provide models. Here, as elsewhere, Americans not only improved on English practices, but institutionalized them and constitutionalized them. This process was of long standing, and by the time of the Revolution colonial ante-

† Thus Theophilus Parsons, in the *Essex Results* of 1778: "A bill of Rights, clearly ascertaining and defining the rights of conscience and the security of persons and property which every member of a State hath a right to expect from the supreme power thereof, *ought* to be settled and established."

cedents to the idea of bills of rights were in all likelihood
more influential than English. Thus, though the immediate
background of the Massachusetts Body of Liberties of
1641 was the wish "to frame a body of grounds of laws, in
resemblance to a Magna Carta which . . . should be received for fundamental laws," the document itself, with its
one hundred provisions, embraced far more than the procedural rights set forth in the Magna Carta or the Petition
of Rights.[1] It included these as a matter of course, and in
addition the right of all freemen to vote and of all men,
"inhabitant or fforreiner, free or not free," to participate in
town meetings; the right to travel; the abolition of monopolies; provision for the "relief" of widows not otherwise
provided for, and beyond this it embraced the rights of children, servants, and even beasts.‡

The Massachusetts Body of Liberties was the most advanced and the most elaborate declaration of rights during
the entire colonial period, but most of the colonial charters
reasserted the traditional rights of Englishmen, and added
elaborate guarantees of due process of law and of a degree of religious freedom quite unknown in the Mother
Country.[2]

Revolutionary documents such as the Declaration and
Resolves of the First Continental Congress, and the Address to the Inhabitants of Quebec elaborated on the
rights of Americans, but collectively, as British citizens,
rather than individually, as men. With independence, however, the new state constitutions returned to the great
theme of the rights of men against Government.

Virginia led the way, and her Bill of Rights, drafted by
George Mason of Gunston Hall, was a model for most of
the others,* and an inspiration to the philosophers of
France, Holland, and Italy.[3] Where Virginia led, others
followed, and soon every State (except of course Con-

‡ "No Man shall exercise any Tirrany or Crueltie towards any brute
Creature which are kept for man's use." Art. 92. See also Arts. 79,
80, 83, 85, 89, and 91.

* It was, in one particular, a model for Jefferson, for it was the first
formal document to include "happiness" as a fundamental right.
Mason, indeed, went beyond Jefferson for he asserted the right both
to pursue and to *obtain* happiness.

necticut and Rhode Island, which made do with their colonial Charters) incorporated guarantees of rights either into the bulk of its constitution or as a separate document. When the Federal Constitution was submitted to the States for ratification without a Bill of Rights, there was an outcry of indignation and alarm. No matter—as Hamilton pointed out so conclusively in number eighty-four of the *Federalist Papers,* that it was illogical to forbid the Federal government from doing what it had no authority to do anyway; the people were not to be fobbed off with arguments they thought sophistical. "A bill of rights," wrote Jefferson to his friend Madison, "is what the people are entitled to against every government on earth, general or particular, and what no just government should refuse or rest on inference,"[4] and he added to the Madisonian proposals a specific declaration of the subordination of the military to the civilian authority and a prohibition of monopolies.[5] Five states ratified the new Constitution subject to an understanding that a Bill of Rights would be added, and just to make assurance doubly sure, many of the states submitted their own lengthy lists of rights that no government should violate or withhold: nine from Massachusetts, twelve from New Hampshire, thirteen from Maryland, fifteen from Pennsylvania, twenty from North Carolina and Virginia, and from New York no less than twenty-four.[6] Most of these duplicated one another, but it was possible to distinguish some two score different proposals: what resourcefulness to identify that many rights against government!

What was most impressive about the American Bills of Rights was not their derivative but their creative character. They differed from their English antecedents not only in philosophy but in substance. In England rights were neither "natural" nor "inalienable"; they were granted or conceded by the Crown, and they could be—and frequently were—alienated by either Crown of Parliament. Thus, the Bill of Rights of 1689 asserted that James I had "endeavoured to subvert the laws and liberties of the Kingdom"—the kingdom, mind, not the people. What Parliament did—Parliament, not a special convention, which was unknown to English law—was "to vindicate and assert their ancient rights and liberties" and to require that his Majesty's ministers shall hereafter recognize that the liberties asserted and claimed in the Bill of Rights are "the true, ancient, and indubitable rights and liberties of the people."[7] That was going farther than any other nation had gone, but it did not go to the root of the matter. For legally the Bill of Rights was a Parliamentary act, and what Parliament did it could undo. As James I was prepared to flout the provisions of the Petition of Rights so, during the wars with France, more than a century later, the younger Pitt was prepared to flout the provisions of the Bill of Rights. But the American Bills of Rights, state and federal alike, rested on constitutional, not statutory, foundations, and recognized that rights were not granted either by a Crown or a Parliament, but inherent. Here is the way George Mason put it in the Virginia Bill of Rights:

> That all men . . . have certain inherent rights, of which, when they enter into a state of society they cannot by any compact deprive or divest their posterity.

John Adams started off with even more elaborate observations on the nature of government, but arrived at the same conclusion:

> The body politic is formed by a voluntary association of individuals; it is a social compact by which the whole people covenants with each citizen and each citizen with the whole people, that all shall be governed . . . for the common good.[8]

What was revolutionary were the substantive differences between the English and the American Bills of Rights. The English played variations on the famous Article thirty-nine of Magna Carta: they reaffirmed due process of law, outlawed cruel and unusual punishments, excessive fines and bail, a standing army without the consent of Parliament, violation of the rights of members of Parliament or interference with the freedom of elections, and reasserted Parliamentary control of the purse. The rights guaranteed in

the American constitutions and bills of rights were not only
procedural but substantive: freedom of religion, freedom
of speech, freedom of the press and of assembly, and
many others as well. Five states forbade self-incrimination;
six specifically asserted the supremacy of the civil over the
military. North Carolina and Maryland prohibited the creation of monopolies, which were pronounced "odious and
contrary to the spirit of free government." Delaware
abolished the slave trade—other states quickly followed
her lead—and Vermont abolished slavery and, for good
measure, most indentured servitude. Virginia and New
York affirmed the right of revolution, and Virginia made
explicit what was everywhere implicit, that "magistrates
are the servants of the people." Pennsylvania and Delaware exempted conscientious objectors from the obligation of military service and, with North Carolina,
imprisonment for debt.† North Carolina required the establishment of schools and universities, and, with Pennsylvania, affirmed the right of its people to migrate across
the mountains and set up their own commonwealths.
New York abolished double jeopardy. Massachusetts, like
Virginia, asserted the equality of all men—whatever that
meant. In Massachusetts it turned out to mean a great deal
more than it meant in Virginia, for "our Constitution,"
wrote Chief Justice Cushing in the Quock Walker case
(1783),

> sets out with declaring that all men are born free and
> equal, and that every subject is entitled to liberty, and
> have it guarded by the laws. . . . and, in short, is to-
> tally repugnant to the idea of being born slaves. This
> being the case, the idea of slavery is inconsistent with
> our own conduct and Constitution, and there can be
> no such thing as perpetual servitude.[9]

Even the rhetoric of the American Bills of Rights
differed from that of the English. It is not merely that it

† Exemption from military service was conditioned on paying an
equivalent (not defined), and exemption from imprisonment for debt
was only on surrender of all real estate and personal property to
creditors. Harsh as this was, it was well in advance of anything to
be found elsewhere.

was Ciceronian, or that it was mercifully uncluttered with what might be called the official jargon of seventeenth-century legalism, but that it was powerful, direct, and unqualified. Thus, Congress shall make *no* law respecting the establishment of religion, or abridging the freedom of speech; there shall be *no* bills of attainder, *no* test oaths, and *no* person shall be convicted of treason except on the testimony of two witnesses, and Treason itself is defined with precision. The right of the people to be secure in their persons, houses, papers, and effects shall not be violated; no person shall be compelled to be a witness against himself; no subordination of any one sect or denomination to another shall ever be established; the people have an incontestable, inalienable and indefeasible right to reform, alter, or totally change their government. So it went, from Constitution to Constitution. On these matters the Founding Fathers did not take refuge in ambiguity or sophistry.

Two additional rights were guaranteed in the first—and in subsequent—constitutions, rights that embodied not limits but claims on government: the right to pursue and obtain happiness, and the right to live under a "republican" form of government. In the genial air of the eighteenth century, religion and politics united to elevate happiness to a natural right.[10] It was, indeed, in the eyes of the philosophes, "our being's end and aim." God or Providence clearly intended that man should be happy; if there could be a suspicion of doubt about this in Italy or Spain, or that Portugal which suffered the Lisbon earthquake (and Candide and Cunegonde sometimes allowed themselves that suspicion), surely there could be none in America. Jefferson had made that almost official when he inserted "pursuit of happiness" into the Declaration, and again when he observed, in his First Inaugural Address, that "Providence, by all its dispensations, proves that it delights in the happiness of man here and his greater happiness hereafter." Clearly it was the duty of the State to carry out the will of Providence. Even the dour John Adams admitted that. "All speculative philosophers," he wrote,

will agree that the happiness of Society is the end of Government, as the divine and moral philosophers

will agree that the happiness of the individual is the
end of Man.[11]

and proceeded to write this axiom into the very first article
of the Declaration of Rights for Massachusetts. What was
surprising in a Calvinist like Adams was natural enough in
a Deist like George Mason or Thomas Jefferson, and it
was Mason who had the distinction of being the first to
write "happiness" into a constitution. "All men," so reads
the Virginia Declaration of Rights, "have certain inherent
rights, among which are the enjoyment of life and liberty,
with the means of acquiring and possessing property, and
pursuing and obtaining happiness." From Virginia the
guarantee spread to the Constitutions of half the States.

The second guarantee was to be found in the body of
the Federal Constitution—"the United States shall guarantee to every State a republican Form of Government." The
word Republican is almost as elusive as the word happiness (and so, too, as it proved, the word "guarantee"),
but to those Americans steeped in the history of the
Roman Republic and in the political principles of the great
seventeenth-century Commonwealthmen,[12] it meant what
indeed it meant to Montesquieu—a government that rested
on a popular basis and on virtue. Madison defined republic
accurately enough as "a government which derived all of
its powers directly or indirectly from the great body of the
people," and Jefferson added that "governments are republican in proportion as they embody the will of their people
and execute it." Probably, to the ordinary American, who
was not steeped in classical history, the sharpest image
conjured up by the term republican was negative. Just as
America herself might be defined as not-Europe, so a
republic was not-despotism, not-monarchy, not-aristocracy,
not-privilege. Democracy was still a pejorative term, but
within a generation the distinction between "republic" and
"democracy" was blurred, and Jefferson's Republican
party became, quite painlessly, the Democratic party. Certainly both in its qualitative emphasis on the origins of
government and the limits of government, and in its quantitative emphasis on majoritarianism, the American Republic differed from the Roman Republic or the English

Commonwealth or the contemporary republics like the United Netherlands or Lucca or Genoa, or that Venice whose extinction Wordsworth was to mourn.[13] It was, as Jefferson and Madison, Barlow and Tom Paine believed, something new under the sun.

* * *

"The last step in human progress is to be made in America," wrote the Reverend Dr. Richard Price of London, who gloried in his honorary citizenship in the United States. But it was not Dr. Price's hopes for his own country that were to be fulfilled, but those of his great antagonist, Edmund Burke, whose *Reflections on the Revolution in France* had been provoked by one of Dr. Price's sermons.[14] Price died within a year of the publication of Burke's masterpiece of reaction, and of the *Thermidor* which followed it, or he might have joined his associates, Dr. Priestley, Benjamin Vaughan, and Tom Paine in flight from that country which was so paradoxically to defend itself against the Reign of Terror in France by inaugurating a Reign of Terror at home. It was not surprising that the example of the American Bills of Rights made no impression on Britain; after all, during these years, the English Bill of Rights made no impression on Britain either.

It was France that welcomed the American example—welcomed it, followed it, and even improved upon it. It was in France that the "American party" triumphed,[15] briefly, to be sure; the party made up somewhat loosely of Lafayette, la Rochefoucauld, Brissot, Condorcet, Beaumarchais, Du Pont de Nemours, Helvétius, the Abbés Sièyes, Raynal, and Mably, and a miscellany of others—followers of Turgot and converts to his doctrines of Physiocracy and of Progress, members of the Amis des Noirs, of the *Club Americaine*, or the Masonic Lodge of the Nine Sisters. Franklin was the pivotal point, Franklin who was a legend, but a very active one, and who saw to it that the American Constitutions, and other State Papers, were translated and published in France.[16] Doubtless it was his influence, or his fame, that accounted in part for the immense popularity of the Pennsylvania Constitution; it was somehow as-

sumed that he had written it as it was assumed that he had
written the anonymously published *Observations on Government*
really by John Stevens, which so skillfully defended the principle of unicameralism.[17] As early as 1778,
Turgot and the Abbé Mably (who had offered to help
John Adams draft a Constitution for Massachusetts) were
familiar with the American State constitutions and had indeed already launched that great debate over them in
which John Adams was to be so inextricably and elaborately involved. For in these years the French were deeply
concerned with the somewhat doctrinaire issue of bicamer-
alism versus unicameralism, and with the separation of
powers, not with Bills of Rights.

That concern came to the fore only with the onset of the
Revolution. In the months before his departure from Paris,
Jefferson was constantly consulted by Lafayette and his associates on the drafting of a Declaration of Rights. "Everyone here is trying their hands at forming declarations of
rights," he wrote to Madison,[18] and sent on to him two
specimens, one of which, at least, met his approval because, "as you will see, it contains the essential principles
of ours accommodated as much as could be to the actual
state of things here." Clearly, his own proposals[19] were far
too moderate "for the actual state of things" in France.
Even the mild and conciliatory Lafayette was prepared to
go a good deal farther than his American mentor here.
Where Jefferson contented himself mostly with procedural
rights, and permitted himself only one really revolutionary
provision—"all pecuniary privileges and exemptions en-
joyned by any description of persons, are abolished"[20]—
Lafayette spoke out for complete equality and the fundamental Rights of Man. "Each man is born with impre-
scriptible rights . . . and the exercise of natural rights has
no limits except those which injure the same rights to society. . . . The principle of all sovereignty rests imprescrip-
tibly in the nation."[21]

The Declaration of the Rights of Man of August
1789,[22] largely the work of Lafayette, Mirabeau, and the
now almost forgotten Jean Joseph Mounier, derived philosophically from the Bills of Rights of the American States,
and practically from the circumstances and exigencies of

France in the year 1789. The anonymous author of *L'Ami de la Révolution*, published the following year, traced the ancestry of most of the provisions of the Declaration to the Constitutions of Virginia, Massachusetts, Pennsylvania, and Maryland. Thus, commenting on the very first article of the Declaration, that "men are born and remain free and equal in rights," our compiler observed that most republics—Venice, Holland, and England among them—had ignored this principle but (forgetting or ignoring slavery) that the principles written into the American Bills of Rights were fulfilled in practice! So, again, commenting on Article Four of the Declaration—that "liberty consists in the ability to do whatever does not harm another"—the compiler concluded that "in Venice the people is slave; in England they enjoy only a shadow of liberty; but the Laws of America have made secure this essential right of the citizen." There was special praise for American guarantees of religious freedom, and a rebuke for the tepid assurances of religious freedom in the Declaration. Of all this the author concludes that "these dispositions of the American constitutions are far superior to ours."

Yet in many and important respects the Declaration of the Rights of Man went beyond anything in the American Bills of Rights. It did away with slavery everywhere under French jurisdiction; abolished the remnants of feudalism and serfdom, including primogeniture and entail, put an end to all honorary distinctions—"titles of nobility, rank, liberties and armorial bearings" and to most of the rights and privileges of nobility and clergy, and admitted Jews to broad political and social rights. It guaranteed the right of work or of a career, enjoined the care of the poor and the aged, and declared education at public expense a right.

What was lacking was as impressive as what was added to the existing fund of rights. There was no recognition that rights were inherent rather than granted by an enlightened government, and no sanctions through which to enforce them—certainly no judicial sanctions. For all the lipservice to the principle of separation of powers, these were not in fact separate or equal: during the early years of the Revolution it was the legislature that was all-powerful; thereafter, with the rise of Napoleon, the executive; at no

time did the judiciary exercise, or even claim, the jurisdiction accorded it in the American system. Not surprisingly, many of the guarantees of the great Declaration
turned out to be shadowy.

All this was in a sense an image of the revolutionary
Enlightenment in Europe and America. Europe could not
realize the Enlightenment without first sweeping away centuries of privilege, toppling Monarchies, overthrowing
Churches, shaking society itself to its foundations and even
shattering it. There the Revolution was, in Jefferson's mag-
nanimous phrase, a spectacle of "infuriated man, seeking
through blood and slaughter his long-lost liberties."[23] In
the eyes of the Old World the task of the American revolution was, by contrast, simple, and the achievements of the
Enlightenment came to seem natural and almost inevitable: no Monarchy to topple (it was enough to repudiate
George III), no Infamy to crush, no ancient privileges to
eradicate, no ruling classes to liquidate, no military to sup-
press, no torture to abolish, no censorship to erase, no
grinding poverty to ameliorate. As Jefferson's friend, Madame d'Houdetot put it, in a letter of 1790:

> The characteristic difference between your revolution
> and ours, is that having nothing to destroy, you had
> nothing to injure, and laboring for a people few in
> number, incorrupted and extended over a large tract
> of country, you have avoided all the inconveniences
> of a situation contrary in every respect. Every step in
> your revolution was perhaps the effect of virtue, while
> ours are often faults, and sometimes crimes.[24]

Neither the Loyalists nor the slaves would wholly have
subscribed to this tribute, but Americans rid themselves of
the first, or silenced them, and did not permit their slaves
to have any opinions at all. Most, though not all, Old
World observers forgot or ignored these exceptions.

Inspired by the American example, French revolutionaries attempted more than they could fulfill, and succeeding regimes circumvented or swept aside most of the
guarantees of the Declaration of Human Rights. If the

American Bills of Rights were less ambitious, they were
more effective and more lasting.

4

The separation of powers along functional lines, Bills of
Rights which limited the scope of governmental powers,
and an independent judiciary which had—or assumed—
authority to set the boundaries of legislative and executive
action—what all this came to was government that rested
more fully on *law* than any other in history. Certainly that
was true in principle. Other societies—from ancient
Athens and the Roman Republic to the Commonwealthmen of seventeenth-century Britain—had celebrated that
principle, but none had ever been able to impose it upon
those who exercised power. Could institutions succeed
where principles had failed?

The dour Fisher Ames of Massachusetts had described
Bills of Rights as mere "cobwebs for lions." But that is not
what they turned out to be; it was the Judges who proved
to be the lions. No Judge in England—not since Lord Coke
had been forced to retreat from the high ground of the Dr.
Bonham case[1]—would have dared pronounce the verdict
that Justice Wythe of Virginia gave in the case of Commonwealth v. Caton, or to indulge in his rhetoric, either.

> I shall not hesitate, sitting in this place, to say to the
> General Court, *fiat justicia, ruat coelum;* and, to the
> usurping branch of the Legislature, you attempt worse
> than a vain thing; for although you cannot succeed,
> you set an example which may convulse society to its
> centre. Nay, more, if the whole legislature . . .
> should attempt to overleap the bounds prescribed to
> them by the people, I . . . will meet the united
> powers at my seat in this tribunal, and, pointing to the
> constitution, will say to them, here is the limit of your
> authority, and hither you shall go but no further.[2]

Nor would any English judge have asserted the authority

that Justice Iredell claimed, as early as 1785, against the
pretensions of the legislature of North Carolina; that

> it is clear that no act they could pass, could by any
> means repeal or alter the Constitution, because if they
> could do this, they would at the same instant of time
> destroy their own existence as a legislature and dis-
> solve the government thereby established. Conse-
> quently the Constitution, standing in the fundamental
> law of the land, [this] act must of course stand as
> abrogated and without any effect[3] . . .

Soon Justice James Wilson, who doubled as a member of
the Supreme Court of the United States and Professor of
Law at the University of Pennsylvania, asserted the authority of the Federal Courts to limit the alleged sovereignty of states, rebuking, in the process, the pretensions of
all governments that sought to arrogate sovereignty to
themselves:

> In almost every nation which has been denominated
> free, the state has assumed a supercilious prëeminence
> above the people who have formed it. Hence the
> haughty notions of state independence, state sover-
> eignty, and state supremacy.[4]

And a decade later the new Chief Justice Marshall provided the authoritative statement not only for judicial
review but for judicial supremacy. The logic was—or
seemed—irrefutable:

> The powers of the legislature are defined and limited;
> and that those limits may not be mistaken or forgot-
> ten, the constitution is written. To what purpose are
> powers limited . . . if those limits may, at any time,
> be passed by those intended to be restrained? The dis-
> tinction between a government with limited and un-
> limited powers is abolished if those limits do not
> confine the persons on whom they are imposed and if
> acts prohibited and acts allowed are of equal obliga-

tion. It is a proposition too plain to be contested, that
the constitution controls any legislative act repug-
nant to it. . . .[5]

It was a proposition too plain to be contested, too, that it
was the right of the judiciary to determine whether the legislative or, for that matter, the executive branch had indeed passed the limits of the Constitution, for "it is
emphatically the province and the duty of the judicial
department to say what the law is." It was another half
century before the Supreme Court once again declared
void an act of Congress,[6] but meantime the principle was
applied to a score of State acts and resoundingly asserted
in scores of cases where it was not applied.

It is difficult to know whether to be more astonished at
the presumptuousness of these claims or at the ease with
which they were vindicated. How paradoxical that the first
nation to base its political philosophy on the principle that
all political authority derives from the people, and that the
people express their will through elected representatives,
should also be the first to embrace the principle that the ultimate interpretation of the validity of the popular will
should be lodged not in the people themselves, or in their
representatives, but in the one non-elective and, therefore,
non-democratic branch of the government.[7]

The paradox was stated in classical form by Jefferson,
himself a champion both of democracy and of limited government, in his first Inaugural Address. All, he said,

will bear in mind this sacred principle, that though
the will of the majority is in all cases to prevail, that
will to be rightful must be reasonable; and that the
minority possess equal rights, which . . . to violate
would be oppression.

It was, indeed, a paradox which even Jefferson could not
resolve. Here he was—like so many others—equivocal,
torn between his faith in democratic majorities and his
passion for protecting the rights of men against governmental usurpation. To Madison he wrote, from Paris, in

1789, that one persuasive argument for a Bill of Rights which carried great weight with him was

> the legal check which it puts into the hands of the judiciary. This is a body which, if rendered independent, and kept strictly to their own department merits great confidence for their learning and integrity. . . . What degree of confidence would be too much for a body composed of such men as Wythe, Blair and Pendleton?[8]

Nor, for all his passion for majority rule did he disapprove of the requirement of a two-thirds majority for changes in fundamental law, or of a bicameral legislature.

The paradox could be explained, but it could not be resolved.[9] The explanation of eventual acquiescence in it is two-fold, philosophical and practical. The philosophical argument is familiar: that constitutions embody fundamental law and that no ordinary legislature can set aside what God or Nature has decreed or a sovereign people ratified. The practical explanation was doubtless more decisive: that a federal system, resting on a delicate distribution of powers among governments, require an umpire to enable it to function, and that the Constitution itself has assigned this role to the Courts,[10] and that if Courts were to exercise judicial review in the federal arena they could not be denied the power to review acts of the legislative and executive branches in the national arena.

All very well, but the problem still remained: why were the American people, who were not all trained either in law or in logic, prepared to accept the judiciary as the interpreter, the umpire, and the authority? It is a question that can be answered only inconclusively, for the ultimate answer, or explanation, lies in the realm of the intangible.[11] First, secularization had made heavy inroads on the claims of the clergy to pre-eminence in the public arena, and by the last quarter of the eighteenth century it was the bench and bar that commanded respect.[12] Second, a government involving complex relationships between the evolving parts of a federal system required an expertise that only those trained in the law could be expected to

command: after all, Americans of that generation can be
said to have invented both constitutional law and the law
school. Third, because for the most part judges held office
for long terms or for good behavior, they could be presumed to be above partisanship and above corruption: the
first assumption did not prove wholly valid, but the second
did. To this should be added the decisive consideration
that early appointments to the Courts, State, and Federal
alike set a high standard: George Wythe and John Blair in
Virginia, Theophilus Parsons and William Cushing in Massachusetts, John Jay and James Kent in New York, Oliver
Ellsworth in Connecticut, James Iredell in North Carolina,
and John Rutledge in South Carolina among them, and in
the new state of Vermont, Nathaniel Chipman, who wrote
one of the best of the early treatises on the nature of the
Union. The first Supreme Court, too, was one of immense
distinction; with the retirement of John Jay its prestige fell,
but with the appointment of John Marshall to the Chief
Justiceship it was restored and enhanced.[13]

There was a fourth consideration making for acquiescence in judicial review, one that emerged with increasing
persuasiveness with the passing of time, namely, that judicial review was not, in fact, inconsistent with the principle
of majoritarianism. How, after all, did it differ in logic or
in principle from those other limitations on majority will—
the bicameral legislature; the executive veto which assigned to governors and Presidents the power to override
the will of the people; limitations on the terms of office to
which the people could elect officeholders; selection of
Senators by State legislatures rather than by popular vote;
indirect choice of the President himself through an Electoral College, and so forth. All of these were theoretical—
and indeed real—limitations on the popular will, but they
were limits that successive majorities not only tolerated but
reaffirmed by writing some of them into the Constitutions
of new States and by retaining what might be called self-
denying arrangements for the choice of a President in successive amendments to the Constitution. What emerged out
of all this was the dramatization of the principle that men
like John Adams, steeped in Old World history, rejected:

that majorities could and in fact did impose limits upon themselves.

Thus, even while the Americans were institutionalizing the revolutionary principle that men can govern themselves, they conceded to their Courts, logically the weakest of the organs of government,[14] responsibility for setting limits on the exercise of majority will. Without a specific mandate, without compelling antecedents,[15] without adequate tools or facilities, with no assurance of support but what came from the weight of their own decisions and the spectacle of their own integrity, they took on the task of settling great constitutional disputes between men and government and between two sets of governments. In the process, they illuminated profound problems of political philosophy, reconciled prodigious social and economic interests, and educated the people and their representatives at every level to the true nature of law and of constitutionalism. This was a judicial, political, historical, educational, and moral enterprise such as no other Court in history had heretofore undertaken[16] and which none thereafter was able or willing to emulate.

Thus, Americans resolved the paradox that Jefferson had put in his first Inaugural Address. Impossible, said Tory philosophers. "The supposition that a large concourse of people in a rude and imperfect state of society, or even a majority of them," as the Reverend Jonathan Boucher put it, "should thus rationally concur to subject themselves to various restrictions, many of them irksome and unpleasant, is to suppose them possessed of more wisdom and virtue than multitudes in any other instancy in real life have ever shown."[17] The morose Loyalist preacher was no doubt right. Yet that is precisely what Americans did. "Who are a free people?" the Pennsylvania Farmer had asked back in 1768. "Not those over whom government is reasonably and equitably exercised, but those who live under a government so constitutionally checked and controlled, that proper provision is made against its being otherwise exercised."

Now there were two formidable objections to this bundle of principles and practices whereby Americans placed restraints upon government, and upon themselves. The first

was practical. Written Constitutions, separation of powers,
checks and balances, bicameral legislatures, executive
vetoes, annual elections, an interlocking network of governments—why the wonder is that with all these, government could function at all. Yet function it did and, for
some time at least, with exemplary efficiency. How the
Americans managed this was, in a sense, their private
joke.‡ And did any other government accomplish so
much that was lasting, in so short a time? Doubtless the
French National Assembly of 1789 did—but how much of
its great accomplishments lasted? At the very time when
Jefferson was triumphantly vindicating the American revolutionary experiment, Napoleon was putting an end to the
French. Or did any of the innumerable states of Germany
or Italy work as well as Massachusetts or Virginia, or even
frontier Vermont? Or was any other people in the eighteenth-century world as content with its government as the
American? Jefferson's expostulation to those who had been
unduly frightened by Shays's "rebellion" remained valid:

> Thus I calculate: an insurrection in one of the thir-
> teen States in the course of eleven years . . . amounts
> to one in any particular state in one hundred and
> forty-three years, say a century and a half. This
> would not be near as many as have happened in every
> other government that has ever existed.[18]

What Jefferson wrote in 1787 remained true until 1860.
Certainly there were no State revolts—except that in
Rhode Island—and the so-called Dorr Rebellion was a
revolt in favor of constitutionalism, not against it.[19] And
because the elements that balanced in America were, on
the whole, harmonious (there was never any balance on
slavery and it was this, in the end, that disrupted the
Union), Americans managed to make of checks and balances not a jumble of disjointed parts, but an engine of
effective government.

The second objection was more serious, for it was philosophical. It was all very well for Americans to conjure up

‡ The phrase is, of course, from Henry James's marvelous essay on
Hawthorne.

the specter of tyranny when they were "slaves to the remorseless oppression" of George III, and "crouched beneath their sufferings . . ." The phrases are those of the Regulators of North Carolina, but they can be matched by Jefferson's more elegant charge of a "design to reduce [the Colonies] under absolute despotism." But did the principle of limits on governments make sense in a democracy, and was it right for a non-elected body of judges to impose limits on the will of the majority as expressed through their representatives? Even more sobering, was it right for one generation to impose its will on future generations?

No more difficult questions than these in the whole range of American political history or philosophy.[20] In theory—even in the American theory—the Parliamentary system was more logical, for there the majority had its way and no Court could or would say them nay. In theory, too, the Jeffersonian gloss on the validity of Constitutions was logical: a formal reconsideration of fundamental law every twenty years, so that the dead would not control the living, or the past control the future.

But all this was only if you assumed that all "rights" were the same and all laws of equal dignity—the rights of conscience, and the right to graze your cattle on the common; the laws of Nature, or the laws governing service in the militia. That was not the view of the Founding Fathers. They knew that some rights were fundamental—so fundamental that they were grafted into the very nature of things, so fundamental that "they could never be erased by mortal hand." Such laws were like the axioms of Euclid or the laws of Newton, and it was as absurd to suppose that they could be repealed or rewritten by popular vote as to suppose that a majority could rewrite the *Elements* of Euclid or the *Principia* of Newton whenever it suited their fancy. It was no more a violation of the majority principle to insist on the supremacy of such law than it was to insist on the validity of the multiplication table.

As it turned out, Americans had the best of both worlds —the world of Newton, and the world of the *Federalist Papers*. It was one of the authors of those papers—himself no friend to majority rule or to limited government—who saw most clearly that limited government was neither a denial of democracy nor a confession of weakness.

> When you have divided, and nicely balanced, the departments of government [wrote Hamilton], when you have strongly connected the virtue of your rulers with their interest, when, in short, you have rendered your system as perfect as human forms can be, you must place confidence, you must give power.[21]

That is what the Americans of this generation did. The principle that inspired separation of powers may have been doctrinaire, but there was nothing doctrinaire about the energy of a Washington or the audacity of a Hamilton or the authority of a Marshall. And, as it turned out, the checks really checked—the history of judicial review testifies to that—and the balances really balanced. And for all the limitations that threatened to paralyze government,* there was energy enough to meet every contingency. Madison's observation that ultimate reliance must be not on "external principles" but on the "internal structure" of government was profound, but even it did not penetrate to the heart of the matter. *Ultimate* reliance was on the virtue, the intelligence, and the sophistication of the people. This was not wanting in the Revolutionary generation.

* John Adams recorded "an event of the most trifling nature," which nevertheless made a strong impression on him. Riding along a country road, in the fall of 1775, he met a horse jockey who saluted him joyfully. 'Oh, Mr. Adams, what great things have you and your colleagues done for us! We can never be grateful enough to you. There are no Courts of Justice now in this Province, and I hope there never will be another.' Is this the object for which I have been contending? said I to myself, for I rode along without any answer to this wretch . . . If the power of the country should get into such hands to what purpose have we sacrificed our time, health, and everything else? Surely we must guard against this spirit and these principles or we shall repent of all our conduct![22]

The Term "Philosophe"

There is no satisfactory English equivalent for the term Philosophe—certainly not philosopher nor savant, nor sage, nor even that term which the French did use to designate the Philosophes, luminaries.[1] Yet the difference between philosopher and Philosophe is fundamental to an understanding of the Enlightenment. There were, to be sure, a few Philosophes who had some claim to be considered philosophers—Helvétius, perhaps, and Condorcet and Condillac, Gaetano Filangieri in Italy and Benito Feyjóo in Spain, and there were philosophers who, by our standards, must be counted among the Philosophes: Hume and Bentham, Christian Wolff and Immanuel Kant among them.

The distinction between the two (we cannot say the two corps or fellowships, because the philosophers did not constitute a corps, though the Philosophes did)[2] is clear enough, but it emerges not from analysis or from definition, but from interpretation and description. The philosopher was a scholar, a savant, one who devoted himself single-mindedly to the search for Truth which was both universal and permanent. The Philosophe was interested chiefly in those truths which might be useful, here and now. The philosopher was preoccupied with the mind and the soul of the individual, and with great questions of theology and morality; the Philosophe was more concerned with society than with the individual, and with institutions than with ideas. Where the philosopher constructed systems, the Philosophe formulated programs. The ideal philosopher was something of a recluse—Kant is the symbol here—but the Philosophe was (not always in Scotland, or Germany) a man of the world, eager to enlighten, to change, to reform, even to subvert, and ready to take an active part in each of these enterprises. The worst fate that could befall a Philosophe would be exile or debarment from the drama that so fascinated him: imagine Voltaire a recluse, imagine Diderot silenced, imagine Franklin restricted to philosophical speculations, or Tom Paine confined to one country!

While many of the Philosophes were prepared to fashion political systems—or Utopias—they were not very interested in moral systems. What distinguished them everywhere was a commitment to the immediate and the practical—government, law, the penal code, censorship, slavery, religious bigotry. They believed ardently in posterity, but were not prepared to wait for it: Patience was not one of their virtues. They were not interested in philosophy, and theology most of them (though not all) found a waste of time. They were Natural Philosophers—what we call scientists—and worshipped at the altar of Newton: A passion for astronomy, mathematics, botany, geology, anthropology, chemistry, physics, and medicine seems to have been their distinctive common denominator. They were educators, and they helped lay the foundations for modern education at every level from Pestalozzi and his kindergarten to Munchausen at Göttingen and Jefferson at the University of Virginia. They were revolutionaries prepared to subvert many of the institutions of society, and reformers ready to reconstruct society on rational lines. They were rationalists and Deists, hostile almost everywhere to revealed religion and to the ecclesiastical institutions which sustained it. They were humanitarians: They crusaded for the end of the debtor's prison, the galleys and the stake, the end of slavery, of torture, and of the Inquisition. They were—all of them—men of letters: the Duke of Gloucester could have addressed them collectively with his famous expostulation; Scribble, scribble, scribble, eh, Mr.

Gibbon, for all of them scribbled incessantly, and the twentieth-century mind boggles at the sheer volume of writing of busy men like a von Haller, a Voltaire, a Diderot, a Priestley, a Goethe, a Jefferson. They were citizens of the world, at home in a half dozen countries: French was their language and Paris their capital (though not for the Americans), but for art they looked to the ancient world, for music to Italy, for philosophy to England and Scotland, for government and law to England, for freedom to Holland, for morality to America, and for their ideal commonwealth to China, which they invented.

They were statesmen, too, but—to use John Adams's phrase—in *posse* rather than in *esse*. They yearned to play an active part in the affairs of government. They wrote elaborately on both the spirit and the substance of the laws and attached themselves, somewhat indiscriminately, to sovereigns they thought enlightened, or whom they hoped to enlighten. Thus, Voltaire rejoiced, for a time, in the company of Frederick the Great, and Diderot basked in the favor of the Semiramis of the North; Sonnenfels faithfully served Joseph II, and Struensee betrayed Christian VII; the American Count Rumford was the alter ego of the Elector of Bavaria and Pedro Campomanes attached himself to Carlos III of Spain, while Goethe was content to overshadow the Duke of Weimar. Only in America did the Philosophes have the happiness to be kings in their own right.

All of this might have added up to a political and a social philosophy, but the Philosophes had neither the desire nor the patience to do the addition: of the major figures only Vico and Montesquieu—both of whom belong to an earlier era—and Hume and Kant wrote formal philosophical treatises, and of these only *The Spirit of the Laws* had any significant influence on events or institutions. Even the American Philosophes, who did play an active role in public affairs, dashed off their political treatises only under pressure: thus Jefferson's *Notes on Virginia,* thus Adams's *Defense of the Constitutions,* thus even the *Federalist Papers,* originally not a political treatise but a journalistic tour de force.

* * *

The most elaborate of contemporary interpretations of the term Philosophe can be read in the various versions of an essay, *Le Philosophe,* published first in 1743 in a volume, *Nouvelles Libertés de penser,* and written (in all likelihood) by an obscure pamphleteer César Dumarsais. This was reprinted, with variations, by Diderot in volume XII of the Encyclopédie,[3] elaborated by Voltaire in various versions of the *Dictionnaire Philosopheque,* and reprinted frequently thereafter. It is the Diderot version in the Encyclopédie that is, for our purposes, central, both because of the authority it derived from Diderot's sponsorship and because through the Encyclopédie it reached if not the largest, then the most distinguished audience.

"We should," wrote Diderot (let us assign it to him for convenience), "have a larger and more accurate conception [*une idée plus vaste et plus juste*] of the Philosophe," and he proceeded to provide it. It is sufficient here to note some of the more perspicacious observations, and we can begin with the most famous of all: "Reason is to the Philosophe what grace is to the Christian."

Let us listen to some of the others:[4]

The Philosophe is a clock which, so to speak, sometimes winds itself.

A Philosophe, even in moments of passion, acts only after reflection; he walks through the night but is preceded by a torch.

Your Philosophe does not think he lives in exile in this world. He does not believe himself to be in enemy territory. He is an *honnête homme* . . . who wishes to render himself useful.

The temperament of the Philosophe is to act out of a feeling for Order and Reason. . . . He is kneaded, so to speak, with the leaven of rule and of order. . . . He is suffused with concern for the good of civil society, and he understands its principles better than other men.

Wickedness is as alien to the idea of a Philosophe, as

is stupidity, and all experience shows us that the more rational and enlightened a man is, the more suited he is for the business of life.

Graft a sovereign onto a Philosophe of this character, and you will get a ruler who is perfect.

Himself perhaps the most nearly perfect example of the Philosophe, Diderot returned to description and definition again and again; nowhere did he catch the public character of the Philosophe more incisively than in his *Essay on the Reigns of Claudius and Nero:*[5]

The magistrate deals out justice; the Philosophe teaches the magistrate what is just and unjust. The soldier defends his country; the Philosophe teaches the soldier what his fatherland is. The priest recommends to his people the love and respect of the Gods; the Philosophe teaches the priest what the Gods are. The sovereign commands all; the Philosophe teaches the sovereign the origins and limits of his authority. Every man has duties to his family and his society; the Philosophe teaches every one what those duties are. Man is exposed to misfortune and pain; the Philosophe teaches man how to suffer.

The Philosophe was a "citizen of the world," not just of France, and one could compile a substantial anthology of European commentary on the term. Thus, Edward Gibbon, himself perhaps more of an érudite than a Philosophe, comparing the two in his youthful *Essay on the Study of Literature* (1761)[6] paid tribute to the Philosophe:

He weighs, combines, doubts and decides. Exact and impartial he yields only to Reason, or to that authority which is the rationale of facts (e.g., drawn from experience). . . . Ready and fertile in resources, he has no deceitful cunning; he is willing to sacrifice the most brilliant and specious theory and does not make his authors speak the language of his own conjectures. A Friend to Truth, he seeks only for those kinds of proof appropriate to his subject and with them he is

content. . . . Far from being satisfied with barren admiration, he dives into the most obscure recesses of
the human heart to obtain a satisfactory explanation
of his likes and dislikes. Modest and sensible he does
not display his conjectures as truths, his inductions as
facts, his probabilities as demonstrations.

In Naples, Gaetano Filangieri, who had created a Science
of Legislation, wrote that a Philosophe "should not be an
inventor of systems but an apostle of truth." It is his duty
"to preach the truth, to sustain it, to promote it, and to illustrate it" for "he is a citizen of all places and ages, and
has the whole world for his country and earth itself for his
school, and Posterity will be his disciples."[7] Goethe—it
was in his *Dichtung und Wahrheit*—was reminiscent
rather than analytical. Everyone, he recalled,

was now entitled not only to philosophize, but little
by little to esteem himself a Philosopher. Philosophy,
too, was taken to be common sense, more or less
sound, which ventured to enter upon the Universal
and to contradict inner and outer experiences. . . .
And so, at last, philosophers were to be found in all
the faculties.[8]

Falling back on Horace for his definition, Kant put it more
succinctly than the others of his era: *"Sapere Aude*
(Dare to think) that is the motto of the Enlightenment."
It was, by implication, the definition of the Philosophe as
well: one who dared to think.

Needless to say, the Philosophes did not have things
their own way when it came to definition or interpretation.
The anonymous author of *Les Choses comme-il-faut les
Voir,*[9] defined the Philosophe as "an impertinent fellow
behind whom lurked a bad man. In our own interests," he
added, "we ought to drive out of society anyone who has
the effrontery to bear the name." And the irrepressible
Horace Walpole wrote from Paris in 1765:

Do you know who the Philosophes are, what the term
means here? In the first place it comprehends almost

everybody, and in the next means men who, vowing war against popery, aim at a subversion of all religion, and still many more at the destruction of regal power.

And he added that the Philosophes were "insupportable, superficial, overbearing, and fanatical. They preach incessantly."[10]

* * *

Curiously enough the distinction between the philosopher and the Philosophe is more appropriate to the American than to the Old World Enlightenment. For America had no philosophers, not after Jonathan Edwards, anyway, or—if you are amiable in your judgment—James Logan of Philadelphia or Cadwallader Colden of New York or Professor John Winthrop of Cambridge, but it was generously and even lavishly endowed with Philosophes. And what we have remarked of the Philosophes in general, was peculliarly true of the American variety: They were men of action rather than of reflection, launching a revolution (a successful one, too), drawing up Constitutions, drafting Bills of Rights, founding new commonwealths, and enlarging a new nation.

The American Philosophes did not differ markedly in their thinking from their Old World associates. They too exalted Reason and worshipped at the altar of Liberty; they too cultivated the natural sciences and worked for a more humane society; they too were cosmopolitans. But there were differences, and these illuminated the larger differences between the Old World and the New World Enlightenment. Consider some of these.

First there is a difference in time. We can date the Old World Enlightenment from the founding of the Royal Society in 1661, or perhaps from the publication of Newton's *Principia* in 1687. It died in the Terror. The American Enlightenment came half a century later—we can date it with some assurance from the founding of the American Philosophical Society in 1741. It lasted until well into the new century and it is permissible to draw down the curtain on it with the dramatic deaths of John Adams and Thomas Jefferson in 1826. The delay and prolongation of the Enlightenment in America was not just a matter of cultural lag; it was, too, a tribute to the elementary fact that in America there was no Terror, no Thermidor, and no counterrevolution to bring the Enlightenment to a dusty climax. Here the Enlightenment blended gently into romanticism.

Second, where in the Old World the Philosophes tended to be a class apart, a distinct and self-conscious element in society, almost a clique, in the New they were drawn from the rank and file of the people, and worked and lived with the people. They were not érudites, for the New nation had no érudites; they were not aristocrats not even aristocrats *manqué*, for there were no aristocrats: if you were a Benjamin Thompson yearning for rank, you went to Europe to become Count Rumford. They did not cultivate monarchs, but denounced them; they did not gather in salons—that came only in the new century; they did not have their own gazettes and journals, or launch their own encyclopedias, but imported these from abroad. They were lawyers and doctors, farmers and planters, merchants and clergymen; they drew strength from each other but more from the people they represented. They did not use the words Philosophe or Philosopher; the distinction of "Doctor" Franklin was about as far as they were prepared to go in the recognition of a special status, and that title was not commonly used for others.

A third distinction between Old World and New Philosophes was in the realm of religion and morals. Of all the major American Philosophes, only Tom Paine—who was after all English—felt compelled to make an issue of his hostility to traditional Christianity, and that ruined him even with most of his fellow philosophers. Deists like Franklin and Jefferson had no trouble in reconciling their private skepticism with public orthodoxy, and a good many of them—Benjamin Rush and David Rittenhouse come to mind—were devout. Nor did the American Philosophe think himself exempted from the standards of conventional morality: How shocked John Adams was at the harmless flirtations of Dr. Franklin, and John Laurens at the immoralities of London. How shocked was even the

sophisticated Jefferson at the wide-ranging amours of his
French and English friends: That was the chief reason he
advised against sending young men abroad for an education.[11] The connection between Enlightenment and *libertinage,* so familiar in France was, if not wholly unknown,
then unacknowledged in America.

This suggests a fourth distinction—that the American
Enlightenment owed less to France than did the European.
Franklin, to be sure, adored the French and Jefferson
adored France, but when they went to France they went as
masters, not as disciples. Rousseau, Voltaire, Diderot, Turgot, the Encyclopédistes—these meant nothing to the
American Philosophes, or meant at best some convenient
intellectual window dressing, and if Montesquieu was a
name to conjure with, he was just a name: It was, after all,
the Americans themselves who invented a true separation
of powers. This is not to say that the American Philosophes were provincial; they were deeply immersed in English antecedents for their philosophy, and in the literature
and history of Greece and Rome. It is interesting that the
ancient world contributed more to the American than to
the French Revolution.

This independence dramatizes a fifth difference between
Old World and New Philosophes, and one with far-
reaching implications. The Old World Enlightenment was
urban. Paris was its capital, but London and Edinburgh,
Geneva and Amsterdam, Berlin and Hamburg, Naples and
Milan—these were provincial capitals, which sometimes
rivaled Paris. The Americans, to be sure, had no capital
cities, though Philadelphia was rapidly becoming another
Edinburgh or, perhaps, Weimar. Franklin was very urban,
and so, too, Hamilton (whose credentials as a Philosophe
were dubious), but the great majority of the American
philosophers shared Jefferson's passion for the simple and
virtuous life of the husbandman: During the whole of the
American Enlightenment, every President was a coun-
tryman. All this was greatly to enhance the romantic element of the American Enlightenment.

The predominantly rural character of the American Enlightenment accounts in part for a sixth distinction: the
meager role that economics played in the thought of the

American Philosophes. Jefferson, to be sure, was committed to agrarianism, and he read both the Physiocrats and the Idéologues,[12] but the commitment, one feels, was more moral than economic. Hamilton, like so many of his Old World contemporaries, thought in terms of economic nationalism and developed an American form of mercantilism, but he was the exception who dramatizes the American rule, for he was neither a Philosophe nor, for that matter, an American—not in his thinking anyway. The New World produced statesmen and jurists who could hold their own with the Old, but it produced no Adam Smith, no Bentham, no Turgot, no Johann Struensee, no Antonio Genovesi. It managed, instead, to do what the Old World Enlightenment was unable to do: It successfully combined mercantilism and physiocracy.

A seventh—and doubtless the most important—difference between Old and New World Philosophes was one with which we are by now familiar: that the American Philosophe did not need to embark upon those crusades which engaged the energies of almost all the European, and was therefore free to follow his own. He was not called upon to uproot ancient abuses (always except for slavery, which he was unable to eradicate) or to topple a ruling class, to end feudalism, to wipe out the Infamy, to oust the Jesuits, to abolish the Inquisition. He could devote himself to activities that were constructive and productive, and that had a very good chance of being realized. Like his Old World associates he was engaged in a crusade, but it was a positive, not a negative, crusade. That is one reason why the literature of the American Enlightenment —except where it is almost ritualistically denouncing British tyranny and corruption—is so different from the literature of the French or the Italian. If the American Enlightenment produced no *Candide,* no *Nathan the Wise,* no *On Crimes and Punishments,* the European produced no *Federalist Papers.*

Another reason for the difference in the literature of the two Enlightenments was the absence of any censorship in America. The American Philosophes did not have to be everlastingly on guard against the censorship of the State, the Church, and the University; they did not have to take refuge in evasion and subterfuge; they did not need to flee to some convenient Geneva or Amsterdam to escape imprisonment—or worse. Nor did they need to invent mythical Persian or Chinese visitors, or imagine Utopias on the Moon, or under the ground, or in Tahiti or the Andes, as a way of criticizing existing institutions. They could write boldly; they could attack the King, the Church, property—whatever they would—without fear of reprisal.

Finally, the American Philosophes were not required to struggle against the Establishment: They *were* the Establishment. They did not wear out their hearts, or their lives, in futile efforts to overthrow the wrongs and tyrannies of the past; they could address themselves to building a future. They did not need to accustom themselves to failure, hoping that Posterity would vindicate them; they could take success for granted, and be confident that Posterity would remember them gratefully—as indeed it has. As they did not construct Utopias because America was itself Utopia, so they did not write treatises on Happiness or on Progress, confident that these could be taken for granted.

Notes

In the following Notes, these abbreviations will be used: Balt. (Baltimore); Bost. (Boston); Calif. (California); Camb. (Cambridge, England); Ind. (Indiana); L. (London); Cambridge (Mass.); N.Y. (New York City); O. (Ohio); Tex. (Texas); Wash. (Washington, D.C.)

CHAPTER ONE

1. See Kant's famous observation: "If some one asks, are we living in an enlightened age? the answer would be No. But . . . we are living in an Age of Enlightenment." Qt. Peter Gay, *The Enlightenment: The Rise of Modern Paganism* (N.Y., 1966), 20, from "Beantwortung der Frage, Was ist Aufklarung?"

2. The debt of the Enlightenment to the classical past is the central theme of the first volume of Professor Gay's *Enlightenment*. Some aspects of this of special interest to America are explored below in chapters three and four.

3. Pope's *Essay on Man* was published in 1732–34.

4. Thus, Terra Australia Incognita, with a land mass as large as the whole of Europe and fifty million inhabitants, was extinguished, as it were, by Captain Cook on the second of his great voyages. See J. A. Williamson, *Cook and the Opening of the Pacific* (L., 1946); John C. Beaglehole, *Captain Cook* (L., 1974); and Vincent Harlow, *The Founding of the Second British Empire*, Vol. I, Ch. ii.

5. A. O. Lovejoy, *The Great Chain of Being* (Cambridge, 1935, and several recent reprints) is the authoritative work. See, too, Charles Gillispie, *Genesis and Geology* (N.Y., 1951). Jef-

ferson paid tribute to the principle in his *Notes on Virginia.* "It may be asked why I insert the mammoth, as if it still existed? I ask in return why I should omit it, as if it did not exist? Such is the economy of nature, that no instance can be produced of her having permitted any one race of her animals to become extinct; of her having formed any link in her great work so weak as to be broken." II Mem. ed., 71; Peden ed., 53–54. Philip Freneau expressed the same notion:

> See with most exact design
> The world revive, the planets shine
> The nicest order, all things meet,
> A structure in itself complete.
> Here beauty, order, power behold
> Exact, all perfect, uncontrolled,
> All in its proper place arranged,
> Immortal, endless and unchanged.

(Qt. Nye, *Cultural Life of the New Nation,* N.Y., 1960).

In his *Lectures on Natural History* (Philadelphia, 1820), the painter Charles Willson Peale quoted with approval the lines from James Thomson's *Seasons:*

> Each shell, each crawling insect, holds a rank
> Important in the plan of Him who form'd
> This scale of beings; holds a rank, which lost
> Would break the chain. . . .

6. Charles C. Gillispie, *Genesis and Geology* (Cambridge, 1951), Ch. 2–3. See also C. L. and M. A. Fenton, *Giants of Geology* (N.Y., 1952).

7. Herschel discovered the planet Uranus in 1781. On Herschel, see A. Abetti, *The History of Astronomy* (N.Y., 1952) and H. C. King, *The History of the Telescope* (L., 1956). On eighteenth-century technology and science in general, see R. Mousnier and F. Labrousse, *Le XVIIIe Siècle: Révolution Intellectuale, Technique and Politique* (Paris, 1955).

8. The reworking of the Encyclopédie was launched in 1782 but not brought to completion until 1832. The text itself was divided by subject matter—Politics, Jurisprudence, Economics, and so forth, and filled 108 volumes and 13 demi-volumes, and the plates required another 8 volumes and 26 demi-volumes. There is an elaborate bibliographical note about this enterprise in E. M. Sowerby, comp., *Library of Thomas Jefferson,* V (Wash., 1959), Ch. xliv.

9. On Buffon and Linnaeus, see below. Réamur's *Mémoires pour servir à l'histoire des insectes* appeared in six volumes in

1734–42, and was one of the more widely read scientific works of its day. See Daniel Mornet, *Les sciences de la Nature en France au XVIIIe siècle* (Paris, 1911).

10. Blumenbach held Haller's chair of anatomy and physiology at Göttingen for almost half a century. His studies of human skulls laid the foundations for scientific work on human anthropology. See ii *Allgemeine Deutsche Biographie* (Leipzig, 1875).

11. See *A Dissertation on Liberty and Necessity, Pleasure and Pain* (first published in London in 1725) in I *Papers of Benjamin Franklin*, ed., L. W. Labaree, 62 (New Haven, 1959).

12. See Leslie Stephen, *English Utilitarians*, I, and the recent biography by Mary B. Mack, *Bentham 1748–1792* (L., 1962).

13. "That Politics May Be Reduced to a Science," in Charles Hendel, ed., *David Hume's Political Essays* (N.Y., 1953).

14. See text and illustrations in John Summerson, *Architecture in Britain 1530–1830* (L., 1953); James Ackerman, *Palladio* (L., 1966); and the sumptuously illustrated *Villas and Palaces of Andrea Palladio*, by Guy Roop (Milano, 1968). Arno Schönberger, *The Age of Rococo* (L., 1966) and Alfred Cobban, ed., *The Eighteenth Century* (L., 1969) are invaluable.

15. *Mémoires sur la Cour de Louis XV*, by the Duc de Luynes, ed. by L. Dussieux and E. Soulie, 17 vols. (Paris, 1860–65).

16. *Les Principes de Menuit* (Paris, 1767). There is a brief note on this book in Arno Schönberger, *Age of Rococo*.

17. Franz Reinhard's *System der Christlichen Moral*, in 5 vols. was published in Wittenberg from 1788 to 1815; Reinhard's sermons fill no less than 39 vols. See his *Memoirs and Confessions*, trans. O. A. Taylor (Boston, 1832).

18. Jonathan Mayhew, "Discourse Concerning Unlimited Submission and Nonresistance to the Higher Powers" (orig. pub., Boston, 1750), reprinted in Bernard Bailyn, ed., *Pamphlets of the American Revolution* (Cambridge, 1965), I, 242.

19. On Monboddo, see Emily Cloyd's short but valuable study, *James Burnett Lord Monboddo* (Oxford, 1972).

20. There is no satisfactory biography of Joseph Banks—that is one of the scandals of English scientific literature—but there is a substantial literature about him. Best of all is J. C. Beaglehole, ed., *The Endeavour Journals of Joseph Banks*, 2 vols. (L., 1962) with a long and brilliant introduction by the editor. The most sympathetic study is by Lord Brougham, "Sir Joseph Banks," in his *Works*, I (L., 1855). Two modern works are Edward Smith, *Life of Sir Joseph Banks* (L., 1911), and H. C. Cameron, *Sir Joseph Banks* (L., 1952). There is a fascinating study of Banks's role as mediator between science and government in Sir Gavin De Beer's *The Sciences Are Never at War*

(L., 1961). See, too, Dorothy Stimson, *Scientists and Amateurs: A History of the Royal Society* (N.Y., 1948); C. R. Weld, *A History of the Royal Society*, 2 vols. (L., 1848); and Lionel Cust, *History of the Society of the Dilettanti*, ed. by Sidney Colvin (L., 1898).

21. Henry Lord Brougham, *Lives of Philosophers of the Time of George III*, 334ff.

22. Sir Gavin De Beer, *The Sciences*, 197.

23. See Harry Woolf, *The Transits of Venus . . .* (Princeton, 1959).

24. See introduction to Beaglehole, ed., *Journal of Joseph Banks*, Vol. I.

25. Ibid., II, 61n.

26. On Mungo Park see articles in *Quarterly Review*, Vols. 22, 38, and 39, and J. N. L. Baker, *A History of Geographical Discovery and Exploration* (L., 1937).

27. On Buffon, see bibliographical note 3 in Ch. Four, Part 2.

28. See the masterly analysis by Clarence Glacken, *Traces on the Rhodean Shore* (Berkeley, 1967), Ch. xiv, and his "Court Buffon on Cultural Changes in the Physical Environment," 50, *Annals of the Assoc. of Amer. Geographers* (1960), 1ff.

29. Three recent works on Linnaeus are Wilfred Blunt's *Compleat Naturalist: The Life and Work of Linnaeus* (N.Y., 1971); Heinz Goerke, *Linnaeus* (N.Y., 1973); and J. L. Larson, *Reason & Experience: The Representation of Natural Order in the work of Carl von Linné* (Berkeley, 1971). As for earlier works, Knut Hagbert's *Carl Linnaeus* (L., 1952) is useful, and something is to be said for the older biography by Benjamin D. Jackson, *Linnaeus, The Story of His Life* (L., 1923), which is adapted from the standard Swedish biography by Theodor M. Fries, and which contains a full bibliography (1903). See, too, Sir J. E. Smith, ed., *A Selection of the Correspondence of Linnaeus*, 2 vols. (L., 1921), and an essay on Linnaeus in L. C. Miall, *The Early Naturalists* (L., 1912). There are some perceptive pages in A. R. Hall, *The Scientific Revolution, 1500–1800* (L., 1954). For Linnaeus's place in literature see Karl Warburg, *Sveriges Literatur Under Frihetstiden och Gustavianska Tidehvartvet* (Stockholm, 1911–12).

30. There is a large literature on the remarkable Haller, but little of it in English. Much the best discussion is in G. de Reynold, *Histoire Littéraire de la Suisse au XVIIIe Siècle*, II, 445–595 (Lausanne, 1912). There are two German monographs of some value: H. E. Jenny, *Haller als Philosoph* (Bale, 1902), and Stephen d'Irsay, *Albrecht von Haller, Eine Studie zur Geistesgeschichte der Aufklärung* (Leipzig, 1930). Haller's med-

ical and anatomical researches have attracted some attention in America. See Henry E. Sigerist, *The Great Doctors* (N.Y., 1958 ed.), Ch. 24; H. Cushing, "Haller and his Native Town," *American Medicine,* 5 October 1901; J. C. Hemmeter, "Albrecht von Haller, Scientific, Literary, and Political Activity," in *Master Minds of Medicine* (N.Y., 1927).

31. See Howard Mumford Jones, "Albrecht von Haller and English Philosophy," *PMLA,* XL (1925), 103. There is a useful bibliography in Margarete Hochdoerfer, *Conflict Between Religious and Scientific Views of Haller* (Lincoln, Neb., 1932).

32. His three Utopian novels are *Usong* (Bern, 1771, and numerous later editions), *Alfred; König der Angel-Sachsen* (Bern, 1773, and numerous later editions), and *Fabius und Cato* (Göttingen, 1774, and numerous later editions).

33. See the delightful book by W. H. Bruford, *Culture and Society in Classical Weimar, 1775–1806* (Cambridge, 1962).

34. Literature on the Aufklärung is enormous. It is perhaps sufficient to cite H. N. Wolff, *Die Weltanschaaung der deutschen Aufklärung* (Berne, 1949); Ernst Cassirer, *The Philosophy of the Enlightenment* (Princeton, 1951); W. H. Bruford, *Germany in the Eighteenth Century* (Cambridge, 1935); John H. Randall, *The Career of Philosophy,* Vol. II (N.Y., 1965); Will and Ariel Durant, *The Age of Voltaire* (N.Y., 1965); Paul Hazard, *European Thought in the Eighteenth Century* (N.Y., 1963); Frederick Hertz, *Development of the German Public Mind,* 2 vols., esp. Vol. II (L., 1962); the early chapters of G. P. Gooch, *Germany and the French Revolution* (N.Y., 1966); and Robert Kahn, *A Study in Austrian Intellectual History* (L., 1960).

35. A. Köster, *Die deutsche Literatur der Aufklärung* (Heidelberg, 1925).

36. There is no biography of Ebeling, but a good deal of miscellaneous information to be gleaned from his letters, and those of his American correspondents. See *Proceedings American Antiquarian Society,* Vol. XXXV (1925); the *Diary of William Bentley,* 4 vols., *passim* (Salem, 1905–14); E. E. Doll, "American History as Interpreted by German Historians," *Transactions American Philosophical Society,* n.s., XXXVIII (1948); and, of great importance, Henry Pochman, *German Culture in America, 1600–1900* (Madison, 1957), 31ff.

37. Doll, op. cit., 477.

38. Passages from the *History* were translated by Peter Duponceau and published in Hazard's Register of Pennsylvania, Vol. I.

39. Quoted in Lane, *Proc. Am. Antiq. Soc.,* XXXV, 413.

40. See Pochman, *German Culture;* O. Long, *Three Literary Pioneers* (Cambridge, 1935); and Doll, op. cit., *passim.*

41. On the acquisition of the Ebeling Library by Harvard, see H. S. Commager, "Science, Learning and the Claims of Nationalism," in *Thoughts from the Lake of Time,* privately printed (N.Y., 1971).

42. On the abortive Dutch Revolution see P. J. Blok, *History of the People of the Netherlands,* Vol. 5, 172ff.; Alfred Cobban, *Ambassadors and Secret Agents* (L., 1954); and the masterly chapter ii in R. R. Palmer, *Age of the Democratic Revolution,* I.

43. There is comparatively little on the fascinating Van der Kemp. See Helen Fairchild, ed., *Francis Adrian Van der Kemp, 1752–1829: An Autobiography Together with Extracts from his Correspondence* (N.Y., 1903), and Harry F. Jackson, *Scholar in the Wilderness: Francis Adrian Van der Kemp* (Syracuse, N.Y., 1963). See also the interchange of letters between Jefferson and John Adams on Van der Kemp (August 1 and 9, 1816) in C. F. Adams, ed., *Works of John Adams,* X, 222–25. They are also in L. J. Cappon, ed., *The Adams-Jefferson Letters* (Chapel Hill, 1959), II, 484–86. See also R. R. Palmer, *Democratic Revolution,* I, *passim.*

44. Quoted in Jackson, op. cit., 34; 30.

45. Quoted in ibid., 42.

46. . . . It all reminded him of an old romance, said Burke: "A chivalrous king, hearing that a princess had been affronted, takes his lance, assembles his knights and determines to do her justice." One sees already his "delightful vision" of Marie Antoinette in the French Revolution, and the ten thousand swords flashing from their scabbards in her defense. . . . (Palmer, *Democratic Revolution,* I, 338–39).

47. On all this, see Jackson, *Scholar,* 58–185, 229–43, 256–97; and Fairchild, *Van der Kemp,* 120–39, 153–200.

CHAPTER TWO

1

1. There is no systematic treatment of the American Enlightenment, or of the Enlightenment in America—not quite the same thing. The nature of that Enlightenment can be reconstructed in part from the writings of its spokesmen—Franklin, Jefferson, John Adams (with reservations and qualifications), Joel Barlow, Benjamin Rush, James Madison, Tom Paine, and others. A useful introduction is Adrienne Koch, ed., *The American Enlightenment* (N.Y., 1965). The most perceptive comparative interpretation is

that by Robert Palmer, *The Age of Democratic Revolution,* Vol. I (Princeton, 1965). See, too, Peter Gay, *The Enlightenment* (2 vols.); Daniel Boorstin, *The Lost World of Thomas Jefferson* (N.Y., 1948); Henry F. May, *The Enlightenment in America* (N.Y., 1976); Daniel Boorstin, *The Americans, The Colonial Experience* (N.Y., 1959); Michael Kraus, *The Atlantic Civilization* (Ithaca, N.Y., 1949); and Perry Miller, *The Life of the Mind in America* (N.Y., 1965). See too, H. S. Commager, *America and the Enlightenment,* in Library of Congress Symposium, Wash., 1972.

2. See E. Alfred Jones, *American Members of the Inns of Court* (L., 1924); William Sachse, *The Colonial American in Britain* (Madison, 1956); Richard Shryock, *Medicine and Society in America* (N.Y., 1960); William T. Whitley, *Artists and their Friends in England, 1700–1799,* Vol. II (L., 1928).

3. On the American Philosophical Society, see Gilbert Chinard, "Am. Philosophical Society and the World of Science" and both in Carl Van Doren, "Beginnings of the *American Philosophical Society,*" 87 *Proc. Am. Phil. Soc.,* 277ff.; Boorstin, *Lost World;* Carl and Jessica Bridenbaugh, *Rebels and Gentlemen: Philadelphia in the Age of Franklin* (N.Y., 1942).

4. Boorstin, *Lost World,* 11.

5. On Logan, see Bridenbaugh, *Rebels and Gentlemen;* F. B. Tolles, *James Logan and the Culture of Provincial America* (Bost., 1957); Brooke Hindle, *Science in Revolutionary America* (Chapel Hill, 1957).

6. Bridenbaugh, *Rebels and Gentlemen,* 307; Brooke Hindle, *David Rittenhouse* (Princeton, 1964).

7. The population of Philadelphia on the eve of the Revolution is variously estimated at between twenty-five and thirty thousand. The only American city that has ever matched the cultural creativity of the Philadelphia of this era is Salem, in the years between the outbreak of the American Revolution and the close of the war of 1812; see James Duncan Phillips, *Salem in the Eighteenth Century* (Boston, 1937), and *Salem and the Indies* (Boston, 1947).

8. Quoted in article on Godfrey by Joseph Jackson in *Dict. Am. Biog.*

9. Jefferson to Rittenhouse, 19 July 1778, Boyd, ed., *The Papers of Thomas Jefferson,* II (Princeton, 1950), 202.

10. On the proposal for the College of Mirania, see Lawrence A. Cremin *American Education: The Colonial Experience* (N.Y., 1970), 378ff. On Provost Smith, see Albert Gegenheimer, *William Smith, Educator and Churchman* (Philadelphia, 1943), and Henry May, *The Enlightenment* (N.Y., 1976).

11. On medicine in colonial Philadelphia, see Bridenbaugh, *Rebels*, Ch. viii; Hindle, *Science in Revolutionary America*, Ch. xiii; William Norwood, *Medical Education in the United States Before the Civil War* (Philadelphia, 1941); and Theodore Hornberger, *Scientific Thought in the American Colonies* (Austin, Tex., 1945).

12. James Flexner, *First Flowers of the Wilderness* (Boston, 1947), *Light of Distant Skies* (Boston, 1964), and *America's Old Masters* (N.Y., 1939); Charles Sellers, *The Artist of the Revolution: the Early Life*, 2 vols.

13. Van Wyck Brooks, *The World of Washington Irving*, Ch. I (N.Y., 1944), and Howard Mumford Jones, *America and French Culture*, Chs. 4 and 5 (Chapel Hill, N.C., 1927).

14. The literature on Franklin is voluminous. It is perhaps sufficient to cite Carl Van Doren, *Benjamin Franklin* (N.Y., 1938); Edward E. Hale, *Franklin in France*, 2 vols. (1887); Paul L. Ford, *The Many Sided Franklin* (1899); and Paul W. Conner, *Poor Richard's Politiks* (N.Y., 1965).

15. Sewall's *Diary* was not published until 1878. A *Vindication of Government of the New England Churches* was published in 1717, and William Byrd's *History of the Dividing Line*—which he surveyed in the year 1728—was first printed in 1841.

16. Infant mortality, even in eighteenth-century America, was appallingly high, but those who survived had a good chance of living to a ripe old age. The longevity of the Founding Fathers is, nevertheless, remarkable. Washington died at 67, Jay at 84, Jefferson at 83, John Adams at 90, John Marshall at 80, Samuel Adams at 81, Aaron Burr at 80, and even Tom Paine lived to be 72—this in an age when life expectancy was somewhere in the thirties.

17. II, *Franklin Papers*, ed., Labaree, 382.

18. The first word was the draft of the Albany Plan of Union of 1754, see Commager, *Documents of American History*, No. 31; the last word was famous "rising not a setting sun" speech on the last day of the Convention: see in Farrand, *Records of the Federal Convention*, II, 648.

19. So said Condorcet, in his *Eulogy* on the death of Franklin: "He had in politics as in morality the type of indulgence which demands little because it hopes much and which pardons the present in favor of the future. . . . His politics was that of a man who believed in the power of reason and the reality of virtue and who had wished to make himself teacher of his fellow citizens before being called to be their legislator." Qt. from Alfred O. Aldridge, *Franklin and his French Contemporaries* (N.Y., 1957), 227.

20. *Works,* ed., C. F. Adams (Boston, 1856), 660. This was written for the Boston *Patriot* in 1811, as part of what was on the whole a critical interpretation. Other parts of this fascinating discussion of Franklin and Adams in Paris are worth quoting. Thus, further on Franklin, Adams wrote:

"While he had the singular felicity to enjoy the entire esteem and affection of all the philosophers of every denomination, he was not less regarded by all the sects and denominations of Christians. The Catholics thought him almost a Catholic. The Church of England claimed him as one of them. The Presbyterians thought him half a Presbyterian, and the Friends believed him a wet Quaker. The dissenting clergymen in England and America were among the most distinguished asserters and propagators of his renown. Indeed, all sects considered him, and I believe justly, a friend to unlimited toleration in matters of religion. . . .

". . . He was thought a profound legislator, and a friend of democracy. He was thought to be the magician who had excited the ignorant Americans to resistance. His mysterious wand had separated the Colonies from Great Britain. He had framed and established all the American constitutions of government, especially all the best of them, *i.e.,* the most democratical. His plans and his example were to abolish monarchy, aristocracy, and hierarchy throughout the world. Such opinions as these were entertained by the Duke de la Rochefoucauld, M. Turgot, M. Condorcet, and a thousand other men of learning and eminence in France, England, Holland, and all the rest of Europe. . . .

"Franklin had a great genius, original, sagacious, and inventive, capable of discoveries in science no less than of improvements in the fine arts and the mechanic arts. He had a vast imagination, equal to the comprehension of the greatest objects, and capable of a steady and cool comprehension of them. He had wit at will. He had humor that, when he pleased, was delicate and delightful. He had a satire that was good-natured or caustic, Horace or Juvenal, Swift or Rabelais, at his pleasure. He had talents for irony, allegory, and fable, that he could adapt with great skill to the promotion of moral and political truth. . . .

". . . Although I am not ignorant that most of his positions and hypotheses have been controverted, I cannot but think he has added much to the mass of natural knowledge, and contributed largely to the progress of the human mind, both by his own writings and by the controversies and experiments he has excited in all parts of Europe. . . ."

See also, 661, 663, 664.

21. Adams's account is in his autobiography, IV *Diary and*

Autobiography of John Adams, ed., L. H. Butterfield, 81 (Cambridge, 1961).

CHAPTER TWO
2

1. The literature on Dr. Rush is voluminous. Perhaps the best introduction is Lyman Butterfield's Introduction to the two-volume edition of his *Letters* (Philadelphia, 1951), and his article, "Benjamin Rush as a Promoter of Useful Knowledge," 92 *Proc. Am. Phil. Soc.,* 26 March 1946. See, too, George W. Corner, ed., *The Autobiography of Benjamin Rush* (Philadelphia, 1934). Brooke Hindle, *Pursuit of Science in Revolutionary America 1735–1789* (Chapel Hill, 1956) has a chapter on Medicine, and Rush figures largely in Carl and Jessica Bridenbaugh, *Rebels and Gentlemen.*

2. Rush read many papers to the Society, and served, successively, as curator, secretary, councilor, and vice-president.

3. For details see bibliography in Nathan G. Goodman, *Benjamin Rush, Physician and Citizen* (Philadelphia, 1934).

4. Biographers of Rush and of Paine give slightly different versions of the role that Rush played in *Common Sense.* Goodman credits Dr. Rush with the idea and with supervising the manuscript as well as suggesting the title; Philip Foner (intro. to *Complete Writing of Paine*), and David Hawke, *Thomas Paine* (N.Y., 1975) credit Rush only with the title. See, however, Rush's own recollection in letter of 1809, Butterfield, ed., *Letters of Benjamin Rush,* Vol. II (Princeton, 1951), 1008.

5. The most successful in the number of students and perhaps in influence; not, certainly, in the number of lives saved, for his commitment to bleeding took a deadly toll.

6. N. G. Goodman has edited a collection of the miscellaneous writings of Rush (Philadelphia, 1934), and so, too, has Dagobert Runes.

7. Butterfield, *Letters,* 2 vols., is a treasure-trove.

8. Rush's argument can be found in *Trans. American Phil. Soc.,* 4 (1799), 289. See discussion in Winthrop Jordan, *White over Black* (Chapel Hill, 1968), Ch. xiv.

9. H. G. Good, *Benjamin Rush and his Services to American Education* (Berne, Ind., 1918).

10. See Butterfield, *Letters,* I, 83, 85.

11. See Leon Howard, *The Connecticut Wits* (Chicago, 1943).

12. The literature on Barlow is voluminous. The most perceptive interpretation is by Howard, *Connecticut Wits.* See also,

Charles Todd, *Life and Letters of Joel Barlow* (N.Y., 1886); Theodore Lunder, *The Early Days of Joel Barlow* (New Haven, 1934); James Woodress, *A Yankee Odyssey* (Philadelphia, 1958), and the somewhat overblown interpretation by John Dos Passos in *The Ground We Stand On* (N.Y., 1941). Several essays illuminate the career of this somewhat elusive figure: Moses Coit Tyler, *Three Men of Letters* (N.Y., 1895), Ch. iii; Milton Cantor, "Joel Barlow, Lawyer and Legal Philosopher," 10, *American Quarterly*, 165; and V. L. Parrington, *The Colonial Mind* (N.Y., 1927), 317ff.

13. The lines are from the *Hasty Pudding*.

14. There are two versions of this elaborate poem. *The Vision of Columbus* was published in 1787; an enlarged *Columbiad* came out twenty years later, handsomely illustrated with engravings by Robert Fulton.

15. See V. L. Parrington, ed., *The Connecticut Wits* (N.Y., 1926).

16. Volney's *Les Ruines ou Méditations sur les révolutions des empires,* first appeared in 1791. Barlow's translation probably appeared in 1802, but the date is uncertain.

17. His "Prospectus of a National Institution to be Established in the United States" appeared in 1805. See David Madsen, *The National University, Enduring Dream of the U.S.A.* (Detroit, 1966).

18. There is no modern biography of Cutler—one of the lamentable gaps in American historical literature. See William and Julia Cutler, *Life Journals and Correspondence of the Rev. Manasseh Cutler*, 2 vols. (Cincinnati, 1888).

19. For Bentley it is sufficient to list the *Diary of William Bentley*, 4 vols. (Salem, Mass., 1905–14); James D. Phillips, *Salem in the Eighteenth Century* (Boston, 1937); and Esther Forbes, *Running of the Tide* (Boston, 1948). For Belknap, see Jane M. Belknap, *Life of Jeremy Belknap* (1847), and J. S. Bassett, *Middle Group of American Historians* (N.Y., 1917). *The Foresters* was published in 1792. For Dwight, see Charles E. Cunningham, *Timothy Dwight* (N.Y., 1942); for Stiles, the masterly biography by Edmund S. Morgan, *The Gentle Puritan* (New Haven, 1962).

20. See for all this the biography by William and Julia Cutler, op. cit.

21. It was Nathan Dane of neighboring Beverly who was chiefly responsible for the Northwest Ordinance, but Dr. Cutler was very part of the whole enterprise, both at New York and in Ohio.

22. Pamphlet on Emigration to Ohio, reprinted in Cutler, *Life*

and Letters, I, 346. The lines of poetry are from Philip Freneau, *The Rising Glory of America.*

23. There is no wholly satisfactory biography of Dr. Priestley, but material for an interpretation can be culled not only from his own voluminous writings, but from histories of science, education, and religion. The standard biography is by John T. Rutt, who edited the *Theological and Miscellaneous Works* in 26 volumes (the "miscellaneous" did not even cover such things as his *History of Electricity*) or the *Life and Correspondence of Joseph Priestley,* 2 vols. (L., 1932). More recent studies are T. E. Thorpe, *Joseph Priestley* (L., 1906); Alice Holt, *Life of Joseph Priestley* (L., 1931); and E. W. Gibbs, *Joseph Priestley, Adventurer in Science and Champion of Truth* (L., 1965). See, too, the observations of Caroline Robbins in *The Eighteenth-Century Commonwealthmen* (Cambridge, 1959). Lord Brougham's essay in his *Collected Works,* Vol. 1, is critical and jaundiced. As for Lord Shelburne, nothing yet has supplanted the 3-vol. biography by E. G. P. Fitzmaurice (L., 1875), but see John Norris, *Shelburne and Reform* (L., 1963).

24. See Irene Parker, *The Dissenting Academies* (Camb., 1914); and J. W. Ashley Smith, *Birth of Modern Education: The Dissenting Academies* (L., 1954). On the Warrington Academy—where Priestley taught—see H. McLachlan, *The Warrington Academy* . . . (Manchester, 1943; reprinted, N.Y., 1969).

25. On the famous Lunar Society, see Robert Schofield, *The Lunar Society of Birmingham* (Oxford, 1963), and three articles in *Country Life,* October 1966.

26. Quote from E. W. Gibbs, *Joseph Priestley,* 168.

27. Priestley had written (*Essay on Government,* 1768) that "The good and happiness of the members, that is of the majority of the members of any state, is the great standard by which everything relating to that state must be finally determined." See Leslie Stephen, *The English Utilitarians* (L., 1900), I, 175ff.

28. For the abortive plan to found a Utopian colony on the banks of the Susquehanna (the location was chosen because of the beauty of the word), see W. H. G. Armytage, *Heavens Above: Utopian Experiments in England* (L., 1961), 62ff. and references to periodical literature.

29. There is no monograph on this fascinating chapter of American intellectual history, but something of Jefferson's relations to and debt to Priestley can be seen by following through the index under Priestley, in E. Millicent Sowerby's *Catalogue of the Library of Thomas Jefferson,* 5 vols. (Washington, 1959).

30. See the elaborate bibliography of Priestley's writing in the *D.N.B.,* Vol. 16, 367–76. The text of the *Familiar Letters* . . . *to*

. . . *Birmingham* may be found in Rutt, ed., *Theological and Miscellaneous Works,* XIX; a good modern selection of Priestley's works is John Passmore, ed., *Writings on Philosophy, Sciences, and Politics* (N.Y., 1965).

31. On Benjamin Thompson, Count Rumford of the Holy Roman Empire, see George Ellis, *Memoir of Sir Benjamin Thompson* (Boston, 1876), and Ellis, ed., *The Complete Works of Count Rumford,* 4 vols. (Boston, 1876). A new edition of Rumford's scientific writings is now in process of publication. For the non-scientific essays, see his *Essays, Political, Economical and Philosophical,* 3 vols. (L., 1797, 1802). J. A. Thompson, *Count Rumford of Massachusetts* (N.Y., 1935), and Lewis Einstein, *Divided Loyalties* (Boston, 1933) are interesting but neither critical nor comprehensive.

32. On the potato in history, see the masterly volume by R. N. Salaman, *The History and Social Influence of the Potato* (Camb., 1949; reprinted 1975).

33. The literature on Thomas Paine is voluminous. Suffice it to list the "standard" biography by Moncure D. Conway (who also edited the *Works*), in two volumes (N.Y., 1892); Ellery Sedgwick, *Thomas Paine* (Boston, 1899); and the recent and admirable biographies of Paine by David Freeman Hawke (N.Y., 1974) and Eric Foner (N.Y., 1976). Moses Coit Tyler, *Literary History of the American Revolution,* Vol. I, is perceptive, and so is V. L. Parrington, *The Colonial Mind,* Bk. III.

34. *Age of Reason,* Ch. XIII.

35. "Royalty," *Works,* ed. Conway, Vol. III, 107.

36. Philip Foner, ed., *The Complete Writings of Thomas Paine,* 2 vols., Vol. II, 21ff. This is the most nearly complete collection of Paine's writings and letters.

37. *The Rights of Man.* This can be found in Vol. I of the Foner edition.

38. "The Eighteenth Fructidor," in *Writings,* II, 594.

39. Introduction to *The Rights of Man.*

40. *Writings,* Memorial ed., Vol. X, 224.

CHAPTER THREE
1

1. For a discussion of the many meanings of the word philosophe, see Appendix.

2. Peter Gay uses the term "family," which seems to me to suggest a closer relationship than in fact existed among the phi-

losophes of western Europe—or even of a single country like France.

3. Quite the contrary. Some, like Hume, disparaged if not reason, then the sovereignty of reason. Others like Diderot and Rousseau in France, Haller and Herder in Germany, exalted the emotions. But even the exaltation of emotions and the disparagement of reason seem to have been an exercise in rationalism. See Gay, *The Enlightenment*, I, 187ff.

4. Herbert Dieckmann has traced the genealogy of this phrase in his fascinating study, *Le Philosophe, Texts and Interpretation* (St. Louis, 1948). See Appendix.

5. See the Plan, reproduced in R. N. Schwab's edition of the *Preliminary Discourse to the Encyclopedia of . . . D'Alembert* (Indianapolis, 1963), 144, and see Arthur Wilson, *Diderot, The Testing Years* (N.Y., 1957), 132.

6. *Essai sur les moeurs*, tr. by Charles Vereker.

7. R. Cantinelli, *Jacques Louis David*, 64 (P., 1930).

8. Jefferson to Justice Johnson, 12 June 1823, X, Ford ed., 227.

9. Jefferson's last known letter, to Mayor Weightman of Washington, breathes his undying faith in progress: "All eyes are opened, or opening, to the rights of man. The general spread of the light of science has already laid open to every view the palpable truth, that the mass of mankind has not been born with saddles on their backs, nor a favored few booted and spurred, ready to ride them legitimately, by the grace of God." X, Ford, 391.

10. On belief in progress, see the classic essay by J. B. Bury, *The Idea of Progress* (N.Y., 1932); Jules Delavaille, *Essai sur l'Histoire de l'Idée de Progrés* (Paris, 1910); R. V. Sampson, *Progress in the Age of Reason* (Cambridge, 1957); and Charles Frankel, *The Faith in Reason* (N.Y., 1948). But see also, H. Vyerberg, *Historical Pessimism in the French Enlightenment* (Cambridge, 1958). Curiously enough, though the idea of progress was more fully and widely accepted in America than in the Old World, the Americans themselves produced no literature on it; the most explicit statements come from transplanted philosophes like Tom Paine and Joseph Priestley, and from cosmopolitans like Franklin and Jefferson. For the differences between New World and Old World concepts of progress, see below Ch. VIII. On the idea of progress in America see: Charles A. Beard, *The American Spirit, A Study of the Idea of Civilization in the United States* (N.Y., 1942); Arthur A. Ekirch, Jr., *The Idea of Progress in America, 1815–1860* (N.Y., 1944); Merle Curti, *Growth of American Thought*, 165ff. (N.Y., 1964); Russel Nye, *Cultural Life of the New Nation*, Ch. ii (N.Y., 1960); Nelson Adkins,

Philip Freneau and the Cosmic Enigma (N.Y., 1949); R. E. Delmage, "American Ideas of Progress, 1750–1760," 91 *Proc. Am. Phil. Soc.* (1947); Gilbert Chinard, "Progress and Perfectibility in Samuel Miller's Intellectual History," *Studies in Intellectual History* (Baltimore, 1953); V. E. Gibbens, "Tom Paine and the Idea of Progress," LXVI *Penna. Mag. Hist. and Biog.*, 191 (April 1942).

11. Qt. Peter Gay, *The Enlightenment: An Interpretation* (N.Y., 1966), 129, from *Scienza della legislazione* (1807 ed.), II, 174. There does not appear to be any book, even in Italian, on this remarkable economist and philosopher. For the cosmopolitanism of the eighteenth-century philosophes see Gavin de Beer, *The Sciences are Never at War* (L., 1960).

12. See above n. 10.

13. "Superstition" is the key word. A good many of the philosophes were deeply religious; thus, for example, Priestley, Dr. Price, the Reverend Van der Kemp, Dr. Rush, and others. Jefferson, John Adams, Tom Paine, Voltaire, Rousseau, all thought of themselves as Deists. A few of the men of the Enlightenment were entirely orthodox: Linnaeus, Haller, Herder, Ludwig Holberg, for example.

14. Qt. in Ernst Cassirer, *The Philosophy of the Enlightenment* (Princeton, 1951), 15, from Duclos, *Thoughts on the Customs of this Century.*

15. Jeremy Bentham, Preface to *Fragment on Government* (1776), reprinted Oxford, 1967.

16. Jean le Rond D'Alembert, *Oeuvres Complètes,* I (Paris, 1821–22), 122–23.

17. Basil Willey, *The Eighteenth-Century Background* (L., 1940, 1962), Chs. ii-v, and Gerald R. Cragg, *From Puritanism to the Age of Reason* (Camb., 1950).

18. Not quite all, to be sure, but an impressive number of them. Adam Smith was a professor of Moral Philosophy; Josiah Tucker was Dean of Gloucester Cathedral; Dr. Price and Dr. Priestley and Thomas Malthus were clergymen. Even Quesnay and Turgot were moralists, after a fashion, while in America Tom Paine and Joel Barlow fancied themselves economists as Hamilton and Gallatin fancied themselves philosophes.

19. Francis Hutcheson published an *Inquiry into the Original of our Ideals of Beauty and Virtue* in 1726; Burke's *Philosophical Inquiry into the Sublime and the Beautiful* was published in 1756, and Lessing's *Laöcoon* appeared in 1764.

20. On Wolff see the masterly introduction to his *Jus Gentium Methodo Scientifica Pertractatum,* Vol. II, by Ottfried Nippold,

in the Classics of International Law series ed. by James Brown Scott, Vol. 13 (L., 1934).

21. Seventeen volumes were published between 1751 and 1765, eleven volumes of plates from 1762 to 1772. The literature on the Encyclopédie is large. The best account in English is still John Morley's *Diderot and the Encyclopaedists*, 2 vols. (L., 1878). See also, L. Ducros, *Les Encyclopédistes* (Paris, 1908); Joseph Le Gras, *Diderot et l'Encyclopédie* (Amiens, 1928); Jacques Proust, *Diderot et l'Encyclopédie* (Paris, 1962); Arthur Wilson, *Diderot, the Testing Years* (N.Y., 1957); Ronald Grimsley, *Jean d'Alembert* (Oxford, 1963); René Hubert, *Les Sciences sociales dans l'Encyclopédie* (Paris, 1923).

22. Ed. by Heinrich Zedler, and published 1732 to 1750. See the admirable account in the Encyclopaedia Britannica, 9th ed., Vol. VIII.

23. "The Encyclopédie," said Arthur Wilson, "purported to be a book of reference but was in fact a sort of political tract" *Testing Years*, 130.

24. See "Preliminary Discourse" in Stephen J. Gendzier, ed. and trans., Denis Diderot's *The Encyclopedia: Selections* (N.Y., 1967).

25. On the vexed and still controversial matter of the authorship of the articles, Proust, *l'Encyclopédie*, seems to be the most reliable authority.

26. See Wilson, *Testing Years*, Ch. 21. "In theological matters" the Encyclopedia indulged in a policy of "pinpricks and knowing winks," op. cit., 279.

27. The story of the censoring of the Encyclopédie, and of the treason of Le Breton has attracted a great deal of attention. "You have stabbed me in the breast," wrote Diderot to his printer, "you have massacred the work of twenty respectable people." (See Gordon and Torrey, op. cit., 32.) Actually, as Gordon and Torrey make clear, it was not that bad. See on all this their *The Censoring of Diderot's Encyclopédie, and the Re-established Text;* Morley, *Diderot and the Encyclopedists*, I, 125ff.; J. P. Belin, *Le Commerce des Livres Prohibés à Paris de 1750 à 1789* (Paris, 1913, and N.Y., 1966), and his *Le Mouvement Philosophique de 1748 à 1789* (Paris, 1913). See, too, Joseph Le Gras, *Diderot et l'Encyclopédie* (Amiens, 1928), and L. G. Crocker, *The Embattled Philosopher: A Biography of Denis Diderot* (L., 1955).

28. *Christianity as Old as the Creation*, 1730. This book, which purported to defend orthodox Christianity, brought forth scores of replies from outraged clergymen who thought it rather an affront to orthodoxy. Among them was Bishop Butler's famous *Analogy of Religion*. Butler wrote somewhat plaintively:

It has come, I know not how, to be taken for granted by
many persons that Christianity is not so much a subject for
inquiry, but that it is, now at length discovered to be ficti-
tious. And accordingly they treat it as if in the present age
this were an agreed point among all people of discernment,
and nothing remained but to set it up as a principal subject
of mirth and ridicule, as it were, by way of reprisals for its
having so long interrupted the pleasures of the world.

> (B. Willey, *Eighteenth-Century,* 81).

29. On Tindal and Butler and Jenyns, see Leslie Stephen, *English Thought in the Eighteenth Century,* Vol. I, 134ff. and 278ff.

30. "Essay on Man," Epistle I, lines 283ff.

31. On Reimarus, see Hazard, *European Thought in the Eighteenth Century.*

32. The best account here too is in Stephen, *English Thought
in the 18th Century,* I (1876; N.Y., 1949), 101ff.

33. On Edelman, see Hazard, *Eighteenth Century,* 56ff.

34. Hume remained a skeptic, and was a bit uncomfortable in
the company of the atheists of the circle of philosophes who
gathered around the hospitable board of the Baron d'Holbach.
Diderot's anecdote of an exchange between Hume and the Baron
is familiar: "The English philosopher took it into his head to
remark to the Baron that he did not believe in atheists, that he
had never seen any. The Baron said to him, 'Count how many we
are here. We are eighteen.' The Baron added, 'It isn't a bad
showing to be able to point out to you fifteen at once; the three
others haven't made up their minds.' " Quoted in Mossner, *Life
of Hume,* 485. On Hume, see E. C. Mossner, *Life of David Hume*
(Edinburgh, 1951); Leslie Stephen, op. cit., I, Ch. vi; and the
admirable discussion by Peter Gay in *The Enlightenment,* Ch. vii.

35. *Man a Machine* was translated and annotated by B. Bussey
(Chicago, 1912). On La Mettrie, see R. Bossier, *La Mettrie*
(Paris, 1931); L. D. Rosenfeld-Cohen, *From Beast-Machine to
Man-Machine* (N.Y., 1940); Hearnshaw, ed., *Social and Political
Ideas of . . . the Age of Reason* (N.Y., 1950).

36. On Baron d'Holbach and his dinners, see W. H. Wickwar,
Baron d'Holbach (L., 1935); Morley, *Diderot,* II, Ch. vi; Kingsley
Martin, *French Liberal Thought in the Eighteenth Century,* Ch.
vii (L., 1929, 1962); D. Mornet, *Les origines intellectuelles de la
Révolution Française* (Paris, 1933); Hearnshaw, ed., *Social and
Political Ideas of some of the Great French Thinkers of the Age
of Reason* (N.Y., 1950).

37. Qt. in Harold Höffding, *History of Modern Philosophy,* I
(L., 1935), 483.

38. Voltaire made an extract of it, *Extrait des sentiments de*

Jean Meslier, in 1762, and it was published in full by d'Holbach
in 1772. There is an English ed., *Superstition in all Ages, or Last
Will and Testament,* trans. by Anna Knoop (N.Y., 1950). On
Meslier, see, too, Hazard, *European Thought,* 54ff.

39. *Supplement de Bougainville,* see below. Ch. III, 2.

40. See below, Part 2.

41. Perhaps the comparative study of religions can be dated
from Leibniz's study of the Chinese, and Wolff's address, *De
Sinarum philosophia practica,* of 1721. It was immensely stimulated by the contributions of the Jesuits, and by the writings of
explorers like Bougainville, de Gentil, and James Cook. See
Reinach, *Cultes, Mythes, et Religions,* Vol. V (Paris, 1923).

42. On Jones, see Garland Cannon, *Oriental Jones: A Biography* (L., 1964).

43. On Hartley, see Leslie Stephen, op. cit., Vol. II, Ch. ix;
Willey, *Eighteenth Century Background,* op. cit., Ch. 8; G. R.
Cragg, *From Puritanism to the Age of Reason,* Ch. iii. There is
an interesting chapter on eighteenth-century psychology in
A. Wolf, *History of Science, Technology and Philosophy in the
11th Century,* 668ff.

44. On Condillac and Materialism, see the perceptive comments in Ernst Cassirer, *The Philosophy of the Enlightenment,*
and G. S. Brett, *The History of Psychology* (L., 1912–21), Vol.
II.

45. There is a large and growing literature on the Marquis de
Sade, little of it of historical interest. See, however, Mario Praz,
The Romantic Agony (Oxford, 1933, 1954), Ch. iii. There is a
new edition of Restif de la Bretonne's autobiographical *Monsieur Nicolas,* trans. and ed. by Robert Baldick (L., 1966).

46. Quoted in Stephen F. Mason, *A History of the Sciences*
(N.Y., 1962), 341.

47. Letter to James Harris, classical scholar, qt. in Lovejoy,
"Monboddo and Rousseau," in *Essays in the History of Ideas,* 57.
On Monboddo, see W. Knight, *Lord Monboddo and Some of his
Contemporaries* (N.Y., 1900). This has been supplemented by
Emily Cloyd's recent *James Burnett Lord Monboddo* (Oxford,
1972).

48. Clarence Glacken, *Traces on the Rhodean Shore* (Berkeley, 1967) is a magnificent study of the history of theories about
the impact of environment on civilization. See, too, Franklin
Thomas, *The Environmental Basis of Society* (N.Y., 1925), and
John K. Wright, *Human Nature in Geography* (Cambridge,
1966), especially Ch. xiv.

CHAPTER THREE
2

1. See John H. Brumfitt, *Voltaire, Historian* (New York, 1958); J. B. Black, *The Art of History* (New York, 1926); Peter Gay, *Voltaire's Politics* (Princeton, 1959); Ira Wade, *Voltaire and "Candide," a Study in the Fusion of History, Art and Philosophy* (Princeton, 1959).
Zadig, L'Ingenue, and *Zaire* are examples of comedy as history.
2. The Philosophical and Political History . . . of the Two Indies, originally published in 1770, and with numerous subsequent editions. See above Ch. II, *passim*.
3. On Hume as historian, see Black, *The Art of History;* Ernest C. Mossner, *The Life of David Hume* (L., 1954), Part III.
4. On Holberg as historian, see Francis Bull, *Holberg some historiker* (Köln, 1913), and Sigurd Höst, *On Holberg's Historisk Skrifter* (Köln, 1913).
5. On Müller, see J. W. Thompson, *History of Historical Writing* (N.Y., 1942), Vol. II; Hubert Butterfield, *Man on his Past* (Camb., 1955), Ch. vi; Georg von Wyss, *Geschichte der historiographie in der Schweiz* (Zurich, 1895).
6. On Williamson see David Hosack, *A Biographical Memoir . . . 1819* (Coll. New York Historical Society for 1821); there is no biography of Belknap, but all histories of American historiography give him some attention, see e.g., Michael Kraus, *A History of American History* (N.Y., 1937), 134–40.
7. On mercantilism it is sufficient to cite the works of C. W. Cole, and Eli Heckscher; on Cameralism, Albion Small, *The Cameralists* (Chicago, 1909). On the Italian economists see Franco Venturi, *Settecento reformatore da Muratori a Beccaria* (Tornio, 1969).
8. Joshua Reynolds, *Discourses on Art,* ed. Roger Fry (L., 1905); Burke, *The Sublime and the Beautiful* in *Works,* Vol. 1 (L., 1792); The Diderot Essay can be found most conveniently in Diderot, *Interpreter of Nature, Selected Writings,* tr. Jean Stewart and Jonathan Kemp (N.Y., 1938). On Winckelmann, see Justi, below. Like Winckelmann, Mengs was for some time at the Court of Dresden, and moved from there to Rome; like Winckelmann, too, he abjured Protestantism for the Catholic faith in order to embrace employment as director of the Vatican School of painting. On Mengs, see Rudolf Zeitler, *Klassizismus and Utopia* (Stockholm, 1954); Carl Justi, *Winckelmann und Seine Zeitgenessen,* 3 vols. (Köln, 1956).

9. John Hadley invented the mirror-sextant in 1731 and John Harrison the chronometer some thirty years later. See René Taton, ed., *The Beginnings of Modern Science, from 1450 to 1800* (L., 1964), 452ff.; E. Guyot, *Histoire de la détermination des longitudes* (La Chaux-de-Fonds, 1955); Stephen F. Mason, *A History of the Sciences*, Ch. xxiii (N.Y., 1962); Mousnier et Labrousee, op. cit., *Le XVIIIé siècle: Rev. technique . . .* (P., 1952), 109ff.; and A. Wolf, *History of Science, Technology and Philosophy*, Ch. vi.

10. On Bowditch, see Robert E. Berry, *Yankee Stargazer* (N.Y., 1941), and Dirk Struik, *Yankee Science in the Making* (Boston, 1948).

11. On limes and scurvy, see J. C. Beaglehole, ed., *Journals of Captain Cook*, 4 vols. (1955–57) and *Life of Captain Cook* (Stanford, Calif., 1974).

12. Thus, Samuel Miller wrote, in his famous 2 vol. *Retrospect of the Eighteenth Century:* "At the beginning of the century almost half of the surface of the globe was either entirely unknown, or the knowledge of it was so small and indistinct, as to be of little practical value. Since that time such discoveries and improvements have been made, that geography has assumed a new face, and become almost a new science. A spirit of curiosity has stimulated mankind to unprecedented activity in exploring remote regions of the earth." (N.Y., 1803), Vol. I, 326–27.

13. The literature on exploration and discovery in the eighteenth century is voluminous; we can mention only a few of the more relevant works here. Indispensable is Edward G. Cox, *A Reference Guide to the Literature of Travel, Including Voyages, Geographical Descriptions, Adventures, Shipwrecks and Expeditions . . .* , Vol. I, "The Old World;" Vol. II, "The New World" (Seattle, Wash., 1938). Most valuable for this era is E. Heawood, *A History of Geographical Discovery in the Seventeenth and Eighteenth Centuries* (L., 1912). More general, but equally useful, is the standard work by J. L. N. Baker, *A History of Geographical Discovery and Exploration* (L., 1937). For general histories, see also A. P. Newton, *The Great Age of Discovery* (L., 1932); J. H. Parry, *The Age of Reconnaissance* (L., 1963). For geographical exploration in different parts of the globe there is nothing better than the pioneer histories, esp., J. Bartlett Brebner, *The Exploration of North America* (N.Y., 1933); J. C. Beaglehole, *The Exploration of the Pacific* (L., 1934); F. A. Kirkpatrick, *The Spanish Conquistadores* (L., 1934), with all bibliographies. See also, Grenfell Price, *The Western Invasion of the Pacific and its Continents* (Oxford, 1963); John Dunmore, *French Explorers in the Pacific*, Vol. I (Oxford, 1965); Bernard

De Voto, *Westward the Course of Empire* (Boston, 1953). Vol. I of Justin Winsor, *Narrative and Critical History of America,* 8 vols. (Boston, 1884–89) is invaluable. The most useful collection for the seventeenth and eighteenth centuries is probably A. and J. Churchill, *A Collection of Voyages and Travels,* 8 vols. (L., 1745 and 1752). Many of the most famous narratives have been republished by the Hakluyt Society.

14. De Brosses, *Histoire des navigations aux terres australes,* was published in 1756. For the quotation see Mousnier et Labrousse, op. cit., 234. See A. C. Taylor, *Le President de Brosses et l'Australie.* Williamson says that the De Brosses volume was "the most weighty combination of history and propaganda as yet devoted to the South Seas." It appeared in English translation in 1766. See "Explorations and Discovery" in Vol. I of *Johnson's England* (Oxford, 1933).

15. On the transit of Venus as an object of international interest, see H. Woolf, *The Transits of Venus* (Princeton, 1959); Beaglehole, *The Endeavor Journal of Joseph Banks,* I, 20ff. (Sydney, 1962); Gavin de Beer, *The Sciences Were Never at War* (L., 1960); A. Wolff, *A History of Science, Technology and Philosophy in the Eighteenth Century* (L., 1938); A. A. Lesueur, *La Condamine* (Paris, 1911); Brooke Hindle, *The Pursuit of Science in Revolutionary America* (Chapel Hill, 1956).

16. Thus, both Franklin and the French Minister M. de Sartines instructed their respective naval commanders during the Revolutionary War "not to molest Captain Cook or his People who were common friends to Mankind." See in De Beer, *The Sciences,* 27.

17. See *Dampier's Voyages,* ed. by John Masefield, 2 vols. (L., 1906).

18. Defoe's *Life and Surprising Adventures of Robinson Crusoe, of York, Mariner,* came in 1719. Other Defoe books with background of exploration were *The Further Adventures of Robinson Crusoe; The King of Pirates; The Life, Adventures and Pyracies of the Famous Captain Singleton; The History and Remarkable Life of Colonel Jacque, Commonly Call'd Col. Jack; A New Voyage Round the World, By a Course Never Sailed Before;* he also wrote tracts on English commerce. See Bonamy Dobrée, *English Literature in the Early Eighteenth Century, 1700–1740* (Oxford, 1959) with elaborate bibliographies.

19. B. G. Corney, *The Quest and Occupation of Tahiti,* 2 vols. (L., 1913–19), Hugh Carrington, *The Discovery of Tahiti* (L., 1948). Bougainville's *Journal of His Voyage Around the Globe* was published in Paris in 1772; an English translation appeared in London in the same year. See Maurice Thiery, *Bougainville,*

Soldier and Sailor (L., 1932), and John Dunmore, *French Explorers in the Pacific,* Vol. I (Oxford, 1965), unfortunately without index or bibliography. Diderot's *Supplement* can be conveniently read in Jonathan Kemp, ed., *Diderot, Interpreter of Nature* (N.Y., 1963).

20. See J. A. Williamson, *Cook and the Opening of the Pacific* (L., 1946). There are numerous editions of *Cook's Voyages;* that edited by Beaglehole and published by the Hakluyt Society (Camb., 1955) is far the best. For literature on Cook see in Cox, *Reference Guide.*

21. No one is better on all this than Van Wyck Brooks, *The World of Washington Irving* (N.Y., 1944).

22. On the Russian advance through Siberia and into America, see Frank A. Golder, *Russian Expansion on the Pacific, 1641–1850* (Cleveland, 1914); *Bering's Voyages,* 2 vols. (N.Y., 1922, 1925); Hector Chevigny, *Russian America* (N.Y., 1965).

23. On the search for a Northwest Passage, see especially L. J. Burpee, *The Search for a Western Sea,* 2 vols. (Toronto, 1935); J. M. Crouse, *In Search of the Western Ocean* (N.Y., 1928); J. B. Brebner, *Explorers of North America,* Ch. xiii (L., 1933).

24. On Spanish expansion into the region north of Mexico see Herbert Bolton, *The Spanish Borderlands* (New Haven, 1921); *Spanish Explorations in the Southwest, 1542–1706* (N.Y., 1916); *The Rim of Christendom, a Biography of Eusebio Kino* (N.Y., 1936). See, too, H. R. Wagner, ed., *Spanish Voyages to the Northwest Coast of America* (San Francisco, 1929), and Charles E. Chapman, *The Founding of Southern California* (N.Y., 1916).

25. On the French explorations of western America, the volumes by Francis Parkman with the collective title *France and England in North America* are still indispensable. See also R. G. Thwaites, *France in America* (N.Y., 1905). For contemporary accounts, the *Original Narratives of American History,* ed., J. F. Jameson include W. L. Grant, *Voyages of Champlain,* while the volumes of the Champlain Society—over forty of them by now —include editions of most of the more famous exploring expeditions.

26. L. J. Burpee has edited, for the Champlain Society, *The Journals and Letters of La Vérendrye and his Sons* (Toronto, 1927). See also J. B. Brebner, *North America,* Ch. xx.

27. Burpee, *Western Sea,* Crouse, *Western Ocean,* Brebner, *North America,* for Northwest Passage. *Mackenzie's Voyages from Montreal on the River St. Lawrence Through the Continent of North America to the Frozen and Pacific Oceans* was first published in 1801, and has been frequently reprinted. See ed.

by J. B. McMaster in the Trail Makers series, 2 vols. (N.Y., 1903). See M. S. Wade, *Mackenzie of Canada* (Edinburgh, 1927), and A. P. Woollacott, *Mackenzie and his Voyageurs* (L., 1927).

28. S. E. Morison, *Maritime History of Massachusetts* (Boston, 1921), Ch. iv; J. Duncan Phillips, *Salem and the Indies* (Boston, 1947); Frederick W. Howay, ed., *Voyages of the "Columbia" to the Northwest Coast* (Boston, 1941), and *Old South Leaflets,* No. 131.

29. Ledyard's *Journal of Captain Cook's Last Voyage to the Pacific,* first printed in Hartford in 1783, has been reprinted (Chicago, 1963). Jared Sparks wrote the first biography of Ledyard, and it is still the best account of that remarkable adventurer (Boston, 1847); see, too, the description of Ledyard in H. B. Adams, *Life and Writings of Jared Sparks,* I, Ch. xii (Boston, 1893), and more popular biographies by Helen Augur, *Passage to Glory* (N.Y., 1946), and J. K. Mumford, *John Ledyard, an American Marco Polo* (Portland, Ore., 1939).

30. Ledyard turned to Jefferson for advice and encouragement, and to John Paul Jones, too. We catch fragmentary glimpses of the relationship in Jefferson's letters which can be followed through the index of Julian Boyd, ed., *The Papers of Thomas Jefferson* (Princeton, 1950); 19 vols. so far carry the record to 1791. This invaluable collection is hereafter referred to simply as Boyd, ed.

31. L'Argens', *Lettres Chinoises* appeared in 1739, and Goldsmith's *Letters from a Citizen of the World to His Friends in the Far East* in 1762.

32. The literature on the rage for China is extensive. See in general, A. Reichwein, *China and Europe: Intellectual and Artistic Contacts in the Eighteenth Century* (N.Y., 1924); A. H. Rowbotham, *Missionary and Mandarin* (Berkeley, Calif., 1942); Lewis Maverick, *China a Model for Europe* (San Antonio, Tex., 1946) with a trans. of Quesnay's *Du Despotisme de la Chine;* Virgile Pinot, *La Chine et la formation de l'esprit philosophique en France, 1640–1740* (Paris, 1932); Henri Cordier, *La Chine en Europe au XVIIIe siècle* (Paris, 1908); Pierre Martino, *L'Orient dans la littérature française sur XVIIe et XVIIIe siècles* (Paris, 1906); Jay Botsford, *English Society in the Eighteenth Century as Influenced from Overseas* (N.Y., 1924); John Steegman, *The Rule of Taste from George I to George IV* (L., 1936); B. Sprague Allen, *Tides in English Taste,* 2 vols. (Camb., 1937). The quotation from Kirchner can be found in Arthur O. Lovejoy, "The Chinese Origins of Romanticism" in *Essays in the History of Ideas* (Baltimore, 1948), 104.

33. In *Novissima Sinica,* published, 1699.

34. Wolff's address of 1721 *De Sinarum philosophia practica,* on the virtues of the Chinese which got him expelled from Halle is reprinted in Vol. VI of his *Philosophical Works,* ed. by G. F. Hagent, and was trans. into English in 1759 under the title, *The Real Happiness of a People under a Philosophical King Demonstrated.*

35. See article on China in the *Philosophical Dictionary,* the opening chapters of the *Essai sur les Moeurs et l'esprit des Nations,* and *Dieu et les Hommes,* 1769.

36. On De Pauw see below, Ch. IV. In 1774 De Pauw published his *Recherches philosophiques sur les Egyptiens et les Chinois.* Frederick was so taken with De Pauw that he offered him a place in the Royal Academy and the Bishopric of Breslau!

37. See Botsford, *English Society,* for furniture, and Allen, *English Taste,* and H. F. Clarke, *The English Landscape Garden* (L., 1948) for gardening. James Cawthorne's poem, "On Taste" (1756) derides the craze for things Chinese:

> On every hill a spire-crowned temple swells,
> Hung round with serpents and a fringe of bells.
> In Tartar huts our cows and horses lie
> Our hogs are fattened in an Indian sty;
> On every shelf a Joss divinely stares,
> Nymphs laid on chintzes sprawl upon our chairs,
> While o'er our cabinets Confucius nods,
> Midst porcelain elephants and China gods.

Goethe satirized the craze for Chinese gardening in the prologue to the fourth act of his *Triumph of Sentiment.*

38. On Chambers and Kew Gardens, see his own *Dissertation on Oriental Gardening* (L., 1772) and see, too, Arthur Lovejoy, *Essays in the History of Ideas,* 99ff., and Lewis S. Maverick, *China Model for Europe* (San Antonio, Tex., 1946). In his *Dissertation on Oriental Gardening,* Chambers took a somewhat unfair advantage of his readers, for he did not allow the Oriental Garden to win on its merits but added extraneous attractions. Thus, he wrote,

> the traveler in China finds him . . . in the splendid pavilions, richly painted and illuminated by the sun; here beautiful Tartarean damsels, in loose transparent robes that flutter in the scented air, present him with rich wines, or invigorating infusions of Ginsing and amber, in goblets of agate; mangostans, ananas, and fruits of Quangsi, in baskets of golden filagree; they crown him with garlands of flowers,

and invite him to taste the sweets of retirement, on Persian
carpets and beds of camusathskin down.

Lovejoy, History of Ideas, 131

For Woburn Abbey, see Apollo, December 1965.

39. S. E. Morison, Maritime History of Massachusetts (Boston, 1921); J. Duncan Phillips, Salem and the Indies (Boston,
1947). Joseph Hergesheimer's Java Head (N.Y., 1919) tells an
interesting and historically authentic story of the impact of Java
on the Salem merchants. See also Phillips, Pepper and Pirates:
Adventures in the Sumatra Pepper Trade of Salem (Boston,
1949); Ralph D. Paine, Ships and Sailors of Old Salem (N.Y.,
1906); and "A Rose from China," Popular Gardening, 29 June
1970.

40. On Turkish romances, see Reichwein, China and Europe,
161. The famous bluestocking, Lady Wortley Montagu, who
lived in Constantinople early in the century and is reputed to
have introduced vaccination against the smallpox from that exotic country, was largely responsible for the interest in Turkey
in Britain. Her Letters during Mr. Wortley's Embassy to Constantinople, were published in 1763, and there have been new
editions of the letters ever since. See, R. Halsband, Life of Lady
Mary Wortley Montagu (Oxford, 1956).

41. On Beckford and Vathek see Guy Chapman, Beckford
(L., 1937) and his Beckford Bibliography (L., 1930).

42. Thorkild Hansen, Arabia Felix (L., 1964).

43. On Freneau, see Louis Leary, That Rascal Freneau (New
Brunswick, 1943), and "Father Bombo's Pilgrimage," LXVI
Pennsylvania Magazine of History. The book was, apparently,
never completed.

44. D. B. Davis, Slavery in Western Culture (Ithaca, N.Y.,
1966) and W. D. Jordan, White over Black (Chapel Hill, 1969)
have explored this fascinating and sobering chapter in history
and psychology with masterly insight. Captain Singleton was first
published in 1720; it is available in Everyman's Library.

45. On the opening up of Africa, see Edward Heawood, A
History of Geographical Discovery in the 17th and 18th Centuries (Camb., 1912), and R. Brown, The Story of Africa and
its Explorers, 4 vols. (L., 1892–95), which deals chiefly with the
nineteenth century. Selections from the original Journal have
recently been reprinted as Travels to Discover the Sources of
the Nile, by James Bruce, selected and edited by C. F. Beckingham (Edinburgh, 1964).

46. On the revival of interest in Greece and Rome, see the
elaborate discussion by Peter Gay in The Enlightenment: The
Rise of Modern Paganism (N.Y., 1967), with elaborate bibliog-

raphy. See, too, Emil Egger, *L'hellenism en France,* 2 vols.
(Paris, 1869); René Canat, *La Renaissance de la Grèce antique*
(Paris, 1913); Louis Hautecoeur, *Rome et la renaissance de
l'antiquité à la fin du XVIIIe siècle* (Paris, 1912); Harold Parker,
The Cult of Antiquity and the French Revolutionaries (Chicago,
1937); Gilbert Highet, *The Classical Tradition* (Oxford, 1949);
and the authoritative J. E. Sandys, *History of Classical Scholarship,* esp. Vols. 2 and 3 (Camb., 1903–8). For the impact of
the ancient world on Germany, see E. M. Butler, *Tyranny of
Greece Over Germany* (Boston, 1958).

47. The best English study of Winckelmann in English is
Butler, *Tyranny.* See also B. Vallentin, *Winckelmann* (Berlin,
1931), and the full-dress and unmanageable biography by C.
Justi, *Winckelmann, sein Leben, sein Werke, und seine Zeitgenos-
sen,* 3 vols. (Leipzig, 1866; recently republished Köln, 1956).
There are some perceptive pages in Vernon Lee's delightful
Studies of the Eighteenth Century in Italy (L., 1880) which
should be reprinted.

48. Winckelmann's *Geschichte der Kunst des Altertums* was
published in 1764, and quickly translated into other European
languages; it made its greatest impact, naturally enough, in Germany, and influenced Goethe profoundly; indeed Goethe later
contributed to a kind of testimonial volume for Winckelmann,
Winckelmann und sein Jahrhundert (1805). Yet his influence
reached France, too; Henri Beyle took his pen name from
Winckelmann's birthplace: Stendhal.

49. On all this, see J. E. Sandys, *History of Classical Scholarship,* Vol. II.

50. On Gluck, see Alfred Einstein, *Gluck* (L., 1964).

51. See the appropriate entries in George Grove, *Dictionary
of Music and Musicians,* new ed. in 9 vols.

52. On Caylus see Peter Gay, *The Enlightenment,* Vol. II,
and Justi, *Winckelmann.*

53. On the society of the Dilettanti, see Lionel Cust, *A History of the Society of the Dilettanti* (L., 1898). For "Athenian"
Stuart, see Lawrence, in 11 *Journal of the Warburg Institute,*
1938. *The Antiquities of Athens* has been reprinted (N.Y.,
1968).

54. Constance Wright, *A Royal Affinity* (N.Y., 1965), 259.

55. The early biography of West by the Scots novelist John
Galt is still valuable (L., 1916). For modern evaluations, see
James Flexner, *First Flowers of our Wilderness* (Boston, 1947);
Lloyd Goodrich, "The Painting of American History," III *Amer-
ican Quarterly,* 283ff. (1951); E. Waterhouse, *Painting in Britain*

1530–1790 (L., 1953); W. T. Whitley, *Artists and Their Friends in England,* 2 vols. (L., 1928).

56. On Canova, Rudolf Zeitler, *Klassizismus und Utopia* (Stockholm, 1954).

57. On Flaxman, W. G. Constable, *John Flaxman* (L., 1927).

58. On Thorwaldsen and Sergel see Erik Moltesen, *Bertel Thorvaldsen* (København, 1929); Julius Lange, *Sergel og Thorvaldsen* (København, 1886); Andreas Lindblom, *Sveriges Kunsthistories,* Vol. III (Stockholm, 1946).

59. On the interest in, or the cult of, antiquity in America, see Richard Gummere, *The American Mind and the Classical Tradition* (Cambridge, 1963), with extensive bibliography; J. J. Walsh, *The Education of the Founding Fathers* (N.Y., 1935); Gilbert Chinard, "Polybius and the American Constitution," I *Journal Hist. Ideas* (1939), 38; Charles Mullett, "Classical Influences in the American Revolution," 35 *Classical J.* (1938), 92; Karl Lehmann, *Jefferson, American Humanist* (N.Y., 1947); Talbot Hamlin, *Greek Revival Architecture in America* (N.Y., 1944). H. Trevor Colbourn, *The Lamp of Experience* (Chapel Hill, 1966) contains a list of classical books in colonial private and quasi-public libraries, as does G. K. Stuart, "Private Libraries in Colonial Virginia," X *American Literature,* 24. There is something in Sandys, *Hist. Classical Scholarship,* Vol. III. H. M. Jones, *Strange New World* has a perceptive chapter on the classical inheritance. There is, of course, no substitute for reading the writings of the Founding Fathers themselves: such documents as Adams's *Defense of the Constitutions,* or James Wilson's *Lectures,* or the *Federalist Papers,* are pervaded with the classical spirit as well as with references to classical history and literature.

60. There are pictures of the Villa Rotunda in James Ackerman, *Palladio,* 1966.

61. Howard Mumford Jones points out that no less than twenty states exhibit Latin mottoes on their seals. Jones, *Strange New World,* 232.

CHAPTER THREE
3

1. The dispute over "Laöcoon" is illuminating. The statue itself was beautifully balanced—the powerful center figure of the father, the two figures of the boys on either side, each with appropriate gestures, all three figures bound together by the python. It was assumed, by the art critics of the Winckelmann era, that even in

their death agony the victims would not give way to expressions or gestures that were violent or undignified, and the point of Lessing's famous essay was that while it was right and proper for the artist to avoid violence or agony or ugliness, it was improper for the poet to do so, for the artist caught merely one glimpse of life, while the poet and dramatist were permitted to embrace the whole of life. Needless to say, the Greeks themselves did not shrink from violence, either in art or drama. Indeed, it is possible to argue that Winckelmann, Canova, Thorwaldsen, and others responsible for the Greek revival of these years misunderstood and misinterpreted them.

2. There is nothing better on this fascinating subject than Howard Mumford Jones, *O Strange New World* (N.Y., 1964), which has a comprehensive bibliography. Equally good, but with a different—and broader—focus is Antonello Gerbi, *The Dispute of the New World*, Jeremy Moyle, trans. (Pittsburgh, 1973). See, too, Edmundo O'Gorman, *The Invention of America* (Bloomington, Ind., 1961); Ray H. Pearce, *The Savages of America* (Baltimore, 1953); Durand Echeverria, *Mirage in the West: A History of the French Image of American Society to 1815* (Princeton, 1957); Gilbert Chinard, *L'exoticisme américain dans la litterature française au XVIe siècle* (Paris, 1911); Leopoldo Zea, *America coma consiencia* (Mexico, 1953). On the El Dorado and legendary island myths, Constantino Bayle, *El Dorado Fantasma* (Madrid, 1943); William Babcock, *Legendary Islands of the Atlantic* (N.Y., 1922); and Howard R. Patch, *The Other World According to Descriptions in Medieval Literature* (Cambridge, 1950).

As part of its celebration of the Bicentennial, the Mellon Museum of Art in Washington put on a magnificent exhibition, "The European Vision of America." Hugh Honour provided an explanatory text for this in his *European Vision of America* (Kent, O., 1976). See also, his *This New Golden Land* (N.Y., 1976).

3. Peter Martyr's *De orbo Novo* is translated into English by F. A. McNutt, 2 vols. (N.Y., 1912). On Peter Martyr, see Milton Waldman, *Americana, the Literature of American History* (L., 1936), Ch. 1; and A. P. Newton, *The Great Age of Discovery* (L., 1931). I have used the translation in Edward Arber, ed., *The First Three Books on America* (Birmingham, 1885).

4. Montaigne, "Of Cannibals." Montaigne's essay was first published in 1580 (*Essays*, I, xxxi); it was probably composed between 1578 and 1580. See Donald M. Frame, *Montaigne: A Biography* (N.Y., 1965), 145, 325. Frame dates the individual essays in an Appendix which is based on the conjectures of Pierre Villey, *Les sources et l'évolution des Essais de Montaigne*, 2 vols., 2nd ed. (Paris, 1933), I, 81 and Table at end of volume.

5. See, e.g., the woodcuts reproduced by R. Proctor, *Jan van Doesborg* (L., 1894); and in Justin Winsor, ed., *Narrative and Critical History of America . . . ,* Vol. I. Hayden, "Archeology of the United States," *Smithsonian contributions,* VIII (1856), gives us pictures of these monsters.

6. Even Buffon accepted the Patagonian giant. See Jacques Roger, ed., *Buffon, Les Epoques de la Nature* (Paris, 1962), lxxvi.

7. On pygmies and Skraelings, see Tryggvi Oleson, *Early Voyages and Northern Approaches 1000–1632* (Canadian Centenary Series, I; N.Y., 1964).

8. All of this, and more, can be found in Corneille De Pauw, *Recherches philosophiques sur les Américains,* 3 vols. (Berlin, 1768–69). See the lavish illustrations in Honour, *European Vision.* As late as 1724 Lafitau presented his readers with pictures of natives with heads in their chests.

9. The literature on the wonders and marvels of the New World is extensive. Some of this is surveyed in Commager and Giordanetti, *Was America a Mistake?: An Eighteenth Century Controversy* (N.Y., 1967). See also the following: Jones, *O Strange New World;* K. B. Collier, *Cosmologies of Our Fathers* (N.Y., 1934); Robert Cawley, *Unpath'd Waters* (Princeton, 1940); Howard Patch, *The Other World;* Pearce, *The Savages of America;* Enrique de Gandia, *Historia critica de los mitos de la conquista Americana* (Madrid, 1929); Antonello Gerbi, *The Dispute,* with a very good full bibliography. For further bibliographical references, see below.

10. Mather, *Frontiers Well Defended,* cited in Roderick Nash, *Wilderness in the American Mind,* 29.

11. René Hubert, *Les Sciences Sociales dans l'Encyclopédie* (Paris, 1923); Joseph Le Gras, *Diderot et l'Encyclopédie* (Amiens, 1928), 89ff.; Beulah Hope Swigart, *Americans as Revealed in the Encyclopédie,* unpub. Ph.D. Dissertation, University of Illinois, 1939.

12. See O'Gorman, *The Invention of America* (Bloomington, Ind., 1961).

13. See references in note 2, and Loren Baritz, "The Ideas of the West," 46 *Am. Hist. Rev.* (1961), 617ff.

14.

> Of Faery Land yet if he more inquyre
> By certein signes, here sett in sondrie place,
> He may it fynd
>
> *Faery Queene*

15. "I am convinced that there is the terrestrial paradise of

'Blessed Isles,'" wrote Columbus. Qt. Fairchild, *Noble Savage*, 6.

16. The narrative of Captain Adamas and Barlow is reprinted in Richard Hakluyt, *The Principal Navigations . . . of the English Nation*, VII, 297ff. (Glasgow, 1904).

17. See Edward Arber, ed., *Travels and works of John Smith*, 2 vols. (1884), and Bradford Smith, *Captain John Smith* (1953).

18. See John Bakeless, *The Eyes of Discovery* (N.Y., 1950), and, in *Original Narratives of American History*, 19 vols. (N.Y., 1906–17), the following: L. G. Tyler, ed., *Narratives of Early Virginia*; J. F. Jameson, ed., *Narratives of New Netherland, and Journal of Jaspar Danckaerts*; A. S. Salley, ed., *Narratives of Early Carolina*; C. C. Hall, ed., *Narratives of Early Maryland*; A. C. Meyers, ed., *Narratives of Early Pennsylvania, West Jersey and Delaware*.

19. William Bradford, *History of Plimoth Plantation* (1630), reprinted by the Commonwealth of Massachusetts (Boston, 1899), 95.

20. C. H. Firth, *An American Garland* (Oxford, 1915), 13–14.

21. Drayton's "Ode to Virginia" can be found most conveniently in the *Oxford Book of English Verse*.

22. The "Summons to Newe England" (1638), is in Firth, *American Garland*.

23. Hammond's *Leah and Rachel . . .* is reprinted in Hall, ed., *Narratives of Early Maryland*, 280–308; the quoted passage is on 297–98. For Alsop see Ibid., 340ff.; William Bartram, *Travels of William Bartram* (N.Y., 1928), 64, 182. Andrew Burnaby, *Travels Through North America* (N.Y., 1904), 73–74. See for these and others, John Bakeless, *Eyes of Discovery*.

24. Imlay was something of a scoundrel. He was deeply involved in French schemes to capture Louisiana from the Spaniards. After his return to England he betrayed and abandoned Mary Wollstonecraft. His *Topographical Description of the Western Territory of North America* (orig. ed., 1792), 169, purported to be written in Kentucky but was written and published in England.

25. Reuben Gold Thwaites has edited *The Jesuit Relations* in 73 vols. (Cleveland, O., 1894–1907). There is a volume of *Selections*, ed. by Edna Kenton (L., n.d.).

26. Hennepin's *New Discovery* appeared in English in 1698, dedicated to King William III; no wonder Louis XIV ordered Hennepin's arrest. R. G. Thwaites edited a new edition, with biography and bibliography, in 1903. On Hennepin, see Parkman, *La Salle and the Discovery of the Great West* (Boston, 1893), Chs. 17, 18.

27. Charlevoix's *Histoire de la Nouvelle France* was published in 1744. An English edition appeared in London in 1761. There was a new translation by J. G. Shea in 6 vols. (New York, 1866–72) which has recently been reprinted. On Charlevoix, see G. Chinard, *L'Amérique et la rêve exotique dans la littérature au XVIIe et XVIIIe siècle* (Paris, 1913).

28. *New Voyages to North America,* by the Baron de Lahontan, reprinted, with introduction by R. G. Thwaites, 2 vols. (Chicago, 1903).

29. The *Dialogues Curieux* was published, with an elaborate introduction by Gilbert Chinard, in 1931.

30. Joseph Francis Lafitau, *Moeurs des sauvages amériquains comparées aux moeurs des premier temps,* 2 vols. (Paris, 1724). A new ed. trans. and ed. by William N. Fenton appeared under the auspices of the Chamberlain Society in 1976.

31. The story comes originally from John Galt's *The Life and Studies of Benjamin West* (1816) reprinted in 2 vols. (1820).

CHAPTER FOUR

1

1. Lester Crocker, *An Age of Crisis, Man and World in 18th-Century French Thought* (Baltimore, 1959).

2. Chauncey B. Tinker, *Nature's Simple Plan* (Princeton, 1922).

3. Qt. in J. B. Bury, *History of the Idea of Progress,* 167.

4. Claude A. Helvétius, *De l'Esprit, or Essays on the Mind* (L., 1807). And see Kingsley Martin, *French Liberal Thought in the Eighteenth Century,* Ch. vii (N.Y., 1962), and W. H. Wickwar, Helvétius and d'Holbach, in Hearnshaw, ed., *Social and Political Ideas of . . . The Age of Reason* (L., 1930). The quotation from Hume is in *Essays and Treatises on General Subjects,* Vol. I, 88.

5. Adams's *Defense of the Constitutions* can be found in vols. IV to VI of *The Works of John Adams,* ed. by Charles Francis Adams, 10 vols. (1850–56). The quotation is in Vol. VI.

William Tudor, who had studied law with Adams, pronounced the same principle on his "Boston Massacre" Address of 1779.

Similar causes will forever operate like effects, in the political, moral and physical world; those vices which ruined the illustrious republics of Greece and the mighty commonwealth of Rome, and which are now ruining Great Britain . . . must eventually overturn every state where their deleterious influence is suffered to prevail.

6. The quotation is from his *Essay on Public Happiness* (L., 1774), 142–43.

7. Joshua Reynolds, *Discourses on Art*, ed. Roger Fry (L., 1905).

8. Qt. in Erik Moltesen, *Thorwaldsens Museums* (København, 1927), 17.

9. Preserved Smith, *History of Modern Culture*, Vol. II: The Enlightenment (N.Y., 1934), 618.

10. Preface to the *Commentaries on the Laws of England.*

11. Consider: "in the course of human events . . . the opinions of mankind . . . all men are created equal."

12. Supplement to Bougainville. I have used the edition of Jonathan Kemp, *Diderot, Selected Writings* (N.Y., 1963). The quotation can be found on 187.

13. *Conquest of Granada*, Pt. I.

14. Qt. in E. M. Butler, *The Tyranny of Greece over Germany* (Boston, 1958), 77.

15. Richmond B. Bond, *Queen Anne's American Kings* (Oxford, 1952); Samuel C. Williams, ed., *Lieutenant Timberlake's Memoirs, 1756–1765* (Marietta, Ga., 1948).

16. On Paoli, see C. B. Tinker, *Nature's Simple Plan.*

17. On Omai, see above, Ch. III. For the country houses see Beaglehole, ed., *Endeavour Journal of Joseph Banks*, Introduction, 102ff.

18. "The favorite," wrote James Bruce, "seemed to me, next to the elephant and rhinoceros, the largest living creature I had met with. . . . A ring of gold passed through her under lip, and weighed it down, till, like a flap, it covered her chin, and left her teeth bare. . . . The inside of her lip she had made black with antimony. Her ears reached down to her shoulders, and had the appearance of wings. . . . The custom of going naked in these warm climates abolishes all delicacy concerning it. I could not but observe that the breasts of each of them (when seated) reached the length of their knees." *Travels to Discover the Source of the Nile*, ed., C. P. Beckingham (Edinburgh, 1964), 234–36.

19. There were some who did not. Thus, Lord Kames, who had a wide following in America, plumped for multiple creation. See, *Sketches of the History of Henry Home, Lord Kames* (Edinburgh, 1807), 360. So, too, Voltaire; see his article "America" in his *Philosophical Dictionary*. But when in 1655, Isaac de la Peyrere propounded the theory of multiple creation he was forced to retract and to spend the rest of his life in a monastery. See Don C. Allen, *The Legend of Noah* (Urbana, Ill., 1949), 134ff. On all of this see "The Progress of Opinion Respecting the Origin

and Antiquity of Man in America" in Justin Winsor, ed., *Narrative and Critical History of America,* Vol. I, 369ff.

20. Don C. Allen, *Legend of Noah.*

21. See his *Six Books of the Commonwealth,* abridged and trans. by M. J. Tooley (N.Y., 1955).

22. *The Spirit of the Laws,* Franz Neumann, ed., Bk. XIX, Ch. 4 (N.Y., 1949).

23. From "Essay on Manners," quoted in John B. Black, *The Art of History, Four Great Historians* (N.Y., 1926), 45.

24. René Hubert observes that "It is primarily to the influence of climate that the Encyclopédistes attributed the diversity which revealed itself in the physical appearance and in the domestic habits of widely varied human groups. Primarily, but not exclusively. Thus color, Diderot explained, 'depends in large part on climate, but not entirely.' . . . We have even stronger grounds for believing this true of moral qualities." Hubert, *Les sciences sociales dan l'Encyclopédie,* 89.

An older book, Abel V. Brandin, *De la influencia de los diferentes climas del universo sobre el hombre, e en particular de la influencia de los climas de la America meridionale* (Lima, 1826) promises much more than it delivers. See the recent work, André Missenard, *L'homme et le climat* (Paris, 1937), and above all Clarence Glacken, *Traces on the Rhodean Shore* (Berkeley, Calif., 1967) which traces with immense learning and profound insight the history of the concept of environment from the days of ancient Greece into the early years of the nineteenth century.

25. This problem is the chief subject of the learned monograph by Antonello Gerbi, *The Dispute of the New World* (Pittsburgh, 1973). See also, R. H. Pearce, *The Savages of America* (Balt., 1953); Gilbert Chinard, "Eighteenth Century Theories on America as a Human Habitat," 91 *Proc. Am. Phil. Soc.,* 27ff.; Henry W. Church, "Corneille de Pauw and the Controversy over his Recherches Philosophiques sur les Americains," *Pub. Mod. Lang. Assoc.,* LI, 178ff.; Howard Mumford Jones, *O Strange New World,* Chs. I and II; Werner Stark, *America: Ideal and Reality* (L., 1947); Silvio Zavala, *America en el espiritu frances del siglo xviii* (Mexico City, 1949).

26. Africa is a special problem in all this conjecture. Clearly, most of Africa was quite as backward as most of America, yet the philosophes and the Naturalists did not concern themselves with the problem of Africa. There were, however, counterarguments that justified this neglect, or oversight. In the first place, Africa at one time had had the most advanced of civilizations; not only Egypt but Carthage, too, had been among the centers of civilization at a time when the ancestors of the French and

the Germans were still barbarians. Second, the Moslems, who had overrun the whole of North Africa and much of Europe, had left some remnants of a high civilization in the North African states. Third, was the persistence of the myth of Prester John and a high civilization in central Africa (and elsewhere, for the locale of Prester John's kingdom was not fixed). Interest in the interior of Africa revived after the middle of the eighteenth century; it was connected, in part, with the new anti-slavery and anti-slave trade campaigns, and in part with the growth of the Cape Colony. The best discussion of the African problem is in Winthrop D. Jordan, *White over Black*, Ch. i (Chapel Hill, 1968).

27. Blackness and lack of blackness engaged the attention of the American philosophes. Dr. Rush, for example, believed that the blackness of the Negro was a form of leprosy, and might, in time, be eradicated: a most progressive theory. See D. Boorstin, *The Lost World of Thomas Jefferson* (N.Y., 1948). See also the more recent works by David Brion Davis, *The Problem of Slavery in Western Culture* (Ithaca, N.Y., 1966) and *The Problem of Slavery in the Age of Revolution 1770–1833* (Ithaca, N.Y., 1975); and Winthrop D. Jordan, *White over Black*, op. cit.

28. Governor Winslow of Plymouth Colony, when he heard that "the Jews in Holland had infallible proofs" of the Ten Tribes being in America, observed that "it was not less probable that these Indians should come from the stock of Abraham than any other nation this day known to the world." From "Epistle, . . . on the Glorious Progress of the Gospel amongst the Indians of New England, 1649," quoted in Mullinger, *History of Cambridge University*, III, 202.

29. The literature on the peopling of America is voluminous. I list all the references, general and particular, in a single package, for most of them touch on more than one theory or inquiry. The first general summary of the various theories was that by Gregorio Garcia, *Origen de los Indios de el nuevo mundo* (1607); Don C. Allen summarizes it in *The Legend of Noah*, Ch. vi. A second important work, that by the jurist Hugo Grotius, *Origine Gentium Americanarum Dissertatio* (Paris, 1642), has been translated into English, *On the Origin of the Native Races of America*, by Edmund Goldsmid, and printed in Amsterdam, 1884. A third major analysis, which is in part a source, in part a history, but certainly a classic, is Alexander von Humboldt, *Vues de Cordillieres et monumens des peuples indignés de l'Amérique* (Paris, 1816). Perhaps a fourth study should be included here, for it too rested in part at least on observation: Herbert Howe Bancroft, *Native Races of the Pacific States*, Vol. V (N.Y., 1876).

The best guide to the literature of the controversy is still, after three quarters of a century, Justin Winsor's chapter in Vol. I of the *Narrative and Critical History of America* (Boston, 1889), "The Progress of Opinion Respecting the Origin and Antiquity of Man in America." This should be supplemented by Samuel F. Havens's "Archeology of the United States . . . ," *Smithsonian Contributions to Knowledge*, VII (1856). The best modern survey is by Don C. Allen, *Noah*, and Enrique de Gandia, *Historia crítica de los mitos de la conquista Americana* (Madrid, 1929). Among the sources of monographs the following are illuminating: Charles G. Leland, *Fusang, or the Discovery of America by Chinese Buddhist Priests* (L., 1875); Thomas Stephens, *Madoc* (L., 1893); William G. Babcock, *Legendary Islands of the Atlantic* (N.Y., 1922); G. M. Gathorne-Hardy, *The Norse Discoverers of America* (Oxford, 1921); Edwin Bjorkman, *The Search for Atlantis* (N.Y., 1927); Howard R. Patch, *The Other World* (Cambridge, 1950); Lewis Hanke, *The First Social Experiment in America* (Cambridge, 1935).

Modern ethnology does not find these conjectures about the multiple origin of the American Indian in the least fantastic. Thus, Macgowan and Hester write of *Early Man in the New World:* "Hooton finds close resemblances to Egyptian skulls among the Arizona Basket Makers and in the Coahuila Caves of northern Mexico, and Dixon identifies ancient Egyptian skulls with skulls from California and skulls of the Iroquois. W. W. Howells sees similarities between 'many forest tribes of South America and certain Indonesian groups in Borneo and the Philippines,' and believes the non-Mongoloid features of the Indians point 'not to the Australoids or the Negroes but towards the White group.' Hooton finds Indians of the Northwest coast who 'resemble Alpine Europeans.' He says that certain Plains Indians seem to be basically White with Mongoloid added, and he points out that although the Eskimo are the most Mongoloid of all the inhabitants of the Americas, they are long-headed, which is a most un-Mongoloid trait. On the basis of skulls from Chancelade, France, and certain late paleolithic traits, Sollas saw the ancestors of the Eskimo living in Europe in Magdalenian times. . . . Hooton puts forward the picturesque and amusing theory that the Maya, with their large curved noses and their mania for flattening their heads between boards, picked up both the nose and the mania from the Armenoids of the Iranian plateau. The Mongoloids provided the characteristic skin, hair and eyelids," 222–23.

30. Rutledge to Jefferson, 23 October 1788, in Boyd, ed., XII, 264.

31. On the persistence of interest in America, Barton's *New*

Views on the Origin of the Tribes of America was published in Philadelphia in 1797. For Mitchill, see views in *Transactions and Collections of the American Antiquarian Society,* I (1820), and see C. H. Hall, *An American Scientist, Samuel Latham Mitchill* (New York, 1933). As late as 1837 Mordecai Noah preached a Discourse on the Evidences of the American Indians Being the Descendants of the Ten Lost Tribes of Israel, see in R. H. Pearce, *The Savages of America,* Ch. 2, especially 61 n. Other early books testify to the abiding interest of the Americans in this subject of origins: James McCulloch, *Researches, Philosophical and Antiquarian, Concerning the Aboriginal History of America* (Baltimore, 1829); A. W. Bradford, *American Antiquities* (N.Y., 1841); James Kennedy, *Probable Origin of the American Indians* (L., 1854).

32. See his *Observations on the Climate in Different Parts of America,* 1811.

33. The three Frenchmen are Buffon, Corneille de Pauw, and Raynal.

CHAPTER FOUR
2

1. *Works,* ed. James Speeding, III, 143.

2. See Don Allen, *The Legend of Noah* (Urbana, Ill., 1949); A. Gerbi, *Dispute Over the New World* (Pittsburgh, 1973); and H. S. Commager and Elmo Giordanetti, *Was America a Mistake?* (N.Y., 1967).

3. On Buffon, see Louis Dimier, *Buffon* (Paris, 1919), which has interesting chapters on Buffon's relations with the philosophes, and on the "Discourses on Style"; P. Flourens, *Buffon: Histoire de ses Traveaux et de ses Idées* (Paris, 1844); L. Roule, *Buffon et la description de la Nature* (Paris, 1924); E. Guyenet, *Les sciences de la vie au XVIIe et XVIIIe siècles; l'idée d'évolution* (Paris, 1946); Jacques Roger, *Les Sciences de la vie dans la Pensée Francaise du XVIIe siècle* (Paris, 1963). The best accounts in English are Otis Fellows, "Buffon's Place in the Enlightenment," *Voltaire Studies,* XXV, 603ff., and Paul Hazard, *European Thought in the Eighteenth Century,* Pt. II, Ch. ii (L., 1954). Buffon permeates Antonello Gerbi, *New World.*

4. *Oeuvres Complètes,* XV, 45. Qt. in Gergi, *New World,* 5 and 6.

5. In the form of a Journal, first published in Stockholm: *En resa til Norra America, pa. Kongl. Swenska Wetenskaps Academiens befallning forratted af Pehr Kalm* (Stockholm, 1753–61).

It was translated into German almost simultaneously and published at Göttingen; a 2-vol. English edition appeared in 1770–71. I have used Peter Kalm's *Travels in North America*, 2 vols., ed., Adolph B. Benson (N.Y., 1937). On Peter Kalm, see C. F. J. Skottsberg, *Pehr Kalm, Levnedsteckning* (1951).

6. See esp. Wm. Darlington, *Memorials of John Bartram and Humphrey Marshall*, Classica Botanica Americana (N.Y., 1967), on Bartram's shipments to Linnaeus and Joseph Banks.

7. *Kalm*, ed., Benson, I, 306.

8. Grimm, *Correspondance Littéraire, philosophique et critique par Grimm, Diderot, Meister, etc.* (16 vols.) (Paris, 1877–82), VIII, 109–10.

9. Jefferson said of the book that "it is really remarkable that in three volumes of small print it is scarcely possible to find one truth"; VII *Papers*, Boyd, ed., 185. On De Pauw, see Henry Ward Church, "Corneille de Pauw and the Controversy over his Recherches Philosophiques sur les Américains," in *Publications of the Modern Language Association of America*, LI, 196.

10. On all this see Gerbi, *New World;* Ralph Miller, "American Nationalism as a Theory of Nature," *William and Mary Quarterly* (January, 1955); Chinard, "Eighteenth-Century Theories . . . ," op. cit.; and Commager and Giordanetti, *America.*

11. Qt. from Gerbi, *New World,* 330, from Kant's lectures on Philosophical Anthropology at Königsberg, in 1772. His notes added that the Americans were "incapable of governing themselves and destined for extermination"; Gerbi, op. cit., n. 14.

12. See the fascinating volume by Alfred Crosby, *The Columbian Exchange: Biological and Cultural Consequences of 1492* (Westport, Conn., 1972).

13. Supplement to the Encyclopédie, I, 351.

14. *The Anarchiad* was first published in the New Haven *Gazette* in 1786–87; it was the joint product of a group of "Connecticut Wits"—Lemuel Hopkins, Joel Barlow, Timothy Dwight, and others.

15. See also, "To the Honorable W. R. Spender," in Moore's *Poetical Works* (Boston, 1856), II, 98:

> Oh! for *such*, Columbia's days were done
> Rank without ripeness, quicken'd without sun
> Crude at the surface, rotten at the core,
> Her fruits would fall, before her spring was o'er.

304 NOTES

CHAPTER FIVE
1

1. See R. A. Humphreys, "William Robertson and His History of America," *Canning House Lecture* (L., 1954).

2. On all this, see Commager and Giordanetti, *Was America a Mistake?* (N.Y., 1967). John Adams, who himself sometimes suspected that America was a mistake, nevertheless protested vigorously against Europeans who deluded themselves on this matter. Thus, at the very beginning of the *Defense* he observed that "The writer has long seen with anxiety the facility with which Philosophers of greatest name have undertaken to write of American affairs, without knowing anything of them, and have echoed and re-echoed each other's visionary language." In IV *Works* (Boston, 1851), 294.

3. See especially Daniel J. Boorstin, *The Lost World of Thomas Jefferson* (N.Y., 1948).

4. See Boorstin, *Lost World,* and Commager and Giordanetti, *Was America a Mistake?* Note, too, the absence of formal speculation about the nature of progress and happiness: see Ch. III above.

5. 20 September 1787. XII Boyd's *Jefferson,* 159. Charles Thomson, the "perpetual secretary" of the Continental Congress, was not only an ardent patriot, but a life-long student of Indian affairs, and an adopted member of the Delaware tribe.

6. Even Noah Webster wrote a 2-vol. *Brief History of Epidemic and Pestilential Diseases* (1799). Of all the American philosophes, it was Dr. Rush who was probably the key figure in this enterprise.

7. There are very general accounts in Daniel Boorstin, *Lost World* and Edwin T. Martin, *Thomas Jefferson, Scientist* (N.Y., 1952); but far and away the best discussion is that by Gilbert Chinard, "Eighteenth Century Theories on America as a Human Habitat" in *Proc. of the Amer. Phil. Soc.,* Vol. 91, No. 1, February 1947. There are illuminating pages in Glacken, *Traces on the Rhodean Shore.* And see, Commager and Giordanetti, *Was America a Mistake?*

8. ". . . The pleasing view of this abundance is never disturbed by the melancholy appearance of poverty. There are no poor in Pennsylvania. All those whose birth or fortune have left them without resources, are suitably provided for out of the public treasury. The spirit of benevolence is carried still further, and is extended even to the most engaging hospitality. A traveler

is welcome to stop in any place, without the apprehensions of giving the least uneasy sensation, except that of regret for his departure . . ." Raynal, op. cit., VII (1783 ed.), 29. The champions of America were not quite as fatuous as the critics, but they too were given to exaggeration. There were indeed poor in Pennsylvania: see Gary Nash, "Poverty and poor Relief in Philadelphia," *William and Mary Qtly.* (January 1976).

9. On Wilson, see Robert Cantwell, *Alexander Wilson, Naturalist and Pioneer* (Philadelphia, 1961). The literature on Audubon is large; see esp. Constance Rourke, *Audubon* (N.Y., 1936); Francis H. Herrick, *Audubon the Naturalist* (N.Y., 1917), 2 vols., and excerpts from Audubon's writings, *Delineations of American Scenery and Character* (N.Y., 1926). There is good material in Van Wyck Brooks, *The World of Washington Irving.*

10. To Rittenhouse, 19 July 1778, II, Boyd's *Jefferson,* 203.

11. *Notes on Virginia,* II, Jefferson, Memorial ed., 95–96.

12. See Eleanor Berman, *Thomas Jefferson Among the Arts* (N.Y., 1947); Karl Lehmann, *Thomas Jefferson, American Humanist* (N.Y., 1947); Fiske Kimball, *Thomas Jefferson, Architect* (Cambridge, 1916).

13. See H. J. Eckenrode, *Separation of Church and State in Virginia* (Richmond, 1910). See, too, Irving Brant, *James Madison, The Nationalist: 1780–1787* (Indianapolis, 1948).

14. See Martin, *Jefferson, Scientist,* Ch. i, and refs. at 224; and Everett E. Edwards, ed., *Jefferson and Agriculture: A Source Book* (Washington, 1943).

15. For Jefferson's Revisal of the Laws of Virginia, see II Boyd's *Jefferson,* 305ff.

16. R. J. Honeywell, *The Educational Work of Thomas Jefferson* (Cambridge, 1931); Gordon C. Lee, ed., *Crusade Against Ignorance; Thomas Jefferson on Education* (N.Y., 1961).

17. Gilbert Chinard, "Polybius and the Founding Fathers," I *Jour. Hist. Ideas* (1939), i. "I prefer the dreams of the future to the history of the past" Jefferson wrote to John Adams in 1816. Jefferson even preferred the pianoforte to the harpsichord, but in architecture and literature he was a classicist.

18. See Edwin M. Betts, *Thomas Jefferson's Garden Book at Monticello* (Philadelphia, 1944). As for music, it is, he wrote, "the favorite passion of my soul." His ability to combine the practical with the aesthetic appears in his request to Mazzei to find him domestic servants who were also musicians. "I retain among my domestic servants a gardener, a weaver, a cabinet-maker and a stone-cutter, to which I would add a vigneron. In a country where, like yours, music is cultivated and practiced by every class of men, I suppose there might be found persons of

306

NOTES

these trades who could perform on the French horn, clarinet, or hautboy, and bassoon, so that one might have a band of two French horns, two clarinets, two hautboys and a bassoon, without enlarging their domestic expenses . . . Perhaps it might be practicable for you . . . to find out such men disposed to come to America." Jefferson to Giovanni Fabbroni, 8 June 1778, II Boyd, 196. See Helen Cripe, *Thomas Jefferson and Music* (Charlottesville, Va., 1974).

19. The text proper runs to 261 pages in the Memorial Ed. The Appendix is made up of documents and letters, with one important essay on the American Indian by Charles Thomson. The best scholarly ed. so far is that by William Peden, pub. at Chapel Hill, in 1955. Mr. Julian Boyd has a more elaborate one in preparation. On the writing of the *Notes,* see Dumas Malone, *Jefferson the Virginian,* Vol. I of *Jefferson and His Times* (Boston, 1948), Ch. xxvi.

20. *Notes on Virginia*—Query VI. II Memorial ed.

21. Jefferson to Rush, 22 January 1797, VII, Ford, ed., *Writings of Thomas Jefferson,* 114. And see too, Julian Boyd, "The Megalonyx, the Megatherium, and Thomas Jefferson's Lapse of Memory," *Proc. Am. Phil. Soc.* 102 (1958), 420ff., and Anna C. Jones, "Antlers for Jefferson," XII *New England Quarterly* 333, and, in a more serious vein, George G. Simpson, "The Beginnings of Vertebrate Paleontology in North America," *Proc. Am. Phil. Soc.* (September 1942).

22. Jefferson discussed the mammoth in his *Notes on Virginia,* where he asserted that "remains of unparalleled magnitude" had been found on the Ohio River. In 1798 he was chairman of a committee of the American Philosophical Society to "Collect Information Respecting the Antiquities of North America." Learning of some fossil bones that might be those of the mammoth in Big Bone Lick, Kentucky, Jefferson employed ten workers for several weeks, at his own expense, to dig up the fossil bones, and had them shipped to him in the White House. Some of the bones went to the collection of the Philosophical Society, others to the National Institute of France. The story is told by Martin, *Jefferson, Scientist,* 99ff. See also Simpson, op. cit.

23. *Notes on Virginia,* II Memorial ed., 60–61.

24. Jones, "Antlers for Jefferson," XII *New England Quarterly* 333, and letters in VI Memorial ed., 324–25 and 328–29.

25. For examples of early American interest in ethnology:

Adair, James, *The History of the American Indians . . .* (L., 1775).

Barton, Benjamin Smith, *New Views of the Origin of the Tribes and Nations of America* (Philadelphia, 1797).

Bartram, John, *Observations on the Inhabitants, Climate, Soil, Rivers, Productions, Animals, and Other Matters* . . . (L., 1751).

Bartram, William, *Travels in Georgia and Florida, 1773–1774.* 33 *Trans. of the Am. Phil. Soc.,* 121ff.

Colder, Cadwallader, *The History of the Five Indian Nations* . . . ed., John G. Shea (N.Y., 1886).

Lawson, John, *The History of Carolina, Containing the Exact Description and Natural History of that Country* . . . (L., 1709; reprinted, Richmond, 1937).

Williams, Samuel, *The Natural and Civil History of Vermont,* 2 v. (Burlington, Vt., 1809).

Williamson, Hugh, *Observations on the Climate in Different Parts of America* (N.Y., 1811).

On all this, see Robert E. Lowie, *A History of Ethnological Theory* (N.Y., 1937); William N. Fenton, ed., *American Indian and White Relations to 1830: Needs and Opportunities for Study* (Chapel Hill, 1957); and Roy Harvey Pearce, *The Savages of America* (Baltimore, 1953).

26. See the Introduction to his *History of the Five Nations,* by John Gilmore Shea (N.Y., 1866).

27. William Bartram, *Travels Through North and South Carolina, Georgia, East and West Florida the Cherokee Country, the Extensive Territories of the Muscogules, or Creek Confederacy, and the Country of the Choctaws* (Philadelphia, 1791). Bartram's *Travels* have been reprinted, ed. by Mark Van Doren (N.Y., 1928). On the influence of the *Travels* on the literary imagination, see Gilbert Chinard, *L'Éxotisme Américain dans l'Oeuvre de Chateaubriand* (Paris, 1918), and I Cambridge *Hist. of Am. Lit.,* 194ff. There is no good biography of William Bartram, but see Ernest Earnest, *John and William Bartram* (Philadelphia, 1940).

28. Stiles, *Letters and Papers* (New Haven, 1953), and Edward S. Morgan, *The Gentle Puritan* (New Haven, 1962), 136–39, 436–37.

29. Logan's speech is to be found in *Notes on Virginia.* See in II Memorial ed., 89, and in Peden, ed., 62–63, 274–75. The speech, says Jefferson, "had circulated in the newspapers through all the then colonies, through the magazines of Great Britain, and periodical publications of Europe. For three and twenty years it passed uncontradicted, nor was it ever suspected that it admitted of contradiction." See Appendix IV of the *Notes.* Peden, ed., 226–58. Yet we may suspect that it was more Jefferson than Logan.

30. *Notes on Virginia.* Thomson's observations are in II Mem. ed., 263ff.

31. Ibid., 267. Here is Hugh Williamson on the same subject: "At a meeting of Indians from different tribes, in the year 1796, I examined near fifty of them, and there was not, in that number, a single Indian without a beard . . . Their beards in general were shaved, but some of the chiefs had suffered whiskers to remain on the upper lip; or they suffered a small portion on the chin to grow to a considerable length." *Observations on the Climate* (N.Y., 1811), 83.

32. In King Philip's War the slaughter on both sides was general and indiscriminate. Jefferson must have been familiar with the Conestoga Massacre of 1763, when the "Paxton Boys" wiped out a settlement of defenseless Conestoga Indians, and the even more atrocious Gnadenhütten Massacre of 1782 when frontiersmen of Washington County killed some one hundred Christian Indians—men, women and children. The indiscriminate slaughter of women and children went on as late as 1864, when Col. Chivington massacred over 400 Indian men, women, and children at Sand Creek, Colorado.

33. The sale of whiskey was, of course, deliberate; the infection with smallpox was not. Yet during the French and Indian War, General Amherst seriously considered supplying the Indians with blankets infected with smallpox as a military device. See Roy H. Pearce, "The Ruins of Mankind," XIII *Jour. Hist. Ideas* (1952), 202; J. C. Long, *Lord Jeffrey Amherst* (N.Y., 1933).

34. This is not to imply that Spaniards uniformly believed Indians unworthy of the benefits of Christianity. Indeed, official Spanish policy from the mid-sixteenth century on sought not only the conversion of the Indians but their protection from greedy colonizers as well. On the Spanish theory of Indian relations, see Lewis Hanke, "The Spanish Struggle for Justice in the Conquest of America," XXIX *Hispanic American Hist. Rev.* J. H. Parry, *The Spanish Theory of Empire in the Sixteenth Century* (Camb., 1940); Lewis Hanke, *Aristotle and the Indians* (Chicago, 1959); and Gerbi, *New World*, Ch. iii.

35. Thus, Robert Cushman of the Plymouth Colony wrote, in 1622, that as the Indians were neither industrious nor skillful, the English had a right to their lands. "As the ancient patriarchs . . . removed from straiter places into more roomy where land lay idle and waste, and none used it, tho there dwelt inhabitants by them . . . so it is lawful now to take a land which none useth and make use of it." Qt. in Pearce, *Ruins of Mankind*, 202, and see John Winthrop's argument to the same effect in Ibid., 203. See also Chester Eisinger, "The Puritans' Justification for Taking the Land," LXXXIV, *Essex Inst. Hist. Coll.*, 131ff.

36. See, in general, R. H. Pearce, *The Savages of America,*

and the highly polemical but not inaccurate book by Helen Hunt Jackson, *A Century of Dishonor* (N.Y., 1881).

37. James Sullivan, *History of the District of Maine* (Boston, 1795), 139.

38. David Ramsay, *History of South Carolina*, 2 vols. (1809), I, 150–51.

39. President Jackson provided an official gloss to this view of the matter in his second annual message to Congress:

> Humanity has often wept over the fate of the aborigines of this country, and Philanthropy has been long busily employed in devising means to avert it, but its progress has never for a moment been arrested . . . What good man would prefer a country covered with forests and ranged by a few thousand savages, to our extensive republic, studded with cities, towns, and prosperous farms . . . and filled with all the blessings of liberty, civilization and religion? (Richardson, *Messages and Addresses of the Presidents*, II, 520.)

This attitude persisted well into the nineteenth century. Thus, the great Prescott, sympathetic as he was to the Aztecs and the Incas, wrote that it was pure sentimentalism for us now to "regret the fall of an empire which did so little to promote the happiness of its subjects or the real interests of humanity." The Aztecs were, for all their achievements, "a fierce and brutal race, little calculated, in their best aspect, to excite our sympathy and regard. Their civilization . . . was a generous graft on a vicious stock, and could have brought no fruit to perfection." Thus, Prescott concludes "it was beneficently ordered by Providence that the land [of the Mexicans] should be delivered over to another race" (I *Mexico*, 85).

40. See *Letters from an American Farmer*, Letters IV to VII.

41. Ibid., Letter XII: "Distresses of a frontiersman."

42. "The Wyoming Massacre" can be found in *Sketches of Eighteenth-Century America*, Ch. viii. This is reprinted in Albert E. Stones's edition of the *Letters of an American Farmer* (N.Y., 1963).

43. "On the Civilization of the Western Aboriginal Country" in *Last Poems of Philip Freneau*, ed. Lewis Leary (New Brunswick, 1945).

44. See Betts, ed., *Garden Book*, and Berman, *Jefferson Among the Arts*.

45. "He has finally returned to his home, amidst the acclaim of his fellow-citizens. I have seen him by his rustic penates at Braintree, where he is busy tending his farm, oblivious of the

time when he struck down the pride of his king, who had put a price upon his head . . . He is like one of the generals or ambassadors of the golden ages of Rome and Greece, an Epaminondes, a Cincinnatus, or a Fabius." Brissot de Warville, *New Travels in the United States of America, 1788,* ed., Echeverria (Cambridge, 1964), 102.

46. See Leon Howard, *The Connecticut Wits* (Chicago, 1943). "The Hasty Pudding" can be found in Parrington, ed. *The Connecticut Wits* (N.Y., 1926).

47. James Woodress, *A Yankee's Odyssey: Joel Barlow* (Philadelphia, 1958). This contains a picture of Kalorama.

48. Henry Adams, *Albert Gallatin* (Philadelphia, 1879), 350ff. The Report itself can be found in 12th Cong. First Sess. v. I, 7–86.

CHAPTER FIVE
2

1. D. V. Glass and E. E. C. Eversley, ed. *Population in History* (L., 1965) is an invaluable collection of somewhat miscellaneous essays on demography in the eighteenth and nineteenth centuries. There is a useful survey of the eighteenth-century population by H. J. Habakkuk on VIII *New Camb. Mod. Hist.,* Ch. ii (Camb., 1965). The growth of American population has not been adequately studied, but see two older works, S. H. Sutherland, *Population Distribution in Colonial America* (N.Y., 1936), and E. B. Greene and V. D. Harrington, *American Population before the Federal Census of 1790* (N.Y., 1932). See, too, the official publication, *Historical Statistics of the United States, Colonial Times to 1957* (U. S. Dept. of Commerce, Washington, 1960). See also a suggestive article by Julian Huxley, "A Factor Overlooked by the Philosophes; the Population Explosion," XXV *Voltaire Studies,* 861. Walter F. Willcox, *Studies in American Demography* (Ithaca, N.Y., 1940) deals mostly with nineteenth- and twentieth-century demography, and see too Gerald Gruman, "Ideas About the Prolongation of Life," in *Trans. Am. Phil. Soc.,* Vol. 56 (1966).

2. Rousseau, *The Social Contract Book* III, Ch. lx. I have used the edition by Frederick Watkins (L., 1953).

3. Raynal, *History of the Indies,* VIII, 264–66.

4. See article "Population" in the Encyclopédie, by Damilaville. In his article on "Population" in John J. Lalor's *Cyclopaedia of Political Science, Political Economy . . . of the United States* (Chicago, 1883–84), Joseph Garnier says that "until the time

of Malthus, legislators, statesmen and philosophers set out with this aphorism, 'where there is population, there is power.' "

5. Goldsmith, *"The Deserted Village,"* lines 51ff.

6. Buffon, II *Histoire Naturelle.*

7. Dorothy George, *London Life in the Eighteenth Century* (L., 1951), Ch. i, "Life and Death in London."

8. Dr. Price has some claim to be considered the most influential of British students of population before Malthus. His *Observations on the Nature of Civil Liberty* was widely read both in Britain and America; his *Essay on the Population of England* (1780) went through many editions. Price asserted that in parts of North America the population could be expected to double every fifteen years. On Price, see Carl B. Cone, *Torchbearer of Freedom* (Lexington, Ky., 1952).

9. S. Peller, in Glass and Eversley, *Population in History*, 92–93. For Breslau, see Brissot, *New Travels*, 285, reporting figures from Edmund Halley, *Degrees of Mortality of Mankind.*

10. Dorothy George, *London Life*, Ch. 1.

11. K. H. Connell, in Glass and Eversley, *Population*, 423; for Finland, Jutikkals, ibid., 568.

12. Estimates for English and Welsh population during these years vary greatly; see the tables in Glass and Eversley, *Population*, Ch. IX, 240. These show that Farr (1861 census) gives the figures for 1700 at 6,122,000 and for 1770 at 7,153,000; Brownlee, writing in 1916 gives the figures for these two years as 5,826,000 and 7,052,000; and Griffith, writing in 1926, as 5,835,-000 and 7,124,000.

13. For Italy see Ibid., 570ff. by Carlo Cippola and C. A. Vianello, *Il Settecento Milanese* (Milano, n.d.) which shows that deaths exceeded births in the State of Milan four years out of eleven (1775–85) and that during this same period the population increased by only 20,000. From 1768–1800 the population of the City of Milan increased from 126,000 to 129,000. See Appendices, 279ff. For France, see chapter by Louis Henry, in ibid., 434ff. For Spain and Portugal see Habbakuk, in VIII *New Cambridge Modern History*, 29. For the German states, Adrian Fauchier-Magnan, *The Small German Courts in the Eighteenth Century*, Ch. I, not scholarly but suggestive.

14. Julian Huxley, "A Factor Overlooked by the Philosophes: the Population Explosion," XXV Voltaire Studies, 861. During the seventeenth century there were serious proposals to legalize polygamy in England; see Alfred Aldridge, "Population and Polygamy in Eighteenth Century Thought," J. Hist. of Med. (1949) IV, 129ff.

15. See note 1, above, and notes 20 and 21 below.

16. Colonial American population as compiled by Stella
Sutherland:

White	Population	Negro	Population
1700	251,000	1700	28,000
1720	466,000	1720	69,000
1740	906,000	1740	150,000
1760	1,594,000	1760	325,000
1780	2,780,000	1780	575,000

Historical Statistics of the United States, 756.

17. See, "Information to Those Who Would Remove to America" in Smyth, ed., *Writings of Benjamin Franklin,* 603ff., and see Norman Hinea, "Benjamin Franklin on Population," III *Economic History Review,* 52 (1934–37).

18. The Polly Baker story can be followed in Max Hall, *Benjamin Franklin and Polly Baker* (Chapel Hill, 1960).

19. *Notes on Virginia,* answer to Query 7. Much of the increase in Negro population came, to be sure, from importation. Rossiter estimates that the total importation of slaves between 1700 and 1790 was between 250,000 and 300,000; the total Negro population in 1790 was c. 760,000. See J. Potter, in Glass and Eversley, *Population,* 63ff.

20. There were, in fact, many conjectures, and not all of them unscientific. Thus, Edward Wigglesworth—he was the Hollis Professor of Divinity at Harvard College, so spoke with authority—predicted a population of five million by 1800, 20 million by 1850, 80 million by 1900, and almost two billion by the year 2000. *Calculations on American Population, 1775.* Ezra Stiles estimated that the population of the United States would reach 50 million in a hundred years, and would eventually outstrip that of China!

21. "Observations on the Probabilities of the Duration of Human Life, and the Progress of Population in the United States of America," in a letter from William Barton, esp. to David Rittenhouse. Read March 18, 1791, III *Trans. Am. Phil. Soc.* (Philadelphia, 1793), 25ff.

22. Carl and Jessica Bridenbaugh, *Rebels and Gentlemen: Philadelphia in the Age of Franklin.* See also Daniel Boorstin, *The Lost World of Thomas Jefferson;* Brooke Hindle, *The Pursuit of Science in Revolutionary America;* and Richard Shryock, "Eighteenth Century Medicine in America," in *Am. Antiq. Soc., Proc.* LIX, 1950, 257.

23. The statement that Barton received a medical degree from Göttingen in 1789 is repeated in most accounts, but that careful scholar Henry Pochmann says there is no record of his attendance

at the university. See Pochman, *German Culture in America, 1600–1900* (Madison, Wisc., 1957), 50.

24. All of this from Dr. Barton's "Observations on the Probabilities of the Duration of Human Life." See n. 21 above.

25. Currie, *Historical Account of the Climate and Diseases of the United States of America . . . Collected principally from Personal Observation and the Communications of Physicians of Talents and Experience . . .* (Philadelphia, 1792).

26. Ibid., 408–9.

27. 23 June 1790, XVI Boyd ed., 550.

28. The whole passage is worth quoting, for it represents so well the point of view of the enlightened Europeans who were looking to America as an example and a model. And of all the Frenchmen who idealized and even romanticized America, none was more eloquent than the unhappy Brissot de Warville. Here is what he had to say about the relation between freedom and life expectancy:

The general causes of longevity are: 1, A healthy climate. 2, Abundant and nutritious food and drink. 3, A regular, active and happy life. Moreover one must take into account such external circumstances as a man's work, his morals, his religion, and the government under which he lives. Wherever property is concentrated in the hands of a few and where employment is precarious, dependent, and uncertain, human life is briefer. It is shortened by worries and cares, which, even more effectively than actual want, cut off the very source of life. Wherever government is arbitrary, where tyranny, descending and subdividing itself at each rank of society, stops only at the members of the very lowest classes, to crush them all, there the life of the common people must be shorter . . . Nor is life long, even for the power-hungry ruling class, for their days are shortened by excesses and worries.

If you apply these moral and political considerations to the United States you must conclude that there cannot be any country in which life expectancy is longer, for, in addition to all their natural advantages, the people enjoy the benefits of a liberty unequaled in the Old World, and it cannot be sufficiently stressed that it is liberty which is the source of health.

Brissot de Warville, *New Travels in the United States, 1788,* ed., Echeverria, 284.

29. Rush, Medical Inquiries and Observations, qt. in Boorstin, *The Lost World of Thomas Jefferson,* 184.

30. *Observations on the Climate in Different Parts of America*
(N.Y., 1811), 123–24, 178. This was eventually incorporated as
an introductory chapter to his *History of North Carolina* (2
vols.). Professor Hamilton asserts that Williamson's observations
on climate brought him an honorary doctorate from the University of Leyden!

CHAPTER FIVE
3

1. The best book on the philosophy of environment, already a
classic, is Clarence Glacken, *Traces on the Rhodean Shore*
(Berkeley, Calif., 1967).
2. *Spirit of the Laws* (Neumann, ed.), Bk. XVIII, Ch. 7. The
whole of Bk. XIV is a gloss upon this theme.
3. *Natural History*, Smellie, trans. quoted in Gilbert Chinard,
"18th Century Theories on America as a Human Habitat," 91
Proc. Am. Phil. Soc. (1947), 31.
4. *Essays upon Field Husbandry in New England, and Other
Papers, 1748–1762*, by Jared Eliot. Ed. by Harry J. Carman and
Rexford Tugwell (N.Y., 1934), 96–97.
5. Raynal, op. cit. (1783 ed.), VII, 161.
6. Brissot, *New Travels*, Echeverria ed., 275.
7. This was written in 1798. Qt. in Martin, *Thomas Jefferson,
Scientist*, 175.
8. On Jefferson's smuggling of rice from Italy, see Michael
Kraus, *The Atlantic Civilization* (Ithaca, 1949), 172.
9. See "Notes of a Tour into Southern Parts of France, etc.
. . . in the year 1787," XI Boyd, ed., 438.
10. Martin, *Thomas Jefferson, Scientist*, 47.
11. Jefferson to Le Roy, 13 November 1786, X Boyd ed., 52.
12. See discussion of authorship of *American Husbandry* by
Harry Carman in Introduction to the book.
13. Best on this is Daniel Boorstin, *Lost World of Thomas Jefferson*. See also, Brooke Hindle, *The Pursuit of Science in Revolutionary America* (Chapel Hill, 1956).
14. See, for example, the rich and fascinating body of material
collected by Oscar and Mary Handlin, *The Popular Sources of
Political Authority: Documents on the Massachusetts Constitution of 1780* (Cambridge, 1966).
15. Montesquieu, Neumann, ed., op. cit., Bk. VIII, Ch. 16, 120.
16. Jefferson to Joseph Priestley, 21 March 1801, VII, *Writings* (Ford, ed.), 21.
17. *American Husbandry*, 304–5. There is, to be sure, some

doubt about the authorship of this book, but the evidence points to Mitchell.

18. It should not be necessary to remind the reader that the term "climate" in the eighteenth century was pretty much the equivalent of our term "environment."

19. Raynal, op. cit., VI, 366. To be sure, it may have been Deleyre, or one of the other anonymous collaborators who wrote this passage. But Raynal allowed it to stand.

20. Turgot to Dr. Price, qt. in John Adams, *Defense of the Constitutions* in IV *Works*, 278ff.

21. Condorcet, *Progress of the Human Mind*, Barraclough, ed. (L., 1955), 173ff.

22. See material in Commager and Giordanetti, *Was America a Mistake?* Intro. Ch. 4, and Pt. II, Chs. 8–10.

CHAPTER SIX

1

1. See under "Climat" in Dictionnaire Philosophique, II, Vol. 48, *Oeuvres Complètes de Voltaire* (Paris, 1870).

2. "Of National Characters," *Essays*, I, 249.

3. Adam Ferguson, *Essay on the History of Civil Liberty* (Boston, 1809), 186ff. There is a new edition with an introduction by Duncan Forbes (Edinburgh, 1966).

4. Priestley, II *Lectures on History* (Philadelphia, 1803), 42.

5. VIII, Raynal, *History of the Indies* (1783 ed.), 366.

6. *Confessions,* Book IX.

7. For Montesquieu I have used the edition of the *Spirit of the Laws* by Franz Neumann (N.Y.; Hafner Classics, 1949). Perhaps the best general book is R. Shackleton, *Montesquieu, a Critical Biography* (Oxford, 1961). Fernand Cattelain, *Étude sur l'influence de Montesquieu dans les constitutions américaines* (Besancon, 1927), and Paul M. Spurlin, *Montesquieu in America* (Baton Rouge, La., 1940) are adequate for that somewhat overworked subject.

8. It is impossible to list the innumerable books that illuminate political thought in the age of the Enlightenment. I list here only those that I have found most helpful, and, for simplicity, I list them in alphabetical order:

Bailyn, Bernard   *Ideological Origins of the American Revolution* (Cambridge, 1967), "Political Experience and the Enlightenment Ideas in Eighteenth Century America," 67 A.H.R. (January, 1962).

Becker, Carl   *The Heavenly City of the Eighteenth Cen-
                       tury Philosophers* (New Haven, 1932).
Bruun, Geoffrey   *The Enlightened Despots* (N.Y., 1929).
Cassirer, Ernst   *The Philosophy of the Enlightenment*
                       (Princeton, 1951).
Cobban, Alfred   "The Enlightenment," Ch. 5 in VII *New
                       Cambridge Modern History* (N.Y., 1960).
                       *In Search of Humanity: The Role of the
                       Enlightenment in Modern History* (N.Y.,
                       1960).
Dorn, Walter   *Competition for Empire* (N.Y., 1940).
Dunning, W. A.   *A History of Political Thought,* Vol. I:
                       From Luther to Montesquieu (N.Y., 1905).
                       Vol. II *Rousseau to Spencer* (N.Y., 1920).
Durant, Will   *The Age of Voltaire* (N.Y., 1965).
  and Ariel   *Rousseau and Revolution* (N.Y., 1967).
Dutcher, George   "The Enlightened Despotism" *A.H.A.* Re-
                       ports, 1920, 187.
Gay, Peter   *The Party of Humanity* (N.Y., 1964). *Vol-
                       taire's Politics* (Princeton, 1959). *The En-
                       lightenment.* Vol. I: "The Rise of Modern
                       Paganism" (N.Y., 1966). Vol. II; "The Sci-
                       ence of Freedom" (1969).
Gershoy, Leo   *From Despotism to Revolution, 1763–1789*
                       (N.Y., 1944).
Halévy, Elie   *The Growth of Philosophical Radicalism*
                       (L., 1938).
Hazard, Paul   *The European Mind, 1680–1715* (L., 1953).
                       *European Thought in the Eighteenth Cen-
                       tury* (N.Y., 1946).
Holm, Søren   *Oplysnings Tiden, Tanker og Livssyn* (Kø-
                       benhavn, 1959).
Lefebvre, Georges   "Le despotisme éclairé," *Annales Hist. de la
                       Rév. Fran.* Vol. 114 (1949), 97ff.
Lheritier, M.   "Le rôle historique du despotisme
                       éclairé . . ." I *Bull. of the International
                       Comm. of Hist. Sciences,* 601 (1928).
Mornet, Daniel   *Les origines intellectuelles de la Révolution
                       française, 1715–1787* (Paris, 1933).
Natali, Giulio   *Il Settecento,* 2 vols. (Milan, 1930).
Palmer, Robert R.   *The Age of Democratic Revolution,* 2 vols.
                       (Princeton, 1959, 1964).
See, Henri   *L'évolution de la Pensée politique en France
                       au XVIIIe Siècle* (Paris, 1925).

Smith, Preserved   *A History of Modern Culture,* Vol. II (N.Y., 1934).

Valsecchi, F.   *L'assolutismo illuminato in Austria e in Lombardia,* Vol. I (Bologna, 1931).

9. See John R. Howe, *The Changing Political Thought of John Adams* (Princeton, 1966).

10. The date is 1790; Europe has entered the Age of Revolution and Reaction, and of Romanticism, too.

11. Rousseau's "Considerations on the Government of Poland" and his "Constitutional Project for Corsica" are reprinted in Frederick Watkins, ed., *Rousseau: Political Writings* (N.Y., 1953).

12. W. W. Stephens, ed., *Life and Writings of Turgot* (L., 1895).

13. Gilbert Chinard has edited the *Code de la Nature,* with an elaborate introduction (Paris, 1950).

14. On Adams's relations to Mably, and Mably's misunderstanding of Adams's casual comments, see Adams's Diary for 5 January 1783, *Diary and Autobiography,* ed. Butterfield (Cambridge, 1961), III, 101. The letter to Mably is printed in Adams, *Works* (C. F. Adams, ed.), V, 491. Mably's "Remarks Concerning the Government and Laws of the United States of America," in *Four Letters,* addressed to Mr. Adams, was published in London in 1783. Haraszti has a chapter on Mably in *John Adams and the Prophets of Progress* (Cambridge, 1952). See also, E. H. Whitfield, *Gabriel Bonnet de Mably* (L., 1930).

15. On Frederick the Great as an Enlightened Despot, see G. Ritter, *Friedrich der Grosse* (Heidelberg, 1954); G. P. Gooch, *Frederick the Great, the Ruler, the Writer, the Man* (L., 1947); P. Gaxotte, *Frederick the Great* (New Haven, 1942); W. L. Dorn, "The Prussian Bureaucracy in the 18th Century," LXVI *Pol. Sci. Qt.* (1931), 402, and XLVI, 75 and 259; W. H. Bruford, *Germany in the Eighteenth Century* (Camb., 1935); Thomas Carlyle, *History of Frederick II of Prussia, Called Frederic the Great,* 10 vols. (L., 1858–65). On Frederick as a philosopher, see the old book by E. Zeller, *Friedrich der Grosse als Philosoph* (Berlin, 1886).

16. On Catherine the Great, see G. P. Gooch, *Catherine the Great, and Other Studies* (L., 1954); I. K. Waliszewski, *The Romance of an Empress* (L., 1894); Zoe Oldenburg, *Catherine the Great* (N.Y., 1965); Ian Gray, *Catherine the Great, Autocrat and Empress* (L., 1961); Morley, *Diderot,* 2 vols.

17. On Gustavus, see R. N. Bain, et al., *Gustavus III and His Contemporaries* (L., 1894), and the more recent work by Beth

318

NOTES

Hennings, *Gustav III* (Stockholm, 1957). Perhaps the best modern treatment of the entire regime is in the large co-operative history by E. Hildebrand and L. Stavenow, *Sveriges Historia Til Vara Dagar,* vols. IX and X (Stockholm, 1919). Verdi's *Ballo in maschera* was first performed in Rome in 1859. To satisfy the still active censor, the scene was laid not in Rome but in *Boston!*

18. On Leopold, see VI *Cambridge Modern History,* Ch. xvi; F. Hirsch, *Leopold II als Grossherzog von Toskana* (Munich, 1878); and Adam Wandruska, *Leopold II,* 2 vols. (Wien, 1963–65).

19. See W. H. Bruford, *Germany in the Eighteenth Century* (the quotation is from p. 32), and his *Culture and Society in Classical Weimar 1775–1806* (Camb., 1962). On Karl August, see W. Andreas, *Karl August von Weimar* (Stuttgart, 1953). On the small states, see also Frederick Hertz, *The Development of the German Public Mind,* Vol. II (L., 1962), Ch. xviii; and Adrien Fauchier-Magnan, *The Small German Courts in the 18th Century* (L., 1958).

20. On Pombal, see F. L. Gomes, *Le Marquis de Pombal* (Lisbon, 1867); Conde de Carnota, *Marquis of Pombal* (L., 1871); Henry Morse Stephens, *The Story of Portugal* (N.Y., 1891). The best account in English is Marcus Cheke, *Dictator of Portugal, a Life of the Marquis de Pombal* (L., 1938).

21. For Floridablanca, see F. Rousseau, *Regne de Charles III d'Espagne,* 2 vols. (Paris, 1907). For the Enlightenment in Spain, see the masterly monograph by Jean Sarrailh, *L'Espagne éclairée de la seconde moitié du XVIIIe siècle* (Paris, 1954).

22. For Sonnenfels, see Robert Kann, *A Study in Austrian Intellectual History* (L., 1960); F. Valscecchi, *L'assolutismo illuminato in Austria e in Lombardia,* 2 vols. (Bologna, 1931–34); G. P. Gooch, *Maria Theresa and Other Studies* (L., 1951); Saul K. Padover, *The Revolutionary Emperor, Joseph II* (N.Y., 1934); Ernst Wangermann, *From Joseph II to the Jacobin Trials* (L., 1959).

23. On Struensee, see H. S. Commager, "Struensee and the Reform Movement in Denmark," unpublished Ph.D. Dissertation, University of Chicago, 1928. The most recent study is that by Svend C. Bech, *Oplysning og. Tolerance,* Vol. IX of *Danmark's Historie,* but *Danmarks Riges Historie,* ed. Joh. Steenstrup et al., Vol. V by Edvard Holm (Copenhagen, n.d.) is still the best account. See, too, *Det Danske Folks Historie,* ed. Aage Friis et al., Vol. VI: *Det Danske Folk under Evevaelden* (Copenhagen, 1928).

24. On Count Rumford, see George E. Ellis, *Memoir of Sir Benjamin Thompson,* Amer. Acad. of Arts and Sciences (Boston,

1870–75); J. A. Thompson, *Count Rumford of Massachusetts* (N.Y., 1935); L. D. Einstein, *Divided Loyalties: Americans in England during the War of Independence* (Boston, 1933).

CHAPTER SIX
2

1. Harold Acton, *The Bourbons of Naples* (N.Y., 1956), 398–400.
2. Gershoy, *From Despotism to Revolution*, 144–45; *Cambridge Modern History*, VI, 607; R. R. Palmer, II, *The Age of Democratic Revolution*, 306ff.; G. B. McClellan, *Venice and Bonaparte* (Princeton, 1931).
3. Palmer, II, *Democratic Revolution*, 142; Morley, *Diderot* (L., 1921), II, 101.
4. See Barton, "Sweden and the War of American Independence," XXIII *William and Mary Qtly.* July, 1966; and Odhner, *Gustaf IIIs Regering*, II, 103–5.
5. B. J. Hovde, *The Scandinavian Countries, 1720–1865*, I, 200ff. (Boston, 1943).
6. Palmer, op. cit., II, 513.
7. W. E. H. Lecky, *Ireland in the Eighteenth Century*, 5 vols. (L., 1892); VI *Cambridge Modern History*, Ch. xiv, with bibliography.
8. Jefferson, *First Inaugural Address*, Commager, *Documents*, No. 106.
9. Robert R. Palmer, *Age of Democratic Revolution*, Vol. II (Princeton, 1964) is the best authority on the counterrevolution. Leopold of Tuscany—and of the Empire—almost alone remained faithful to the principles of the Enlightenment, but he died within two years of coming to Vienna. See, too, the admirable biography of Leopold by Adam Wandruszka.

CHAPTER SEVEN
1

1. *Spirit of the Laws*, Neumann, ed., Bk. XI, Ch. 6, 162.
2. *Common Sense*, Ch. iii.
3. But not in the generation of the American Revolution. That, indeed, is one of the things the Revolution was about.
4. XV, Mem. ed., 75. To Tracy himself, Jefferson, 26 January 1811, wrote that his book was "the most precious gift the present age has received," IX Ford, ed. 305.

5. *A Commentary and Review of Montesquieu's Spirit of the Laws* (Philadelphia, 1811), 107. Jefferson supervised, if he did not actually make, the American translation of this book.

6. The Estates General of France did not meet between 1614 and 1789, and by 1789 the Estates of Denmark, Bavaria, Portugal, and other continental states had ceased to meet altogether, I Palmer, *Age of the Democratic Revolution,* 34. Some of those which did meet from time to time had no authority. Thus, the German publicist A. G. F. Rebmann described the Diet of Saxony as "a farce performed every six years, in which all the actors have to say is 'yes.'" Bruford, *Germany in the Eighteenth Century,* 23.

7. The literature on class and rank in the eighteenth-century world is voluminous, and there is no point in an elaborate presentation here. Suffice it to note E. Lousse, *La société d'ancien regime: organization et représentation corporatives* (Paris, 1943); H. Brocher, *Le rang et l'étiquette sous l'ancien régime* (Paris, 1934); Franklin L. Ford, *Robe and Sword, the Regrouping of the French Aristocracy after Louis XIV* (Cambridge, 1953); A. Goodwin, ed., *The European Nobility in the Eighteenth Century* (L., 1953), with admirable bibliographies. Something is to be gleaned from the lively pages of A. Fauchier-Magnan, *The Small German Courts in the Eighteenth Century* (L., 1958). On Magnates and Regents, see Henrik Marczali, *Hungary in the Eighteenth Century* (Camb., 1910); on Spain, F. Rousseau, *Regne de Charles III d'Espagne,* 2 vols. (Paris, 1907).

8. On the emergent bureaucracy see Walter Dorn, "Prussian Bureaucracy in the XVIII Century," XLVI *Political Science Quarterly,* 403–23; XLVII, 79–94, 259–73; Hans Rosenberg, *Bureaucracy, Aristocracy and Autocracy* (Cambridge, 1958).

9. The first phrase is from the Constitution itself. The other two are from *Cohens v. Virginia,* 8 Wheaton 264, and can be paralleled in many other judicial opinions by Marshall and Story.

10. I use the verb "invented" deliberately. I am aware of the long antecedents, philosophical and legal, but only in the United States did these crystallize into the institution of judicial review. On this there is still nothing better than A. C. McLaughlin, *The Courts, the Constitution, and the Parties* (Chicago, 1912).

11. See the whole of Ch. iv of J. L. De Lolme, *The Constitution of England.* The quotation is on p. 273 of the 1812 ed.; the reference was to Rome, but De Lolme generalized from Roman to universal experience.

12. Catherine's Instructions (1767) can be found in W. F. Reddaway, *Documents of Catherine the Great* (Camb., 1931), 215ff.

13. See *Die politischen Testamente Friedrich's des Grossen* edited by G. B. Volz (Berlin, 1920); see also Walter Dorn's illuminating articles in *Pol. Sci. Qtly.*, op. cit.

14. Bruford, *Germany in the Eighteenth Century*, 18.

15. On Lamprecht, see Fritz Hartung, *Enlightened Despotism*, 12 (L., 1957).

16. These are collected and edited in Holger Hansen, ed., *Kabinetstyrelse i Danmark*, 3 vols. (København, 1916–25).

17. Qt. Thomas Erskine May, *The Constitutional History of England, 1760–1860* (L., 1822), II, 312.

18. The words of Joseph II are characteristic of the enlightened despots. "Since I have ascended the throne," he said, on his accession in 1781, "and wear the first diadem of the world, I have made philosophy the legislator of my empire. In consequence of its logic, Austria will assume another form. . . . Thus, after the lapse of centuries, we shall have Christians; thus, when I have executed my plan, the people of my empire will better know the duties they owe to God, to the country, and to their fellow-creatures. . . ." Qt. in Herbert Rowen, ed., *From Absolutism to Revolution* (N.Y., 1963), 174–75.

CHAPTER SEVEN

2

1. These figures are all, in a sense, arbitrary. The population of the thirteen United States was somewhere between two and one half and three million in 1776; of these perhaps four hundred thousand or five hundred thousand were Negroes. Males were slightly less than half the total population, which might put their total at roughly one and a quarter or one and a third million. Of these it is improbable that more than five or six hundred thousand were adult.

2. Jefferson and Adams lived, and were active, until 1826; Jay lived to 1829, Monroe to 1831, Marshall to 1835, Madison to 1836, and Gallatin to 1849!

3. See my article on this subject in *Daedalus*, Fall, 1961.

4. *Notes on Virginia*, II Memorial ed., Query VI.

5. Palmer, *Age of Democratic Revolution*, Vol. I, and A. G. Porritt, *The Unreformed House of Commons*, 2 vols. (Camb., 1903).

6. *Notes on Virginia*, Query XIV, 206.

7. On the position of the lawyer in early American society, see Charles Warren, *A History of the American Bar* (Boston, 1911); Roscoe Pound, *Formative Era of American Law* (Boston,

1938); F. R. Aumann, *Changing American Legal System* (Columbus, O., 1940); Perry Miller, *The Life of the Mind in America from the Revolution to the Civil War*, Bk. 2 (N.Y., 1965). Not until Marshall's day can it be said that it was possible to make a national reputation at the bar.

8. On the romantic John Izard Middleton of Charleston, who spent most of his life on archeological studies in Rome, and who was reputed to be the original for Lord Nevil in Madame de Stael's *Corinne*, see Van Wyck Brooks, *The Dream of Arcadia* (N.Y., 1952) and the article in the Dictionary of American Biography.

9. The story can be followed in the *Journal of William Maclay, 1789–1791*, ed. Charles A. Beard (N.Y., 1927).

10. See Joel Larus, "Pêle-mêle Along the Potomac," in XVII *William and Mary Qtly.* (July, 1960), 349.

11. See Benjamin Wright, *Consensus and Continuity, 1776–1787* (Boston, 1958).

12. Most of them were modeled on those of Virginia and Massachusetts. The English Bill of Rights were concerned with protection against the abuse of power, guarantees of due process, and so forth; they made no reference to such things as freedom of religion or press or speech. See Robert A. Rutland, *The Birth of the Bill of Rights, 1776–1791* (Chapel Hill, 1955), and chapter X below.

13. Some scholars disagree with this interpretation of our early party history. I have in mind chiefly the readiness of the Republicans, when in control, to adopt broad construction principles, and the inclination of the Federalists, when not, toward state rights and narrow construction. John Quincy Adams joined the Republicans and Joseph Story shifted over to the Federalists without any great soul-searching, and it is difficult to know where we should place John Adams after 1808.

14. *Familiar Letters of John and Abigail Adams*, ed., C. F. Adams (Boston, 1863), 120.

15. To Joseph Cabell, 2 February 1816, XIV Mem. ed., 422.

16. Perhaps Willie Jones is an exception to this generalization. He was a man of wealth and education; he had attended Eton College, taken the grand tour, associated with the Royal Governor; he would no doubt have been acceptable in British politics. Yet he was a disciple of Thomas Jefferson and a precursor of what came to be an American state "boss."

17. See David Jacobson, *The English Libertarian Tradition, from the Writings of John Trenchard and Thomas Gordon* (Indianapolis, 1965), esp. introduction. See, too, Caroline Robbins, *The Eighteenth-Century Commonwealthman* (Cambridge, 1959).

18. William Tudor, *Life of James Otis* (Boston, 1823), 144.
19. Josiah Quincy, *Memoir of the Life of Josiah Quincy, Jr.*
(Boston, 1825), 289.
20. The Dissertation can be found in *Works of John Adams*,
III, 448ff. (Boston, 1851); it is conveniently reprinted in George
A. Peek, ed., *The Political Writings of John Adams* (N.Y., 1954).
21. *Works of John Adams*, IV, 469.
22. Jefferson to John Adams, 21 January 1812, XIII Mem.
ed., 124.
23. Partly, to be sure, because there was no national capital,
in the Old World sense of the term, until much later, while many
of the state capitals were but small towns. Certainly Washington
preferred Mt. Vernon to New York or Philadelphia, and Jefferson, Monticello, while Adams was happiest in Braintree. Both
Gallatin and Priestley took to the Pennsylvania woods. Aaron
Burr, who was the least typical of American statesmen, had a
hankering for the flesh pots and indulged it in the capitals of
the Old World. Joel Barlow is almost the only one of the philosophes who deliberately chose to live in, or near, the national
capital, but he had been spoiled by almost twenty years residence abroad and really had no American home. Hamilton, too
—if he can be considered a philosophe—preferred the city, but
then Hamilton was in so many respects more European than
American.

CHAPTER SEVEN

3

1. Quoted in Commager and Morris, eds., *Spirit of Seventy-
Six*, I, 12.
2. Quotation from Thomas Chandler, "What Think Ye of the
Congress Now?" in B. Bailyn, *Ideological Origins of the American Revolution*, 281.
3. Quoted in J. T. Main, *The Social Structure of Revolutionary
America* (Princeton, 1965), 213.
4. From Canto III, "The Liberty Pole." *M'Fingal* can be
found in V. L. Parrington, ed., *The Connecticut Wits*. On Trumbull, see Leon Howard, *The Connecticut Wits* (Chicago, 1943).
Barbé-Marbois wrote that "no form of activity is considered
ignoble here as long as it is useful to society. Sometimes we
learned that the keeper of an inn was a colonel in the forces of
the State; sometimes we saw a priest [he means a minister] himself getting in the crops or working in his fields . . ." *Letters of
Barbé-Marbois*, ed., Eugene Chase (N.Y., 1929), 88–89.

324

5. Which is how the Chevalier de Rohan-Chabot treated the young Voltaire.

6. Quoted in A. Fauchier-Magnan, *The Small German Courts in the 18th Century*, 52. It can be found in VI *Oeuvres de Frédéric le Grand*, ed., Preuss (Berlin, 1846), 95.

7. Forgotten, that is, until Palmer rescued him from oblivion; see I *Age of the Democratic Revolutions*, 61ff.

8. *Commentaries on the Laws of England*, I, 128, cited in Palmer, op. cit., 63.

9. The Duke of Wellington on the Order of the Garter.

10. I. B. Christie, *Wilkes, Wyvill, and Reform* (L., 1962), 16 n. The *Hollis Memoirs* are almost unobtainable. On Hollis, see Caroline Robbins, *The Eighteenth Century Commonwealthman*, and her luminous articles on "Library of Liberty Assembled for Harvard College by Thomas Hollis" in *Bulletin of the Harvard Library*, V (1951), 5, 181.

11. W. F. Rae, in IX *Encyclopaedia Britannica*, 9th ed., 498.

12. See the Trial of Thomas Paine, in Howell's *State Trials* (L., 1817), Vol. XXII, 357ff.

13. Lewis Namier, *Structure of Politics at the Accession of George III*, I, 82–83. In this discussion of voting and office holding in eighteenth-century Britain I have relied chiefly on Namier's two volumes, and on E. and A. G. Porritt, *The Unreformed House of Commons*, 2 vols. (Camb., 1903); W. E. H. Lecky, *A History of England in the Eighteenth Century*, 8 vols. (L., 1883–87); Thomas Erskine May, *The Constitutional History of England, 1760–1860*, 3 vols. (L., 1882); H. E. Witmer, *Property Qualifications for Members of Parliament* (N.Y., 1943); Charles Seymour, *Electoral Reform in England and Wales* (New Haven, 1915). On matters of interpretation I have found Porritt more persuasive than Namier.

14. Technically, non-conformists could "attend" the universities, but could not take degrees; this, in turn, excluded them from many of the learned professions.

15. II May, *Constitutional History*, 292ff. The Trial is in *State Trials*, XIX. On the Duke of Richmond's reform bill, see I May, op. cit., 395, citing XXI *Parliamentary History*, 686.

16. I May, op. cit., 332.

17. I Lecky, *England in the Eighteenth Century*, 436; I Porritt, *House of Commons*, 221.

18. I Porritt, op. cit., 313; I May, op. cit., 332ff.

19. I Porritt, op. cit., 76 and I May, op. cit., 354.

20. I May, op. cit., 333. According to Porritt, 84 patrons returned 157 members, and as many as 307 may have been returned by patronage. Lewis Namier's somewhat more prudent

calculation concludes that 51 peers controlled 101 seats and 55 commoners, 91 seats, while the Administration controlled, more or less firmly, another 60 seats—a total of 252. Porritt, op. cit., I, 31, and Namier, *Structure of Politics*, I, 174ff.

21. I May, op. cit., 332.

22. Burke, *Speech on Conciliation with America* (Buchan ed.), 179.

23. See Lecky, *Leaders of Public Opinion in Ireland*, I, 78ff. and I May, op. cit., 360ff.

24. I list here alphabetically the chief books on which I have relied for this somewhat impressionistic and highly selective commentary on the European scene.

C. B. A. Behrens, *The Ancien Régime;* John Blum, *Lord and Peasant in Russia from the Ninth to the Nineteenth Century; Cambridge Modern History,* Vol. VI, and *New Cambridge Modern History* (alas without bibliographies), Vols. VII and VIII; F. L. Carstens, *Princes and Parliaments in Germany;* Walter Dorn, *Competition for Empire, 1740–1763;* L. Ducros, *French Society in the Eighteenth Century;* A. Fauchier-Magnan, *The Small German Courts in the 18th Century;* Franklin Ford, *Robe and Sword;* Peter Gay, *Voltaire's Politics: The Poet as Realist;* Leo Gershoy, *From Despotism to Revolution, 1763–1789;* A. Goodwin, ed., *European Nobility in the Eighteenth Century;* R. Heer, *The Eighteenth Century Revolution in Spain;* Hajo Holborn, *History of Germany,* Vol. I; B. J. Hovde, *Scandinavian Countries, 1728–1865,* 2 vols.; H. J. Kerner, *Bohemia in the Eighteenth Century;* Ernst Lavisse, ed., *Histoire de France Illustrée . . . ,* Vol. VII, Pt. 2, and Vol. IX, Pt. 1; H. Marczali, *Hungary in the Eighteenth Century;* W. Oecheli, *History of Switzerland, 1499–1914;* David Ogg, *Europe of the Ancien Régime;* Robert E. Palmer, *The Age of Democratic Revolution,* 2 vols.; Penfield Roberts, *The Quest for Security, 1715–1740;* P. Sagnac, *La Fin de l'ancien régime et la Révolution américaine, 1763–1789;* Alexis de Tocqueville, *The Ancient Regime and the Revolution.*

25. I May, *Constitutional History,* 250–52.

26. Marczali, *Hungary in the Eighteenth Century;* C. A. Macartny, Hungary, in Goodwin, *European Nobility* (L., 1953); Lindsay, in VII *New Cambridge Modern History,* 56–57.

27. Bruford, *Germany in the Eighteenth Century,* 23. On Rebmann see II Palmer, *Democratic Revolution,* 442–43.

28. Fauchier-Magnan, *Small German Courts,* 45.

29. On all this see I Palmer, op. cit., 37–38.

30. Bruford, *Classical Weimar,* 91.

31. On Moser, see August Schmid, *Das Leben Johan Jacob*

Mosers (Stuttgart, 1868); Fauchier-Magnan, *Small German Courts*, 210. On Süss Oppenheimer see Fauchier-Magnan, 154ff. There is a biography by Joseph Zimmer (Stuttgart, 1874). Leon Feuchtwanger's *Jud Süss* is one of the best of historical novels.

32. Fauchier-Magnan, op. cit., 53, and 215ff.

33. I Palmer, op. cit., 34.

34. J. O. Lindsay, in VII *New Cambridge Modern History*, 282.

35. Franco Venturi, *Settecento riformatore Da Muratori a Beccaria* (Torino, 1969), and *Utopia and Reform in the Enlightenment* (Cambridge, 1971), Ch. 1.

36. Arel Lindvald, in VI *Det Danske Folks Historie*, Sec. 1; E. Holm, *Danmarks Riges Historie*, V, Sec. 3.

37. J. O. Lindsay, in VII *New Cambridge Modern History*, 57.

38. *The Cambridge History of Poland*, ed. W. F. Reddaway, et al. (Cambridge, 1941), Vol. I. And see the illuminating chapter in I Palmer, op. cit., "The Lessons of Poland."

39. I Palmer, op. cit., 35ff. Bonjour, Offler, and Potter, *A Short History of Switzerland*, 201–2.

40. The story is set forth elaborately in Peter Gay, *Voltaire's Politics*. See, too, I Palmer, op. cit., Ch. v.

41. Gay, op. cit., 231.

42. P. J. Blok, *History of the People of the Netherlands*, Vol. V; Helen Fairchild, *Francis Adrian Van der Kemp, an Autobiography with Extracts from his Correspondence* (N.Y., 1903); I Palmer, op. cit., Ch. xi.

43. This piece of rhetoric comes from the *Reflections on the Revolution in France*, and in quotation in I Palmer, op. cit., 338. See, too, Alfred Cobban, *Ambassadors and Secret Agents* (L., 1954).

CHAPTER SEVEN

4

1. Pope, *Essay on Man*, IV, lines 49ff.; *Moral Lessons*, III, lines 161–62.

2. Soame Jenyns, *Free Inquiry into the Nature and Origin of Evil*, quoted in Arthur Lovejoy, *Great Chain of Being*, 207.

3. Letter 65. Reprinted in David Jacobsen, ed., *The English Libertarian Heritage*, 152ff.

4. *Spirit of the Laws*, Neumann ed., Bk. III, Chs. 5, 6.

5. IX Lavisse, *Histoire de France*, 57, 66.

6. Fauchier-Magnan, *Small German Courts*, 57; in the end these states gave little help to Louis.

7. Porritt, *Unreformed House of Commons*, I, 354–57; I May, *Constitutional History*, 359. Competition from the Nabobs returning from the East Indies in the sixties and seventies raised the price to four or five thousand, and George Selwyn sold the seat for the borough of Ludgershall for nine thousand. Some seats were rented by the year. Namier dismisses the "East Indian Nabobs" as a legend; not until 1780, he says, did the "so-called Bengal Squad make its appearance, with adventurers of doubtful character." I *Structure of Politics*, 210.

8. George Grove, *Dictionary of Music and Musicians*, "Mozart."

9. I Lecky, op. cit., 454.

10. This is the theme of Bernard Bailyn's penetrating study of *The Origins of American Politics* (N.Y., 1968). It is the theme, too, of many earlier historians, and it finds support not only in Lecky but in George Otto Trevelyan's classic "Whig" *History of the American Revolution*.

11. Jack P. Greene, ed., *Diary of Landon Carter*, 58 (Charlottesville, Va., 1965).

12. XIX *Parliamentary History*, 183ff.

13. I May, *Constitutional History*, 342; John Norris, *Shelburne and Reform*, 163–64 (L., 1963).

Sir Lewis Namier rejects the interpretation that historians like Lecky and Sir Thomas May put upon the political methods of men like Walpole, Newcastle, Bute, and North, but actually his analysis of the situation under George III does not differ in important particulars from that set forth by Shelburne. Thus, Namier writes: "Bribery to be really effective has to be widespread and open; it has to be the custom of the land and cease to dishonour the recipients, so that its prizes may be attractive for the average self-respecting man. Such was the political corruption in Great Britain about the middle of the eighteenth century, and the true mystery about the secret service fund of that time is why it should have existed at all when . . . nine-tenths of the subsidizing of politicians was done in the full light of the day." (I *Structure of Politics*, 219). No doubt Sir Lewis is right in insisting that, by the time of George III, open bribery of members of Parliament was a thing of the past, and in explaining away as extravagant but not immoral the private pension lists of monarchs. Much of the corruption of this period was what later came to be known as "honest graft"—pensions, jobs, contracts, favors, access to power. But the point is not so much whether these practices and malpractices are corrupt in our more sophisticated eyes, but how they appeared to eighteenth-century Americans who read about them in the diatribes of a Cato or a Burgh, the novels of

Fielding, the plays of John Gay, who saw them at first hand, or who suffered their consequences. On all this, see Bernhard Knollenberg, *The Origin of the American Revolution 1759–1766*, Ch. 16, and Bernard Bailyn, *The Origins of American Politics*.

14. See O. M. Dickerson, *American Colonial Government, 1696–1775* (Cleveland, 1912); E. B. Greene, *Provincial Governor in the English Colonies* (N.Y., 1898); L. W. Labaree, *Royal Government in America* (N.Y., 1930).

15. Knollenberg, op. cit., 274.

16. Habbakuk in Godwin, *European Nobility*, 7.

17. The expectation from stamp taxes from the mainland colonies was between 30 and 50 thousand pounds annually, from Townshend duties perhaps 40 thousand—a total of not more than 80 or 90 thousand at best. A few years later, according to Lord Lansdowne, the sinecures in the Customs alone cost the Treasury 26,000 pounds for London and 140,000 for the Outposts. Norris, *Shelburne*, 287. See also Vincent T. Harlow, *The Founding of the Second British Empire*, I (L., 1952), 189.

18. III Lecky, op. cit., 228.

19. Franklin to John Galloway, 25 February 1775, in *Writings*, Smyth, ed., VI, 311–12.

20. W. H. Lewis, *The Scandalous Regent* (L., 1961), 175–76. This is a scholarly book, notwithstanding its title.

21. Lavisse, *Histoire de France*, IX, *passim*, and Georges Lefebvre, *The Coming of the French Revolution* (Princeton, 1947), Pt. I.

22. J. F. Bosher, in VIII *New Cambridge Modern History*, Ch. 20, 565ff.

23. In addition to books already cited above, see W. H. Lewis, *Master of the Bedchamber* (L., 1966); Nancy Mitford, *The Sun King* (L., 1966); R. B. Mowat, *The Age of Reason* (Boston, 1934); Maurice Vaussard, *Daily Life in 18th Century Italy* (L., 1962); Louis Ducros, *French Society in the Eighteenth Century* (L., 1926); Frederick Green, *Eighteenth Century France* (L., 1929); F. Funck-Brentano, *The Old Regime in France* (L., 1929); J. B. Perkins, *France Under the Regency* (Cambridge, 1892); P. Nors, *The Court of Christian VII of Denmark* (L., 1928).

24. H. S. Commager, "Struensee and the Reform Movement in Denmark" (Unpublished Ph.D. Dissertation, University of Chicago, 1928).

25. Lion Feuchtwanger, *Jew Süss* (L., 1926), gives an accurate picture of this episode.

26. Roberts, in Godwin, ed., *European Nobility*, 140.

27. Harold Acton, *Bourbons of Naples* (N.Y., 1956).

28. *Spirit of the Laws,* Neumann, ed., Bk. IV, Ch. 2.

29. Jerome Blum, *Lord and Peasant in Russia* (Princeton, 1961), 357.

30. Qt. in Vaussard, op. cit., 96.

31. Hertz, *German Public Mind* (L., 1962), 342.

32. Baroness d'Oberkirch, *Mémoires,* cited in Fauchier-Magnan, *Small German Courts,* 201.

CHAPTER SEVEN

5

1. A note here on the term "democracy" may be relevant. There is a curious reluctance on the part of contemporary historians to use this word to describe colonial or early American history and institutions. This reluctance is rooted in a two-fold confusion: one between democracy and absolute majoritarianism, and the other between democracy and equality. If, as I believe, democracy means, quite simply, that men make government—that government comes from below, not above, and *derives* its authority from the people—then democracy began, in America, with the Mayflower Compact. If it means—and I think there is a good case here—that a substantial part of the existing body politic is involved in the process, then again, as I have argued below, there was a great deal more democracy in the American colonies than elsewhere in the seventeenth- and eighteenth-century world. If it can be assumed that democracy requires the participation in political processes of a clear majority of the adult inhabitants of any society, then we are reduced to the absurdity of supposing that the United States suddenly became a democracy in 1920 with the ratification of the Nineteenth Amendment and the even more confusing difficulty of concluding that because a majority of the adult population, e.g. of those over eighteen, rarely participate in the political process, we still do not have a democracy. What democracy does quite clearly require is the opportunity for a majority of the existing and recognized body politic to participate, and we must keep in mind that the concept of the body politic has changed steadily for the past two centuries, and that it may continue to change, though not radically. That democracy does not require, or depend on, social or economic equality is clear; England and Sweden are more democratic than the United States but (always ignoring American racial inequalities) not more equalitarian, and, for that matter, the Soviet Union is equalitarian without being democratic.

2. As students turn away from generalizations to careful statis-

tical analyses, the literature on voting and office holding in the American colonies and the states grows rapidly. It is no exaggeration to say that so far the findings tend to confirm the insights—or perhaps the recollections—of Bancroft's generation rather than the conclusions of Beard's. I have drawn on the following critical studies for my own generalizations: Robert E. Brown, *Middle-Class Democracy and the Revolution in Massachusetts* (Ithaca, N.Y., 1955); Robert E. and B. Katherine Brown, *Virginia, 1705–1786: Democracy or Aristocracy* (East Lansing, Mich., 1964); Fletcher Green, *Constitutional Development in the South Atlantic States, 1776–1860* (Chapel Hill, 1930); C. S. Grant, *Democracy in the Connecticut Frontier Town of Kent* (N.Y., 1961); Staughton Lynd, "Who Should Rule at Home?" *William and Mary Quarterly*, July 1961; A. E. McKinley, *The Suffrage Franchise in the Thirteen American Colonies* (Philadelphia, 1905), long the standard account; Jackson Turner Main, *The Social Structure of Revolutionary America* (Princeton, 1965); Allan Nevins, *The American States During and After the Revolution* (N.Y., 1924), still, after fifty years, an admirable general account; J. R. Pole, *Political Representation in England and the Origins of the American Revolution* (L., 1966); J. Paul Selsam, *The Pennsylvania Constitution of 1776* (Philadelphia, 1936); Anson Phelps Stokes, *Church and States in the United States*, 3 vols. (Washington, 1909), the basic documentary collection; Chilton Williamson, *American Suffrage, from Property to Democracy* (Princeton, 1960).

3. Brown, *Massachusetts*, 60; Williamson, *American Suffrage*, 83.

4. IX *Works of John Adams,* 377.

5. Ibid., IV, 360.

6. Pole, *Political Representation,* 560.

7. It is equally interesting that the great majority of those entitled to vote did not do so, and that almost everywhere (as far as we have data) and for a quarter of a century, voting in local and state elections was substantially heavier than in national.

8. Brown, *Virginia,* 146; Pole, op. cit., 562.

9. Pole, op. cit., 563.

10. Williamson, op. cit., 85.

11. Poore, ed., II *Charters and Constitutions,* 1541, 1542.

12. Pole, op. cit., 553.

13. It is an interesting, but unanswerable, question whether property qualifications on office holding in some states in the early Republic were more or less effective in excluding the poor from office than present-day costs of candidacy for almost any office.

14. On religious qualifications see the mass of miscellaneous materials in A. P. Stokes, *Church and State*, Vol. I, Sec. 8.

15. For southern states see the admirable monograph by Fletcher Green, *Constitutional Development*.

16. Oscar and Mary Handlin, *Commonwealth, Massachusetts*, Appendix I, 267–68.

17. Leonard Labaree, *Conservatism in Early American History* (Ithaca, N.Y., 1948).

18. 18 October 1790, in VI *Works*, 417.

19. L. J. Cappon, ed., *Adams-Jefferson Letters* (Chapel Hill, 1959), II, 389.

20. Labaree, *Conservatism*, Ch. 1, makes much of the importance of family, especially in Connecticut and Virginia, but his analysis is confined entirely to the colonial period, while my concern is with the situation after Americans took charge of their own affairs and wrote their own constitutions. IV, Elliot's Debates, 192.

21. See "The Economic Interpretation of the Constitution Reconsidered" in H. S. Commager, *Search for a Usable Past* (N.Y., 1967), 56–73.

CHAPTER SEVEN

6

1. A brief 1-vol. summary of Adams's *Defense of the Constitutions* reached the Federal Convention at the beginning of its deliberations, and caused quite a stir. Charles Warren has devoted an Appendix to letters from members of the convention about the Adams book in his *The Making of the Constitution* (Boston, 1928), 815ff.

2. The five quotations are from: a) *Federalist Papers*, No. 75; b) III Elliot, 32; c) W. C. Ford, *Essays on the Constitution*, 379; d) quoted in C. Kenyon, *The Anti-Federalists*, xviii; e) II Elliot, 225.

3. Jefferson in the Kentucky Resolutions of 1797, in Commager, *Documents*, No. 102. See, too, the observation in the earlier *Notes on Virginia*: "Nor should our assembly be deluded by the integrity of their own purposes and conclude that these unlimited powers will never be abused. . . . They should look forward to a time, and that not a distant one, when a corruption in this as in the country from which we derive our origin, will have seized the heads of government and be spread by them through the body of the people; when they will purphrase the voices of the people and make them pay the price. Human Nature

is the same on every side of the Atlantic, and will be alike influenced by the same causes. The time to guard against corruption
and tyranny is before they shall have gotten hold of us." Answer
to Query XIII, II Mem. ed., 164–65.

4. This is one of the theses of William W. Crosskey's erudite
and slashing two-volume study of *Politics and the Constitution
in the History of the United States* (Chicago, 1953). The book is
dedicated "To the Congress of the United States in the Hope that
it may be led to claim and exercise for the common good of the
country the powers justly belonging to it under the Constitution."

5. Two occasions were, of course, *Marbury v. Madison* and
Dred Scott v. Sanford. The first rejected what might have been
an intention by Congress to confer on the Supreme Court original
jurisdiction to issue a writ of mandamus; the second nullified part
of an Act which had been repealed three years earlier.

6. VII Ford, ed., 174.

7. To William Hamilton, 2 May 1797, in XXI, Squetted, 78.

8. See "Jefferson and the Book-Burners" in H. S. Commager,
Search for a Usable Past (N.Y., 1967), 99ff.

9. On judicial salaries, see L. B. White, *The Federalists* (N.Y.,
1948); Francis Aumann, *The Changing American Legal System:
Some Selected Phases* (Columbus, O., 1940), Ch. viii.

10. Jean De Lolme, *The Constitution of England* (L., 1810
ed.), 271ff.

11. 7 July 1775, in VI *Writings*, Smyth, ed., 408.

12. Samuel Williams, *Natural and Civil History of Vermont*
(1794), 343–44. I have changed the order of the two parts of this
quotation.

CHAPTER EIGHT

1

1. Henry's "Give me liberty or give me death" speech can be
found in W. W. Henry, *Patrick Henry: Life, Correspondence, and
Speeches*, I (N.Y., 1891), 266; Paine's statement is in *The Crisis
Papers*, No. 13.

2. The achievement of nation making has not been accorded
the attention it merits. See Hans Kohn, *American Nationalism*
(N.Y., 1957) and his *The Idea of Nationalism* (N.Y., 1944), Ch.
vii; C. J. H. Hayes, *Essays on Nationalism* (N.Y., 1937); Boyd C.
Shafer, *Nationalism: Myth and Reality* (N.Y., 1955); William P.
Murphy, *The Triumph of Nationalism* (Chicago, 1967); and
H. S. Commager, "The Origins and Nature of American Nation-

alism," in *Jefferson, Nationalism, and the Enlightenment* (N.Y., 1975), Ch. 7.

3. Lewis Mumford, *Sticks and Stones* (N.Y., 1924), and see also the opening pages of his *Golden Day* (N.Y., 1926).

4. *Letters from an American Farmer*, Letter III.

5. Merle Curti, *Roots of American Loyalty* (N.Y., 1946), and Max Savelle, "Nationalism and Other Loyalties in the American Revolution," LXVII *American Historical Review* (July 1962), 901ff.

6. It is not surprising that Tom Paine and Crèvecoeur, both of whom came to America when mature, saw this more clearly than did most Americans except perhaps Jefferson himself. See S. William Sachse, *The Colonial American in Britain* (Madison, Wis., 1956) which unfortunately stops with the outbreak of the Revolution. See too some passages in H. S. Commager, *The Defeat of America* (N.Y., 1975), Ch. 1. See also, for illuminating insights, Hans Huth, *Nature and the American* (Berkeley, Calif., 1957); Daniel J. Boorstin, *The Americans: the Colonial Experience* (N.Y., 1958); Perry Miller, *Nature's Nation* (Cambridge, 1967); Howard Mumford Jones, *O Strange New World* (N.Y., 1964); John Bakeless, *Eyes of Discovery* (N.Y., 1950); Roderick Nash, *Wilderness and the American Mind* (New Haven, 1967); Charles Sanford, *The Quest for Paradise* (Urbana, Ill., 1961); and Leon Baritz, "The Idea of the West," LXVI *American Historical Review* 618 (1961).

7. Letter to Galloway, 25 February 1775, in VII *Writings*, ed., Smyth, 82.

8. Jefferson to the Earl of Buchan, 10 July 1803, *Memorial Edition*, 400.

9. Quoted in Goodman, *Rush* (Philadelphia, 1934), 285.

10. *Letters from an American Farmer*, Letter III.

11. The literature on the impact of the Indian on the American imagination and history is immense. See William Fenton, ed., *American Indian and White Relations to 1830* (chiefly bibliographical) (Chapel Hill, 1957); Roy Pearce, *The Savages of America: A Study of the Indian and the Idea of Civilization* (Baltimore, 1953); and, for contemporary material, *The Travels of William Bartram* (various editions) and Jefferson's *Notes on the State of Virginia* (various editions).

12. William Bradford, *Of Plymouth Plantations*, S. E. Morison, ed. (N.Y., 1952), 61.

13. Bernard Sheehan, *Seeds of Extinction: Jeffersonian Philanthropy and the American Indian* (Chapel Hill, 1973).

14. Logan's speech is reproduced in Jefferson's *Notes on the State of Virginia* (Query VI), and can be found in Ford's edition

of the *Writings,* III, or in the recent editions of the *Notes* by Thomas P. Abernethy (N.Y., 1964), or by William Peden (Chapel Hill, 1955), 62–63, 226–58, 274–75.

15. George R. Stewart, *Names on the Land: a Historical Account of Place-naming in the United States* (N.Y., 1945).

16. On religion and the Great Awakening, see Anson Phelps Stokes, *Church and State in the United States,* Vol. I (N.Y., 1950); Wesley Gewehr, *The Great Awakening in Virginia* (Durham, N.C., 1930); Cedric B. Cowing, *The Great Awakening and the American Revolution* (Chicago, 1971); William W. Sweet, *Religion in Colonial America* (N.Y., 1942); Alan Heimert and Perry Miller, eds., *The Great Awakening* (Indianapolis, 1967); Edwin S. Gaustad, *The Great Awakening in New England* (N.Y., 1957); Herbert L. Osgood, *The American Colonies in the Eighteenth Century* (N.Y., 1924), Vol. III, Pt. III, Ch. 1.

17. Stokes, *Church and State,* analyzes some of these figures in Vol. I, 228ff.

18. Carl Bridenbaugh, *The Spirit of Seventy-Six* (N.Y., 1975), Ch. III, and 118.

19. See references in Note 16 above.

20. On Whitefield, see L. Tyerman, *The Life of the Rev. George Whitefield:* 2 vols. (L., 1876–77); and Stuart Clark Henry, *George Whitefield: Wayfaring Witness* (N.Y., 1957).

21. James Thomas Flexner, *Washington: The Indispensable Man* (Boston, 1974); and the Introduction to Richard H. Kohn, *Eagle and Sword* (N.Y., 1975).

22. Kohn, *Eagle.,* 9ff.

23. H. S. Commager, *The Search for a Usable Past* (N.Y., 1967).

24. See Irving Brant, *James Madison: The Virginia Revolutionary* (Indianapolis: 1941), Ch. xviii.

25. *Crisis,* No. XIII.

26. Richard Frothingham, *Rise of the Republic of the United States* (Boston, 1872).

27. See E. D. Collins, "Committees of Correspondence in the American Revolution," *Am. Hist. Assoc. Annual Report* 1901, Vol. I; J. Leake, *The Virginia Committee System* (Baltimore, 1882); Frothingham, op. cit.

28. Stanley Elkins and Eric McKitrick, "The Founding Fathers: Young Men of the Revolution," 76 *Pol. Sci. Qtly.* 181ff.

29. All the major histories of the Revolution cover this: John Fiske, *Critical Period;* A. C. McLaughlin, *Confederation and Constitution;* E. C. Burnett, *The Continental Congress;* John C. Miller, *Origins of the American Revolution;* C. H. Van Tyne,

Causes of the War of Independence; Merrill Jensen, *The New Nation;* and so forth.

30. Carl and Jessica Bridenbaugh, *Rebels and Gentlemen: Philadelphia in the Age of Franklin* (N.Y., 1942).

31. On Washington idolatry, see Gilbert Chinard, *Washington as the French Knew Him* (Princeton, 1940); W. S. Baker, ed., *Character Portraits of Washington* (Philadelphia, 1867); Bryan, "George Washington: Symbolic Guardian of the Republic," *Wm. and Mary Qtly.,* 3d series, VII (January, 1950); and the portrait in W. M. Thackeray's *The Virginians.* Jefferson did not always approve of Washington's policies, but his final judgment of Washington was just and sagacious: "On the whole, his character was, in its mass, perfect, in nothing bad, in few points indifferent; and it may be truly said that never did nature and fortune combine more perfectly to make a man great, and to place him in the same constellation with whatever worthies have merited . . . an everlasting remembrance." Letter to Dr. Walter Jebb, 2 Jan. 1814, *Writings,* ed., H. A. Washington, VI (Washington, 1855).

32. J. Tucker, *Cui Bono.* (Gloucester, Mass., 1781), 117.

33. The Turgot letter to Dr. Price is printed in C. F. Adams's edition, IV *Works of John Adams,* 273ff.

34. Commager, *Jefferson, Nationalism, and the Enlightenment,* 176.

35. *Common Sense* (Foner edition, N.Y., 1945), I, 29.

36. *Poetical Works of Thomas Moore* (Boston, 1856), I, 95–96.

37. Thomas Jefferson to John Adams, 13 November, 1787, XII Boyd, 351.

38. Goethe, "Amerika, du hast es besser." Hans Kohn has translated this poem—one difficult to render into English—in his book on *American Nationalism,* 250:

America, thou are more fortunate than our old continent. Thou hast no ruined castles, no venerable stones. No useless memories, no vain feuds, harry thee in thy soul when thou wishest to live in the present. Make something happy out of today. And when thy children start to write, may a kind Providence preserve them from tales of chivalrous knights, robber barons, and ghosts.

CHAPTER NINE
1

1. Tocqueville's *Democracy in America* has some penetrating observations on the "aristocracy of the robe." See, too, Charles

Warren, *History of the American Bar* (Cambridge, 1912); Perry Miller, ed., *The Legal Mind in America* (N.Y., 1962); Lawrence Friedman, *History of American Law* (N.Y., 1973).

2. For the American debt to the ancient world, see above, Ch. III. For the debt to Britain, see Clinton Rossiter, *Seedtime of the Republic* (N.Y., 1953); Max Savelle, *Seeds of Liberty* (N.Y., 1948); Charles Mullett, *Fundamental Law and the American Revolution* (N.Y., 1933); R. G. Adams, *Political Ideas of the American Revolution* (Durham, N.C., 1922); Roscoe Pound, *The Development of Constitutional Guarantees of Liberty* (New Haven, 1957); Caroline Robbins, *The Eighteenth-Century Commonwealthman* (Cambridge, 1959); David L. Jacobsen, ed., *The English Libertarian Heritage* (Indianapolis, 1966); A. C. McLaughlin, *Foundations of American Constitutionalism* (N.Y., 1932); Howard M. Jones, *O Strange New World* (N.Y., 1964).

Bernard Fäy's *Revolutionary Spirit in France and America* (N.Y., 1927) attempts to prove a close relationship between the American Revolution and the French Enlightenment.

Gladys Bryson emphasizes the debt to Scotland, *Man and Society: the Scottish Inquiry of the Eighteenth Century* (Princeton, 1945); and so, too, Douglas Adair, "Hume and the Tenth Federalist," 20 *Huntington Library Qt.* 345 (August 1957), and Gottfried Dietze in *The Federalist, A Classic on Federalism and Free Government* (Baltimore, 1960), 316–19. Yet we know that Jefferson detested Hume, and we do not find, in the libraries of the Fathers, evidence of the influence of Ferguson or of Adam Smith. See H. Trevor Colbourn, *The Lamp of Experience* (Chapel Hill, 1966).

3. Paine, *The Rights of Man,* Bk. II, Ch. 4.

And see Jefferson to Major Cartwright, 5 June 1824: "Our Revolution . . . presented us an album on which we were free to write what we pleased. We had no occasion to search into musty records, to hunt up royal parchments, or to investigate the laws and institutions of a semi-barbarous ancestry. We appealed to those of nature and found them engraved on our hearts." XVI Memorial ed. 44.

4. Mayflower Compact, Commager, *Documents,* No. 11. The quotation is from Bradford's Journal, on board the Arbella: "The work we have in hand is by mutuall consent . . . to seeke out a place of cohabitation and Consorteshipp under a due forme of Government both civil and ecclesiastical. . . . Thus stands the cause between God and us. We are entered into a Covenant with Him for this worke. . . . The Lord hath given us leave to drawe our own articles." etc. *Journal,* in M.H.S. *Coll.* 3d ser. VII, 45–46.

5. Most of these can be found in Commager, *Documents*. See also, Anson Phelps Stokes, I *Church and State in the United States* (N.Y., 1905), 203ff.

6. This is the way the philosophes imagined it. Thus, Hilliard d'Auberteuil, in his *Essais historiques et politiques sur les Anglo-Américains*, 1782, wrote that "In Virginia the members chosen to establish the new government assembled in a peaceful wood . . . , in an enclosure prepared by nature with banks of grass, and in this sylvan spot they deliberated on who should preside over them." Palmer, *Age of Democratic Revolution*, I (Princeton, 1959), 254.

7. The best analysis of this is A. C. McLaughlin, *Foundations of American Constitutionalism*, Ch. i (N.Y., 1932, 1961).

8. Commager, *Documents*, No. 16.

9. Quoted in A. P. Stokes, I *Church and State*, 203.

10. Peter Force, ed., *American Archives*, 5th Series, II (Washington, 1837–53), 567–77, quoted in H. S. Commager and R. B. Morris, eds., *The Spirit of Seventy-Six*, I (N.Y., 1975), 383. Among other quotations from Town Meetings in this volume is the following from the town of Ashfield: "Voted that we will take the Law of God for the foundation of the Forme of our Government, for as the Old Laws that we have Ben Ruled by under the British Constitution have Proved Inefectual to Secuer us from the more than Savige Crualty of Tiranical Opreseans and Sense the God of Nature hath Enabled us to Brake that yoke of Bondage we think our Selves Bound in Duty to God and our Country to Opose the Least Apearanc of them Old Tiranical Laws taking Place again." (Ibid., 348).

11. Commager, *Documents*, No. 67.

12. For the Massachusetts Bill of Rights, Commager, *Documents*, No. 70. All of the colonial and revolutionary bills of rights are assembled in Ben: Perley Poore, ed., *Federal and State Constitutions, Colonial Charters, etc.*, I, 817.

C. S. Lobengier, *The Peoples Law* (N.Y., 1909) emphasized the familiar and common-sense tradition of forming governments. See, too, Amasa Eton, "The Right to Local Self-Government," XIII *Harvard Law Review* (1900), 441, 638.

13. Commager and Morris, *Spirit of Seventy-Six*, 370ff.

14. Fletcher Green, *Constitutional Development in the South Atlantic States, 1776–1860* (Chapel Hill, 1930), 36ff. And see W. B. Stevens, II, *History of Georgia*, 18ff. (Philadelphia, 1859).

15. Ray Billington, *The Far Western Frontier* (N.Y., 1956), 126ff.

16. Ibid., 166. The whole proclamation can be found in Simeon

Ide, *A Biographical Sketch of the Life of William B. Ide* (Claremont, N.H., 1880), 138.

17. Benjamin F. Shambaugh, "Frontier Land Clubs or Claim Associations," *American Historical Association Report*, 1900, I, 67ff.

18. Robert G. Clark, *History of the Willamette Valley, Oregon*, 3 vols. (Chicago, 1927), vol. I.

19. A meeting of a band of California-bound emigrants on the banks of the Missouri, May 6, 1850, unanimously adopted a body of regulations, with the following preamble: "Whereas we are about to leave the frontier, and travel over Indian territory, exposed to their treachery and knowing their long and abiding hatred of the whites; also many other privations to meet with. We consider it necessary to form ourselves into a Company for the purpose of protecting each other and our property during our journey to California." The resolutions are given in *The Oregon Trail*, W.P.A. American Guide Series (N.Y., 1939), 40–41.

20. Quoted in S. E. Morison and H. S. Commager, *Growth of the American Republic*, II (5th ed., N.Y., 1952), 144.

21. Charge to the Grand Jury of Kingston County, 9 September 1777, in H. Niles, ed., *Principles and Acts of the Revolution in America* (Baltimore, 1822).

22. David Ramsey, "Oration on the Advantages of American Independence," in H. Niles, *Principles and Acts*, 64–72 (quotation on 68).

23. On all this see John Fenton, Jr., *The Theory of the Social Compact and its Influence upon the American Revolution* (1891); A. C. McLaughlin, "Social Compact and Constitutional Construction," V *Am. Hist. Rev.*, 467; J. W. Gough, *The Social Contract: A Critical Study of its Development* (Oxford, 1936); Ralph Barton Perry, *Puritanism and Democracy* (N.Y., 1944); Thad W. Tate, "The Social Contract in America, 1774–1787: Revolutionary Theory as a Conservative Instrument," *William and Mary Quarterly* (July, 1965), 375–91.

24. On Adams's contribution to the Massachusetts Constitution see Page Smith, *John Adams* (Garden City, 1962); C. M. Walsh, *The Political Science of John Adams* (N.Y., 1915); Edward Handler, *America and Europe in the Political Thought of John Adams* (Cambridge, 1964); John R. Howe, *The Changing Political Thought of John Adams* (Princeton, 1966).

25. III *Diary and Autobiography*, ed., Butterfield (Cambridge, 1961), 352, 355–57.

26. For these and many other resolutions and declarations of like tenor, see Oscar and Mary Handlin, eds., *Popular Sources of Political Authority: Documents on the Massachusetts Conven-*

tion of 1800 (Cambridge, 1966). Some of these are quoted in Commager and Morris, eds., *Spirit of Seventy-Six*, 391ff.

27. See S. E. Morison, *History of the Constitutions of Massachusetts*, in Manual of the Constitutional Convention of 1917.

28. Niles, ed., *Principles and Acts*, 52. There is a new and unfortunately abbreviated edition of the *Principles and Acts* (N.Y., 1965).

29. Thomas Cooper, *Some Information Respecting America* (L., 1794), 209.

30. *Reflections on the Revolution in France*, various eds. For immediate background, see VI *Correspondence of Edmund Burke*, ed., Alfred Cobban (Camb., 1967).

The institution of the constitutional convention swiftly spread to most of the states of the union and from America to other nations and continents. Yet, oddly enough, philosophers of the Old World went right on writing just as if it had never been contrived. Hume and Burke might differ on other matters, but they agreed in rejecting the "compact" origin of government as a myth. And well into mid-nineteenth century, with the whole of American experience before them, political philosophers continued to intone the old litanies. Thus, at mid-century the learned Jacob Burckhardt, "The hypothesis of the State as founded on an antecedent contract is absurd. . . . No state has ever yet been erected by a genuine contract." *Force and Freedom: Reflections on History* (N.Y., 1943), 109. Professor Burckhardt may not have regarded the Constitution of Massachusetts as "genuine," but the people of Massachusetts did.

CHAPTER NINE
2

1. There is a fascinating and instructive discussion of this question by Jefferson and Madison in Vol. XV of Boyd's edition of *Jefferson's Papers*, 384ff. See, too, Adrienne Koch, *Jefferson and Madison: the Great Collaboration* (N.Y., 1950), 62ff.

2. Burke, IX *Works* (1836 ed.), 449.

There is a penetrating critique of Burke's later political philosophy in R. R. Palmer's *Age of Democratic Revolutions*, I, 308ff. For Burke, see further John Morley, *Burke* (L., 1887); Thomas Copeland, *Our Eminent Friend, Mr. Burke* (New Haven, 1949); Carl B. Cone, *Burke and the Nature of Politics*, Vol. II (Lexington, 1965). There are some relevant observations by Leslie Stephen in his *English Thought in the Eighteenth Century*, II, 219ff. "The methods of constitution-mongers and of the ab-

stract theorists were equally beneath his notice," says Stephen
(230). True enough; he did not even notice the making of the
most important constitution of modern history, that of the United
States, nor did he anywhere permit the experience of Americans
in constitution making, democracy. or social equality to ruffle
the polish of his arguments. So much for his vaunted empiricism!

3. The phrase is, of course, from Jefferson's First Inaugural
Address.

4. "Dissertation on First Principles of Government," in Philip
Foner, ed., *The Complete Writings of Thomas Paine*, II (N.Y.,
1945), 576.

5. XV Boyd, *Jefferson*, 391–92.

6. XV Ibid., 392ff.

7. XVI Boyd, 153–54.

8. Jefferson to Kercheval, July 12, 1816, in XV *Memorial
Edition*, 32ff., esp. 46–48.

9. XV *Memorial Edition*, 48.

10. II Elliot's *Debates*, 116.

Jefferson made the same point in a letter to M. Dumas, 10
September 1787: "A more able assembly never sat in America.
Happily for us, that when we find our constitutions defective,
and insufficient to secure the happiness of our people, we can
assemble with all the coolness of philosophers, and set it to
rights, while every other nation on earth must have recourse to
arms to amend or to restore their constitutions." XII Boyd, 113.

11. II Elliot's *Debates*, 422–23. Later in the debate Wilson
enlarged on this consideration. "I confess," he wrote, "I feel
a kind of pride in considering the striking difference between
the foundation on which the liberties of this country are declared
to stand in this Constitution, and the footing on which the liberties of England are said to be placed. The Magna Charta of
and to all the freemen of this our realm, these liberties following
. . . But . . . from what source does that instrument derive the
liberties of the inhabitants of that kingdom? Let it speak for
itself. The king says, '*We* have *given* and *granted* to all arch-
bishops, bishops, abbots, priors, earls, barons, and to all the
freemen of this our realm, these liberties following . . .' But
here, sir, the fee-simple remains in the people at large, and by
this Constitution they do not part with it." Ibid., 435.

12. The difference between the "radical" 1776 constitution
and the "conservative" 1790 constitution has been greatly exaggerated. The chief differences were in the mechanics of government, not in its philosophy.

13. On the amending process see Walter F. Dodd, *The Revision and Amendment of State Constitutions* (Baltimore, 1910).

See, too, Allan Nevins, *American States During and After the Revolution, 1775–1789* (N.Y., 1924) and, from another point of view, C. H. McIlwain, *The American Revolution: A Constitutional Interpretation* (N.Y., 1923).

14. XXX, *Writings*, Fitzpatrick, ed. (Washington, 1931–42), 301. And see, too, Tench Coxe on the ability of Americans to change their constitutions: "When the public judgment is decided upon any one or more derelictions of those principles of magnitude sufficient to induce an effort for reform, the will of the people cannot be successfully resisted or even suspended. The consequences of this state of things will be, that the mass of error will not easily accumulate so as to become insupportable, being kept down by these orderly natural exertions of the community, to relieve themselves at an earlier stage of inconvenience." *A View of the United States of America* (Philadelphia, 1794), 375.

CHAPTER NINE

3

1. On Federalism see E. A. Freeman's classic *History of Federal Government* (L. and Camb., 1863); A. C. McLaughlin, *Foundations of American Constitutionalism* (N.Y., 1932, 1961), Ch. vi; Gottfried Dietze, *The Federalist: A Classic on Federalism and Free Government* (Baltimore, 1960). Interestingly enough, federalism has attracted more attention on the European continent than in Britain, or even in the United States. There was a French translation of the *Federalist Papers* as early as 1798, but the British did not get around to issuing an English edition of this classic until the twentieth century. American scholarship has not yet provided a scholarly commentary on the *Federalist* nor a searching examination of the origins and history of the philosophy of the Papers. There are, however, a number of recent foreign studies listed in Dietze's bibliography: Wilhelm Samuel, *Die Idee des Fëderalismus* (Dissertation, Halle, 1928); Gaspare Ambrosini, *Il Federalista* (Pisa, 1955); Gaston Jese, ed., *Le Federaliste* (Paris, 1902); Aldo Garosci, *Il Pensiero Politico degli Autori del "Federalist"* (Milan, 1954); Wilhelm von Kisselbach, *Der Amerikanische Federalist—Politische Studien für die Deutsche Gegenwart* (Bremen, 1864).

The late Douglas G. Adair has left a body of writing whose importance far exceeds its bulk. See his dissertation (Ph.D., Yale University, 1943), "The Intellectual Origins of Jeffersonian Democracy: Republicanism, Class Struggle, and the Virtuous

Farmer," and the articles collected and edited by H. Trevor Colbourn in *Fame and the Founding Fathers: Essays of Douglas Adair* (N.Y., 1974).

2. See Richard Gummere, *The American Colonial Mind and the Classical Tradition* (Cambridge, 1963), Ch. x, and Gilbert Chinard, "Polybius and the American Constitution," *J. Hist. Ideas,* I (1939), 38.

3. Nos. 18, 19, and 20. See, too, III (Hunt) *Writings of James Madison,* 369ff.; G. E. Bourne, *Essays in Historical Criticism* (N.Y., 1896), 165ff.; John C. Ranney, "Bases of American Federalism," III, *William and Mary Quarterly,* January 1946; Maynard Smith (Principles of Republican Government in the Federalist), Ph.D. Dissertation, The New School, 1957.

4. The *Federalist,* No. 15.

5. The *Federalist,* No. 15.

6. The *Federalist,* No. 46.

7. Madison to Jefferson, 24 October 1787, XII, Boyd, 271.

8. To be sure we have had very little experience with the unicameral legislature. The government of Pennsylvania, however, was not perceptibly different before and after 1791, nor that of Vermont before and after 1836, while it will not be contended that Nebraska's experiment with a unicameral legislature in the mid-twentieth century has exposed that state to radical experiments or the tyranny of the majority.

9. The political party did not, to be sure, influence one feature of the balance assured by a separation of powers, judicial independence. But, then, Adams paid little attention to the judiciary (nor did Montesquieu), and failed wholly to anticipate the role of judicial review.

10. The *Federalist,* No. 51.

11. On this, see Justin Winsor, *Westward Movement* (Boston, 1897); Homer C. Hockett, "Federalism and the West," in G. S. Ford, ed., *Essays in American History . . .* (N.Y., 1910; reprinted, 1951); F. J. Turner, "Western State-Making," in his *Significance of Sections in American History* (N.Y., 1932); A. C. McLaughlin, *Confederation and Constitution* (N.Y., 1905); Francis Philbrick, *The Rise of the West* (N.Y., 1965); Burke Aaron Hinsdale, *The Old Northwest, the Beginnings of our Colonial System* (N.Y., 1891).

12. It is extraordinary that so little of a critical or philosophical nature has been written on the institution of colonies and colonization. The classic attack on colonization and imperialism is, of course, the Abbé Raynal's *Philosophical and Political History . . . of the Indies,* which we have discussed in an earlier chapter. Only second to this in importance is Adam

Smith's *Wealth of Nations,* 2 vols., 1776. Thomas Pownall, himself a leading figure in colonial administration, produced what is probably the most important contemporary treatise on the English colonies in his *The Administration of the Colonies* (L., 1766). Just after the turn of the century Lord Brougham, who had one of the most original minds of his generation, produced a two-volume essay on *The Colonial Policy of the European Powers* (Edinburgh, 1803). Of modern treatises the following are helpful: H. E. Egerton, *History of Colonial Policy* (L., 1898); George L. Beer, *Origins of the British Colonial System* (N.Y., 1908) and *The Old Colonial System,* 2 vols. (N.Y., 1912); Charles de Lannay, *Histoire de l'expansion coloniale des peuples européens,* 3 vols. (1907–21); E. P. Cheyney, *European Background of American History* (N.Y., 1904); W. C. Abbott, *The Expansion of Europe* (N.Y., 1928); R. H. Tawney, *Religion and the Rise of Capitalism* (N.Y., 1926); J. H. Parry, *Europe and a Wider World* (L., 1949) and *The Age of Reconnaissance* (L., 1963); E. F. Heckscher, *Mercantilism,* 2 vols. (1935).

13. On mercantilism, see E. F. Heckscher, op. cit.; Gustav Schmoller, *The Mercantile System* (N.Y., 1884).

14. Franklin to Lord Kames, 25 February 1767, in XIV *Papers,* ed., Labaree, 65.

15. Lecky, *History of Ireland in the Eighteenth Century* (L., 1892). And see Howard Mumford Jones, *Strange New World,* Ch. V.

16. "The provinces of absolute monarchies are always better treated than those of free states. Compare the *pais conquis* of France with Ireland and you will be convinced of this truth . . . Corsica is also an obvious instance to the same purpose." So wrote David Hume, in "That Politics May Be Reduced to a Science," *Political Essays,* ed., Charles Hendel (N.Y., 1927), 17.

17. Dallas D. Irvine, "The Abbé Raynal and British Humanitarianism," III *Journal of Modern History,* December 1931.

18. E. Holm, in V. *Danmarks Riges Historie* (Copenhagen, n.d.).

19. A. C. McLaughlin, *Confederation and Constitution,* Ch. vii; Justin Winsor, *The Westward Movement;* Francis S. Philbrick, *The Rise of the New West,* Ch. iv and v.

20. These can be found in Commager, *Documents,* Nos. 75–78, 82, 87. The simple phrases of the Congressional Resolution of 1780 proved decisive: "Resolved, that the unappropriated lands that may be ceded or relinquished to the United States, by any particular States, . . . shall be disposed of for the common benefit of the United States, and be settled and formed into distinct republican States, which shall become members of the Fed-

eral Union, and shall have the same rights of sovereignty, freedom and independence, as the other States. . . ."

21. On Spanish viceroys, see Don E. Smith, "The Viceroy of New Spain in the Eighteenth Century," *Ann. Rep. Am. Hist. Assoc.*, 1908, I, 169; Herbert Priestley, *Jose de Galvez, Visitor General of New Spain*, 1765–1771 (Berkeley, 1916); C. H. Haring, *The Spanish Empire in America* (N.Y., 1947); John Lynch, *Spanish Colonial Administration* (L., 1958). In a curious way, this distinction persists, notwithstanding the relatively greater affluence of the United States. The salary of the President of the United States was until recently one hundred thousand dollars; in mid-summer of 1966 the Dutch raised the salary of their Queen to £520,000, or roughly a million and a half dollars, while £82.5 thousand was allotted to the upkeep of the royal palaces! *London Observer*, July 31, 1966.

22. For St. Clair and American territorial government, see W. H. Smith, ed., *The St. Clair Papers: The Life and Public Services of Arthur St. Clair* (Cincinnati, 1882), 2 vols.; Beverly Bond, *The Civilization of the Old Northwest* (N.Y., 1934), and his "An Experiment in Colonial Government," XV *Miss. Val. Hist. Rev.*, September 1928; Randolph Downes, *Frontier Ohio, 1788–1803* (Columbus, O., 1935); Leonard B. White, *The Federalists* (N.Y., 1948).

23. Qt. White, *The Federalists*, p. 366.

CHAPTER TEN
1

1. *Common Sense*, 1.

2. "Letter to the Town of Providence," VI *Publications of the Narragansett Club* (1874), 268. The rest of the argument is worth quoting. "We have not felt the new chains of Presbyterian tyrants, nor in this Colony have we been consumed with the over-zealous fire of the godly christian magistrates. Sir, we have not known what an excise means; we have almost forgotten what tithes are, yea, or taxxes either, to church or commonwealth. We could name other special privileges, ingredients of our sweet cup, which your great wisdom knows to be very powerful. . . ."

3. Autobiography, III *Adams Papers* (Cambridge, 1961), 276; and see Adams himself, to the same effect:

"But what Plan of Government would you advise? A Plan as nearly resembling the Governments under which we were born and have lived as the Circumstances of the Country will admit. Kings we never had among Us. Nobles we never had.

Nothing hereditary ever existed in the Country; Nor will the Country require or admit of any such Thing. . . ." III *Diary and Autobiography*, 356.

4. *Political Sketches, Inscribed to . . . John Adams*. By a Citizen of the United States (L., 1787), 4.

5. Jonathan Mayhew, "Discourse Concerning Unlimited Submission," January 1750. Reprinted in Bailyn. *Pamphlets of the American Revolution*, Vol. I (Cambridge, 1965), 203ff. See, too, Alice Baldwin, *The New England Clergy and the American Revolution* (Durham, N.C., 1928).

6. Adrien Fauchier-Magnan, *The Small German Courts* (L., 1958); and *Karl-Eugen von Wuerttemberg und seine Zeit*, ed., Württemberg Geschichtes-verein, 2 v., 1907.

7. See Zoltan Haraszti, *John Adams and the Prophets of Progress* (Cambridge, 1952), 53–54. "You have Lord Bolingbroke by heart," said one of Adams's friends. Ibid., 49.

8. Montesquieu, *Spirit of the Laws*, Bk. XI. See comments on this subject by the editor, Franz Newmann (N.Y., 1949), esp. at lixff. On Montesquieu and England, see F. T. H. Fletcher, *Montesquieu and English Politics, 1750–1800* (L., 1939), and Joseph Dedieu, *Montesquieu et la tradition politique Anglaise en France* (Paris, 1909). On the influence of *Montesquieu in America*, see Paul Sperlin, *Montesquieu in America*. Destutt de Tracy's formidable attack on Montesquieu, *A Commentary and Review of Montesquieu's Spirit of the Laws* (Philadelphia, 1811) had the enthusiastic approval of Jefferson, who thought Tracy the ablest political thinker of his age. Most commentators exaggerate the influence of Montesquieu on American politics and constitutional thinking; it was in fact meager. Montesquieu was widely read, but his role was chiefly that of intellectual window dressing. Americans had long antecedents for the separation of powers, and their constitutions went much farther toward true separation than anything set forth by Montesquieu, or by any other political thinker of eighteenth-century Europe.

9. I *Commentaries on the Laws of England*, Cooley, ed. (Chicago, 1884), Pt. I, Ch. 2, 103 (orig. p. 161). See Daniel Boorstin, *The Mysterious Science of the Law* (Cambridge, 1941).

10. The Declaratory Act can be found in Commager, *Documents*, Doc. No. 41.

11. See A. E. Porritt, *The Unreformed House of Commons*, Vol. I (Camb., 1909); Thomas E. May, *Constitutional History*, Vol. I, Chs. iv and vi (N.Y., 1880).

12. "Two Letters to Gentlemen in the City of Bristol," II *Works*, 135.

13. *The Spirit of the Laws*, Bk. XI, 156.

14. Qt. in Stanley Pargellis, "Theory of Balanced Government," in Conyers Read, ed., *The Constitution Reconsidered* (N.Y., 1939), 37.

15. Porritt, op. cit.; L. B. Namier, *Structure of Politics at the Accession of George III*, Vol. I, Ch. iv (L., 1929); I am well aware that Namier takes a somewhat more amiable view of this matter of representation, but it seems clear that such independence as most members of Parliament enjoyed was a testimony not so much to the good intentions of the Crown and patrons, but to their inefficiency. On all this, see part 4 of Ch. VII, above, particularly text accompanying n. 13.

16. See below, Part 2, n. 7.

17. Richard Hooker's *The Laws of Ecclesiastical Politie* was published in 1594.

18. "The rich, the well born and the able acquire an influence among the people that will soon be too much for simple honesty and plain sense, in a house of representatives. The most illustrious of them must, therefore, be separated from the mass, and placed by themselves in a senate: this is, to all honest and useful intents, an ostracism." Adams, *Defense of the Constitutions*, IV *Works*, 290–91. And how interesting that Adams, who had himself served in the General Court—which was in effect the House of Representatives of the Bay Colony—should have thought so poorly of the intelligence of his fellow members.

19. VI Madison, *Writings*, ed., Hunt, 83. This was in the course of his debate with Hamilton over the nature of executive power in the conduct of foreign relations, conducted in the *National Gazette* in 1792.

20. In the decade before the Declaration of Independence the Board of Trade had repeatedly disallowed colonial laws abolishing the importation of slaves.

21. It was perhaps Crèvecoeur who saw this most clearly, or at least explained most clearly the forces that accounted for it; see his *Letters from an American Farmer*. This is the theme, too, of Herbert Agar's *The Price of Union* (Boston, 1950).

22. 7 June 1787. See I Farrand, *Records of the Federal Convention* (New Haven, 1911–37), 153.

23. Charles Warren, *The Making of the Constitution* (Boston, 1928), 155–56 and Appendix C.

24. 18 June 1787, Farrand, *Records of the Federal Convention*, I, 282.

25. Pinckney's speech, ibid., 397ff.

CHAPTER TEN
2

1. Carl Bridenbaugh, *Mitre and Sceptre* (N.Y., 1962), 10–11.
2. Hofstadter, *The Idea of a Party System* (Berkeley, 1969), 60 n.
3. Edmund S. Morgan, *The Gentle Puritan: A Life of Ezra Stiles 1727–1795* (New Haven, 1962), 205–6.
4. *Notes on Virginia.* Query XIII, 20.
5. H. S. Commager, *Majority Rule and Minority Rights* (N.Y., 1943). For these and other expressions of Jefferson's views on majority rule see under "Majority" in John Foley's *Jeffersonian Cyclopaedia* (N.Y., 1900).
6. Ben: Perley Poore, *The Federal and State Constitutions*, 2 vols. (Washington, 1877).
7. On separation of powers, see W. R. Gwyn, *The Meaning of Separation of Powers* (Tulane Studies in Political Science, Vol. IX); M. J. C. Vile, *Constitutionalism and the Separation of Powers* (1967); Benjamin Wright, "Origin of Separation of Powers in America," *Economica*, XIII (1933); and M. P. Sharp's magisterial essay, "The Classical American Doctrine of Separation of Powers" 11 *University of Chicago Law Rev.* (1935).
8. On legislative usurpations of power, see E. S. Corwin, "Progress of Constitutional Theory" in 30 *Am. Hist. Rev.* (1925), 511ff., and Julius Goebel, *History of the Supreme Court*, Vol. I, Ch. 3 (N.Y., 1971). Simeon Baldwin points out that the practice of legislative interference in the judicial arena persisted in Connecticut well into the nineteenth century. *The American Judiciary* (N.Y., 1905).
9. This was, in a sense, the heart of what we may call the Turgot-Adams controversy: see Turgot's letter to Dr. Price in Adams, *Works*, IV, 469, and Zoltan Haraszti, *John Adams and the Prophets of Progress* (Cambridge, 1952).
10. Madison in *Federalist*, no. 66.

CHAPTER TEN
3

1. The Massachusetts Body of Liberties can be found in Z. Chafee, *Documents on Fundamental Human Rights*, I, 79ff. (printed, not pub.).
2. All of the colonial charters can be found in Ben: Perley

Poore, ed., *The Federal and State Constitutions, Colonial Charters and other Organic Laws*, 2 v. (Washington, 1877).

3. For Virginia Bill of Rights, see Commager, *Documents,* No. 67, with bibl. references.

4. XII Boyd, *Papers,* 371.

5. Ibid., 440.

6. I Elliot's *Debates,* 319ff.

7. Chafee, I *Documents,* Nos. 66 and 67.

8. Commager, *Documents,* Nos. 67 and 70.

9. Commager, *Documents,* No. 71.

10. H. M. Jones, *The Pursuit of Happiness* (Camb., 1953); Commager, "The Pursuit of Happiness," in *Jefferson, Nationalism and the Enlightenment,* 93ff.

11. IV, *Works of John Adams,* 193.

12. On eighteenth-century concept of republicanism, see Caroline Robbins, *The Eighteenth-Century Commonwealthman* (Camb., 1959); R. W. Shoemaker, "Democracy and Republic as Understood in late 18th Century America," 41 *American Speech,* 1966; W. Paul Adams, "Republicanism in Political Rhetoric," in 80, *Pol. Sci. Qtly.* 397. There are some perceptive observations in Y. Arieli, *Individualism and Nationalism in American Ideology* (Cambridge, 1964).

13. See Franco Venturi, *Utopia and Reform in the Enlightenment,* Ch. I (Cambridge, 1971).

14. Price preached this famous sermon, "On the Love of Our Country," in November 1789. See Carl Cone, *The English Jacobins* (N.Y., 1968) and his biography of Price, *Torchbearer of Freedom* (Lexington, Ky., 1952); and Anthony Brown, *The French Revolution in English History* (1918).

15. There is voluminous literature on the impact of the American Revolution on France, but no definitive study has as yet been written. See older books like E. E. Hale, Jr., *Franklin in France,* 2 vols. (N.Y., 1887–88); Bernard Fäy, *Revolutionary Spirit in France and America* (N.Y., 1927). See also contributions by Gilbert Chinard, Nicholas Hans, and others to Franklin volume of the *Proc. of the Am. Phil. Soc.,* Vol. XCVIII (1954); Alfred Aldridge, *Franklin and his French Contemporaries* (N.Y., 1957); and Dumas Malone, *Jefferson, and the Rights of Man* (Boston, 1951).

16. See Fäy, *Revolutionary Spirit,* 270; and Henri Peyre, "Influence of Eighteenth-Century Ideas upon France," 10 *J. Hist. of Ideas,* 63ff.

17. See Joyce Appleby, "America as a Model for the Radical French Reformers of 1789," XXVIII *Wm. and Mary Qtly.* 267 (1971).

18. Letter of 12 Jan. 1789, in XIV Boyd, ed. 437.
19. XV Boyd, ed. 167.
20. XV Boyd, ed. 168.
21. G. Chinard, ed., *Letters of Lafayette and Jefferson*, 136ff. (Baltimore, 1929).
22. "The Declaration of the Rights of Man" is most easily available in E. L. Higgins, *The French Revolution as Told by Contemporaries*, 111ff. (Boston, 1938); and in the Appendix to G. Lefebvre, *The Coming of the French Revolution* (Princeton, 1947). See also the classic George Jellinek *Declaration of the Rights of Man* (N.Y., 1901).
23. The phrase is from Jefferson's First Inaugural Address.
24. Qt. in G. Chinard, ed., *Les Amitiés Américaines de Madame Houdetot* (Paris, 1924), 56.

CHAPTER TEN
4

1. On the Dr. Bonham case, see T. F. Plunckett, "Bonham's Case and Judicial Review," 40 *Harvard Law Rev.* (1926), 30, which has elaborate bibliographical annotation.
2. *Virginia Reports*, 4 Call, 5. Reprinted in part in Commager, *Documents*, No. 73.
3. *North Carolina Reports*, 1 Martin, 42. Reprinted in part in Commager, *Documents*, No. 89. See also, G. F. McRee, *James Iredell*, 2 vols. (1857).
4. *Chisholm v. Georgia*, 2 Dallas, 419.
5. *Marbury v. Madison*, 1 Cranch, 137.
6. *Dred Scott v. Sanford*, 19 Howard, 393 (1857). In between, of course, there had been innumerable instances when the Court declared void some act of a state, or considered and questioned the constitutionality of acts of the Congress and of the executive. All these cases are in Commager, *Documents*.
7. Eugene Rostow has two perceptive essays on judicial review and democracy in *The Sovereign Prerogative* (New Haven, 1962).
8. XIV Boyd, ed., *Jefferson*, 659.
9. See Edwin Mims, Jr., *The Majority of the People* (1941); and H. S. Commager, *Majority Rule and Minority Rights* (N.Y., 1943).
10. The "law of the land" clause of Article VI of the Constitution. Yet there is some ambiguity here, for the clause read that "the Judges of every State shall be bound" by the Constitution, "anything in the Constitution or Laws of any State to the

contrary notwithstanding." The explanation of this wording is simple enough: the Constitution did not provide specifically for a federal judiciary (aside from a Supreme Court); that was left to the Congress, which did create a federal judiciary.

11. The literature on judicial review is voluminous, but no student has yet resolved this apparent paradox. A flood of light, or of something, is thrown on the problem by the testimony of witnesses before the Senate Judiciary Committee on Senate Bill 1342—the so-called Court reform (or court packing) bill of 1937, 6 vols., 75 Cong., 1st Sess., 1937.

12. This can be traced in Charles Warren, *History of the American Bar* (Cambridge, 1912); Vol. I of the same author's *Supreme Court in American History* (N.Y., 1922); Albert Beveridge's biography of John Marshall, 4 vols. (Boston, 1916–19), esp. Vols. 2 and 3; Simeon Baldwin, *The American Judiciary* (N.Y., 1905); and Lawrence Friedman, *A History of American Law* (N.Y., 1973).

13. See Justice Holmes, "John Marshall," first printed in his *Speeches* (Boston, 1913) and available in *Collected Legal Essays* (N.Y., 1920), where he observed sagely that part of Marshall's greatness was "in being *there.*" There is, alas, no satisfactory history of the American Bar after independence; this story must be followed in the numerous—and usually filiopietistic—Bench and Bar volumes dealing with particular states.

14. *Federalist Papers,* No. 81.

15. Louis Boudin, *Government by Judiciary* (1932), cuts most of these precedents down to size, leaving us with no satisfactory explanation of the general acquiescence in judicial review.

16. On this, see H. S. Commager, "Democracy and Judicial Review," in *Freedom and Order* (N.Y., 1966).

17. Jonathan Boucher, "Of Civil Liberty" in *A View of the Causes and Consequences of the American Revolution: Thirteen Discourses* (L., 1797). The qt. is on p. 520. On Boucher, see perceptive chapter by Moses Coit Tyler, *Literary History of the American Revolution,* II, Ch. 14; Mary B. Norton, *Loyalist Exiles in England* (Boston, 1972); Wallace Brown, *The Good Americans* (N.Y., 1969).

18. Jefferson to David Hartley, 2 July 1787, XI *Papers* Boyd, ed., 526.

19. Arthur Mowry, *The Dorr Rebellion* (Providence, 1901).

20. See Benjamin F. Hallett, *Right of the People to Establish Forms of Government* (Boston, 1848). This was his argument for the defense in *Luther v. Bordon;* it is a masterly survey of the history of the problem of revolution and should be reprinted.

21. Hamilton, in *Federalist,* No. 22.

22. II Diary, ed. C. F. Adams, 420–21.

NOTES FOR APPENDIX

As the Appendix is itself an enlarged note, I confine myself here to those items which require annotation.

1. Oddly enough there is no substantial monograph on the Philosophes, though all of the major treatises on the Enlightenment inevitably deal with them. Most perceptive is no doubt Peter Gay's first volume, *The Enlightenment: The Rise of Modern Paganism* (N.Y., 1966). But see also Will Durant, *Age of Voltaire*, Ch. 28 (N.Y., 1965). Herbert Dieckmann's, *Le Philosophe* is largely textual analysis, see below, n. 3. There are a number of anthologies of Enlightenment literature which illuminate the character of the Philosophe. Thus, Peter Gay, ed., *The Enlightenment* (N.Y., 1973); Lester Crocker, ed., *The Age of Enlightenment* (N.Y., 1969); Isaiah Berlin, *Age of Enlightenment* (N.Y., 1956); Norman Torrey, ed., *Les Philosophes* (N.Y., 1960). Better yet are biographies of the leading Philosophes such as Diderot, Voltaire, Helvétius, the Baron d'Holbach, d'Alembert, Hume, Beccaria, and others, all far too numerous to list here.

2. Peter Gay has assigned the word "family" to the Philosophes, see Ch. 1 of *The Enlightenment*, Vol. 1.

3. For an analysis of *Le Philosophe*, a discussion of authorship, and a printing of some of the texts, see Herbert Dieckmann, *Le Philosophe: Texts and Interpretations*, Washington University Studies in Language and Literature, Vol. 18 (St. Louis, 1948).

4. For an English translation of the article in the Encyclopédie, see N. S. Hoyt and T. Cassirer, eds., *The Encyclopédie* (Indianapolis, 1965). I have modified some of the translations.

5. This quote can be found in Gay, *Enlightenment*, at 14.

6. The *Essay on the Study of Literature* was originally written in French. It can be found in trans. in John L. Sheffield, ed., *Miscellaneous Works of Edward Gibbon* I (1837), 643.

7. See Gay, *Enlightenment*, Vol. I, 129.

8. See trans. by Parke Godwin (N.Y., 1850), Bk. VII, 57.

9. Qt. in Marius Roustan, *Pioneers of the French Revolution* (Boston, 1926), 19.

10. To H. S. Conway, 28 October 1765, in *Letters*, IV, 427, ed., Peter Cunningham (1906).

11. See the famous letter to John Bannister, 15 October 1785, in VIII Boyd, ed., 635.

12. See Gilbert Chinard, *Jefferson et les Idéologues* (Baltimore, 1925).

Index

Amendments, constitutions
and, 200–6
American Academy of Arts
and Sciences, 12
American Enlightenment,
16–42, 92ff. (*see also* Enlightenment; Philosophes;
specific aspects, developments, events, individuals);
compared to European,
xi–xiii, 16ff., 77ff., 262ff.;
dating, 262
American Husbandry, 115
American Philosophical Society, 12, 16, 17, 20, 23, 93,
115, 262
American Revolution, xi,
xii–xiii, 6, 41, 42, 117, 127,
139, 182–84 (*see also* Col-
onies; United States of
America; specific aspects,
developments, individuals);
French Revolution com-
pared to, 243–47, 253
Americans no Jewes, 84
Ames, Fisher, 128, 247
Ami de la Révolution, L', 245
Ami des Hommes, L', 104
Amsterdam, 105, 150, 153,
264
Anarchiad, The, 91
Ancient History (Rollin), 52,
68
Ancient regime, 156–57,
159–60
Anderson, James, 105
Anglican Church, 180–81,
230
Ansbach, Margrave of, 149
Anson, Captain, 56
Antarctic explorations, 54, 56
Anthropophagi, 69, 81
Anti-Federalists, 138
Anti-Machiavel, 124
Antiquities in Athens, 67

*Apology for the Rational
Worship of God,* 49
Arabia, 56, 64–65, 78
Arabian Nights, 64
Aranda, Count of, 126
Arbieux, Laurent d', 64
Architecture, 3
Arctic explorations, 54, 56, 61
Argens, Marquis d', 47, 62
Aristocracy (nobility, pa-
tricians), as ruling class,
144ff., 173, 192 (*see also*
Classes; Monarchs; specific
developments, individuals,
places); limits on power of,
217ff., 224, 226, 229; *no-
blesse de race,* 149; *no-
blesse de robe,* 149
Aristotle, 217
Art (arts, artists, art-
philosophers), 37, 44,
65–68, 79, 162, 258 (*see
also* specific artists, kinds,
places, works); American
Enlightenment and, 19;
classical revival of, 65–67
Articles of Confederation, 14,
20, 184, 187, 207ff.
Asia, 212. *See also* specific
places
Association of Ideas, 51
Astronomy, 2, 4, 29, 53, 55,
257
Atala, 57
Atlantis, 84
Aufklärung, 10
Augustus II (Augustus the
Strong of Saxony), 161
Augustus III, 65
Australia, 1, 7, 54, 55, 69–70
Austria, 10, 44, 123, 125, 145,
175
Authority. *See* Power
Aztecs, 83

366

INDEX

HENRY STEELE COMMAGER did his graduate work in history at the universities of Chicago and Copenhagen. He has taught American history at New York University, Columbia University, and at Amherst College, where he now holds the position of Simpson Lecturer.

Mr. Commager has held the Pitt Chair of American History at Cambridge University, the Harmsworth Chair at Oxford University, and the Gottesman Chair at Uppsala University. He is an Honorary Fellow of Peterhouse, Cambridge, and holds an Honorary Professorship at the University of Santiago de Chile. In 1972 he was awarded the Gold Medal for History by the American Academy of Arts and Letters.